W9-BHG-727

Advance Praise

"This book is a beautiful example of the notion that 'sensing, naming, and identifying what is going on inside is the first step to recovery.' Deb Dana lucidly guides you to travel deep inside of yourself to become aware of how your internal surveillance system—the safety settings of your autonomic nervous system—is the foundation of the way we feel, act, and think. This is a valuable manual to help you address your inner physiology and thereby create the necessary conditions for safety and connection."

—**Bessel A. van der Kolk, M.D.,** President, Trauma Research Foundation, Professor of Psychiatry, Boston University School of Medicine, author of NYT #1 Bestseller *The Body Keeps the Score: Brain, Mind, and Body in the Healing of Trauma*

"Deb Dana's book is a must-have for any experientially oriented clinician and a double must for those working with trauma. It unequivocally de-pathologizes both dysregulation/activation and shut/down dissociation as wired in, biologically based, evolutionary responses to perceptions of stress, threat, and danger. For the neuroscience nerds among us, Deb Dana has a crystal-clear writing style that allows her to teach the complex science of Polyvagal Theory in a way that is highly accessible. The early chapters are a must-read for anyone who has wanted to understand this crucial theory but until now has not quite grasped it. With its very clever, doable, and well-articulated exercises this book can be a direct resource for even the most traumatized clients. It's a vital contribution to the trauma clinician's tool kit."

—**Diana Fosha,** Ph.D., developer of AEDP and Director of the AEDP Institute, editor of *AEDP 2.0: Undoing Aloneness and the Transformation of Emotional Suffering into Flourishing*

"Whether or not you are familiar with Polyvagal Theory, I highly recommend this invaluable resource and guide. Deb Dana eloquently explains the physiology of fight/flight/freeze responses and offers creative strategies to increase self-awareness while simultaneously providing resourcing for re-grounding, self-soothing, resilience, and the capacity for safe connection with others. Step-by-step guidance for incorporating breathwork, guided imagery, somatic resourcing, journaling, art modalities, and movement provide a terrific roadmap for healing work that can be achieved both in and out of the therapist's office."

—**Lisa Ferentz,** LCSW-C, DAPA, trauma therapist, consultant, educator, and author of *Treating Self-Destructive Behaviors in Trauma Survivors: A Clinician's Guide, Letting Go of Self-Destructive Behaviors: A Workbook of Hope and Healing,* and *Finding Your Ruby Slippers: Transformative Life Lessons From the Therapist's Couch*

"Written with great intelligence and clarity, Deb Dana's *Polyvagal Exercises for Safety and Connection* provides clinicians with everything they need to help clients become adept at managing the dysregulating survival responses of their nervous systems. Clients can immediately learn to implement a wealth of precise and practical tools, within and beyond the therapy room, to respond to and recover from the challenges of daily living with competence and courage."

—**Linda Graham,** MFT, author of *Resilience: Powerful Practices for Bouncing Back from Disappointment, Difficulty, and Even Disaster*

"Deb Dana has given a very clear, illuminating guide for therapists to help their clients embody deep healing. This essential book has excellent, user-friendly, and practical interventions that support polyvagal-informed treatment based on Stephen Porges' research, which validates the success underlying all somatic therapies. She gives therapists relevant insights that help us facilitate a process from fear-induced threat responses towards healthy relational social engagement following natural physiological pathways and sequences. This book is a must-read for any therapist working with trauma and interested in efficient and effective treatment."

—**Diane Poole Heller,** Ph.D., SEP, LPC, Developer of the DARe: Dynamic Attachment Re-patterning experience therapy model, author of *Crash Course, Healing Your Attachment Wounds,* and *The Power of Attachment*

POLYVAGAL
EXERCISES

FOR SAFETY
AND
CONNECTION

THE NORTON SERIES ON
INTERPERSONAL NEUROBIOLOGY

Louis Cozolino, PhD, Series Editor
Allan N. Schore, PhD, Series Editor (2007–2014)
Daniel J. Siegel, MD, Founding Editor

The field of mental health is in a tremendously exciting period of growth and conceptual reorganization. Independent findings from a variety of scientific endeavors are converging in an interdisciplinary view of the mind and mental well-being. An interpersonal neurobiology of human development enables us to understand that the structure and function of the mind and brain are shaped by experiences, especially those involving emotional relationships.

The Norton Series on Interpersonal Neurobiology provides cutting-edge, multidisciplinary views that further our understanding of the complex neurobiology of the human mind. By drawing on a wide range of traditionally independent fields of research—such as neurobiology, genetics, memory, attachment, complex systems, anthropology, and evolutionary psychology—these texts offer mental health professionals a review and synthesis of scientific findings often inaccessible to clinicians. The books advance our understanding of human experience by finding the unity of knowledge, or consilience, that emerges with the translation of findings from numerous domains of study into a common language and conceptual framework. The series integrates the best of modern science with the healing art of psychotherapy.

POLYVAGAL EXERCISES
FOR SAFETY
AND
CONNECTION

50 CLIENT-CENTERED PRACTICES

DEB DANA

FOREWORD BY STEPHEN W. PORGES

W. W. NORTON & COMPANY
Independent Publishers Since 1923

Note to Readers: Standards of clinical practice and protocol change over time, and no technique or recommendation is guaranteed to be safe or effective in all circumstances. This volume is intended as a general information resource for professionals practicing in the field of psychotherapy and mental health; it is not a substitute for appropriate training, peer review, and/or clinical supervision. Neither the publisher nor the author(s) can guarantee the complete accuracy, efficacy, or appropriateness of any particular recommendation in every respect.

For information about permission to reproduce selections from this book, write to Permissions, W. W. Norton & Company, Inc., 500 Fifth Avenue, New York, NY 10110

For information about special discounts for bulk purchases, please contact W. W. Norton Special Sales at specialsales@wwnorton.com or 800-233-4830

Manufacturing by Sheridan Books
Production manager: Katelyn MacKenzie

Library of Congress Cataloging-in-Publication Data

Names: Dana, Deb, author. | Porges, Stephen W., writer of foreword.
Title: Polyvagal exercises for safety and connection : 50 client-centered practices / Deb Dana ; foreword by Stephen W. Porges.
Description: First edition. | New York : W.W. Norton & Company, [2020] | Includes bibliographical references.
Identifiers: LCCN 2019050472 | ISBN 9780393713855 (paperback) | ISBN 9780393713862 (epub)
Subjects: LCSH: Autonomic nervous system. | Psychic trauma—Treatment. | Affective neuroscience. | Clinical psychology. | Client-centered psychotherapy.
Classification: LCC QP368 .D358 2020 | DDC 612.8/9—dc23
LC record available at https://lccn.loc.gov/2019050472

W. W. Norton & Company, Inc., 500 Fifth Avenue, New York, N.Y. 10110
www.wwnorton.com

W. W. Norton & Company Ltd., 15 Carlisle Street, London W1D 3BS

4 5 6 7 8 9 0

To my fellow travelers on this autonomic journey...

CONTENTS

FOREWORD

As a professor whose research career has spanned five decades, I have had ample time to contemplate personal goals. During my career, I have observed the trajectories of my colleagues as they matured and transitioned through the academic ranks. Some welcomed becoming emeritus and continued to be actively involved in their science through research, writings, and presentations. Others seamlessly left the academic world and retired.

Being a professor is a demanding position that includes managing laboratories, teaching undergraduate students, mentoring graduate students and junior colleagues, writing grants and generating resources for research, networking within a discipline, welcoming professional tasks such as reviewing colleagues' manuscripts and grant proposals, and serving on committees within institutions. Some of us also have served in administrative roles within institutions and professional societies, while others have built liaisons with government agencies and industry.

This complex portfolio of experiences has given me insight

into how I developed and accepted the specific benchmarks that define my personal goals. As I observed my colleagues, I realized that many professors were frustrated at the end of their careers. They seemed to feel that they were not successful and had not accomplished anything meaningful. This self-evaluation was often structured by their institutions encouraging them to retire and their sense that they had not received the recognition that they felt that they deserved. They felt that no one remembered them and their contributions. My colleagues had spent decades defining themselves in terms of the structure of academic evaluations, and when they were no longer able to fund their research through federal grants, they felt abused and neglected. Basically, from a Polyvagal perspective, the academic world with its chronic evaluation strategies had triggered the bodies and minds of my colleagues into a chronic state of defense. For many who did not have a positive transition narrative, the experience of being a professor ended up abusive and isolating. Consistent with Polyvagal Theory, these experiences of vulnerability and chronic defense would retune autonomic state, leading to mental and physical health issues. Thus, we see that the experience of being a professor shares many attributes with abusive families and relationships. However, there is an important distinction: the experience of being a professor provides a powerful skillset that may be applied outside the university. Thus, if the professorial experiences are internalized as preparatory—enabling the scientist to deal with the challenges of the world outside of the university— then the personal narrative changes from one of abuse to one of adaptive resilience. This resilience is associated with autonomic states that may lead not only to better mental and physical health, but also to bold expansive thinking and rewarding social interactions.

Metaphorically, professors age out within the university. In professional circles, their peer group starts to disappear due to retirements and health issues. This change in social interactions marginalizes professors and their narratives become negative. When I was about 50, I started to think about personal transitions within academics. I realized that a passive stance toward what the institution defined as success would lead only to disappointment and frustration as I aged. I started to operationalize what I, personally, needed to accomplish to feel that my journey was successful. I focused on the realization that for me, the translation of my ideas into practice was my personal goal. However, I was ill-prepared to take my research ideas and move them into clinical practice, education, or public awareness. Thus, as an academic, I had structured my narrative to apply the tools that I had and focused on having an opportunity to archive my ideas and methods. I set my personal goals to publish papers that would present an integrative theory and provide the methodology to study the theory.

At the time I was contemplating the dimensions of academic success, I developed the initial formulation of the Polyvagal Theory. The theory stimulated interest in the clinical world and rapidly gained traction in the study and treatment of trauma. This good fortune supported my personal need to move ideas into practice. During the 25 years since the initial presentation of the theory, I have had the good fortune to have the opportunity to support insightful and talented therapists who have embraced Polyvagal Theory as a manual outlining the body's responses to safe, danger, and life-threat. These bold, passionate, and compassionate therapists have used this information to help their clients organize and make sense of their reactions to danger and life-threat. As therapists embraced Polyvagal Theory, their therapies became Polyvagal-informed.

Deb Dana is one of these special therapists. Her books take the principles of Polyvagal Theory and provide therapists with a toolkit of therapeutic skills designed to enable the client—and often the therapist—to explore their bodily responses; to become reacquainted with a body that may have become numb. Through her clear and brilliant translation of Polyvagal Theory into practice, the client is guided to honor both the adaptive numbness that follows severe trauma, and vulnerabilities that are experienced when the portals to the nervous system are awakened through cues of safety. Through her exercises, the client is able to experience an unacknowledged intelligence of the nervous system as it initially rejects the validity of cues of safety. This skeptical reaction illustrates the disparity of the personal narrative with the narrative of the body (i.e., nervous system). The personal narrative that brings the client into therapy pleads for trusting relationships, while the narrative of the body emphatically screams that it will not be fooled again and will protect the survivor by not trusting that cues are truly well-intentioned cues of safety.

In this book, *Polyvagal Exercises for Safety and Connection*, Polyvagal Theory becomes a living, felt process that can be shared with clinicians and clients. Deb Dana provides exercises that systematically unwrap the adaptive layers of neural regulation of the autonomic nervous system that shift, and at times distort, our perspective of events and others. Through these exercises we shift autonomic state and start to have an understanding that the personal narrative is not a documentary of events, but a documentary of feelings. This does not minimize the importance of events, but it emphasizes the importance of feelings in distorting, amplifying, or buffering the impact of events.

It is through Deb's creative and compassionate vision and the welcoming, expanding family of Polyvagal-informed therapists that Polyvagal Theory is being translated and embedded into tools that are transforming the practice of trauma-informed therapies. As a witness of this process, I am humbled by the impact that a vision of understanding our evolutionary heritage can, in the hands of Deb Dana and other gifted therapists, have on reducing the burden of personal pain and suffering that survivors of trauma have experienced. I am looking forward to Deb's continued brilliant insights in translating the principles of Polyvagal Theory into an accessible language and useful toolkit for therapists.

—Stephen W. Porges
Author of *The Polyvagal Theory*

ACKNOWLEDGMENTS

There are "before and after" moments in life. These are the moments when the world we are inhabiting changes and we find ourselves in uncharted territory. The publication of my first book, *The Polyvagal Theory in Therapy*, was, for me, one of these life-changing moments. People read about my way of working and wanted to know more. I started traveling and teaching and my small polyvagal family grew into a global polyvagal community. In person and through email, I heard clinical case descriptions and personal stories of suffering. What all of these had in common was the recognition that looking through the lens of the autonomic nervous system changed the way people understood their stories and engaged with the world.

I came to realize that the simple activities of daily living offered ongoing opportunities for autonomic shaping. Everyday practices to nurture the nervous system are the foundation of *Polyvagal Exercises for Safety and Connection*, so it's only fitting that this book was written not in quiet, uninterrupted stretches of time that is my preferred writing rhythm, but in smaller moments I lay claim to in the flow of my daily life. In the process of writing, I became a student of my own system; discovering patterns I wanted to savor and patterns I was ready to change. I learned from personal experience that shaping the nervous system in new ways requires patience, persistence, and is possible.

Writing *Polyvagal Exercises* was an autonomic adventure I couldn't have navigated without the support of many people. There is a special place in my heart for the participants in my workshops who were willing to be my test pilots. Together we learned that some exercises were helpful in theory, but didn't translate to practice, and others worked well with a bit of revision. Tina Zorger has been with me on this adventure since the beginning and was the person I trusted to listen to my frustrations and help me find a way forward. She knew when I needed to slow down and savor and how to support me in continuing to create. My trusted guide Linda Graham invited me to see beyond the places I was stuck and trust my inner wisdom. Fellow author Gary Whited brought his gift of deep listening to our connection, offering me a safe place to talk about my writing challenges. My friend Marilyn Sanders shared my love of early mornings and many mornings, wherever we each woke up in the world, we would start our day with a cup of coffee and a polyvagal-inspired conversation.

This book would not have been possible without the support of my wonderful editor, Deborah Malmud, and her great team at Norton. She believed in this work, connected me with Trish Watson (who helped me organize the exercises so they would be easy to understand and access) and was always open to exploring new ideas. Deborah understood my moments of dorsal vagal despair and never failed to respond with a message of ventral vagal hope.

My life has been shaped in wonderful and unexpected ways by my friendship with Stephen Porges. Steve was always ready to help me understand the science of connection in a more nuanced way, showed up without question to offer a much needed moment of co-regulation when I lost my way, and continues to shape my world with invitations to join him on new polyvagal-inspired adventures.

My deepest appreciation is for my husband Bob who supported me every day during what often felt like a never-ending book writing adventure. He was there to celebrate with me when I found just the right words and helped me keep going when I was ready to give up. His love continues to fill my heart with joy.

While writing *Polyvagal Exercises*, countless people showed up with an offer of connection just when it was most needed. Friends checked in, colleagues tried out practices, and people shared their stories. To everyone who joined me on this journey, may your days be filled with ventral vagal abundance…

or polyvagal-informed, the exercises offer a pathway to autonomic reorganization.

The Appendix completes the book, offering personal progress trackers for each of the BASIC components and presenting the exercises in a format that can be copied and shared with your clients. One important predictor of change is the perception of moving toward a goal. Studies show that even when you identify a goal as important and meaningful, you don't automatically track changes and, when you do, you tend to take in some pieces of information and ignore others (Webb, Chang, & Benn, 2013). Having a way to see and measure progress supports change. The personal progress trackers for Chapters 4–8 are simple evaluation tools designed to help your clients bring explicit attention to the subtle shifts that show their autonomic nervous systems are reorganizing. The trackers are intended to be used at regular intervals, first while working with the exercises in the chapter and later to see how ongoing autonomic change is continuing to impact behaviors and beliefs. Complete them in your sessions, return to them later as an ongoing check-in, and invite your clients to use them at home on their own.

Polyvagal Exercises for Safety and Connection gives you a way to help your clients keep the process of autonomic awareness and reorganization alive outside of the therapy hour. The organizing principles outlined in Section I will help you understand how the autonomic nervous system works and create a platform for teaching the exercises in Section II. The BASIC exercises will help your clients attend to the actions of their autonomic nervous systems between sessions, begin to reshape their autonomic pathways, and strengthen their movement toward safety and connection. "Joy lowers the neural thresh-old for perceiving life events as being positive and hopeful, while raising the threshold for perceiving events as negative and hopeless" (Lucardie, 2014, p. 440). With this book, you and your clients have a guide to building the autonomic foun-dation for ventral vagal–inspired joy.

THE AUTONOMIC NERVOUS SYSTEM: PATTERNS AND PATHWAYS

I realized that there was a thrilling undiscovered country to be explored in the mechanisms of the mammalian nervous system.

—WILDER PENFIELD

The ability to respond to and recover from the challenges of daily living is a marker of well-being and depends on the actions of the autonomic nervous system. When you think about the autonomic nervous system, where do your thoughts go? Perhaps you have a fuzzy memory of biology learned long ago and a feeling that this system is somehow important to survival. With the development of Polyvagal Theory, Stephen Porges has provided a modern map of the territory of the autonomic nervous system and a new understanding of the ways it shapes moment-to-moment experiences of connection and protection.

The three organizing principles of Polyvagal Theory are:

1. **Autonomic hierarchy**

   The autonomic nervous system is divided into three parts, each with its own set of protective actions.

   - The earliest dorsal vagal system brings strategies of immobilization.
   - The sympathetic system, next to arrive, adds fight and flight.
   - The most recent ventral vagal system offers the ability for safety through connection and social engagement.
   - Recognizing where on the hierarchy your client's autonomic nervous system has taken them is fundamental to the success of therapy. When the autonomic nervous system has moved into a dysregulated dorsal vagal or sympathetic state, your client's body and brain have been hijacked and they are held in a survival response. When the ventral vagal state is active, body and brain work together, and processing and change are possible.

2. **Neuroception**

   Neuroception, detection without awareness, describes the way the autonomic nervous system interfaces with the world.

   - Working below the level of awareness, the autonomic nervous system listens inside the body, outside in the environment, and in the relationships between people.
   - Reshaping the autonomic nervous system involves first making the implicit experience explicit by bringing perception to neuroception and then adding context through the lens of discernment.

- Neuroception is at work in every moment of the therapy session. The ability to tune into the implicit autonomic conversations that are happening between you and your clients is an essential part of creating therapeutic presence and building trust in the therapy process.

3. **Co-regulation**

Co-regulation is a biological imperative. It is essential to survival.

- The ability to self-regulate is built on ongoing experiences of co-regulation. Through co-regulation we connect with others and create a shared sense of safety.
- With a reliable, regulating other, we engage in the rhythm of reciprocity and build experiences of safety in connection. For many of your clients this earliest experience of being with a safe person in a safe place is missing.
- As a therapist, you are responsible for being a regulated and regulating presence for your clients. Without your predictable, ongoing offer of co-regulation in the therapy session, your clients will struggle to engage in the therapeutic process of change.

Over the course of evolution both the brain and the autonomic nervous system have grown and changed. John Hughlings Jackson proposed a hierarchy of brain structures in which higher levels regulate the function of lower levels; he defined *dissolution* as a sort of evolution in reverse that happens when higher brain structures no longer inhibit lower structures

(Franz & Gillett, 2011; York III & Steinberg, 2011). You see this when your client's prefrontal cortex shuts down in response to a situation that feels overwhelming, leaving their limbic system to mount a response. The autonomic nervous system can likewise be seen through the lens of hierarchy and dissolution. Looking at the evolution of the autonomic nervous system, there is an emergence of a three-part system that is distinct and measurable, creating a predictable hierarchy of response (Porges & Carter, 2017). The autonomic nervous system also follows a predictable pathway of dissolution, moving from ventral vagal safety and connection down the hierarchy into the sympathetic mobilization of fight and flight and finally to the earliest state of dorsal vagal shutdown.

Using images, you can feel the flavor of each autonomic state. Humans evolved from ancient reptiles similar to turtles (Porges, 2015a). The image of the turtle hiding in its shell is an apt one for the dorsal vagal state of disconnection. Continuing to the sympathetic nervous system, imagine the darting movements of a fish reacting in an instant to avoid a predator. Finally, arriving in the uniquely mammalian ventral vagal state, picture people talking and smiling in a shared moment of connection.

Darwin understood that the brain and the heart were connected and engaged in a two-way conversation through what was then known as the pneumogastric nerve, now called the vagus or Cranial Nerve X (Darwin, 1873). William James (1890) wrote that, "A purely disembodied human emotion is a nonentity" (p. 194) and that intellectual feeling must be connected to "a bodily reverberation of some kind" (p. 201). This early understanding of the two-way conversations between the body and brain was abandoned in favor of envisioning the brain as the dominant force directing daily experience. Polyvagal Theory reestablished the understanding that through bidirectional pathways, psychological processes influence body state and body state colors your perceptions (Porges, 2009). Sensory fibers send information to the brain and motor fibers bring information back, initiating a response. Corticobulbar (cortico for cortex and bulbar for a region of the medulla) pathways connect the brain's motor cortex to the autonomic nervous system via the vagus, giving the cortex a way to exert some control over brainstem responses (Porges, 2011).

Until recently, scientists had no way to understand this brain-heart connection except through using animal models to test hypotheses and postmortem study of body systems. Researchers are now able to study the autonomic nervous system and patterns of brain activity in living humans in real time. Through the use of EEGs, biofeedback, and wearable devices, we can listen in on the conversations that travel the pathways between the autonomic nervous system and limbic and cortical networks. Heart rate variability, the naturally occurring changes in the beat-to-beat rhythm of the heart, is indicative of the state of the autonomic nervous system and might be a biomarker of general stress and health (Evans et al., 2013). High and low variability is associated with changes in the ability for the brain (prefrontal region) to promote cognitive and emotional self-regulation (Park & Thayer, 2014). Another rhythm, respiratory sinus arrhythmia, tracks the changes in heart rate associated with breath patterns (Sahar,

Shalev, & Porges, 2001). This beat-and-breath rhythm shifts in response to both physical and psychological needs. In clinical work, you sense body-brain communication in how deeply your clients respond to an experience, how long their response lasts, and how often it occurs. You see your clients' body-brain conversations in action. As technology advances, you may soon be able to see changes in autonomic state as a session unfolds through numbers tracking moment-to-moment shifts and changing colors that illustrate the autonomic experience. It is interesting to consider what a dual lens of observing your client's body and behaviors in combination with the next generation of physiological measurement tools might bring to the clinical interaction.

The autonomic nervous system shapes the way you experience your life. Beliefs, behaviors, and body responses are embedded in the autonomic hierarchy. Physiology and psychology are interconnected. State and story work together in a persistent and, if not interrupted, enduring loop. Polyvagal Theory invites you into the science of feeling safe enough to fall in love with life and take the risks of living. By bringing explicit awareness to the implicit workings of the autonomic nervous system you can learn to become a regulated and regulating resource for your own well-being and for the people around you. In the next chapters we'll look beneath the behaviors and beliefs and begin to answer the question of how physiology can create the conditions that support safety and connection.

CHAPTER 1

THE AUTONOMIC HIERARCHY

The body will reorganize when it feels safe.

—STEPHEN PORGES

Everyday living is a complex experience of autonomic navigation. Trauma, which might be thought of as "what happens to a person where there is either too much too soon, too much for too long, or not enough for too long" (Duros & Crowley, 2014, p. 238), creates an autonomic demand that shapes the system away from connection toward protection. The autonomic nervous system responds moment to moment to what are often competing needs to survive and to be social. In a state of protection, survival is the only goal. The system is closed to connection and change. In a state of connection, health, growth, and restoration are possible.

IN SERVICE OF SURVIVAL

Clients are faced with the dilemma of balancing the drive to survive with the longing to connect. The responses that were necessary and adaptive for survival in the past bring suffering in the present. Trauma stories are held in autonomic pathways that are tuned to a low threshold–high intensity pattern of responding. A question to ask when your client feels the rise of an adaptive survival response is, "Does this autonomic shift feel familiar?" The activation in the present moment often leads them back to the autonomic origin in their past.

The autonomic nervous system learns through experience. Even before birth, this system is taking in and responding to the environment. Prenatal exposure to a variety of adverse experiences including socioeconomic hardship, inadequate social support, and the use of substances influences the baby's autonomic function (Alkon et al., 2014; Fifer, Fingers, Youngman, Gomez-Gribben, & Myers, 2009; Hambleton et al., 2013). Maternal mood is transmitted, with anxiety and depression impacting the developing baby's level of activity and heart rate (Kinsella & Monk, 2009). First in the womb and then in the family, early experiences influence the autonomic nervous system, creating habitual response patterns. Through repeated experiences of co-created regulation, the intimate interactions between mother and baby shape the baby's system (Ostlund, Measelle, Laurent, Conradt, & Ablow, 2017). Mother and child "sharing at the autonomic level" create the experience of attunement (Manini et al., 2013, p. 2). Held in a relationship with a responsive caregiver, the dyadic dance of connection, falling out of connection, and a return to connection, creates the foundation for a regulated nervous system. With a reliably regulated and regulating person, rhythms of reciprocity build experiences of safety in connection. When family dynamics are based in experiences of autonomic misattunement, there is little chance for experiences of repair. When the adults in a family carry their own patterns of dysregulation, habitually triggered into states of protection and unable to return to regulation and offer the safety of connection, the child's autonomic nervous system responds by creating its own patterns of protection. "Without the experience of an organizing other, the nervous system is stunned" (Fisher, 2014). Without intervention, a legacy of dysregulated autonomic organization is passed from one generation to the next.

Trauma survivors often suffer from unpredictable, rapid, intense, and prolonged states of dysregulation. This autonomic imbalance and lack of flexibility leads to health problems. Physical problems include impaired immune function, digestive problems, respiratory problems, diabetes, increased risk of heart disease, stroke, and chronic fatigue (Andersson & Tracey, 2012; Dorrance & Fink, 2015; Mazur, Furgała, Jabłoński, Mach, & Thor, 2012; Merz, Elboudwarej, & Mehta, 2015; Thayer & Sternberg, 2006; Vaillancourt et al., 2017; Van Cauwenbergh et al., 2014). In addition to physiology, psychology is impacted. Social isolation and loneliness, a vigilance for angry faces, distraction from tasks, inability to discern meaningful cues from trivial ones, and increased depression and anxiety are some of the consequences of an out-of-balance autonomic nervous system (Grippo, Lamb, Carter, & Porges, 2007; Hawkley & Cacioppo, 2010).

The hopeful news for you and your clients is that since the autonomic nervous system learns from experience, ongoing experiences can reshape the system. Habitual response patterns can be interrupted and new patterns can be created. Autonomic flexibility is a hard-won outcome of therapy as you help your clients discover their autonomic vulnerabilities and together look toward resourcing autonomic resilience.

THE EVOLUTIONARY HIERARCHY

As illustrated in Figure 1.1, the autonomic nervous system is made up of two branches (parasympathetic and sympathetic) and, with the division of the parasympathetic system, three distinct pathways, each working in service of survival. As each

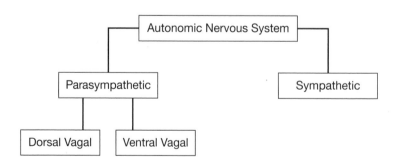

FIGURE 1.1. The Shape of the Autonomic Nervous System: Two branches–Three pathways

new pathway emerged, the older one was retained, continuing to bring its unique survival response (Porges, 2006). When you follow the evolution of the three pathways of the autonomic nervous system, you see the autonomic hierarchy, the first organizing principle of Polyvagal Theory, and find the emergent properties and adaptive strategies for each of the three autonomic states.

Imagine the autonomic nervous system as a nested system. Over the course of evolution, what began as a single dorsal vagal system of immobilization that our reptilian ancestors used for survival was added onto first with the sympathetic system of mobilization and options for fight and flight and then with the ventral vagal system of social communication and connection. As each new system was built and the older system retained, the autonomic hierarchy emerged (Figure 1.2).

The earliest dorsal vagal system runs in the background, regulating organs below the diaphragm, including the digestive system. The sympathetic nervous system, next to arrive,

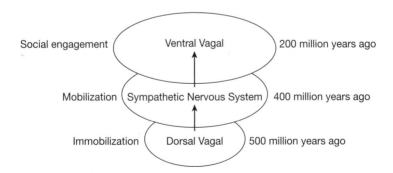

FIGURE 1.2. Nested Evolutionary Relation of Three Pathways

works to circulate blood, shape normal heart rhythms, regulate body temperature, respond to changes in posture, and provide energy to the system to support passion and play. The most recent system, the ventral vagal system, brings the ability for connection and social engagement. The ventral vagus is tasked with overseeing the autonomic nervous system, metaphorically holding the sympathetic and dorsal vagal systems in a warm embrace. When the newest autonomic pathway is directing the system, healthy homeostasis is the result.

The vagus nerve is the major component of the parasympathetic branch of the autonomic nervous system. Not a single nerve, the vagus is actually a "family of neural pathways" that wander (vagus means wanderer in Latin) throughout the body (Porges, 2011, p. 27). Beginning in the brainstem, the dorsal vagus primarily influences organs below the diaphragm and the ventral vagus mainly affects organs above the diaphragm. Through the dorsal and ventral vagal pathways, messages are sent in two directions. Sensory information travels from the body to the brain and motor information returns from the brain to the body, making this a rich, bidirectional information highway. The two vagal pathways represent either end of the evolutionary history of the autonomic nervous system. The oldest dorsal vagal (our reptilian ancestors) and the newest ventral vagal (uniquely mammalian) are at opposite ends of the continuum of response from dorsal vagal immobilization and disconnection to ventral vagal social engagement. This is reflected in the maturation of these pathways in a developing baby. Autonomic function develops over the course of pregnancy, dorsal vagal and sympathetic systems emerging first and the ventral vagus myelinating during the last trimester of pregnancy and over the first year of life (Fukushima, Nakai, Kanasugi, Terata, & Sugiyama, 2011; Porges & Furman, 2011).

Activity of the ventral vagus, often referred to as vagal tone, can be measured through heart rate variability. While heart rate measures the number of beats per minute, heart rate variability measures the variation in time between heartbeats. A high level of variability indicates the ventral vagus is active and results in a flexible autonomic nervous system and the ability to adjust to the demands of daily living (Laborde, Mosely, & Thayer, 2017). In recent years heart rate variability measurement has moved beyond laboratories and expensive ECGs to the general public with widely available, low-cost, user-friendly devices that can be worn during daily activities (Georgiou et al., 2018). There is increasing understanding about the impact of the autonomic nervous system on well-being and the need to attend to ventral vagal pathways.

Where sympathetic and dorsal vagal states activate an either/or experience constricting the ability to see beyond limited options, the ventral vagal state at the top of the hierarchy brings alive the expansive world of both/and that is filled with possibilities and choices. The ventral vagal experience is one of being a part of the world, connected to self, able to reach out to others, open to change and willing to look at possibilities. Here, solitude and social connection, excitement and rest, joy and sadness, and frustration and flow are found. The glue for the diverse ventral vagal experiences is a sense of safety.

> — MINI EXERCISE —
> - Is there an experience of ventral vagal energy that comes to mind?
> - By yourself? With others?

Philosophers and poets have long memorialized the face as the mirror to the soul. What is felt in the heart can be seen in the face. As the autonomic nervous system evolved and the ventral vagus emerged at the top of the hierarchy, the roots of five cranial nerves (trigeminal, facial, glossopharyngeal, accessory, and vagal) came together in the brainstem to create an integrated social engagement system. The ventral vagal pathway from the heart connected with pathways that control muscles of the face and head, regulating how you see, hear, speak, express emotions with your face, and turn and tilt your head, forming a "face-heart" connection (Porges, 2003). This social engagement system is both a sending system and a receiving system, constantly uploading and downloading information about connection. You are continuously posting information about yourself and gathering information about others. Each individual element of the social engagement system sends signals either inviting or discouraging connection and at the same time tunes into other social engagement systems looking for signs of warning or welcome.

Imagine the social engagement system as your autonomic safety circuit. Your eyes send signals of safety and look into other eyes for signs of welcome. Your ears tune in to conversations, listening for the sounds of friendship while your voice broadcasts the meaning underneath your words. Your shoulders move, your head turns and tilts, sending signals that you are safe to approach. When you encounter looks, sounds, and gestures that invite connection, you move closer. Meeting looks, sounds, and gestures that send signals of unsafety, you move into watchfulness. The social engagement system, with its exquisite ability to sense moment-to-moment actions in other systems, filters the stream of cues inherent in social interactions and responds by welcoming or discouraging physical proximity and social engagement (Porges & Furman, 2011).

MOVING DOWN THE HIERARCHY

Events are sometimes beyond the capacity of the ventral vagus to regulate the system. Illness and traumatic events predictably tax the system, but everyday experiences can also trigger dysregulation. Feeling alone, having too many responsibilities in a day, working in a challenging environment, and being in a distressed relationship are just some of the experiences that can overwhelm the ventral vagal system.

--- MINI EXERCISE ---

- What are some of the ordinary difficulties that predictably overwhelm your system?
- Is there an extraordinary distress that is too great a challenge for your system?

Following the predictable path of the autonomic hierarchy, when your ventral vagal capacity is depleted, you move one step down the hierarchy and enter the energy of the sympathetic nervous system and the experiences of fight and flight. This survival response is fueled by adrenaline and cortisol. Here you are a system in motion, or more accurately a system in commotion. Flooded with mobilizing energy, you no longer look for connection; you are now focused simply on survival. The body moves into action while the ability for complex, flexible reasoning is impacted (Maran et al., 2017).

—— MINI EXERCISE ————————————————

- What does mobilization look like for you?
- Where does mobilization take you?
- Into fight? Into flight?

It is when mobilization doesn't bring a resolution to the distress that the autonomic nervous system takes the final step down the hierarchy collapsing into dorsal vagal lifelessness. Sometimes called the primitive vagus, the dorsal vagal response takes the entire system offline and into conservation mode. The dorsal vagal experience is a response to what seems inescapable. The autonomic nervous system creatively finds a way out through numbing, disconnection, and dissociation. From a dorsal vagal state, it is difficult to find the way back to ventral vagal connection. In the beginning move out of dorsal vagal collapse, there is a moment of mobilization from the sympathetic nervous system. If not regulated, this necessary infusion of energy elicits the more typical sympathetic actions of fight and flight. Without a reg- ulating influence (internal resourcing, connection with another person, an organized way to use the energy) the onset of mobili- zation is too much. Rather than moving through action into ven- tral vagal connection, there is a return to dorsal vagal shutdown.

— MINI EXERCISE ——————————————————

- Is the experience of dorsal vagal shutdown familiar to you?
- How does the sense of disconnection hap- pen for you?

MEETING THE DEMANDS OF THE DAY

The ability to return to regulation is the essence of resilience. When you establish and resource pathways to ventral vagal regulation, you recover your innate abilities for resilience. The ventral vagus connects with the heart's pacemaker—the sinoatrial node—that regulates the rhythms of the heart. This pathway has been named the vagal brake because it describes the actions of the ventral vagus to slow down or speed up the heart, supporting a flexible response to the challenges of every- day living (Porges, 2017a). A well-functioning vagal brake brings the ability to rapidly engage and disengage, energize and calm, and experience ease in making these transitions. With a flexible vagal brake, you can reflect and respond rather than react. (See Chapter 7 for a full description and a vagal brake exercise.)

In describing five stages of neuroplastic healing, Norman Doidge (2015) identifies the influence of the autonomic nervous system on neuromodulation and restoring the balance in a busy brain. With the ventral vagal system overseeing sympathetic and dorsal vagal responses, the brain quiets and there is a powerful healing effect. Doidge says the state of parasympathetic rest and repair " . . . also recharges the mitochondria, the power sources inside the cells . . . reenergizing them" (p. 111). The ventral vagal system truly powers the journey to well-being.

*The natural healing force within each one of us
is the greatest force in getting well.*
—HIPPOCRATES

—— MINI EXERCISE ——————————

Use the following prompts to consider your autonomic nervous system. Spend a few moments exploring this important and often unacknowledged relationship.

– My autonomic nervous system is . . .

– When I think about my autonomic nervous system I . . .

– I'm grateful to my autonomic nervous system for . . .

– I wish my autonomic nervous system would . . .

CHAPTER 2

NEUROCEPTION

Listen to the wind, it talks. Listen to the silence, it speaks.
Listen to your heart, it knows.

—NATIVE AMERICAN PROVERB

Since humans first appeared on earth, we have been finding ways to safely move through the world. From ancient navigational aids like the North Star and the Viking sunstone to 20th-century machines that use echoes of radio waves, sound, and light, we map what is unseen and navigate to safety. Using the process of neuroception, the second organizing principle of Polyvagal Theory, the autonomic nervous system listens intently, searching for cues of safety and watching for signs of danger to help you orient and take action.

BENEATH AWARENESS

Through neuroception, the autonomic nervous system is listening *inside* to what is happening in your internal organs;

outside, scanning the environment; and *between,* sensing the connection to another nervous system. Cues of life-threat bring a shift into a dorsal vagal state of immobilization or collapse. With cues of danger you step into sympathetic fight and flight. Cues of safety activate the ventral vagal branch and the social engagement system. A pang of hunger, the size and temperature of a room, the feel of a chair, a face with a smile or a frown are just some of the experiences that are taken in by the process of neuroception and bring an autonomic response.

--- MINI EXERCISE ---

Consider your personal neuroceptive cues.
- What is a cue of safety or unsafety from inside your body?
- From the environment?
- Between you and another person?

Neuroception is a passive pathway always running in the background moving your clients up and down the autonomic hierarchy. Beneath awareness, neuroception assesses present moment demands initiating some actions while inhibiting others. A neuroception of safety calms, connects, and dampens the need for protection. By first regulating the passive pathways of neuroception, a platform of safety is created that provides support for engaging the voluntary pathways involved in the process of change (Porges & Carter, 2017).

Neuroception is a deeply subcortical experience that happens below the realm of conscious thought and outside of awareness (Porges, 2017a). This internal surveillance system takes in a constant stream of information and responds by making autonomic adjustments that move you either toward connection or into protection. Always working in service of survival, neuroception activates "the most adaptive [behavior] as interpreted by the nervous system" (Porges, 2017a, p. 176). Long before the information reaches the brain to form a thought, biology has taken action. While you are often unaware of the cues of safety or danger, you feel the autonomic response. Reactions are felt on the inside, (e.g., warmth in the heart, ease of breathing, stomachache, or dry throat) and are sometimes seen on the outside (e.g., smiling, blushing, a relaxed or stiff posture).

—— MINI EXERCISE —————————————————

Consider some of the ways you experience autonomic reactions.

- Which are known only to you?
- Which are visible to others?

SAFETY VERSUS DANGER

Neuroception is tuned through individual experience to take in cues in particular ways as safe, dangerous, and life-threatening. Based on interactions with people and places, neuroception creates habitual patterns of connection or protection. Over time, your internal radar is calibrated to respond in particular ways. Shaped in an environment that is safe and supportive, the system reads cues accurately and inhibits defense systems in safe environments or activates them when there is risk (Porges, 2004). Shaped in an environment that is unpredictable and filled with unexpected events, an environment in which you feel unsafe or unseen, neuroception is biased toward protection which leads to a mismatch between autonomic state and actual safety or risk (Porges, 2015a). This mismatch activates strategies that keep you from accurately sensing safety and inhibiting defense responses, or identifying danger and initiating protective responses. These early autonomic patterns live on through neuroceptive tendencies that create an autonomic profile.

A neuroception of safety is incompatible with a neuroception of danger or life-threat, making this an either/or experience (Porges, 2015a). Through neuroception, your autonomic nervous system is either open to connection and the possibility of change or locked in a protective response and stuck in a survival story. Patterns of connection arise from cues of safety that the down-regulate your defense systems and activate the social engagement system (Porges 2015a). Research has shown that health effects of positive affect, including greater longevity and better immune function, are more than the absence of negative affect (Segerstrom & Sephton, 2010). An embodied sense of safety requires both the reduction or resolution of cues of danger and the experience of cues of safety (Porges & Lewis, 2009). One without the other may not be enough to move out of a state of protection into readiness for connection. The nervous system needs the active appearance and experience of cues of safety (Porges, 2015a).

The hopeful message from Polyvagal Theory is that autonomic patterns and autonomic profiles can be reshaped. While early experiences shape the system, ongoing experiences can reduce or even resolve cues of danger. Cues of safety, often missed in the midst of cues of danger, can be recognized and over time become more abundant. One of the ways to reshape your system is to first bring perception to neuroception and then add context through the lens of discernment. Bringing attention to the present moment invites you to consider the origins of cues of danger. Has a cue from the past reached into the present? While it was a necessary survival response when it first activated, is it needed now?

--- MINI EXERCISE ---

Stop for a moment to notice your neuroception. Take in the environment through sight and sound. See the people and things around you.

What are the cues of safety and danger? Are there enough cues of safety to bring you into a readiness for connection? Or do the cues of danger keep you poised for protection?

Use this question to look through the lens of discernment: In this moment, with this person, in this place, surrounded by these things, are you actually in danger, or are you safe?

BACK TO BEGINNINGS

Neuroception launches a cascade of embodied events that become a story. When entering into an autonomic state, the information about that state travels up the autonomic pathways to the brain. There, a story is created to make sense of the experience. The physiological state creates a psychological story. Using the metaphor of a river, imagine the flow of experience. At the river's source is neuroception and at the river's mouth is the story. In between lie perception, autonomic state, feelings, and behaviors (Figure 2.1).

FIGURE 2.1. From Neuroception to Story

We're accustomed to entering the river downstream with feelings, behavior, or story. But neuroception happens at the farthest point upstream. You need to make your way back to the starting point, leaving behind story, behavior, and feelings to identify the state and bring perception to neuroception. It is when you travel back upstream to consider neuroception that you become aware of how your internal surveillance system begins the sequence of events that eventually leads to the way you are feeling, acting, and thinking.

Attitudes, actions, and the way you see the world are the result of the autonomic nervous system moving between states of connection and protection. The stories you inhabit begin far away from the thinking brain in the autonomic nervous system with a neuroception of safety, danger, or life-threat.

— **MINI EXERCISE** —————————————

Bring to mind an experience and make your way to the river's source. Bring perception to the neuroception that was the starting point. What was the cue of safety or danger that you followed downstream into feeling, behavior, and finally story?

Through understanding the process of neuroception, you can begin to honor the ways the autonomic nervous system listens and acts in service of your safety and survival. Knowing that neuroception shapes the first part of your story, you can begin to listen in new ways and learn to become a skilled story editor.

CHAPTER 3

CO-REGULATION

*We cannot live only for ourselves. A thousand fibers
connect us.*

—HERMAN MELVILLE

Connection is a biological imperative, vital to our survival
(Porges, 2015a). Through our biology, we are wired for connection. Our autonomic nervous system longs for connection
with another system and sends signals out into the world,
searching for signals in return. By means of co-regulation, the
third organizing principle of Polyvagal Theory, we connect
with others and create a shared sense of safety.

WIRED FOR CONNECTION

Belonging to a group or being part of a tribe has been a survival
strategy throughout evolutionary history. Humans are social
beings "and our nature is to recognize, interact, and form relationships" with others (Cacioppo & Cacioppo, 2014, p. 1). We

find purpose in our social connections and when our belongingness needs aren't met, we feel less meaning in our everyday lives (Stillman et al., 2009). Connection is a wired in biological necessity; isolation, or even the perception of social separateness, leads to a compromised ability to regulate our autonomic states and impacts our physical and emotional well-being (Porges & Furman, 2011). When we feel alone in the world we suffer. When that feeling is chronic, medical and mental health risks multiply. Cardiovascular disease and death, an exaggerated inflammatory response, cognitive decline, sleep disturbance, and depression are just some of the consequences of being stuck in a loneliness loop (Cole et al., 2015; Hawkley & Cacioppo, 2010).

Beginning with the way we are welcomed into the world the autonomic nervous system starts to build a story about relationships. How much of that story is about connection and how much is about protection depends on whether we have regulated and regulating people surrounding us. At birth we move from anatomical connection through the umbilical cord to autonomic connection through face-to-face, nervous system to nervous system co-regulation. Kangaroo care, skin-to-skin contact between mothers or fathers and babies, has become common practice in hospital nurseries and neonatal intensive care units. Positive outcomes for babies include heart, breathing, and temperature stabilization; more organized sleep; rapid improvement in state organization; and parents report feeling more sensitive to their babies and more able to adapt to their baby's signals (Jefferies, 2012). In these earliest interactions, babies depend on their caregiver to bring a regulated nervous system to the connection.

In attuned parent-child relationships, parents recognize their child's changing autonomic needs and respond appropriately. In this co-regulation of autonomic states, there is a shared autonomic experience, a shared emotional experience, and a shared experience of safety. The attuned dyad creates a biological synchrony that forms the foundation for navigating interpersonal relationships (Manini et al., 2013). Uninterrupted attunement isn't necessary to develop a regulated autonomic response system. In fact, that match needs to happen only about a third of the time (Ostlund et al., 2017; Tronick & Gianino, 1986). The essential ingredient is what happens after the mismatch. A regulated, flexible, and resilient system is built when the ruptures are recognized and repairs are made.

The ability to self-regulate is built on ongoing experiences of co-regulation. Yet, even as we develop self-regulating capacities, the need for social interaction and co-regulation remains throughout our lifetime (Porges & Furman, 2011). We depend on the people around us for co-regulation and try to offer experiences of co-regulation in return. Sometimes, however, rather than a co-regulating experience we find we are engaged in mutual dysregulation. We follow a friend into anxiety, lose hope along with our partner, or find ourselves in a state of opposition to others.

MISSED CONNECTIONS

When there is ongoing misattunement, when ruptures aren't recognized and repaired, the autonomic experience of persistent danger shapes the system away from connection into

—— MINI EXERCISE ————————————————

Think about the people in your life and consider which connections are most often coregulating and which more often bring mutual dysregulation.

- When do you feel an autonomic match?
- When do you feel an autonomic mismatch?

patterns of protection. Loneliness is a subjective experience. It emerges not from the objective facts of social isolation but out of a perception of social isolation (De Jong Gierveld & Van Tilburg, 2010). Loneliness is a common human experience. A study of 20,000 people in the United States (Cigna U.S. Loneliness Index) found that 46% reported feeling lonely sometimes or always, 46% reported feeling left out sometimes or always, and only 27% feel as if they belong to a group. A 2017 survey in Britain (Jo Cox Commission on Loneliness) found over nine million people reported feeling often or always lonely. Loneliness prompts us to reach out to others but can also activate patterns of protection (Cacioppo & Cacioppo, 2014). We feel both the pull to connect and the fear of rejection. Cues of danger and life-threat interrupt the ability for co-regulation and the creation of relationships (Porges & Carter, 2017). When we move into hypervigilance for threat, it's difficult to send signals of welcome to others. Through the cues of safety and danger we send out into the world people feel our *social temperature*—warm and welcoming, hot and bothered, or cold and calculating (Ijzerman et al., 2012).

Social connection is the subjective experience of being connected to others (Seppälä, Rossomando, & Doty, 2013). Social support on the other hand may be an exchange relationship in which services, information, and advice are offered. While social support has a necessary place in your life, if you don't also experience social connection, you can feel a deep sense of loneliness. In fact, in studies of social support it appears that it is the quality and not the quantity of the support that impacts life satisfaction (Utz & Breuer, 2017). Interestingly, studies indicate that *perceived* social support shows higher correlations with well-being than *received* support (Utz & Breuer, 2017). When offers of social support and acts of social interaction include the sense of companionship, then co-regulation and social connection ease the sense of loneliness. When social support is being delivered from a state of misattunement, then the autonomic experience is one of needing protection from harm (Porges, 2012). It's the "perception of safety [that] is the turning point in the development of relationships . . ." (Porges, 2003, p. 39).

─── **MINI EXERCISE** ───────────────

Take a moment to consider the people around you. Notice which category (support or connection) people belong in. Some people may be in one category while others may be in both.

– Who is in your social support network?

– Who do you feel socially connected to?

RECONNECTING

The research on loneliness proves what your autonomic nervous system knows; you need social connection and suffer both physically and emotionally when you don't experience enough of it. The UCLA Loneliness Scale, a 20-question survey that you can locate easily on the internet, assesses the perception of social isolation and is used extensively in research. One way to begin to consider your experience of loneliness is with the short, three-item version of this scale:

On a scale of Hardly ever, Some of the time, Often,

1. How often do you feel that you lack companionship?
2. How often do you feel left out?
3. How often do you feel isolated from others?

According to Porges (2016, p. 5), "Survival is dependent on opportunities to successfully co-regulate." With enough experiences of co-regulation you become able to successfully self-regulate as well. He goes on to state that " . . . a history of successful and predictable co-regulation tunes the nervous system to be sufficiently resilient to function during periods of separation" (Porges, 2016, p. 6). With this understanding of co-regulation and self-regulation comes the recognition that being alone does not always equate with feeling alone and being alone is not always an experience of suffering. When you suffer from loneliness, being alone means being isolated, but with a foundation of social connection and predictable opportunities for co-regulation, you can safely enter into the experience of solitude. "[Language] has created the word 'loneliness' to express the pain of being alone. And it has created the word 'solitude' to express the glory of being alone" (Tillich, 1963). What are the autonomic differences between isolation and solitude? Isolation arises from a state of protection. This may be the sympathetic nervous system mobilizing a desperate search for connection or the dorsal vagal system bringing a collapse into despair and disconnection. On the other hand, solitude is a ventral vagal–resourced experience of choosing to be alone and feeling a sense of peace in the separateness.

—— MINI EXERCISE ————————————————
- When do you feel lonely?
- When do you feel the sweetness of solitude?

If a core component of well-being is the predictable opportunity for co-regulating relationships, then trauma might be described as the chronic disruption of connectedness (Porges, 2014). Trauma creates ongoing adaptive survival responses that keep the autonomic nervous system from finding safety in connection. Without experiences of co-regulation, and without trust that ongoing opportunities for co-regulation are available, the autonomic pathways that support moving out of protection into connection aren't exercised and strengthened. The autonomic nervous system remains on guard, ready to act in service of survival. When two people co-regulate and share a state of safety, their autonomic nervous systems create the possibility for health, growth, and restoration. Within a co-regulated relationship, your quest for safety is realized and you can create a story of well-being.

SECTION I **SUMMARY**

If civilization is to survive, we must cultivate the science of human relationships.

—FRANKLIN D. ROOSEVELT

Life is experienced from the inside out through neuroception and state changes and from the outside in through co-regulating or dysregulating connections with others. Experiences are carried in autonomic pathways: trauma stories rooted in states of sympathetic and dorsal vagal dysregulation and stories of well-being anchored in the ventral vagal state of safety and connection.

The autonomic nervous system is designed to help you successfully navigate the challenges of daily living. Formed through the history of human evolution and individually shaped by day-to-day experience, the autonomic nervous system continuously assesses risk, inhibiting some responses while initiating others, all in service of survival. Cues of safety and danger, often outside of your awareness, activate autonomic states that are translated into patterns of protection or connection. Through the lens of Polyvagal Theory, these experiences of moving toward or away from people, places, and things become understandable and predictable.

The autonomic nervous system shapes the ways you experience your life. Through your physiology, you hear the call to connect and feel an autonomic response. Where does your autonomic nervous system take you? Moving toward or backing away? Extending a hand or clenching a fist? When you learn to partner with your autonomic nervous system, you can reshape the system and rewrite your stories. When you are anchored in a state of ventral vagal safety, you can open the door to change.

SECTION II

NAVIGATING AUTONOMIC PATHWAYS: THE BASIC APPROACH

There is more wisdom in your body than in your deepest philosophy.

—NIETZSCHE

OVERVIEW: THE BASIC FRAMEWORK

How can you recruit the power of the autonomic nervous system not only in service of survival but also in service of healing? Using the same physiological processes that shape the system, it is possible to move out of habitually activated reactions and bring flexibility back to a system that has become rigid in patterns of protection. Following the organizing principles of Polyvagal Theory, you can help your clients reshape their systems and rewrite their stories.

The BASIC framework—Befriend, Attend, Shape, Integrate, Connect—helps your clients develop skills in autonomic regulation leading to increased flexibility of response and resilience. Repatterning the nervous system depends on bringing explicit awareness to implicit experiences, interrupting automatic response patterns, and engaging the ventral vagal safety circuit.

Befriend. Transient experiences of disconnection from the body are common in the general population and prevalent with your clients who have experienced traumatic events. The greater the awareness of body-based feelings, the more control your clients have over their lives. Befriending is learning to *tune in and turn toward* autonomic state and story with curiosity and self-compassion.

Attend. Attending practices create the ability to name autonomic states, track the movement between states, and develop a moment-to-moment habit of noticing large shifts and nuanced changes. Learning to attend to these autonomic experiences sets the stage for shaping the system.

Shape. Trauma interrupts the ability to regulate autonomic state and flexibly transition between states. Just as the brain has the capacity to rewire, the autonomic nervous system can also establish new patterns. Shaping the system away from habitual survival responses into patterns of connection involves bringing mindful attention to practices that increase the capacity for staying anchored in the ventral vagal system.

Integrate. Through the lens of the autonomic nervous system, resilience is the ability to return to ventral vagal regulation following a move into sympathetic mobilization or dorsal vagal shut down. Autonomic state shifts in response to the challenges of daily living are a normal and expected experience. For many people, the shifts are slight, and even in the moments of large-scale changes there is enough resilience to return to a regulated state. For others, the response is extreme and a return to regulation is unreachable. Integrating brings attention to the new autonomic patterns that are emerging and engages them to shape new, resilient pathways.

Connect. The autonomic nervous system shapes the way we connect. The way your clients experience self, create relationships, and move through the world is built through their autonomic pathways. With new abilities for regulation, creating safe connections is possible.

When the autonomic nervous system has been shaped by trauma, there is often a disconnection between physiological state, psychological story, and behavioral response. Cues of danger seem to be everywhere and the smallest reminder of a traumatic experience activates a survival response. The ability to find regulation in the ventral vagal state is compromised. This leaves your clients unable to either become quiet and calm or activated and outspoken without moving out of connection into a state of protection (Williamson, E. C. Porges, Lamb,

& S. W. Porges, 2015). When the regulating influence of the ventral vagal system is missing, your clients feel as if they are locked in a state of protection, unable to either reach out or let anything in. Interrupting the automaticity of a response pattern through awareness supports the process of change (Neal, Wood, Wu, & Kurlander, 2011). Bringing perception to neuroception mobilizes higher brain structures and stimulates awareness. With awareness, your clients can see cues in present time rather than through the lens of the past.

It's important to help your clients cultivate a ventral vagal–powered attitude of self-compassion when working with the BASIC exercises. Self-compassion can reduce sympathetic activity and bring increased ventral vagal flexibility in responding to stressful situations (Homan & Sirois, 2017; Kirby, Doty, Petrocchi, & Gilbert, 2017; Luo, Qiao & Che, 2018). Self-criticism activates ancient defense systems that take your clients out of safety into a state of protection. From a survival state, access to higher levels of thinking is impaired, reflection is replaced with reaction, and the ability to engage in the process of change is shut down. Self-compassion offers your clients a safe pathway to explore their autonomic response patterns.

HOW TO USE THE EXERCISES IN THIS SECTION

Research on the way humans make and sustain change highlights the importance of having confidence in the ability to change, having positive beginning experiences of change, and having a belief that with practice change takes less effort to sustain (Lally, Wardle, & Gardner, 2011). Following a process of making and repeating small changes brings these possibilities to life.

Chapters 4–8 offer exercises to introduce to your clients during sessions, with the intention that they will continue to work on their own between sessions. The exercises are designed to bring autonomic patterns into explicit awareness, and it is helpful for clients to use a notebook or journal as a way to track changes. Grounded in the clinical philosophy that therapists don't ask their clients to do anything they have not already tried I encourage you to complete the exercises yourself before inviting your clients to try them. The BASIC framework is designed so the exercises in one chapter build the foundation for the next. A natural confidence emerges as your clients begin to engage new autonomic patterns that support well-being. My suggestion is that you go through the chapters with your clients in order. Sometimes, though, you may decide that a client would benefit by engaging in a specific exercise at a certain point in your work. You could choose to introduce the exercise out of sequence and then return to earlier exercises. The exercises are not meant to be a one-and-done activity. The goal is for your clients to use the exercises over time to create competence and confidence with a specific skill and then select certain ones to become ongoing autonomic practices.

Personal progress trackers for Chapters 4–8 are found in the Appendix. These are designed to track the subtle shifts that are an integral part of autonomic change. Invite your clients to use the personal progress trackers on their own and also follow your clients' progress by periodically using the trackers to check in during your sessions. Change is not an event but rather a lifelong process and autonomic reorganization is ongoing. The personal progress trackers are a way for your clients to routinely check in with the ever-changing state of their systems.

EXPECTED OUTCOMES

The BASIC framework guides your clients into a new experience of actively engaging with their autonomic nervous systems. The exercises offer opportunities for your clients to experiment with skills to navigate differently. Over time, new skills become sustainable practices. As your clients learn to partner with the autonomic nervous system, they feel more competent and more confident, and they experience the well-being that comes from living with an integrated body-mind system. With greater capacity for staying anchored in ventral vagal regulation, clients discover they have an expanded ability to feel safe and connect to the inherent wisdom of the autonomic nervous system. For many clients this is the longed-for therapeutic outcome and once they are able to predictably regulate, they are ready to move on. For other clients, this is the platform that supports moving deeper into trauma processing. For all clients, engaging in the Befriend, Attend, Shape, Integrate, and Connect exercises builds the ability to look through the lens of the autonomic nervous system and recognize what is happening, find a toehold in ventral to be able to regulate and respond in a different way, and begin to write new stories of safety and connection.

CHAPTER 4

BEFRIENDING THE AUTONOMIC NERVOUS SYSTEM

The first step toward change is awareness.
The second step is acceptance.

—NATHANIEL BRANDEN

How do you help your clients learn to tune in and turn toward their bodies and, in particular, the autonomic nervous system? Befriending establishes the ability to safely feel autonomic states, identify individual aspects of each state, and activate and maintain curiosity and compassion during the process. Many of your clients live in their stories, disconnected from the body states from which those stories emerge. And as van der Kolk (2014) reminds us, "You can be fully in charge of your life only if you can acknowledge the reality of your body, in all its visceral dimensions" (p. 27).

By putting things in categories, your clients' perception of them changes and they gain expertise in recognizing and differentiating between them (Petersen, Schroijen, Mölders, Zenker, & den Bergh, 2014). "Sensing, naming, and identifying what is going on inside is the first step to recovery" (van der Kolk, 2014, p. 68). Recognizing sympathetic mobilization and dorsal vagal immobilization as adaptive survival responses triggered by too many cues of danger and not enough cues of safety helps your clients reappraise their responses as actions in service of survival. Research shows that rethinking states of arousal as functional responses reduces the intensity of activation and supports a connection to regulating resources; thinking about physiological activation as a resource to meet a challenge brings positive outcomes (Jamieson, Nock, & Mendes, 2011). The simple act of labeling responses impacts autonomic activity and likely supports vagal function (Kanbara & Fukunaga, 2016).

When your clients learn to mindfully meet their autonomic nervous systems, bring compassion to their embodied experiences, and honor each autonomic response, they have begun to befriend the nervous system. The befriending exercises are presented in three categories: Accurate Autonomic Awareness, the Art of Befriending, and the Practice of Reconnecting. Accurate Autonomic Awareness presents one exercise to help your clients create personal archetypes of each state and a second exercise that brings ventral vagal experiences into concrete usability. The Art of Befriending offers your clients exercises to deepen the connection to their autonomic hierarchy through the use of art, writing, and movement. The final section, the Practice of Reconnecting, offers four exercises to explore the range of responses possible within each autonomic state.

ACCURATE AUTONOMIC AWARENESS

Before your clients can explore new ways to regulate, they first need to recognize their autonomic state. The ability to regulate is dependent on how accurately incoming information is interpreted. Being able to correctly identify autonomic states is the necessary first step in the process of shaping the system in a new way.

──── EXERCISE ────────────

Autonomic Landmarks—Stories
of Landmark Moments

This exercise is a good way to introduce clients to recognizing autonomic responses by focusing on key experiences. Clients can write their experiences in their journal and share them with you during a future session.

BACKGROUND

Landmarks give structure to our environments, forming cognitive anchors, marking points of orientation, and becoming references for communication. Autonomic landmarks are the internal reference points that mark the experience of states. We have personal landmarks that represent the embodied experience of a state and are stored in our memory. This is a moment that stands out from all the others, a moment you can look back on as a defining experience of an autonomic response.

Identifying the landmark moment for each state is a way to quickly bring the properties that personify the state to mind.

STEPS

1. What are the stories of your dorsal vagal (collapse or shutdown), sympathetic (fight or flight), and ventral vagal (safe and connected) landmark moments? To make it easier to think about your states, you can give them descriptive names in addition to the physiological ones. Take time to look back and locate the moments in your memory. Find the times that stand out and become the archetype for each state.

2. Landmarks are recognizable by their names and characteristics. Write a story describing the landmark moment. Make sure to identify the concrete details of what happened, how you responded, what your body felt like, and what you thought.

3. When you are done, read through the story and identify the crucial moment. Use this to give the story a name.

TIPS

Identifying clients' key autonomic moments and giving them a name can create useful anchors to use during therapy sessions as you explore your clients' experiences. Your clients may benefit from examples of stories to get a feel for the experiences to explore (the autonomic hierarchy from dorsal vagal to sympathetic to ventral vagal) and the level of detail for their descriptions. You can provide your own examples or use the following ones.

Dorsal Vagal Bowl-Shattering Moment: In my commitment to eating in a healthier way, I took time to make a salad for lunch. I used the special bowl that I brought back from France and enjoyed cutting up and layering vegetables making a lunch that was nutritious and looked inviting. As I walked out of the kitchen, my arm caught on the counter and I dropped the bowl. It shattered, spreading vegetables and pieces of pottery across the floor. I stood there unable to move, just staring at the mess, and then walked to the living room and sat down on the couch. It felt like an overwhelming disaster, not a dropped bowl of salad, and I went into a full collapse. I sat and stared and felt numb. The only thing I could say was "I'm done"—without even knowing what that meant. It took 15 minutes to begin to feel the stirring of enough energy to clean the kitchen floor. Lunch was a thing of the past and my attention was now focused on simply putting one foot in front of the other. While the intensity of collapse I experienced in response to the accident made no sense in isolation, in a larger context it was the last straw for my nervous system that couldn't keep up with the overwhelming demands of daily living. This "bowl-shattering moment" is for me the epitome of a dorsal vagal experience.

Sympathetic Jack-in-the-Box: I learned growing up that it was safer to be seen and not heard—ever. I've worked hard to find my voice as a grown-up, and now, instead of the shutdown experience of my childhood, when I feel someone is minimizing my experience, I'm immediately mobilized to fight. I'm like a Jack-in-the-Box—coiled tight and ready to spring. I feel the lever turning and then I pop. The moment that sticks in my mind is a phone call with my brother during the holidays. I had been estranged from my sister for some time and my brother made an innocent comment about holidays and families being together and POP! I stopped hearing what he said, hung up on him, and threw the phone. When I regained enough regulation to look back on that moment, I knew it wasn't what my brother said, it was that my rupture with my sister was unacknowledged and my experience dismissed.

Ventral Vagal Wise Woman: I was on a 2-week meditation retreat struggling with doubt, fear, self-criticism, and boredom—all the kinds of feelings that find their way into awareness when you sit silently for hours a day. One day, when I was sitting with tremendous sadness, I saw the image of an old woman silently sitting in a warm, dark room, next to an enormous, glowing, pulsing shape that I knew was my own heart. In that moment I knew there was nothing in the world that would stop her from sitting next to that heart. Her presence was unconditional. Her warmth and regard unchangeable. She was sitting with my heart. The tremendous sadness I was feeling didn't go away, but it was somehow eased and seen in such a way that I wasn't burdened by it anymore. For me, in that moment, *being with* became the essence of the ventral vagal state.

Encourage your clients to explore the details of their experiences. If they have trouble getting in touch with a state, talk with them about some of their memories. Have them write a few words, short phrases, or sentences to begin their landmark story. They can then take their beginning story home and continue the work on their own. You can return to this exercise the following week(s) and revisit it later in the therapy process to expand your clients' stories and understanding.

—— EXERCISE ——
Ventral Vagal Anchors—Anchoring in Safety

This exercise helps your clients identify the experiences that anchor them in a ventral vagal state, using the categories of who, what, where, and when. Invite your clients to work on this at home and share their anchors with you during a session. This is an exercise to return to as your clients add ventral vagal anchors and update their lists.

BACKGROUND

The Merriam-Webster dictionary defines an anchor as "something that serves to hold an object firmly; a reliable support." A ventral vagal anchor holds the connection to the energy of your ventral vagal system when experiences threaten to pull you into a sympathetic or dorsal vagal state. Your ventral vagal anchors help you find the way back to regulation and stay there. These are autonomic cues of safety that can be found in the categories of who, what, where, and when. You can use your anchors by reconnecting to the anchor or by activating the memory of the anchor. With regular practice, ventral vagal anchors strengthen your capacity to return to regulation.

STEPS

1. **Who.** Reflect on the people in your life and make a list of the ones who bring you a feeling of being safe and welcome. You might also have a pet who fills that role. First identify a person or pet who is present in your life. Then, if you wish, you can expand your search to also include people who are no longer living, people you haven't met but who bring your ventral vagal state alive, and spiritual figures.

2. **What.** Think about what you do that brings your ventral vagal state alive. Look for small actions that feel nourishing and inviting of connection. Keep track of the things that bring moments, or micro-moments, of ventral vagal regulation.

3. **Where.** Take a tour of your world and find the physical places that bring you cues of safety. Look around your home, your neighborhood, your community, your workplace, a place you feel a spiritual connection. Bring to mind the everyday places you move through. Take note of the environments and name the ones that activate your ventral vagal state.

4. **When.** Identify the moments in time when you feel anchored in your ventral vagal energy. Take a moment to go back and revisit those experiences. Bring them into conscious awareness and write them down.

5. **Create a portfolio of your ventral vagal anchors.** Decide how you want to gather your anchors together in one place: write them in a notebook, illustrate them in a journal, make a list and hang it in a prominent place,

write on sticky notes and put them around your home and at work in places that are easy to see. Experiment and find the way that works for you, making sure you have easy access to your anchors.

TIPS

You might share your own anchors to prompt your clients, or they may readily identify anchors on their own. The following are some examples of anchors in each category that can be used to start the exploration.

Who: Sometimes one person is identified as an overarching anchor.

- My old friend from childhood is my anchor. I have been sharing stories with her for almost 60 years and know I can count on her to be there no matter what I need.
- At other times different people are identified as anchors for specific kinds of moments.
  - I have someone who is my "happy moments" anchor, someone who is my "angry moments" anchor, and someone who is my "lonely moments" anchor.
  - I have a person who is an anchor in my professional world and another person who is a personal anchor.

What:
- My walk to work, checking my horoscope, looking out the window, holding my lucky stone, watering my plants

Where:

- By the ocean, at my local coffee shop, under my favorite tree, in my car, at my friend's house, in the kitchen, in the garden

When

- The very early hours of the morning, climbing into bed at the end of the day, Sunday afternoon, in the evening when the kids are asleep, leaving work and heading home

Just as the ancient Greek philosopher Epictetus wisely recommended that we not moor a ship with one anchor, having a variety of ventral vagal anchors to choose from makes it easier to find an anchor to hold onto when needed. During the course of therapy, you've probably heard your clients identify anchors (although not named in that way), and they can bring their awareness to those. Many clients begin by finding one anchor in each category and add more as time goes on. Because trauma often happens in relationships, the *who* category can be the most challenging for your clients. In the beginning, they may not have safe, regulated people in their lives and may identify you as the person who is their ventral vagal anchor.

THE ART OF BEFRIENDING—AN ILLUSTRATED HIERARCHY

The autonomic hierarchy can be visualized in many ways. The autonomic ladder presented in *The Polyvagal Theory in Therapy* (Dana, 2018) is one way that has proven to be easy to understand and use.

Art, writing, and movement are other options for your clients to get to know the autonomic hierarchy. Art is a means of self-expression and communication that supports experiencing emotions in a safe way (McPherson, Barrett, Lopez-Gonzalez, Jiradejvong, & Limb, 2016). Making visual art has been shown to have an impact on resilience (Bolwerk, Mack-Andrick, Lang, Dörfler, & Maihöfner, 2014) and is a way to explore, understand, and express experiences that may be difficult to put into words (Stuckey & Nobel, 2010). Writing brings together cognition, emotions, and biology and offers a new way of understanding experiences of self (Pennebaker, 2018) while movement has been shown to support self-awareness (Stuckey & Nobel, 2010). Once your clients have a feel for the states of the autonomic nervous system, the ways to illustrate the hierarchy are unlimited.

---------- **EXERCISE** ----------

Befriending the Hierarchy

This exercise uses a simple vertical line to represent the hierarchy. Clients explore a variety of design options and a range of ways to illustrate their personal experiences of moving between states. Invite your clients to work on these at home and bring their completed designs to sessions.

BACKGROUND

With the ability to name your states and recognize the shifts that happen between states, you can represent your experience of moving along the hierarchy. Portraying these movements in different ways expands that connection. As you engage in the process of designing hierarchies, you are engaging in an act of befriending.

STEPS

1. Draw a vertical line, divide it in thirds, and mark the three states (ventral, sympathetic, dorsal, or the words you choose to name your states).

2. Imagine moving along that line and feel the autonomic state shifts.

3. Illustrate the small increments of change that happen as you travel down and up the hierarchy using:

   • color to represent your states and transitions from state to state, blending shades to illustrate the full range of the autonomic hierarchy

   • words to label the continuum of your experience from dorsal through sympathetic to ventral

   • photos of faces to show the many ways your states are expressed

   • images of animals to represent states

   • pictures of places that bring the points along the continuum to life

   • nature scenes that portray the many stops you make along the hierarchy

   • names of songs that carry the energy of states

4. Create a few illustrated hierarchies to get a sense of how different designs work for you. See if you resonate with one particular way of representing the hierarchy or if you connect with several different styles.

5. Choose one or more hierarchies and create an ongoing practice of using it (or them) to find your place and name your state.

TIPS

Encourage your clients to create their first hierarchy using the style they feel most comfortable with and then experiment with other designs. Have them share their completed hierarchies in session. Discuss how they connect with each and compare their autonomic experiences.

─── **EXERCISE** ───────────────────
Autonomic Trees

This exercise is a multifaceted way to help clients safely create connection to their autonomic states. Three modalities—art, writing, movement—are used to help clients come into connection with their regulated and reactive responses in new ways. Clients can create variations at home and share their different autonomic expressions in sessions.

BACKGROUND

A tree is a commonly used metaphor. The tree of life is often used to illustrate both evolutioniionary processes and patterns of relationships. Using a tree metaphor, you can investigate your autonomic experiences: with trees representing regulated responses and ones representing reactive systems. There are many ways to dive into discovering the qualities of autonomic trees, and each brings its own pathways to befriending the embodied experience of your autonomic nervous system.

Art: Making art is a safe way to explore autonomic states. Creating images of regulated and reactive trees invites you to bring your autonomic states to life and befriend them through color and design.

Writing: Sitting down to write the stories of regulated and reactive autonomic trees requires a stance of curiosity that lends itself to befriending.

Movement: Imagined or enacted movement is a way to feel the rhythms of your regulated and reactive trees. Autonomic trees can feel as if they are stomping and swaying, their trunks bending or twisting, their branches reaching up and out, and their spring buds emerging or autumn leaves falling.

STEPS FOR AUTONOMIC TREE ART:

1. Set up your creative space. Gather various-sized papers and other art materials.
2. There are thousands of species of trees, many living only in one specific place in the world. Your regulated and reactive trees live in your personal world and have their own unique characteristics. Visualize their roots, branches, and leaves. See their forms, shapes, and colors.
3. Create your trees. You might design one tree that illustrates all three states, one regulated and one reactive tree, or a family of regulated and reactive trees (Figure 4.1).

FIGURE 4.1. Autonomic Tree by David Keevil; Autonomic Tree by Rebecca Gerbig

4. Reflect on your designs. What autonomic experiences do they represent?
5. Periodically return to your trees and connect to your personal tree kingdom.

TIPS

Clients' art trees are useful tools to explore ventral, sympathetic, and dorsal states. Because the images can be brought to life quickly, they become easy reference points to use in sessions.

STEPS FOR WRITING TREE STORIES

1. If you have created your tree maps, you can use those as an entry point for listening. Otherwise, bring your regulated and reactive trees to life by focusing on an internal image.

2. Use the following prompts to begin to write a story for each of your trees:
   - The (roots, trunk, branches) of my tree bring . . .
   - When I sit under my tree, I . . .
   - When I put my arms around my tree, I . . .
   - When I listen to my tree, I hear . . .

3. Read your story and add any other information you want to complete it.

4. Give your story a title.

TIPS

Similar to art trees, clients can create tree stories for more than one regulated and reactive state. Have your clients share their tree stories with you. Get to know the particular words that are meaningful for each client as they describe their experiences of being with each tree. The act of reading a story and having a story read to you evokes different experiences. Invite your clients to read their tree stories to you and also read their tree stories to them. Explore what happens when they speak and hear their stories.

STEPS FOR MOVING TREES

1. Visualize your tree and feel its movement inside your body.

2. Either see the movement in your mind's eye or let the movement come into physical expression. Choose the way that brings a neuroception of safety.

3. Explore the ways your tree moves. Ventral vagal regulation is experienced in many different ways along the continuum of stillness to joy-filled passion. Reactivity includes both the intensity of sympathetic mobilization with fight and flight and the absence of energy in dorsal vagal disappearance, disconnection, and collapse.

4. Repeat the process with all of your trees.

5. Build an ongoing practice of moving with your trees.

TIPS

Regulated and reactive trees have a multitude of movements. Just as living trees are impacted by daily weather and changing seasons, the shifts in your client's *autonomic weather* affect their embodied trees and can be seen in the changing movements.

THE PRACTICE OF RECONNECTING

A common posttraumatic response is a sense of disconnection from the body. Since 80% of the information from the vagus is sent through afferent pathways from the body to the brain, learning to turn toward and listen in to what the autonomic nervous system is communicating is an important part of befriending.

——— **EXERCISE** ———————————

Body Language

Safe embodiment is a challenge for many clients, so intro-duce this exercise and experiment with it during a session where you are there to be a co-regulating presence. Once safety with this way of listening has been established, your clients can continue the practice at home.

BACKGROUND

With an ability to safely connect to your autonomic states and bring that embodied experience into explicit awareness, you have access to the important autonomic information that is guiding your daily experience.

STEPS

1. Find the place in your body where you feel most con-nected to your ventral vagal state. Bring the qualities of that experience into explicit awareness and add lan-guage to describe it.

2. Find the place in your body where you feel most con-nected to your sympathetic state. Bring the qualities of that experience into explicit awareness and add lan-guage to describe it.

3. Find the place in your body where you feel most con-nected to your dorsal vagal state. Bring the qualities of that experience into explicit awareness and add lan-guage to describe it.

4. Connect to the three places in your body where you

identified feeling each state most fully. Move from one place to another. Feel the ways your experience changes as you shift your focus.

5. Connect to your ventral vagal state of safety and connection. Tune in to how this is expressed in your body. Identify the qualities of your breath, muscle tone, and posture. Track the flow of energy throughout your body and notice any movements connected with this state.

6. Move to your sympathetic nervous system and consider the activation of the mobilizing energy of fight and flight. Tune in to how this is expressed in your body. Identify the qualities of your breath, muscle tone, and posture. Track the flow of energy throughout your body and notice any movements associated with this state.

7. Move to your dorsal vagal state and consider the ways collapse and shutdown are experienced. Tune in to how this state is expressed in your body. Identify the qualities of your breath, muscle tone, and posture. Track the flow of energy throughout your body and notice any movements associated with this state.

8. Move from state to state and notice the changes that happen. Become familiar with the ways your body moves through states.

TIPS

Bringing safe awareness to the embodied experiences of states is more challenging than working with cognitive awareness. This is an exercise where *small and often* is an important guideline. Support your clients in listening for small moments to make connecting to this autonomic information a natural, uncomplicated, and ordinary practice.

——— EXERCISE ———

The Continuum Between Survival and Social Engagement

This exercise brings explicit awareness to the experience of being safe and engaged or disconnected and in danger. Since this is often experienced as an either/or event, the use of a continuum helps identify the subtle autonomic shifts that happen between the two opposite ends of experience.

BACKGROUND

Between the two ends of autonomic responses, there are many points along the way. Some bring a nuanced experience of an autonomic shift while other points are where you make a bigger step from one state to another. Using a continuum is a way for you to map the progression of small steps that connect two opposite end points. To create this continuum, bring focused attention to the particular ways you move between protection and connection.

STEPS

1. Draw a horizontal line and name the two ends of your continuum. What is your label for engagement? What is your label for disconnection?

2. Start at either end. Identify the first small step out of that state toward the other end. Repeat this, marking small steps along the way until you reach the other end.

3. Mark the midpoint where you feel the larger shift from connection to protection. The midpoint is a good way to identify this moment of change.

4. Remember you are always moving along this continuum, sometimes firmly planted in one place and other times pulled from one end to the other. Stop and see where you are. Use the midpoint to first see if you are on the side of protection or closer to the state of connection. Then identify more precisely where you are on your range of responses.

5. Return to your continuum and practice placing yourself on it until it becomes second nature for you to know where you are and in which direction your autonomic nervous system is taking you.

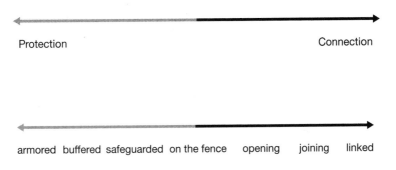

FIGURE 4.2. Between Protection and Connection Continuum and Example

TIPS

By using the continuum illustrated in Figure 4.2, your clients learn to see the flow of experience and move away from thinking in all-or-nothing terms. They create skill in feeling the nuanced shifts that lead to large scale changes. Once your clients have worked with this continuum, this becomes a useful template to create other continuums. Just identify a particular experience, name the two ends, find the midpoint, and then fill in the steps that lead from one end to the other.

——— EXERCISE ———

The Social Engagement Scale

This exercise is a way for clients to identify their personal experiences of the ebb and flow of social engagement that happens within the ventral vagal state. With the social engagement scale, clients are able to track the level of participation that is resourcing in the moment.

BACKGROUND

Rather than a straightforward on or off mode, the social engagement system can be online and bring a range of responses. Sometimes you may feel a pull to enter into conversations and at other times feel a deep contentment in sitting back and listening. One moment you may be moving in synchrony with another person, while the next brings the joy of being an observer. Between the two ends of engagement there are a variety of experiences. In addition to the expected everyday fluctuations, the capacity for social engagement is impacted by illness and wellness. In a state of illness, the social engagement system retracts, responding to the physiological demand to attend to internal conditions. In a state of wellness, the social engagement system is at work in the external environment, seeking and signaling readiness for connection.

STEPS

1. Use the scale to fill in your personal experience of the points between "open and engaged" and "internal and engaged." Start by naming each end and then label the points between.
2. Consider where you are right now. Stop and find your place on your scale.
3. Reflect on recent experiences and see where you were on your scale.
4. Look at when your place on the scale fits with the environmental and relational demands of the moment and when there is a mismatch.
5. Recognize any patterns to your placement on the scale. Look for people, places, and experiences that predictably take you to a certain point along the scale. Become curious about the characteristics of those interactions that activate that response. Get to know your personal social engagement profile.

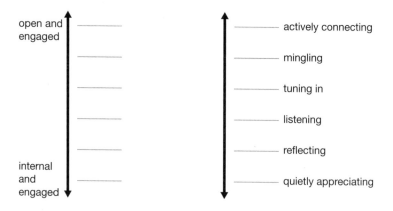

FIGURE 4.3. Social Engagement Scale and Example

TIPS

Clients often assume they are in a protective response and move into self-criticism when they are in fact nearer the "internal and engaged" end of the Social Engagement Scale. Help your clients understand the range of responses that are still within the state of ventral vagal safety. Using the scale shown in Figure 4.3, your clients can begin to bring curiosity and self-compassion to their personal patterns of engagement.

——— **EXERCISE** ————————————

A Neuroception Notebook

This exercise brings the implicit experience of neuroception into explicit awareness where it can be used to understand activation of autonomic states. Neuroception is working in the background below the level of awareness. Bringing perception to this flow of information is a foundational skill. This is a good exercise to introduce to clients early in the therapy process.

BACKGROUND

Neuroception, the messages the autonomic nervous system receives and records from inside your body, in the environment around you, and between you and other people, provides a valuable stream of information when brought to conscious awareness. When you bring perception to neuroception, you can find reminders of ventral vagal possibilities and identify moments of messiness and distress. Keeping a neuroception notebook is one way to bring explicit awareness to the ways the autonomic nervous system is working in the background shaping your life.

STEPS

1. Divide a notebook in sections for the three categories of neuroception: ventral vagal safety, sympathetic danger, and dorsal vagal life-threat. Use your own words to name the sections.
2. Carry the notebook with you and write in it as you feel your state shifting. Or create time at the end of the day to look back and reflect on your experiences.
3. Look for the specific cues that activated your state changes. Write down the cues of safety, danger, or life-threat you have identified.
4. Find any predictable patterns in the cues that move you toward connection or into protection.

TIPS

Tracking neuroception is an important skill. Introduce the neuroception notebook exercise in a session and then use it during the session. Stop several times to ask your clients to identify their neuroceptive experiences. With this practice, clients begin to bring explicit awareness to their implicit experiences. Have your clients continue to use their notebooks to track experiences and routinely bring their notebooks to therapy to share with you what they are learning. Things that bring a neuroception of safety become resources while things that bring a neuroception of unsafety (sympathetic or dorsal vagal) often become a focus of therapy.

CHAPTER 4 **SUMMARY**

Know thyself.

—INSCRIPTION AT THE TEMPLE OF APOLLO AT DELPHI

The practice of recognizing autonomic states is a neural exercise and a step in the process of creating a more resilient system (Sullivan et al., 2018). As a physiological system, the autonomic nervous system doesn't attach moral meaning to states and state changes; it simply acts in service of survival. Through the skills of befriending, your clients learn to nonjudgmentally recognize the connecting and protecting actions of their autonomic nervous systems and bring curiosity to the patterns that have been created. The exercises presented in this chapter offer a guide to recognizing the full range of autonomic states. With ongoing practice, your clients build a habit of connecting with compassion. When you help your clients create a pattern of tuning in and turning toward without self-criticism, they build the important habit of befriending.

CHAPTER 5

ATTENDING TO AUTONOMIC STATES

Pursue some path, however narrow and crooked, in which you can walk with love and reverence.

—HENRY DAVID THOREAU

Attending is the ability to track autonomic states, see the movement between states, and create a moment-to-moment habit of noticing both large shifts and nuanced changes. For your clients, having an autonomic sense of where they are and where they are heading is the first step to finding their way home to autonomic regulation. Autonomic awareness can be thought of as a "protective factor for psychological well-being" (Fustos, Gramann, Herbert, & Pollatos, 2012, p. 915). The more skilled your clients are at autonomic attending, the more flexible they can be in their autonomic responding. The more attuned they are to their own physiology, the greater their ability to attune and be compassionate to others (Halifax, 2012).

Over a century ago William James described a "continuous cooperation between the body and emotions" (1890, p.

192). More recently research has underscored the importance of the body-mind connection, noting that the "orientation of our emotional compass" is directly connected to our physiology (Furman, Waugh, Bhattacharjee, Thompson, & Gotlib, 2013, p. 780). The ongoing flow of information from the body to the brain influences the experience and intensity of emotion (Critchley & Harrison, 2013). Studies show that a reduced awareness of autonomic state results in decreased experiences of positive moments and more difficulty with decision making (Furman, Waugh, Bhattacharjee, Thompson, & Gotlib, 2013). Posttraumatic response limits awareness of autonomic responses and fosters a biological bias toward looking for cues of danger (Rabellino et al., 2017). Research on resilience shows that low resilience corresponds with less awareness of physiological signals, and an inability to monitor and use moment-to-moment autonomic information to guide decision making (Haase et al., 2015).

The experience and awareness of who you are is shaped by your physiology (Critchley & Harrison, 2013). You know yourself through your autonomic state, or as Internal Family Systems (Schwartz, 2001) might say, you know your "selves" through your autonomic state shifts. Chapter 5 is divided into five sections, offering your clients a variety of different ways to follow their nervous systems: Attending to the Nervous System, Attending to Autonomic Pathways, Playfulness, Rethinking Solitude, and Moments to Savor. Narrative writing has been shown to be an emotional regulator (Herbert, Sfärlea, & Blumenthal, 2013), and the exercises in Attending to the Nervous System use writing as a way to bring clarity to the many flavors of autonomic states and track moment-to-moment changes. Attending to Autonomic Pathways offers three exercises designed to move into awareness of how multiple pathways join to create a larger perspective. With an understanding that play and stillness are challenging for many clients, the Playfulness and Rethinking Solitude sections present exercises that help your clients explore how to create conditions that support safe engagement with these experiences. Finally, Moments to Savor provides three exercises that bring into practice ways to connect with and deepen moments of ventral vagal regulation. Each of the exercises in these sections will help your clients begin to know *where* they are and *how* they are and help them get to know *who* they are.

ATTENDING TO THE NERVOUS SYSTEM

Autonomic state shifts sometimes activate a move down or up the hierarchy and other times bring subtle changes in the way a state is experienced and expressed. Your clients feel the shifts between states as their body systems respond, their behaviors change, and their stories reshape. The nuanced changes that happen within a state are more difficult to track and may go unnoticed. Helping your clients learn to first notice and then follow the changes that happen as they move within a state and between states brings attention to the ways the autonomic nervous system responds to meet their individual needs.

——— EXERCISE ———

Autonomic Alphabets

In this exercise, clients are asked to use the letters of the alphabet to move beyond the broad category descriptions of states and attend to the variety of experiences each state offers.

BACKGROUND

Looking beyond the primary description of a state creates an expanded understanding of the ways each of your states can be experienced. Finding the variety of flavors of each state encourages you to become aware of the subtle ways your states shift.

STEPS TO CREATING YOUR ALPHABET:

1. Find a word that begins with each letter of the alphabet to describe the qualities of your three autonomic states. (You may have to get creative with the letter X.)
2. Begin by creating your dorsal vagal alphabet.
3. Move up the hierarchy and create your sympathetic alphabet.
4. Continue to the top of the hierarchy and create your ventral vagal alphabet.
5. Use your alphabets. When you notice a familiar feeling, a quality you identified in one of your alphabets, stop and name the state. When you notice you are in a state, go to your alphabet and find the quality.

TIPS

Creating an alphabet is a way to look at the qualities of the three states from a safe distance. Once your clients have created their alphabets, you can then use them in sessions to attend to the nuance of states and shifts.

You may want to create your own alphabets to use with your clients, but samples are included here as examples to share.

Dorsal: Absent, Blank, Collapsed, Despairing, Exhausted, Foggy, Grim, Hopeless, Impenetrable, Judged, Knocked out, Lost, Missing, Numb, Overwhelmed, Pathetic, Queasy, Retracted, Shutdown, Terrified, Unloved, Void, Without, eXpressionless, Young, Zoned out.

Sympathetic: Alarmed, Buzzing, Claustrophobic, Deranged, Envious, Frightened, Grasping, Harried, Irrational, Judgmental, Knotted, Looping, Manic, Nasty, Overdoing, Pressured, Quick, Raging, Stuck, Troubled, Unwanted, Vibrating, Worried, eXtreme, Yearning, Zigzagging.

Ventral: Awesome, Benevolent, Courageous, Devoted, Eloquent, Free, Grateful, Happy, Joyful, Kind, Loving, Mellow, Nice, Open, Playful, Quiet, Relaxed, Skilled, Trusting, Uplifted, Vibrant, Whole, eXtraordinary, YES, in the Zone.

——— EXERCISE ———
Autonomic Names

In this exercise, clients are asked to use the letters of their name to move beyond the broad category descriptions of states and attend to the variety of experiences each state offers.

BACKGROUND
In Shakespeare's *Romeo and Juliet*, Juliet asks "What's in a name?" In fact, your name is often the first label you are given, and is an important way you identify who you are. Looking at your name through the qualities of autonomic states invites you to experience who you are in different ways.

STEPS TO WRITING YOUR NAME:
1. Use the letters of your name to describe who you are in a dorsal, sympathetic, and ventral state.
2. Create several autonomic name descriptions for each state and compare the effects.

TIPS
When your clients write their names using autonomic state descriptors, the exercise feels very personal and often brings connection to a larger story. Different words evoke particular flavors of a state. Invite your clients to write several variations of their names for each state and see what stories emerge. You can use your own name if you choose or here is my name as an example to share.

Name: *DEB.*

> *Dorsal = **D**isconnected, **E**mpty, **B**roken*
>
> *Sympathetic = **D**istracted, **E**rratic, **B**attling*
>
> *Ventral = **D**elighted, **E**xcited, **B**enevolent*

———— **EXERCISE** ————

Autonomic Short Stories

This exercise is a way for clients to intentionally add narrative to an autonomic experience. The five prompts offer a structure for clients to connect body and brain, create an integrated story, and reflect on the ways autonomic activation begins the story-creation process.

BACKGROUND

Adding language to autonomic events is a way to become acquainted with states and state changes. The plots of your short stories illustrate a slice of an autonomic experience. This is a quick writing exercise designed to bring attention to a specific autonomic point in time and spend a moment getting to know it.

STEPS

1. Use these five prompts to write your autonomic short story. Spend no more than a minute or so on each.
   - My autonomic state is . . .
   - My system is responding to . . .
   - My body wants to . . .

- My brain makes up the story that . . .
- When I review my short story, I notice . . .
2. When you feel a state change, take a couple of minutes to listen in and follow the five prompts.
3. When you want to appreciate where your autonomic nervous system has taken you, follow the prompts and write a short story.
4. Track how your stories change as your autonomic responses begin to reshape.

TIPS

This is a good exercise to have your clients use regularly. The short stories offer your clients a way to notice both the impact of state to story and the ways their stories change as therapy progresses and their autonomic patterns begin to reshape. It is often a good idea to have your clients write their first stories with you during a session. After that, invite your clients write stories at home and share them with you in their sessions. Remind your clients this is a quick dip into listening to their autonomic experience; they should spend no more than a minute or so with each prompt.

An example of an autonomic short story is included here:

My autonomic state is moving into sympathetic.

My system is responding to the people around me who are arguing about how to meet the deadline for our project.

My body wants to get up and run away.

My brain makes up the story that it's all my fault. I'm a total failure and I'm going to be fired.

When I review my short story, I notice how quickly I lose control and think about the worst-case scenario. As I look back now, I recognize the familiar, childhood pattern of my sympathetic state being triggered by raised voices. I can reflect on the ways that in my adult life raised voices are not the same sign of danger.

―――― **EXERCISE** ――――――――――――――――――
Attending over Time

The first exercise creates skill in following autonomic movement and feeling the ways autonomic states shift in nuanced and large-scale ways in short periods of time. The second exercise uses a longer period of time to notice how patterns evolve and consider whether to continue or interrupt a response.

BACKGROUND
While atomic clocks measure time with precision and accuracy, it seems your personal experience of time is changed by your state of engagement with it. Time sometimes seems to stand still and other times fly by. You can feel stuck in a state of dysregulation or unable to hold onto a state of regulation. Using increments of time to attend to state changes adds

chronology to your understanding of how you move through daily experiences. Attending over time, both in short and long intervals, invites you to see the ongoing ebb and flow of your autonomic nervous system and the ways it responds both in moment-to-moment shifts and in patterns over time.

SHORT-DURATION ATTENDING STEPS

1. Decide on a 5- or 10-minute increment as your measure of time. Use the following series of prompts to check in three times over that span of time.
   - In this moment my autonomic state is . . .
   - And I am feeling . . .
   - Now my autonomic state is . . .
   - And I am feeling . . .
   - And now my autonomic state is . . .
   - And I am feeling . . .
2. Repeat this exercise a few times a day for several weeks.
3. Look for any patterns that emerge. When are the times you respond flexibly and when are the times you get stuck? Are any changes happening over the course of tracking?

LONG-DURATION ATTENDING STEPS

1. Longer time periods offer an expanded, bird's eye view of your experience. Decide on a timeframe to use. You can experiment with doing the exercise in the morning, at the end of the day, or even once a week.

2. Answer the following four questions.
   - *Where am I?* The starting point is where you are right now. Begin with noticing your current state.
   - *Where have I been?* From your present reference point, reflect back and notice any state changes.
   - *What does this mean for where I might be heading?* With an understanding of your movement from past to present, bring curiosity to the trajectory you have found. Is there a pattern? Does it make sense to you when you see it clearly?
   - *What do I want to do now?* Is this a path you want to follow or a pattern you want to interrupt?
3. Repeat this exercise over successive days or weeks and track emerging patterns.

TIPS

Your clients often see their autonomic state changes as individual moments in time not connected to a larger experience. Autonomic shifts are interconnected experiences that lead your clients deeper into or out of a state. By adding the dimension of time to track autonomic change, your clients can begin to notice the flow of their experience. The two Attending Over Time exercises help your clients bring attention to moment-to-moment change and build their awareness of how moments combine to create patterns.

Included here is an example of the first exercise.

At the first minute:

In this moment my autonomic state is . . .

In this moment my autonomic state is slightly dorsal vagal

and I am feeling . . .

and I am feeling a little collapsed

Now my autonomic state is . . .

Now my autonomic state is a bit more dorsal

and I am feeling . . .

and I am feeling some disconnection

And now my autonomic state is . . .

And now my autonomic state is moving just a fraction toward sympathetic

and I am feeling . . .

and I am feeling as if I might be able to move

At 3 minutes:

In this moment my autonomic state is . . .

In this moment my autonomic state is becoming more sympathetic

and I am feeling . . .

and I am feeling the need to get going

Now my autonomic state is . . .

Now my autonomic state is heading to ventral

and I am feeling . . .

and I am feeling that I can look at my list for the day

And now my autonomic state is . . .

And now my autonomic state is much more ventral

and I am feeling . . .

and I am feeling that the day might be ok

At 5 minutes:

In this moment my autonomic state is . . .

In this moment my autonomic state is a bit sympathetic

and I am feeling . . .

and I am feeling some anxiety about getting ready to go to work

Now my autonomic state is . . .

Now my autonomic state is moving into ventral

and I am feeling . . .

and I am feeling organized

And now my autonomic state is . . .

And now my autonomic state is fully ventral

and I am feeling . . .

and I am feeling ready to meet the day

ATTENDING TO AUTONOMIC PATHWAYS

Reflection invites awareness of where clients are and where they have been and often leads to thinking about where they might be heading. Making time to slow down and become curious leads to an awareness of the many states and state changes that clients naturally experience while navigating the demands of the day and an appreciation of the autonomic pathways that they have traveled.

───────── **EXERCISE** ───────────────────────────────

Daily Pie Charts

This exercise uses the visual design of a pie chart to tune into the ways a day is comprised of a blend of dorsal vagal, sympathetic, and ventral vagal states and the relationship between states during the day. As soon as clients can predictably name their three states, this exercise becomes a useful tool.

BACKGROUND

We tend to give our days a label—this was a good day or a difficult day, a quiet day or a busy day—based on one particularly intense moment or on a string of related experiences. When you name your days in this way, you often miss the moments that didn't fit the pattern. When considering the day through an autonomic lens, looking at the relationship between states and the relative amount of time spent in each gives a more complete picture of your daily experience. With a pie chart, ventral vagal, sympathetic, and dorsal vagal experiences are seen as part of an integrated autonomic system. The global flavor of your day is a result of the contributions of each. The design of a pie chart (Figure 5.1) offers an uncomplicated image of the overall sense of a day and brings the feeling of the day alive in shape and color. What name would you use to describe each of the days illustrated here?

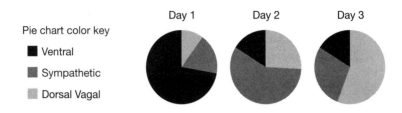

Pie chart color key
- ■ Ventral
- ▨ Sympathetic
- ▧ Dorsal Vagal

FIGURE 5.1. Daily Pie Charts

STEPS

1. What does your autonomic pie chart look like? Use a blank circle each evening to review your day.

2. Choose the colors you want to represent each state and divide your pie into ventral vagal, sympathetic, and dorsal vagal pieces.

3. Name your day.

4. Make a collection of your daily charts. Use your collection of daily charts to get a sense of your autonomic experience over a period of time. With a series of charts, you can look at the ebb and flow of states and the impact on your autonomic experience.

   • Is there a day of the week that repeatedly brings the same autonomic responses?

   • What is the overall tone of a week?

   • Is there a pattern to your weekends?

   • If you are in a time of transition, use your pie charts to see how your autonomic nervous system is responding.

TIPS

Many clients identify with a specific state and miss the everyday mixture of states that make up their day. A pie chart is an easy way for your clients to bring attention to their combinations of states and notice how much time they actually spend in each state during a day. Invite your clients to periodically bring their pie charts to a session. Look for patterns and track change over time.

--- **EXERCISE** ---

Daily Tracker—Three Different Things

This exercise brings explicit awareness to the ways a client's autonomic patterns are shifting. In the midst of the therapy process, it's easy to miss the small moments that mark the beginning of change. This exercise is an easy way to create a habit of recognizing and naming the hopeful signs of a system that is reorganizing.

BACKGROUND

An end-of-the-day reflection during which you listen to the subtleties of autonomic change is a good way to look back at the autonomic path you've traveled. With a habit of autonomic reflection, implicit knowing and explicit awareness combine to bring you into a deeper understanding of the ways the autonomic nervous system shapes your days. Remembering that the autonomic response is always considered an adaptive one, don't look for what is better, but instead look for what is different. A regular tracking practice brings attention to the small shifts in patterns that highlight the ways your system is reorganizing.

STEPS

1. Review the day and identify three different ways your autonomic nervous system responded.
2. Bring attention to what happened. You might notice a slightly less intense response to an event or an easier recovery into regulation. Or maybe you recognize a different kind of response—sympathetic mobilization in place of a dorsal vagal collapse or a moment of ventral vagal connection instead of fight or flight.
3. It's equally important to attend to what didn't happen. The absence of a reaction is also a good measure that a response pattern is changing and that your system is moving toward regulation.
4. Keep a journal of your daily "three different things" experiences. As small changes begin to add up, new autonomic patterns take root.
5. Review your daily journal periodically to see how your responses are changing. Look back over the range of autonomic responses and consider the larger picture of change that is happening. Is there a shift? If so, in what direction? Consider the intensity, frequency, and duration of your states and state changes in your reflection.

TIPS

Because clients are used to naming responses as good and bad, it is important to remind them that this exercise is about noticing difference. Some clients resonate with asking what happened while others find asking what didn't happen to be a more useful question. Encourage your clients to use both. Seeing the small changes that are tracked with this exercise keeps the focus on the fact that autonomic patterns are shifting.

——— EXERCISE ———

The Autonomic Request for Connection

This exercise brings explicit attention to the implicit signals being sent between autonomic nervous systems. By focusing on the pathways of the social engagement system, clients learn to discern signs of welcome and warning and use that knowledge in making decisions about connection.

BACKGROUND

The autonomic nervous system is a relational system. Through your biology you are wired for connection. Eyes, voices, faces, and gestures telegraph cues that it is safe to explore a relationship. The elements of the social engagement system are essential to assessing safety and danger. Yet, through the ways the nervous system has been shaped by your personal experiences, you might miss or misread those invitations.

An ongoing stream of signals of welcome and warning

are received and sent through the pathways of the social engagement system. The muscle around the eyes (the orbiculares oculi) opens and closes the eyelid and contributes to the wrinkles around the eyes that express emotions. This is where the nervous system looks for signs of warmth and an invitation to connect. Prosody (patterns of rhythm, tone, frequency in the voice) is an important nonverbal signal and sends messages of welcome or warning to another nervous system. Facial expressions convey social information. An unmoving face is seen as a sign of danger, while a mobile face is experienced as alive and sending social information. Finally, turning and tilting the head signals availability and interest.

You can begin to understand the conversation that is taking place between two nervous systems when you are aware of the cues you are sending and can accurately interpret the cues you are receiving. As you become familiar with this way of listening, you'll find you are able to navigate relationships more skillfully.

STEPS

1. Make a practice of looking at eyes, listening to voices, seeing facial expressions, and watching for social gestures. Bring explicit awareness to your present-moment experiences with another social engagement system. Use the following prompts to build skill in noticing:
   - Their eyes are signaling . . .
   - Their tone of voice sounds . . .
   - Their face is expressing . . .
   - Their gestures convey . . .

2. Identify the specific characteristics that invite connection or prompt a move into disconnection. Exactly what is it about the other person's eyes, voice, face, and movements that sends cues of safety or danger to your nervous system?

3. Ask yourself if your response is a match for the present-moment situation or linked to a prior experience.

4. As you get to know your responses to another social engagement system, bring attention to your own end of the interaction using the same questions.

   • My eyes are signaling . . .
   • My tone of voice sounds . . .
   • My face is expressing . . .
   • My gestures convey . . .

TIPS

This is a good exercise to practice during sessions before asking your clients to try it in their daily environments. Clients are often unaware of both their responses and of the cues they are sending. Experiment with sending different signals via your eyes, tone of voice, facial expressions, and gestures to help your clients find the matches and mismatches in their neuroceptive response to your signals. Reverse the process and give your clients feedback about the signals they are sending.

PLAYFULNESS

"Playfulness occurs in a protected context and is easily disrupted by stress" (Bateson, 2014, p. R13). Playfulness is a state of mind supported by the autonomic state of ventral vagal regulation and a great way to exercise the vagal brake (Porges, 2015b). Studies suggest playfulness is a quality that is not set but can be enhanced and invited into daily living (Neyfakh, 2014).

While we are serious beings, problem solvers wanting to make sense of the world, we are also playful beings wanting to let go of our problems for a moment in time.

——— EXERCISE ———

Pathways to Playfulness

To play is a challenging experience and is especially difficult for many clients. In order to play, clients have to stay in the safety of a ventral vagal state while feeling the mobilizing energy of the sympathetic nervous system. This exercise explores building a capacity for playfulness.

BACKGROUND

You can be playful both by yourself and with others. Playfulness and a sense of well-being go together. A playful attitude supports seeing new perspectives and being able to cope with adversity. As Dr. Seuss (1960) said, fun is good.

STEPS

1. Get to know yourself as a playful person. Look at the conditions that support your sense of playfulness:
   • Identify where, when, and with whom you feel your sense of playfulness emerge.

2. Identify where, when, and with whom you feel your sense of playfulness disappear.

3. Track your experiences of the different kinds of playfulness. Identify where you find yourself on your autonomic hierarchy when you engage in, or think about engaging in, these kinds of playfulness:

   • playing with others
   • playing with thoughts and ideas
   • spontaneous play
   • daydreaming

TIPS

Your clients may be occupied by the serious issues that bring them to treatment and think they've lost the ability for playfulness. They may think there's no place in their lives for being playful, that it's a luxury rather than an everyday experience, something to look at once therapy has ended. Playfulness is an important part of well-being and emerges when there is a neuroception of safety and an active ventral vagal state. Help your clients discover who they are as playful people.

EXERCISE

Playful Moments

As clients begin to understand how they play, the next step is to create time to play. This exercise helps clients find moments to play and expand their repertoire of playful experiences.

BACKGROUND

Playfulness is an important quality that contributes to well-being. As you find ways to create opportunities for moments of playfulness, you can become a more playful person and experience the joy and creativity that accompanies play.

STEPS

1. Notice how often, easily, and intensely you engage in a playful experience.
2. Increase your playful experiences. Find the ones that bring a smile and the ones that bring energy and play in those ways a little bit more.
3. Expand your playfulness. Experiment with experiences in the kinds of play that aren't in your play repertoire.

TIPS

Play is often a missing experience in your clients' lives. When an environment is filled with cues of danger, the autonomic nervous system remains on guard, focused on protection, making play a nonessential and even unsafe choice. Many of your clients have had limited opportunities to engage in play. With the clinical focus on the challenges that bring your clients to therapy, play is often overlooked in the therapy process. Yet, play is an essential element of healing. Find ways to routinely bring moments of play into your sessions. Play can be as simple as sharing a moment of laughter and friendly banter. Introduce play early in therapy as a reminder that even in the midst of complicated trauma work, the autonomic nervous system has the capacity to engage in moments of play.

RETHINKING SOLITUDE

Humans are inherently social beings, yet also have a desire for moments of solitude to "cultivate the inner word of the self and experience self-discovery, self-realization, meaning, wholeness, and an enhanced awareness of one's deepest feelings and impulses" (Hollenshorst & Jones as cited in More, Long, & Averill, 2004 p. 224). Solitude has been shown to have a deactivating effect on the intensity of high-arousal responses, such as excitement and anger, and to be activating of low arousal responses, such as calm and ease (Nguyen, Ryan, & Deci, 2018). In experiences of solitude, many people report feelings of intimacy and a stronger feeling of closeness to another person while others feel a religious or secular spiritual connection (Long & Averill, 2003). Creativity often blossoms in solitude, as does self-reflection that can lead to self-transformation (Long & Averill, 2003).

"Unique among the species, we have the ability to sit and mentally detach ourselves from our surroundings and travel inward . . ." (Wilson et al., 2014, p. 75). "Stillness is the moment when the buried, the discarded, and the forgotten escape to the social surface of awareness . . ." (Seremetakis as cited in Lepecki, 2001). Stillness is a joining of the ventral and dorsal vagal circuits that allows you to sit alone in silence and feel restored or share a moment of quiet with a friend. As these two pathways come into connection, with the sympathetic nervous system quiet in the background, you feel immobilization from the dorsal vagus joined with the experience of safety from the ventral vagus and can enter into the state of being safely still (Porges 2017c).

——— **EXERCISE** ———————————————————

Personal Preferences Around Solitude

This exercise brings attention to the autonomic experience of solitude and helps clients identify where and when they look for solitude and how much solitude they need. When clients understand the concrete elements that support their ability to safely find moments of solitude, they are more likely to attend to their needs for time alone.

BACKGROUND

Distinct from loneliness, which has been shown to have a multitude of negative physical and psychological outcomes, entering into moments of solitude has positive benefits for well-being. Practicing a moment of solitude is an autonomic exercise that creates an experience of feeling centered and peaceful.

STEPS

1. Locate the experiences of solitude and loneliness on your autonomic hierarchy. Feel the difference between them.
2. Explore where in your daily environment you find solitude.

   Nature is often where people go to find a private place to escape to when they are surrounded by the demands of the day and the autonomic nervous system is needing room to breathe.

   • Reflect on your daily experiences to discover where you choose to find solitude.

- Identify what kind of natural habitat are you drawn to.
- Notice where in your everyday natural environment are the places you can predictably visit and feel the benefits of solitude.

Solitude is a state of being and doesn't have to take place in isolation. Solitude is also found in spaces where there are other people.

- Identify the places and spaces you visit every day that include other people and also offer you an opportunity for a moment of solitude.

3. Notice when you reach for solitude.

Consider what is happening in your life that prompts you to seek quiet.

- Look at your physical environment.
- Consider the actions of people around you.
- Reflect on the number, frequency, and kinds of requests for your time and attention.

4. Identify how much solitude you need.

Focus on your moments of solitude and the length of time that brings a sense of nourishment.

- Consider when a few moments of solitude meet your need.
- Compare that to when you need a longer experience of solitude to feel nurtured.
- Notice how you know when your system has taken in enough solitude and you're ready to rejoin the world outside yourself.

TIPS

Solitude is often confused with loneliness. Solitude is an experience of feeling safe while loneliness activates a survival response. Use the autonomic hierarchy to help your clients understand the difference between these two states.

EXERCISE

Attending to Stillness

This exercise continues the exploration of autonomic experiences of quiet with attention to exploring the conditions that support a client's ability to rest.

BACKGROUND

Over the course of evolution, humans developed the ability to become still as a way to rest and renew. Sometimes, instead of feeling nurtured by stillness, the beginning of calm can bring cues of danger and a sense of vulnerability. As your autonomic nervous system begins to move from action to quiet, you might feel your sympathetic nervous system reacting with mobilizing energy or you might feel pulled into dorsal vagal collapse. Bring curiosity to identifying the elements that add safety to your experiences of rest so you can find your way to the places where you can receive the benefits of moments of quiet.

STEPS

1. Identify restful and restless environments.

Many people label environments with lots of people, activity, sound, and movement as restless. Workplaces and the daily commute are two environments that are often cited as mobilizing and not restorative. In comparison, the natural environment and at home are often identified as places to rest and renew.

- Identify environments at the two ends of your experience—places that bring you a feeling of restlessness and places that offer you the opportunity to rest.

2. Attend to the qualities of the spaces that bring you a rhythm of rest.
   - location
   - size and shape of the space
   - colors, sounds, and textures
3. Consider when you want to be by yourself and when you want to be with others (people or pets).
4. Make a list of the combination of qualities you've identified. Go out and find places that offer those.
5. Create a plan to regularly visit the places you identified as offering the opportunity for rest.
6. Create your own space, incorporating qualities you identified that support you in resting in a moment of stillness.

TIPS

Stillness is a complicated autonomic experience and many clients find sympathetic mobilization interrupts their ability to rest, or they get pulled into dorsal vagal collapse when they begin to become quiet. By helping your clients attend to the qualities of places that support safety in quiet, this exercise helps them first identify where they can safely experience stillness and then experiment with entering those places.

MOMENTS TO SAVOR

Savoring is a process of attending to and appreciating positive life events (Bryant as cited in Geiger, Morey, & Segerstrom, 2016). Trauma can disrupt the ability to savor. Feeling negative emotions in a normally positive moment and an inability to experience positive affect can create secondary guilt and shame at the inability to experience joy (DePierro, D'Andrea, & Frewen, 2014). These experiences then set up a pattern of ongoing dysregulation. The practice of savoring is an active strategy to build ventral vagal resources. Savoring is linked to psychological resilience, positive health outcomes, and a sense of well-being (Geiger, Morey, & Segerstrom, 2016; Phillipe et al., 2009; Speer, Bhanji, & Delgado, 2014). Momentary savoring enhances positive mood, while an ongoing practice of savoring maintain levels of happiness (Jose, Lim, & Bryant, 2012).

───── **EXERCISE** ─────
Savoring Snapshots

This exercise helps clients recognize moments or micro-moments of ventral vagal experience. It is a way to remember that the autonomic nervous system regularly moves into moments of regulation and a way to capture those moments and bring them into explicit awareness. This exercise is applicable both in times of relative ease and in a time of ongoing challenge.

BACKGROUND

To savor is to take a moment of ventral vagal regulation and the feeling of a sense of safety and experience a story of connection to self, to another, or to nature. Savoring is a quick practice whereby you capture a ventral vagal moment and hold it in your conscious attention for just a short time. Moments to savor routinely happen in the course of everyday living. Because a 20- to 30-second snapshot is all that is needed to benefit from the practice, it is easy to savor during the natural flow of your day.

STEPS

1. Look for a ventral vagal moment to savor, bring it into conscious awareness, and place your attention on it for 20–30 seconds. In the beginning, if the experience of savoring is challenging, start with micro-moments of savoring (5–10 seconds). Each micro-moment shapes your system. Over time, your ability to savor will build to the 20–30 second maximum that defines a savoring experience.
2. Practice savoring each day. Begin with finding one moment to savor each day. As savoring becomes easier, increase the number.
3. Track your savoring moments.
   - Keep a savoring notebook or a joy journal.
   - Reflect at the end of the day to find and savor moments you may have missed.

- Create an agreement to share savoring moments with a friend using technology or in person.
- Organize a savoring circle—online, in person, or a combination of the two.
- Create a savoring album using simple illustrations of your savoring moments and adding captions.

4. Establish a habit of savoring.
   - Remind yourself that moments to savor are common occurrences in everyday life.
   - Be on the lookout for the small moments that bring you into a ventral vagal state.
   - Set a goal to see and savor a certain number of moments each day.
   - Invite a friend to savor with you.

TIPS

In addition to the routine appearance of moments to savor in daily life, opportunities to savor also happen regularly during therapy sessions. The essence of savoring is the 20–30 second timeframe, making it easy to incorporate into the therapy session. Introduce this skill to your clients and then stop and notice moments during your session. Help your clients build confidence in their ability to savor so they can create a successful everyday practice.

EXPANDING OUTWARD—CONNECTING TO ART AND NATURE

Connecting inward to attend to the challenges of sympathetic and dorsal vagal survival responses along with the resources of the ventral vagal system is a foundational skill. Expanding outward to identify ways you are resourced through connecting to art and nature is also important. Each offers connection to the ventral vagal state of regulation through easy to access experiences.

Art can move you to tears with its beauty, prompt a moment of transformation, and change your self-image or world view (Pelowski, Markey, Lauring, & Leder, 2016). Viewing art is a complex experience that engages the body and mind in a process that unfolds over time (Brieber, Nadal, Leder, & Rosenberg, 2014). "Art viewing engenders myriad emotions, evokes evaluations, physiological reactions, and in some cases can mark or alter lives" (Pelowski et al., 2016, p. 1).

Your ability to return to autonomic regulation following a stressful event is supported through connection with nature (Brown, Barton, & Gladwell, 2013). Nature scenes are autonomically regulating and restorative. Technology that simulates the natural world brings an autonomically regulating effect (Kahn, Severson, & Ruckert, 2009), while listening to the sounds of nature brings an increase in autonomic regulation (Gould van Praag et al., 2017). Another way to connect with nature is through fractals—the simple patterns in nature that repeat over and over with increasing complexity (e.g., the nautilus shell, a leaf, a pinecone, broccoli buds, dandelions, ice crystals, clouds). Viewing fractals reduces physiological stress levels (Taylor & Spehar, 2016). The regulating autonomic response to fractals appears to be universal and is elicited in periods of time as short as 10 seconds (Taylor, 2006).

Intentionally bringing experiences of art and a connection

with nature into daily life is an uncomplicated, easily accessible way to enter into moments of ventral vagal regulation.

―――――― **EXERCISE** ――――――――――――――――
Attending Through Art

Viewing art opens up possibilities for seeing the world in new ways. Both the body and the mind are involved in the experience. Engaging with forms of art that bring a ventral vagal response can change the way clients think and feel. This exercise invites clients to investigate their autonomic response to different kinds of art and make art a part of their everyday lives.

BACKGROUND
Art comes in many forms and no special training is necessary to benefit from seeing it. Art speaks to the body through your autonomic pathways and brings responses that can lead to new ways of thinking about yourself and the world. Finding ways to invite art into your life is an act of listening to your autonomic nervous system and discovering the particular ways you connect.

STEPS
1. Explore the ways that are easily available to you to see and be with art. Museums, artists' workshops, public art spaces, arts festivals, and an illustrated art book are just some of the options.
2. Identify the kinds of art you are drawn to. View differ-

ent kinds of artwork (photography, sculpture, drawing, painting, ceramic, mosaic, textiles, and other forms of art) and notice how you respond.

3. Decide how and how often you need to connect to art in order to feel as if you have enough art in your life.

TIPS

Clients may feel that art is a luxury they don't have time for or that it doesn't fit in their lives. Help them understand that art is all around, comes in many forms, and has an impact that can easily evoke the qualities of the ventral vagal system.

——— EXERCISE ———
Attending in Nature

This exercise brings attention to the naturally occurring autonomic benefits found in nature. With the recognition that nature is nourishing both in live experiences and through images, attending to a connection with nature becomes an easily accessible regulating activity.

BACKGROUND

Nature, both in real life and through viewing images, offers relaxing and restorative opportunities. Abundant in the natural world are fractals, simple patterns that repeat over and over creating increasing complexity (the nautilus shell, a leaf, a pinecone, broccoli buds, dandelions, ice crystals, clouds).

Viewing fractals for just a few moments brings a regulating autonomic response. Find the particular places and ways to connect with nature that bring your ventral vagal system alive.

STEPS

1. Attend to the natural environment around you and track your responses. Identify the places that bring you into ventral vagal regulation, sympathetic mobilization, and dorsal vagal disconnection.

2. Visit the places that are regulating for you either in person, through images, or in a combination of both.

3. Look for fractals as you move through your day. Stop for a just a few seconds to take them in.

4. Find images of fractals or objects that have the characteristics of fractals and notice the ones that bring an intense ventral vagal response. An internet search will bring up a wealth of images, and the plants and trees around you offer living examples.

5. Display fractal images or objects in a way that you can easily return to them. (A screen saver, photos on your phone, or a flowering plant or cactus in your home or office are some suggestions.)

TIPS

Clients are exposed to the regulating influences of the natural world as they move through their daily lives. By bringing attention to these experiences nature becomes an active resource. Helping your clients learn to intentionally connect with nature is a way to build their ventral vagal capacities.

CHAPTER 5   **SUMMARY**

If there is a feeling change, there is an autonomic change.

—STEPHEN PORGES

Each autonomic state holds within it a multitude of flavors. The practice of attending creates skill in discerning these micro-states. Ventral vagal is more than regulated and calm. It also brings joy, passion, excitement, celebration, interest, alertness, ease, and rest. Sympathetic is sometimes fight and other times flight, and dorsal vagal can feel collapsed, foggy, numb, or invisible. The three autonomic states are always moving in relationship with each other. As ventral, sympathetic, and dorsal energies ebb and flow how your clients experience the world changes. By engaging in attending, your clients create moments of mindfulness. These small practices interrupt the automaticity of habitual patterns and make space to see autonomic responses in a new way. Making intentional choices about what to attend to offers opportunities to use everyday experiences to build ventral vagal capacity.

CHAPTER 6

SHAPING THE AUTONOMIC NERVOUS SYSTEM

The natural healing force within each one of us is the greatest force in getting well.

—HIPPOCRATES

The autonomic nervous system "plays a central role in regulating energy and information flow between the brain, body, and environment" (Rejeski & Gauvin, 2013, p. 660). Trauma interrupts the ability to regulate and flexibly move between autonomic states. Fight, flight, or shutdown prevail, while the state of calm and connection is fleeting (Williamson et al., 2015). When the ventral vagal state of safety is missing, life is an exhausting mix of intense mobilization and withdrawal. Navigating daily living is focused on limiting the possibility of being activated into a state of dysregulation. The path to regulation and social connection is hidden by habitual protective responses.

Shaped by experience, the autonomic nervous system acts in service of survival, responding to cues of safety and danger in the present moment based on experiences in the past. "Visiting the past in therapy should be done while people are, biologically speaking, firmly rooted in the present and feeling as calm, safe, and grounded as possible" (van der Kolk, 2014, p. 70). Regularly engaging in practices to retune neuroception and reshape habitual response patterns helps your clients build this biological platform. The continuing opportunity to exercise the neural circuits of regulation and connection is essential for physical and psychological well-being (Flores & Porges, 2017). This chapter presents daily practices in the categories of energy, sound, movement, breath, environment, and reflection to help your clients shape their autonomic nervous systems toward safety and connection.

THE RIGHT DEGREE OF CHALLENGE

Finding actions that stretch but don't stress the autonomic nervous system is at the heart of shaping. When the autonomic flavor is one of dorsal vagal protection through conservation of energy, taking small steps toward mobilization begins to create new patterns. When the system is in the mobilizing energy of sympathetic protection, an intentional release of that energy begins to build new pathways. When in a state of ventral vagal regulation, it is essential to celebrate and deepen the experience.

——— **EXERCISE** ———

Energy and Actions Map

This exercise offers clients a way to map the range of actions they can use to find their way back to ventral vagal regulation and stay there when they arrive. Each state is individually mapped, identifying actions on a scale of passive to active in the two categories of self- and co-regulation. It is helpful to regularly review this scale and revise it as new resources are recognized.

BACKGROUND

Activities that shape the autonomic nervous system fall along a scale of passive to active. There are times when thinking about moving, remembering a connection with a friend, or simply looking up toward the sky is the right choice and other times when you need to take action, put your body in motion, or head out into the world and seek social connection. Choose an experience that brings a return of energy when the dorsal vagal immobilizing collapse is present, a way to safely discharge energy when feeling the frenetic activity of the sympathetic state, and an action that deepens the feeling of regulation when anchored in the safety of ventral vagal.

STEPS

1. Label your state in the box at the top of the Energy and Actions map. Identify your state through its biological name (dorsal, sympathetic, ventral) or name it in a way that has meaning for you.

2. For sympathetic and dorsal vagal states, move along the line between passive and active and identify actions that take you in the direction of a return to the ventral vagal state of regulation. Use the left side to identify self-regulating actions and the right side to identify co-regulating actions.

3. For your ventral vagal state, move along the line between passive and active and identify actions that deepen your experience of safety and connection. Use the left side to identify self-regulating actions and the right side to identify co-regulating actions.

4. Complete a map for each state.

5. Use your maps to find a resource that is in the range of energy that fits your needs in the moment.

6. Update your maps as you create additional resources.

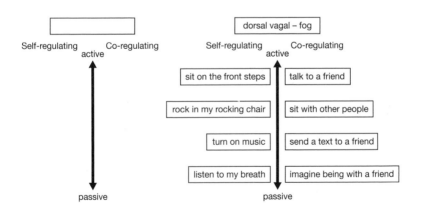

FIGURE 6.1. Energy and Actions Map and Example

TIPS

A resource is an action that moves your clients up the hierarchy toward ventral and, once there, helps them stay there. Goldilocks and her experiences with *too much, not enough, and just right* can be useful in helping your clients understand how the autonomic nervous system connects with resources. When your clients can match the energy they have available with the energy that is required for a particular resource, they can choose the action that fits the autonomic need of the moment (Figure 6.1).

GLIMMERS AND GLOWS

Sometimes simply navigating a day filled with responsibilities feels like an autonomic challenge. These are *glimmer days*, when noticing micro-moments of ventral vagal energy can help you stay regulated and ready for connection. Other days feel more open with time to pause and deepen into the longer experience of a glow. Both experiences shape your system and strengthen your connection to ventral vagal regulation.

——— **EXERCISE** ———————

Finding Glimmers

This exercise engages clients in an active search for micro-moments of regulation. Looking for these moments brings a new level of autonomic awareness. Finding them begins to change clients' expectations around their daily experience.

BACKGROUND

Glimmers are the micro-moments of ventral vagal experience that routinely appear in everyday life yet frequently go unnoticed. To ensure survival, human beings are built with a negativity bias. This means you are biologically wired to pay more attention to negative events than positive ones and can often miss the ventral vagal moments that coexist with moments of dysregulation. Things like seeing a friendly face, hearing a soothing sound, or noticing something enjoyable in the environment go unnoticed. A fundamental step in shaping your system is seeing a glimmer, pausing to take it in, and then beginning to look for more.

STEPS

1. Set an intention to look for a certain number of glimmers each day. Choose a number that feels doable to begin. If glimmers are an unfamiliar experience, watch for a single glimmer. As finding glimmers becomes easier, set a new goal.
2. Notice when you feel a spark of ventral vagal energy. Look for glimmers in your daily activities. Glimmers happen regularly, but because they are micro-moments you need to be on the lookout for them.
3. See, stop, and appreciate your glimmers. Create an easy way to acknowledge a glimmer when it happens. You might bring attention to the moment by simply saying "glimmer" or with a small movement (perhaps your hand on your heart).

4. Track your glimmers. Create a daily glimmers notebook or keep a running list.

5. Look for glimmers in specific places, with particular people, at certain times. Find the ways your glimmers routinely appear.

6. Share your glimmers. You might text your glimmers to a friend, make talking about daily glimmers a family nighttime ritual, or share your list of weekly glimmers with your therapist. Find the way that works for you.

TIPS

As glimmer experiences accumulate, your clients naturally turn toward finding more. Creating a practice of recognizing glimmers is a reminder to your clients that among many experiences of dysregulation, there are also regularly occurring micro-moments of regulation. Just a simple acknowledgement of those moments can temper the intensity of your clients' responses to the challenges in their daily lives. Glimmers also predictably happen in your therapy sessions. Look for them and stop to name them.

——— **EXERCISE** ———————————————

From Glimmer to Glow

This exercise builds on the skill of recognizing glimmers to create a more expansive ventral vagal experience. When clients hold a glimmer in their awareness for a longer period of time, the experience deepens and the story that accompanies it comes to life.

BACKGROUND

When you recognize the micro-moment of a glimmer, you feel the spark of your ventral vagal system. Just as sparks can be used to ignite a fire, glimmers can be turned into the deeper experience of a glow. With a glimmer, you pause just long enough to acknowledge that a ventral vagal moment is happening in the flow of your day. With a glow, stop and celebrate the glimmer. Take time to soak it in and give it deeper meaning.

STEPS

1. Notice a glimmer and stop and let the experience fill you. Move beyond a few seconds and stay with the experience for a half a minute or more. Give the glimmer time to become a glow.
2. Feel what happens as you move from connecting for a micro-moment to a longer experience of taking in.
3. Listen to the story that accompanies the glow.
4. Describe your experience of the glimmer and the glow. Notice how the experience changes. For example, a particular glimmer moment might be described as a quick hit of happiness that brings a smile, and when you turn it into a glow, the experience feels like basking in the warmth of the sun while breathing a sigh of contentment.

TIPS

Once your clients are skilled at noticing glimmers, introduce this exercise. Practice in your sessions so your clients get the feel of holding a glimmer in awareness for a longer length of time. Glow moments are still relatively short (up to a minute), which makes them accessible for most clients but can, for some clients, activate a sympathetic or dorsal vagal survival response. Work with your clients to increase the time they hold a moment in awareness and stay in the experience of ventral vagal deepening.

SHAPING YOUR STORY THROUGH SOUND

The world is never quiet.

—ALBERT CAMUS

Sound is one of the ways the autonomic nervous system experiences the world. When you speak, you are not only creating a story through language, but with prosody (the music of the voice that is felt in rhythm, loudness, and pitch) you are also telling a story about your autonomic state. In interesting research, people reported that when their voice was computer altered, their level of anxiety changed. This self-reported experience was measurable in physiological changes (Costa et al., 2018). In one project, participants recorded a short story that was then computer altered so their voices reflected happiness, sadness, and fear. As participants listened to the modified recordings, their physiological responses changed and they reported feeling the emotions portrayed in each recording (Aucouturier et al., 2016).

When listening to music you often experience a state of absorption or flow (Hall, Schubert, & Wilson, 2016). Music is a portal to safely connecting to, and even enjoying, distressing emotions (Herbert, 2011). The tempo of a piece moves you: heartbeat, breath, movements, and likely cognition all synchronizing with the music (Chanda & Levitin, 2013), while the frequency of music in the range of the human voice is a kind of musical prosody that encourages physiological regulation (Porges, 2010). Since music is an autonomic regulator, you can choose musical selections that safely move you in and out of states of activation. (See *The Polyvagal Theory in Therapy,* pp. 88–90 for a description of using musical maps.) Face and head muscles are used when you both listen to and produce music, and the middle ear muscles support listening (Porges, 2010), so whether you are listening to music or making music, you are engaged in an autonomic exercise.

EXERCISE
The Sound of Your Voice

This exercise is a way for clients to get to know how different tones of voice change the way they feel. By manipulating their tone of voice and tracking responses, clients begin to become aware of how the way they speak impacts their own experience and can begin to look at how the sound of their voice impacts the way they are experienced by others.

BACKGROUND

The autonomic nervous system uses tone of voice as a way to discern safety. You respond to intonation before you take in information. The way you speak changes the way you feel, the story you tell, and changes the way people around you hear what you are saying.

STEPS

1. Experiment with the ways your voice impacts the way you feel. Tell, or record, a short story in different tones of voice. Notice where the different tones of your voice take you on your autonomic map.

2. Track the way the same word spoken in different tones of voice elicits a different state and feeling. Choose a word, speak it in different ways, and follow the ways your states and feelings shift. Try out a variety of words and notice the specific ways of speaking that elicit certain states and feelings.

3. Talk about a difficult experience using different tones of voice. Track what happens to your autonomic state. Find the way of speaking that brings you into a ventral vagal state. Notice the way of speaking that helps you see options and take regulated actions.

4. Find a friend and experiment with sound. Talk in different tones of voice and get feedback on their responses.

Ask your friend to do the same and track your own responses.

TIPS

Tone of voice is a fundamental way neuroception assesses safety or unsafety. A small change in the way a word is spoken can create a large-scale shift in autonomic state. Pay attention in sessions to the messages that are being sent through your and your client's tone of voice. Bringing these messages into explicit awareness often leads to a new insight. Help your clients create a habit of listening to the way they are speaking.

--- **EXERCISE** ---

The Music in Your Life

BACKGROUND

Music is all around you, affecting your physiology and your feelings. Along with activating a ventral vagal response, music has a paradoxical effect that allows you to safely connect to, and even enjoy, your sympathetic and dorsal vagal states.

STEPS

1. Take an inventory of the way music is a part of your life.
   - Music listening: Do you regularly listen to music? Have a favorite radio station? Favorite songs or artists? Do you go to hear live music?

- Music making: Do you make music? Do you play an instrument or sing by yourself or with others?

2. Assess how much music is in your everyday life.
   - Is there enough music in your daily experience?
   - Do you miss music and want to hear more?

3. If your everyday experience is already filled with music, acknowledge the role of music in your life and identify the ways music is a regulating resource.

4. If your inventory brings a recognition that you have a desire for more musical moments, begin to look for ways to add music to your daily experience.

5. Identify the particular pieces of music that take you to different places on the autonomic hierarchy. Sing along, play along, or move along with the music. Use different selections to safely join with your sympathetic and dorsal vagal states and dive into all the flavors of ventral vagal.

TIPS

Music is a readily available resource, which makes it something your clients can easily explore on their own and you can bring into your sessions. Create connection by listening with your clients to their selections. Add the experience of reciprocity by sharing your own music preferences.

SHAPING THROUGH MOVEMENT

All that is important is this one moment
in movement.

—MARTHA GRAHAM

Movement is an essential life process. When you catch something moving out of the corner of your eye, you turn your attention to look for something that is alive. A leaf blowing, a candle unexpectedly flickering, and shadows in the sunlight each bring a sudden sense that something alive is nearby. Humans, like all living things, respond to stimuli with movement and how that happens is in part regulated by the autonomic nervous system.

The ability to turn toward and fully experience body sensations as you move is therapeutic (Lucas, Klepin, Porges, & Rejeski, 2018; Rejeski & Gauvin, 2013). Movement practices are a form of autonomic exercise that shapes the system. Both the actual physical act of moving and bringing movement to life in your imagination activate the autonomic nervous system (Collet, Di Rienzo, El Hoyek, & Guillot, 2013; Demougeot, Normand, Denise, & Papaxanthis, 2009).

─────── **EXERCISE** ───────────────────────

Moments of Movement

This exercise helps clients identify a continuum of movements for each autonomic state. The continuum can then be used as a guide to safely navigate dorsal vagal and sympathetic moments and maintain a ventral vagal experience.

BACKGROUND

Movement occurs along a continuum of expression: simple through complex, micro-movements to full body motions. Each autonomic state has different levels of energy that you can connect with and use to shape your experience. Intentional use of movement is a way to engage your dorsal vagal and sympathetic states, making them less intense and persistent, and it's also a way to deepen your ventral vagal capacities.

STEPS

1. Choose an autonomic state. Using a line to represent ways you move, identify movements at either end. Look for movements that engage the least and most energy available to you in the state.

2. Identify movements that happen between the ends. In dorsal vagal, look for movements that begin to gently energize you. In sympathetic, look for movements that use the activated energy in organized and safe ways. In ventral vagal, look for movements that prolong the experience.

3. Design a series of movement lines to bring awareness to the range of movements that are possible in each autonomic state.

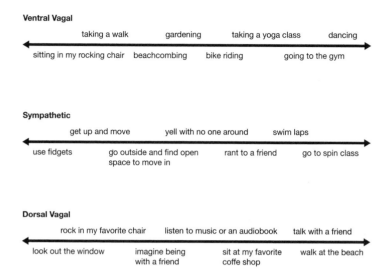

FIGURE 6.2. Movement Continuums

TIPS

Clients are often surprised to realize they can use organized movements (Figure 6.2) to shape their experiences of dysregulation. From a state of dorsal vagal conservation, movement needs to be gentle and often involves imagining a movement before enacting a movement. Simply being in a place where other people are present without a requirement to connect can bring the right degree of autonomic challenge to support beginning mobilization. In the intensity of sympathetic mobilization your clients are looking for an organized way to use and safely discharge their energy. Because the ability for clear thinking is impaired in a dorsal vagal or sympathetic state, having a movement continuum as a guide supports your clients when their autonomic state makes it difficult for them to make a choice and is a reminder to recognize and savor their ventral vagal experiences.

―――― **EXERCISE** ―――――――――――――――――――――

Imagined Action

Movement is not always an option. Personal and environmental circumstances sometimes make it difficult to take an action. When that happens, imagined movement is the next best choice. This exercise helps clients connect to the benefits of movement through imagery.

BACKGROUND

Motor imagery is a way for you to be in motion when the environment you're in doesn't support moving, when physical challenges make moving difficult, or when making a movement doesn't feel safe and instead activates a protective survival response. Imagined movement practices, either as a replacement for or as a complement to movement, are another way to get the benefits of moving and experience safely moving through space.

STEPS

1. Identify a movement you are drawn to but haven't brought into action yet. Play with it. Imagine yourself safely bringing the action to life. See yourself doing it. Sense your body moving on the inside. Feel the emo-

tions that accompany your moving. Hear the story of who you are as you move.

2. Once you get the feel for imagined movement, create a series of movements. Use your imagination to move in ways you have always wanted.

3. Make time each day to bring one of your moments of movement to life on the inside.

4. Notice if, over time, using motor imagery invites bringing the movement out of your imagination into the world or if it is autonomically nourishing when it remains an imagined experience.

TIPS

Movement is a good example of needing to find the right degree of challenge to have an action be resourcing rather than dysregulating. Some of your clients will find that imagining certain actions supports their ability to feel safe enough to then enact the action in real life. Other clients are nourished through imagining a movement, but a sympathetic flight or dorsal vagal immobilization response takes over when they think about their private, internal experience becoming visible. However your clients sense and see themselves safely bringing a movement to life, the experience of being a mover brings new information that can be integrated into the story of who they are.

——— EXERCISE ———
Labyrinth Walking

Walking a labyrinth activates a subtle pattern of mobilization and calm and opens the mind to new experiences. This exercise offers clients multiple ways to engage with labyrinths, create repeated experiences of autonomic shifts, and explore new ways of thinking.

BACKGROUND

People have been walking labyrinths for centuries. Unlike a maze, a labyrinth has one path and no dead ends. Often thought of as a path to transformation, when you enter a labyrinth, there is a release of connection to the everyday world, a sense of receiving wisdom when you reach the center, and a subtle shift in your sense of yourself and the world when the circuit is completed. When walking a labyrinth there is first a slight increase in mobilization followed by a return to calm making this a gentle autonomic exercise.

STEPS

1. Investigate labyrinth-walking options. The location of thousands of labyrinths around the world as well as access to virtual and printed ones are available at https://labyrinthsociety.org
   - Walk a full-size labyrinth.
   - Navigate a virtual labyrinth on your computer.
   - Trace a printed labyrinth.

- Walk a labyrinth with your fingers using a finger-walking guide.
2. Identify your physiological response to each of the different labyrinth-walking options. Which ones feel the most regulating?
3. Notice any ways your thinking shifts over the course of your labyrinth walk.
4. Keep track of the stories about yourself and the world that you connect with on your labyrinth walks.
5. Find an easily accessible form of labyrinth-walking you can use to return to regulation when you notice a rise in stress.
6. Combine different forms of labyrinth-walking to create a regular practice.

TIPS

With the variety of ways to connect with a labyrinth, this becomes an accessible way for your clients to reduce psychological and physiological stress and gently shape their systems. While using labyrinth walking as an autonomic shaping exercise, your clients may experience an accompanying shift in the ways they think about themselves and see the world.

SHAPING THROUGH BREATHING

> *We live in an ocean of air like fish*
> *in a body of water.*
>
> —ALEXANDER LOWEN

Breathing, thinking, and feeling are tied together through the autonomic nervous system (Ma et al., 2017). Autonomic regulation and a story of safety happen when the heart and the breath are in harmony. This cardiorespiratory synchronization is a function of the vagal pathways. While breath is an autonomic process that works without need for conscious attention, breath can also be consciously shaped. Intentionally regulated breath practices can initiate a state of calm, activate a needed moment of mobilizing energy, increase the capacity for attention and alertness, and enliven the social engagement system (Gerbarg & Brown, 2016).

Engaging in simple breath practices has a positive effect on physical, emotional, and relational well-being. Breath counting increases heart rate variability while decreasing sympathetic activation (Kim, Bae, & Park, 2016). The general rules around breath practices are slow extended exhalations and resistance breathing bring more ventral vagal tone; fast, forceful, and sharp inhalations or irregular breathing mobilize a sympathetic nervous system response; matched inhalations and exhalations maintain the system in a ventral-sympathetic balance (Gerbarg & Brown, 2016). Because breath practices dynamically alter the autonomic nervous system, they are both therapeutic and preventative interventions (Jerath, Edry, Barnes, & Jerath, 2006).

——— **EXERCISE** ———————————————————

Find Your Breath

This exercise uses a breath map to help clients bring attention to the particular ways of breathing that accompany their dorsal vagal, sympathetic, and ventral vagal states (Figure 6.3).

BACKGROUND

There are many ways of breathing. Sometimes breath comes in a quiet and rhythmic cycle and other times it arrives in an erratic and stressed way. Different rhythms of breathing change your physiology, making breath a direct route to shaping your autonomic responses. Use the autonomic hierarchy to map the many kinds of breaths you breathe each day.

STEPS

1. Begin by bringing awareness to what kind of breathing happens in your ventral vagal, sympathetic, and dorsal vagal states.
2. Experiment with different kinds of breath. Notice how each impacts your autonomic state. Identify breaths that are mobilizing, calming, disconnecting, and connecting.
3. Create a breath map.
   - Using a line to depict the autonomic hierarchy, come into connection with each state and feel the ways of breathing that happen there.
   - Breathe in different ways and see where the breath takes you. Place those breaths on your breath map.
4. Use your breath map to find your place on the hierarchy.

TIPS

Since this is an exercise that identifies rather than modifies breath, creating a breath map is a good way for your clients to get to know how their autonomic state and breathing are connected and sets the stage for the next exercises.

ventral vagal	full, deep, easy, steady, slow, long, calming, filling, even, regular, flow between heart and belly, healthy, sustaining
sympthetic	sharp, short, fast, loud, forced, irregular, tight, restricting, fiery, gasping
dorsalvagal	shallow, silent, unfulfilling, flat, empty, weak, depleting

FIGURE 6.3. Sample Breath Map

——— **EXERCISE** ———

Understand Your Breath

This exercise offers clients a way to experience how breath is affected by the actions of the diaphragm and begin to play with shaping their breath in different ways.

BACKGROUND

The diaphragm is the most important muscle in the process of breathing. The diaphragm divides your torso into two parts: the chest cavity inside the ribcage where the lungs and heart reside and the abdominal cavity where the stomach, liver, intestines, and adrenal glands are found. With each breath cycle, the diaphragm changes shape. On an inhalation the muscles of the diaphragm contract and the diaphragm flattens, stretching the lungs to make room for more air. On the exhalation the muscles of the diaphragm relax, restoring the natural curve of the diaphragm to help push air out. When you need extra strength to lift things, during exercise, or in a sympathetically charged state of fight or flight, your breath moves up from your belly to your chest. While this is necessary in the moment, if used for prolonged periods, chest breathing brings anxiety and fatigue. Belly breathing on the other hand emphasizes moving the abdomen, letting it fill and expand on the inhale, empty and contract with each exhale. Belly breathing engages the diaphragm, deepens the breath, and activates the ventral vagal system, inviting a return to regulation.

STEPS

1. Get a feel for the way your diaphragm works.
   - Hold your hands in front of you, fingers interlaced, elbows at your side. In this position, your hands take on the shape of the curve of the diaphragm.
   - Inhale, raising your elbows pointing them outward and let your fingers flatten.
   - Exhale, relaxing your arms letting your elbows fall to your side as your fingers return to the shape of the curve.
   - Follow this cycle, letting your motion reflect the rhythm of your breath as you imagine the action of your diaphragm.
2. Play with changing the rhythm of the motion and syn-

chronizing your breath. Speed the motion up and slow it down. Track the ways your autonomic state shifts with different breath rhythms.

3. Listen to the stories that accompany state shifts.
   - Practice connecting the action of your diaphragm with your breath and listening to the story.
   - Breathe into your chest and track the way your autonomic state changes. Bring awareness to the stories that accompany the change.
   - Breathe into your belly and track the way your autonomic state changes. Bring awareness to the stories that accompany the change.

TIPS

Beginning to attend to the mechanics of breath is a safe starting point for most clients. Do these exercises with your clients to support their ability to bring attention to the interactions of the diaphragm and breath and stay in a ventral vagal regulated state. Once your clients have confidence in that ability, they can continue to explore breath on their own.

——— EXERCISE ———

Follow Your Breath

This exercise offers clients simple and safe ways to actively engage breath as a way to resource regulation.

BACKGROUND

Some of the ways to follow your breath are to attend to each cycle, track the ways your breath moves in your body, add movement to your breath cycle, and create a mantra to tie intention to inhalation and exhalation.

STEPS

1. Count your breaths. Breath counting (counting each exhalation) has been a part of mindfulness training for over 1500 years.
   - Begin with short sets—between 3 and 10 exhalations. Experiment until you find the number that brings you into the ventral vagal place on your breath map.
   - Count to that number of exhalations and begin again. Experiment with repeating the cycle two or three times to find the number of repetitions that brings a balance between challenge and nourishment.
2. Find the places you feel breath moving in your body.
   - Some of the common places to find your breath are the abdomen, chest, heart, throat, just under the breastbone, in the side ribs, and in your lower back.
   - Choose two places and put one hand on each. As you inhale and exhale, feel your breath moving between your hands. Find places that offer an easy pathway to feel the breath flowing between your two hands.
3. Create a mantra. The use of mantras is common in

mindfulness practice and is a way to bring focused intention to your breath.

- Find a word or a phrase for each inhalation and exhalation that brings awareness to:
  - the feeling of energy rising and falling (mobilize, calm)
  - sensing inward and outward connection (tune in, reach out)
  - moving between action and rest (attentive, peaceful)

Honor the ways your autonomic nervous system and breath are interconnected. Let your breath and body guide you in finding your own words and phrases.

4. Take breath outside your body and add movement.
   - There is a strong connection between breath and posture. Experiment with changing postures (lying down, sitting, or standing; posture slumped, straight, or slightly curved) and listen to the story that accompanies each shift.
   - Integrating breath and arm movements strengthens the muscles used in breathing and increases lung capacity. Experiment with adding arm movements to your breath cycle. Try it both seated and standing. Let your body lead the way. Invite your arms to illustrate your inhalation and exhalation. Notice how your movements change when the quality of your breath changes. Find a pattern that feels restorative and create a daily practice of moving with your breath.

5. Add a sigh. Sighing resets the respiratory system, affects your physiological state, and impacts the story that emerges. Humans sigh many times an hour and those spontaneous sighs are a sign your autonomic nervous system is looking for regulation. You can intentionally sigh to engage your system in that process.

- Become aware of the times you spontaneously sigh as your system looks for regulation. Make a practice of noticing. Spend a moment actively appreciating the wisdom of your biology.

- Intentionally sigh. Experiment with a sigh to interrupt a sympathetically activated moment or to bring some energy into a dorsal vagal moment of collapse. Create a habit of bringing a sigh to a difficult situation. Breathe a sigh of relief or sink into a sigh of contentment to deepen a state of regulation and nourish a story of well-being.

TIPS

Breath is an autonomic action that can be intentionally manipulated and is a direct route to influencing autonomic state. When your clients use these exercises between sessions, they are practicing regulation. When you join your clients in following their breath it becomes a co-regulating activity. Watch for your clients' sighs during a session and name them as a way their autonomic nervous system is helping them regulate.

SHAPING THROUGH THE ENVIRONMENT

Outdoor Environments

> *And into the forest I go, to lose my mind and find my soul.*
>
> —JOHN MUIR

The American naturalist and conservationist John Muir found spirituality in nature. He intuitively knew the importance of connecting to nature for well-being. Decades after his death, science confirms what Muir knew: nature nourishes the autonomic nervous system. We now know that nature contributes to resilience (Wells & Evans, 2003) and is associated with feelings of safety (Maas et al., 2009). Walking in a forest environment is an autonomically regulating, restorative experience (Kobayashi et al., 2018; Song, Ikei, & Miyazaki, 2017, 2018), and following a period of distress is a way to calm intense emotions, evoke a state of relaxation, and bring a return of ventral vagal energy (van den Berg, et al., 2015). Looking out at a forest landscape or just viewing an image of a forest scene can restore autonomic balance (Joung et al., 2015; Kobayashi et al., 2018; Song et al., 2018). Both mental health and general health are also positively impacted around environments that include water (de Vries et al., 2016). We have a deeply embodied, emotional, and communal connection to coastlines (Bell, Phoenix, Lovell, & Wheeler, 2015). In the same way viewing forest scenes is restorative, images with water bring an autonomically regulating effect (White et al., 2010).

Because we can't always get out into nature, we bring nature inside. Caring for indoor plants reduces sympathetic activity (M. S. Lee, J. Lee, Park, & Miyazaki, 2015). Flowers in offices bring physiological and psychological relaxing effects (Ikei, Komatsu, Song, Himoro, & Miyazaki, 2014). Simply having flowers in a room can reduce feelings of loneliness (Mojet et al., 2016), and the presence of a single flower invites people to move closer (Haviland-Jones, 2005).

Connecting with nature is a restorative experience, bringing the autonomic nervous system into a state of ventral vagal regulation. Creating an ongoing connection with nature is a preventative experience and an autonomic exercise that shapes the system toward well-being.

─────── **EXERCISE** ───────────────────

Green, Blue, and Flowering

This exercise offers ways for clients to use the natural environment, either in reality or through images, to come into a ventral vagal state and deepen the experience.

BACKGROUND

It is a generally accepted that the *green effect* (the impact of being in green spaces) is a powerful contributor to physical and psychological well-being and that being in a *blue environment* (around or in the water) reduces stress and enhances well-being. Even the simple act of directly connecting to the earth's surface, known as grounding, is an autonomically regulating experience. Drawing on the power of the environment and feeling nurtured by nature is a natural way to shape your system toward well-being.

STEPS

1. Head outside into the natural world.
   - Walk in the woods. Forest bathing, a term coined in Japan in the 1980s denoting the benefits of being in a forest environment, is regulating and restorative.
   - Find the green spaces around your home and work. Regularly return to the places that bring you into a ventral vagal state.
2. Find your way to water.
   - Being by the water is an autonomically regulating and restorative experience. Locate the places around you that offer you the opportunity to be in a *blue environment.* Look toward the ocean, rivers, lakes, ponds, streams, and fountains in city parks.
   - Being in the water brings its own benefits. Cool water experiences have been shown to bring a sympathetic nervous system response, and immersion in warm water lowers sympathetic activation and increases ventral vagal influence. Find a way to immerse yourself in the temperature of water that fits your autonomic need in the moment.
3. Make a physical connection to the earth's surfaces.
   - Walk barefoot in the grass, on the ground, or in the sand.
   - Dig your hands in the dirt or in the sand.

4. Bring the outside in.

- Add flowers and plants to your home and work environments and benefit from their autonomically regulating effects.

- The smell of clean air and wet earth is something all animals and especially humans are sensitive to. Track what happens in your body and where your autonomic nervous system takes you when you encounter those smells.

- Experiment with scent. The smells found in nature are powerful activators of autonomic states. Juniper, lavender, rose oil, and bergamot are some of the scents that have been shown to bring relaxation and regulation. Rosemary, grapefruit, and fennel increase alertness.

- Discover the fragrances that your autonomic nervous system finds renewing. Experiment with different ways to use them. Living or dried objects from the natural world, candles, essential oils, and body creams are some possibilities. Incorporate your chosen fragrances into your everyday experience.

5. View nature.

- Looking out a window at the natural world for as little as 5 minutes facilitates the return to regulation following a distressing experience.

- Images can be used to complement your time in nature or as a stand-in for spending time in nature when opportunities in real time are limited. Find pictures of nature that are autonomically regulating for you.

TIPS

Whether or not your clients have physical access to water or green spaces, they can realize the autonomic benefits of connecting to nature. Help your clients find ways to get out into the natural world when possible and use images as another way to connect to nature. If you work in a place where you have access to outside spaces, consider moving outside for a session.

Indoor Environments

> *This happiness consisted of nothing else but the harmony of the few things around me.*
> —HERMAN HESSE

Along with the outdoor environments you move in, you inhabit indoor environments. Through the pathways of neuroception, your homes and workplaces send cues of connection to meet your needs for co-regulation or signals of protection that bring feelings of isolation.

───── **EXERCISE** ─────────────────

A Ventral Vagal Space of Your Own

This exercise brings clients' attention to the indoor environments they inhabit. Using their autonomic responses to places and objects, clients assess what brings comfort or discomfort and create spaces to nourish their nervous systems.

BACKGROUND

Danish people have one all-encompassing word for a lifestyle that brings well-being. *Hygge* describes a way of living that is cozy, caring, content, friendly, and safe. This speaks to our longing to create and inhabit environments that are filled with cues of safety and inspire an enlivening of ventral vagal energy. Bringing these qualities into your home and workplace in small and simple ways is an act of autonomic shaping.

STEPS

1. Listen to your autonomic nervous system and become aware of what is present in your environment.
   - Look around your home and see where your sympathetic and dorsal vagal systems begin to activate. Identify what brings those states alive.
   - Consider the objects around you that bring a flavor of dissatisfaction or unease.
   - Look around your home and find the places that feel cozy, comforting, and connecting. Identify what makes them feel that way.

- Notice the objects around you that inspire safety, contentment, and warmth.
- Do the same with your workplace.

2. Make a list of the places and things in your home and work environments that bring a feeling of safety and connection. Identify the specific qualities that feel regulating and nourishing to your nervous system.

3. Bring curiosity to what might be possible. Look for spaces at home and at work (a room, a corner, or even a shelf) that could become a place of ventral vagal inspiration for you.

4. Find objects that bring your ventral vagal system alive and bring them into your space. Make small changes and track your autonomic response to each. Remember, small moments add up to a tipping point. Look for the moment when a space feels welcoming. Stop and take that in.

5. Ventral vagal spaces are filled with abundance, but abundance does not mean that your spaces are filled with lots of things. Abundance and scarcity are felt not in the presence of absence of objects but in your autonomic states. Find the balance of open and filled spaces that brings you an autonomic feeling of abundance.

TIPS

When your clients look at their homes and workplaces, they come into contact with a range of autonomic experiences, including disorganized and chaotic environments that mobilize the sympathetic system, ones that are dull and disconnecting and bring a dorsal vagal deactivation, and places that feel safe and welcoming and inspire a ventral vagal response. Because there may be a disproportionate number of elements of dysregulation, it is important to help your clients stay connected to the formula for change—small and often—and track the subtle shifts that happen. Creating ventral vagal-inspired places utilizes processes of closely tracking autonomic responses.

SHAPING THROUGH REFLECTION

Time and reflection change the sight little by little till we come to understand.

—CÉZANNE

For centuries, people have used writing as a way to make sense of their lives. Writing brings a special kind of awareness to thoughts and feelings. Expression in written form has short-term and long-term autonomic regulating effects (Beckwith McGuire, Greenberg, & Gevirtz, 2005). Writing about a past distress can reduce your autonomic response to a new stressor (DiMenichi, Lempert, Bejjani, & Tricomi, 2018), and writing about satisfying experiences can decrease stress, anxiety, and depression (Bhullar, Schutte, & Malouff, 2011).

Compassion practices increase heart rate variability, a marker of ventral vagal influence (Kirby et al., 2017), and self-compassion practices show an increased flexibility of response to stressful experiences (Friis, Consedine, & Johnson, 2015). Loving-kindness mediation has been shown to increase baseline vagal tone, which in turn impacts positive emotions and social connection (Kok et al., 2013).

Your brain and body are intimately connected, autonomic state and psychological story forming experiences and expectations that are sometimes nourishing and sometimes painful. Through the art of reflection, you have the power to shape your system in the direction of safety and connection.

EXERCISE

Writing Your Reflections

This exercise uses writing to add language to autonomic experiences. Creating a practice of listening and using the information to write stories of sympathetic and dorsal vagal challenges and ventral vagal victories helps clients bring explicit awareness to what are otherwise implicit experiences. Adding that awareness often leads to new insights.

BACKGROUND

Your autonomic states carry a wealth of information. Adding words brings a different kind of awareness to your autonomic stories. Even if you don't think of yourself as a writer, your autonomic nervous system benefits as you listen to your state and begin to put words on paper.

STEPS

1. Think of a time when you experienced a dysregulated response. Take just a few minutes to write about it. Lis-

ten to your sympathetic or dorsal vagal survival state and write what you hear.

2. Think of a time when you felt the flow of ventral vagal energy. Turn toward that experience. Listen and write what your ventral vagal state wants you to know.

3. Choose a period of time and set an intention to write about an experience from each autonomic state. A suggested timeframe is once a week over the course of 6 weeks. After the initial writing period, if it feels like a positive experience, set the next intention.

4. Find someone to share your writing with or bring your writing to your therapy sessions. You hear your stories in a new way when you tell them to someone. In the telling, deeper awareness and different insights often emerge.

TIPS

For many clients, writing about autonomic challenges and successes becomes a part of their ongoing shaping practices. Invite your clients to share their stories with you and notice with them any ways their perceptions change as they put language to their experiences. Sometimes this is a subtle shift in understanding and sometimes there is a transformative insight.

In the midst of therapy, these autonomic experiences can be missed, and writing is one way to bring them into awareness.

─────── **EXERCISE** ───────────────────────────

Reflecting with Compassion

This exercise is based on the practice of loving-kindness meditation. Using the focus of the four traditional phrases— happiness, health, safety, ease—clients are asked to find the particular language that represents their autonomic experiences and write their own statements.

BACKGROUND

Compassion emerges from a ventral vagal state and then shapes your system toward experiencing more ventral vagal energy. Loving-kindness meditation is an ancient practice that focuses on self-generated feelings of love, compassion, and goodwill toward oneself and others. Loving-kindness meditation engages the power of the ventral vagal system first through self-compassion and then by offering compassion to others.

The traditional four phrases of loving-kindness meditation are, "May I be happy. May I be healthy. May I be safe. May I live with ease." Some variation of these four phrases has been used for centuries. Jack Kornfield and Sharon Salzberg, two giants in the field of meditation, note that it's okay to adjust the words to find the phrases that are most personally meaningful. What words bring these statements alive for you? Let your ventral vagal state guide you.

STEPS

1. Look at the four categories (happy, healthy, safe, and living with ease) through the language of the autonomic nervous system.
   - Find the words that you would use and write your own four phrases. Here is one example of the four phrases:
     - May I find glimmers every day.
     - May I be nourished by the flow of ventral vagal energy.
     - May I be filled with a neuroception of safety.
     - May I live in the rhythm of a regulated nervous system.
2. Say your phrases out loud. Listen to the words and feel how they land in your system. You'll know you've found the right words when you feel a deep connection to your ventral vagal system.
3. Say the phrases to yourself ("May I"). Then send the phrases to others ("May you") beginning with someone you feel safe and connected to, then a neutral person, then someone you may have an unrepaired rupture with, and finally to all living beings.
4. Share your four phrases with someone else. This might be a friend, a family member, or your therapist. Say the phrases to the other person and also have them read your phrases back to you. Notice what happens when you offer and receive your unique phrases. Track your autonomic response to

the experience of first offering compassion and then of receiving compassion.

TIPS

This exercise uses the ancient practice of Metta meditation as a structure for your clients to find language that reflects the ways their ventral vagal system can be engaged for well-being. Particular words bring different autonomic responses. Help your clients move out of a cognitive decision-making process and discover the wording for each phrase by attending to their autonomic experience.

CHAPTER 6 **SUMMARY**

Neural exercises create a resilience platform for everyday regulation (Flores & Porges, 2017). When your clients have ongoing experiences of returning from protection to the regulation of connection, their autonomic nervous systems are working out. As with other forms of exercise, autonomic exercising is good for physical and psychological well-being. Over a century ago, William James (1890) implored us to see the nervous system not as an enemy but as an ally. It's important for your clients to cultivate an attitude of understanding and respect for the rhythms the autonomic nervous system has created as they enter into practices to shape their systems. Shaping is not about one specific practice. It's through multiple autonomic pathways that a more flexible pattern of response is created, and the autonomic nervous system begins to move toward connection. Some exercises in this chapter involve active engagement while others quietly invite in a new pattern. Help your clients consider what fits their needs in the moment. Learning to listen to the wisdom of the autonomic nervous system and honoring the right degree of challenge is the foundation for change.

CHAPTER 7

INTEGRATING NEW AUTONOMIC RHYTHMS

The whole is greater than the sum of its parts.

—ARISTOTLE

Integration is a process of establishing new autonomic rhythms. Living creatures are amazingly flexible in adapting to the environment and, in fact, change some of their physiological characteristics in order to survive. Fascinating research shows that the tiny water flea grows a helmet or spikes in response to cues of danger from predators in the environment (Reger, Lind, Robinson, & Beckerman, 2017). Although humans may not grow actual helmets or spikes, experiences leave an autonomic imprint and over time create autonomic habits. "Our nervous system grows to the modes in which it has been exercised" (Blanco, 2014, p. 1). If your clients' autonomic patterns were created in an environment of unsafety, they often still move through life in ways that were once adaptive and are now limiting. When your clients predictably experience cues of safety and bring them into explicit awareness, they can shape their response patterns to match the new environment. With practice, an integration process unfolds and repeatedly activated states become new embodied traits (Siegel, 2007).

When autonomic patterns begin to change, your clients find themselves in the unfamiliar experience of being between—not held in old patterns and not yet predictably in new ones. They may feel untethered, ungrounded, unsure of how to engage with others or how to move through daily living experiences. Attending to the beginnings of change and wiring in new neural expectations is an essential part of the integration process.

The integration process takes the small shifts that are the essence of autonomic shaping, brings implicit experiences into explicit awareness, and utilizes the emergent properties of the new patterns to create a new story. There is a gap between intention and action and adding an implementation intention increases the likelihood that your clients will reach their goals (Achtziger, Gollwitzer & Sheeran, 2008; Gollwitzer & Sheeran, 2006; Milne, Orbell, & Sheeran, 2002). When your clients use an implementation intention, they keep moving toward their goals even when they are feeling the high levels of cortisol and increased heart rate that are signs of a sympathetically dysregulated state (Wieber, Thürmer, & Gollwitzer, 2015). The first section, A New Rhythm of Regulation, offers a series of five exercises that help your clients use autonomic awareness to identify and implement goals.

The second section focuses on resilience. Resilience

emerges when, either in perception or in reality, there are more resources than stressors (Ruini, Offidani, & Vescovelli, 2015). Autonomic overload occurs when an environment is filled with frequent cues of danger, when the autonomic nervous system can't adjust to the needs of the moment, or when a survival response keeps going long after it should turn off. Resilience emerges when your clients can accurately detect and effectively respond to cues of safety and danger. Resilience is teachable, learnable, recoverable, and takes practice and awareness (Graham, 2018). The second section, Resilience, offers two exercises to build resilience; Engaging the Vagal Brake and Building Resilience Routines. The capacity to manage distress and keep a healthy balance of resources to stressors relies on the actions of the vagal brake. The vagal brake exercise brings the biology of this ventral vagal circuit into useful form through metaphor. The second exercise gives your clients a way to create a personalized plan to build resilience by choosing actions that resource the capacities of their vagal brake and bring a flow of ventral vagal energy.

A NEW RHYTHM OF REGULATION

Let us not look back in anger, nor forward in fear,
but around in awareness.
—JAMES THURBER

We are all creatures of habit. In fact, some studies have shown that 90% of daily actions are so routine they can be predicted by a few mathematical equations (Buchanan, 2007). "We establish physiological and behavioral set points or default patterns that, once established, the brain and nervous system strive to maintain" (McCraty & Zayas, 2014, p. 7). Your clients see the world through the lens of their autonomic expectations. Awareness of body state and awareness of emotional state are interconnected experiences that make it likely that more awareness of autonomic states will be of benefit in regulating emotions (Fustos et al., 2012).

Habitual autonomic patterns work in the background, bringing a familiar rhythm to your clients' everyday experiences. When those patterns are anchored in a flexible autonomic nervous system, ventral vagal energy supports their ability to safely and successfully meet challenges and move through the day. This is a rhythm to deepen and celebrate. Ongoing activation of sympathetic or dorsal vagal energy creates rigid response patterns, and with rigidity comes suffering. Here you need to help your clients gently shake up the system, interrupt the engrained patterns of protection, and enliven their ventral vagal capacities. Using practices to recognize, reflect, regulate, and re-story, your clients can create a new rhythm of regulation.

───── EXERCISE ─────────────────────

Recognize

This exercise is the foundation for building new autonomic patterns. The simple two-step process is an easy way for clients to build the habit of knowing moment to moment what autonomic state is active.

BACKGROUND

Autonomic awareness is a protective factor. Without the ability to recognize states and state changes, you are at risk for remaining stuck in dysregulation. The question, "Where am I on my autonomic map?" is a simple way to build autonomic awareness.

STEPS

1. Notice. Bring awareness to your autonomic state. Use what you learned about your autonomic states from the exercises in Chapters 4 and 5 to tune in.
2. Name. Stay out of your story and identify your state. Where are you on your autonomic map?
3. Repeat these two steps often. Create ease with this practice until you can quickly and accurately place yourself on your autonomic map.

TIPS

While a seemingly simple skill, it takes repeated practice for your clients to become expert state detectors. Stop in your sessions to notice and name and help your clients create confidence with this skill. Take time with this step to build the foundation for the next steps.

—— **EXERCISE** ———————————————
Reflect

Building on clients' ability to recognize their autonomic states, this exercise adds the next step of turning toward the state and spending a moment listening to the essential information held in the state.

BACKGROUND
Once the notice-and-name practice becomes easy and automatic, add the next step of turning toward your autonomic nervous system to listen for just a quick moment to what it is telling you. Don't spend a long time hearing the full story. Just take long enough to get the general idea of what is happening.

STEPS
1. Be curious about what just prompted a mobilization of your sympathetic system, a descent into dorsal vagal conservation mode, or an experience of ventral vagal regulation.
2. Listen to what your state wants you to know.
   • My sympathetic mobilization is telling me . . .
   • My dorsal vagal state is letting me know . . .
   • My ventral vagal system is inviting me to . . .
3. Listen for just a brief moment with curiosity and without judgment. Don't spend more than a minute or so listening. This practice is a quick experience of listen-

ing to the outlines of your story and not diving deeply into the details.

TIPS

This exercise builds your clients' ability to turn toward their autonomic experiences and reflect without getting pulled in. Your clients should spend just long enough to hear the essential information and not a full story. As clients listen, they begin to hear how their sympathetic and dorsal vagal states are a way their autonomic nervous system is activating an adaptive survival response and how their ventral vagal state is offering a moment of regulation and connection.

——— EXERCISE ———

Regulate

Building on the Recognize and Reflect exercises, this exercise uses clients' awareness of their autonomic patterns to move into goal setting.

BACKGROUND

Everyday navigation of daily living involves setting goals and then acting to make your goals a reality. Goals are helpful in identifying what you want to achieve and are often stated in the form of an intention.

STEPS

1. Consider the autonomic goals you want to set. Ask yourself:
   - Where do I want my autonomic patterns to take me?
   - What do I want to change?
   - What do I want to deepen?
2. Write goals that address what you discovered. Begin each statement with the words "I intend to." For example: I intend to not get stuck in dorsal vagal collapse. I intend to more quickly manage my sympathetic response. I intend to find moments of ventral vagal happiness to savor. Find the words that express your autonomic goals and write your personal intentions.

TIPS

Autonomic goal setting helps your clients work with the autonomic states that underlie their personal narratives. Working with their biology first, your clients can shape new response patterns that create a foundation for new behaviors and beliefs.

EXERCISE

Create "If-Then" Statements

This exercise shows clients how to add an implementation intention to autonomic goals. Using the proven if-then formula, clients write goals to shape their responses to dorsal vagal, sympathetic, and ventral vagal experiences.

BACKGROUND

Once you identify your autonomic goals, the next step is to translate your intention into action by adding what is called an implementation intention. An implementation intention is an if-then statement that identifies when, where, and how you plan to respond to a situation. Writing implementation intentions brings awareness to experiences by creating a link between cues and responses, making it easier for you to recognize situations and take action.

STEPS

1. Set goals for responding to cues of safety and danger in new ways. Set goals for all three states. Make sure your goals aren't too big (unrealistic as a starting point), too broad (undefined and hard to put into action), or too bland (uninteresting and don't keep your attention). Set goals that begin with small steps and lead to a larger change, are well defined with tangible ways to measure, and entice you to want to see what happens when you follow through.

2. Use the beginning statement, "If this happens then I will" to write if-then statements for each of your identified goals.

3. Write statements for external cues (response to certain people, places, or events).

4. Write statements for internal cues (response to autonomic state changes).

5. Read your if-then statements and check your autonomic response. Make sure each statement brings a

neuroception of safety. Rewrite any statements that trigger a move into a sympathetic or dorsal vagal response.

6. Use your statements and track what happens. As your responses shift you may want to add new goals and write new if-then statements.

TIPS

The neuroception of safety is an essential element in the change process. To be successful, your clients' autonomic goals and if-then statements have to bring the right degree of challenge. Too much and the system moves into a survival response. Not enough and the system won't recognize the invitation to repattern. Help your clients track their movement toward a goal, celebrate reaching their goal, and then create new goals and if-then statements when they successfully realize their original ones.

The following examples are offered as a guide. If the goal is to return to regulation more easily, if-then statements might be written like this:

For external cues:

- If I'm going to be around my family, then I will make sure my talisman stone is in my pocket so I can reach it easily.
- If my work to-do list seems overwhelming, then I'll take a quick break to get up and move every hour.
- If I go to the coffee shop with friends, then I will tell them how much I like being there with them.

For internal cues:

- If I feel the beginning of disconnection, then I will send a text to my friend.
- If I notice my sympathetic system beginning to rev up, then I will use my sighing practice.
- If I get back to my state of ventral vagal ease, then I will put my hand on my heart and celebrate.

——— **EXERCISE** ————————————————————

Re-Story

Resisting the pull of old stories and giving new stories time to take shape is an integral part of the change process. This exercise helps clients follow the subtle shifts that bring a new rhythm of regulation and bring attention to concrete markers of change.

BACKGROUND

Humans are meaning-making beings, automatically pulled toward story. Working with the skills of recognizing, reflecting, and regulating brings you to the important step of re-storying. As you integrate new patterns, you move out of your old stories and head toward new ones. This transition often brings with it discomfort and you can easily be pulled back into old familiar stories about yourself and the world. The re-storying process disrupts the habit of listening to an old story and encourages the development of a new one. Re-storying invites you to become an active author of your own autonomic adventure.

STEPS

1. What are the ways your autonomic nervous system is responding differently? Fill in the following sentences to bring awareness to the shifts that are happening.
   - Instead of my expected sympathetic mobilization I . . .
   - Instead of my familiar dorsal vagal disconnection I . . .
   - I notice I am more . . .
   - I notice I am less . . .
2. Write a story that speaks to your new pattern. Choose words that come from your ventral vagal state and keep that state online and active. For example, "I'm strong when I interact with other people" might bring sympathetic mobilization while "I have inner strength that serves me when I'm interacting with others" could keep you anchored in ventral.
3. Write about qualities and not behaviors. Use sentences that begin with "I am" (a quality) rather than "I do" (a behavior). *I am kind* is a different story than *I do kind things*.
4. Create a story that illustrates your new autonomic responses.
   - Use *I am beginning to* or *It is possible that* as the opening line to the new story.

- Write in small increments. In the re-storying process, a short story is more effective than a long essay.

TIPS

Through their stories your clients define who they are and how they find their way in the world. Embedded in their old stories are acts of protection that come from sympathetic or dorsal vagal states. Help your clients create new stories that are anchored in their ventral vagal energy and nourish their nervous systems.

RESILIENCE

Resilience—the capacity to bend with the wind, go with the flow, bounce back from adversity, is essential to the survival and thriving of human beings and human societies.

—LINDA GRAHAM

Through the lens of the autonomic nervous system, resilience is the ability to return to a ventral vagal state following a move into sympathetic or dorsal vagal responses. Autonomic state shifts in response to the challenges of everyday life are a normal and expected experience. The goal is not to always be in a state of ventral vagal regulation but rather to be able to flexibly navigate the small, ordinary shifts that a part of everyday life and build enough resilience to weather the ones that are traumatic. Your clients build resilience by moving through cycles of regulation, dysregulation, and the restoration of regulation.

Before birth, the capacity for resilience is shaped as a mother's levels of stress impacts the prenatal programming of her baby's autonomic nervous system (Bush et al., 2017). As we mature, ventral vagal activity measured through heart rate variability (HRV) is associated with resilience. People who have high HRV score higher on resilience questionnaires, recover more efficiently from acute psychological stress, and are less vulnerable to the development of PTSD-and depression-related symptomatology (Carnevali, Koenig, Sgoifo, & Ottaviani, 2018).

Resilience helps your clients stay hopeful when things feel hopeless, engage an effective survival response in the face of danger, manage levels of stress in an ongoing stressful environment, and keep moving forward when the world around them is filled with suffering.

——— EXERCISE ———
Exercise the Vagal Brake

This exercise brings attention to the role of the ventral vagal pathway to the heart's pacemaker (the sinoatrial node) in regulating autonomic responses. Through the use of image and movement, clients are able to access and exercise the important regulating capacities of the vagal brake.

BACKGROUND

The vagal brake is responsible for speeding up and slowing down your heart rate. The vagal brake allows you to feel more sympathetic nervous system energy while keeping your ventral vagal system online and in charge. As the vagal brake begins to release, the mobilizing energy of the sympathetic nervous system that is in the background begins to move into the foreground. Then as the vagal brake reengages, the process is reversed, sympathetic energy moving to the background and ventral vagal back to the foreground. Think about the vagal brake working similarly to the brakes on a bicycle. Imagine you are riding a bike down a hill and you want to go a little faster. Release the brakes a bit and feel the wheels spin faster. Gently squeeze the brakes to slow down.

When your vagal brake relaxes but doesn't fully release, you have access to a range of responses, including feeling calm, engaged, joyful, excited, passionate, playful, attentive, alert, or watchful, while still safely anchored in the ventral vagal system. You can bring the energy necessary to respond to what is needed in the moment. When working well, the vagal brake supports flexibility in your responses and creates a sense of ease to transitions.

Using metaphor and imagery you can experiment with engaging, relaxing, and reengaging the vagal brake and experience the ways this part of the ventral vagal system helps you safely navigate everyday challenges. With ongoing practice, you create more flexibility in your responses and feel the benefits of a resilient autonomic nervous system.

STEPS

1. Find an image of your vagal brake that brings to life your sense of regulating the increase and decrease of energy

in your ventral vagal pathways. Look for an image that gives you the feeling of controlling the dimensions of something. Some commonly used images include bicycle brakes, a door, a bridge, a gate, a water faucet, a volume control knob, and a dimmer switch. Let your imagination guide you as you find an image that you can manipulate and measure the changes.

2. Write a simple story about your vagal brake using the image. Describe your image and how you use it to increase energy and return to calm.

3. Use a movement. Not everyone creates imagery to come into connection with inner experience. For some people movement is the preferred method. Find a movement that changes shape to illustrate the increase and decrease of energy.

4. Connect your vagal brake image and/or movement to your breath cycle. A subtle pattern of relaxation and reengagement happens with every breath cycle. With each inhalation, the brake relaxes just a bit, allowing a slight speeding up of the heart, and then reengages on the exhalation to bring a return of the slower beat. Take a moment and play with these two pathways. Feel your vagal brake relax, then reengage with each breath in an ongoing cycle. Move through several breath cycles until it begins to feel natural.

5. Use the image and/or movement to intentionally engage, relax, and reengage the brake.
   • See yourself as an active operator of your vagal brake, shaping the rise and fall of energy. Bring the

image to life—see it, hear it, feel yourself adjusting it, and feel your energy moving in synchrony with the changing image.

- Bring the movement connected to your vagal brake into awareness either in outward action or inward experience. Change the movement and feel the increase and decrease of sympathetic energy in your system.

6. Play with the experience of intentionally exercising your vagal brake.

- Start with a small challenge, perhaps something that is commonly experienced in your day-to-day life. On a scale of intensity from 1–10, choose something in the 1–3 range.

- Use your image and/or movement to relax the brake to meet your chosen challenge and reengage the brake when the challenge is over. Feel the influence you have over the ways your vagal brake works in service of managing the challenge.

7. Experiment with a variety of challenges. Build confidence in using your vagal brake to meet everyday challenges.

- Once you feel confident in successfully meeting small challenges, choose a slightly stronger challenge. Notice how your vagal brake relaxes, allowing your energy to rise in the face of more intense challenges while maintaining the ventral vagal state of safety. Then reengage the brake and return to your ventral vagal starting point.

- Practice using your vagal brake with environmental experiences.
- Practice using your vagal brake with relationship stressors.

TIPS

The vagal brake is an embodied system of regulation that you can help your clients intentionally access and exercise. Without the vagal brake, your clients lose their anchor in the ventral vagal state of safety and connection and move into the sympathetic nervous system's protective states of fight and flight. Without the vagal brake they may stay stuck in sympathetic mobilization or continue the descent into dorsal vagal collapse. With ongoing practice, clients create more flexibility in their responses, learn to safely access the mobilizing energy of the sympathetic system, and feel the benefits of a resilient autonomic nervous system.

Here are some examples of vagal brake imagery:

- Open a bridge to allow big ships to pass through safely and then close it for the usual boat traffic.
- Open and close a door, letting in the amount of light and air wanted. Make the opening the right size just to look through or to walk through.
- Use a dimmer switch for a light fixture. There are many adjustments between on and off. Decide how much light is needed moment to moment and move the dimmer switch up or down.

──── EXERCISE ────────────
Resilience Routines

This exercise helps clients take what they have learned about their autonomic patterns and choose practices that fit their personal needs around feeling nourished and increase their capacity to respond with resilience. Since resilience is a quality that can be enhanced over time, this exercise combines ongoing core practices with regularly changing practices.

BACKGROUND
Resilience is an emergent property of a ventral vagal state. As you build resilience, instead of responding to a challenge with an automatic move into a survival response, you are able to respond with more flexibility. And in the times when you are pulled into a survival response, rather than getting stuck there, you're able to return to the state of ventral vagal regulation. As resilience builds, your capacity for flexibility of response deepens.

STEPS
1. Create resilience routines that draw from practices that engage your body and brain in a variety of ways. Revisit Chapter 6 and see if there are shaping exercises from the different categories that fit into your resilience routine.
2. Experiment with actions that bring moments of ventral vagal experience.

- Look inward to breath and reflection practices.
- Look outward into the environment of your home and nature.
- Look at the way you move in the world and the people who accompany you.

3. Choose experiences that feel nourishing and ones that feel a bit challenging. You want a mix of practices that feel comfortable and are easy to engage with and ones that take concerted effort. Building resilience is about both deepening into ongoing practices that feel sustaining and inviting in new practices that bring the right degree of neural challenge for your system.

4. Find a few core practices that will remain constant in your resilience routine.

5. Create a second category of practices that routinely change.
   - Decide on the length of time you want to use. The time period can be anywhere from 1 week to 6 months.
   - Choose a few new practices to experiment with over your chosen time period. At the end of that time some practices may become core practices while you let others go. As you try out new practices, your resilience routines continue to develop.

6. Regularly review and revise your resilience routines. Some practices will become lifelong, while others will serve you for a time and then be replaced with new ones.

My Core Practices	Changing Practices This month I will . . .
vagal brake image with breathing	use breath counting once a day
intentional sighing	find a place I feel safe to be quiet
glimmers with my hand on my heart	try a different yoga class each week

FIGURE 7.1. Sample Resilience Routines

TIPS

Resilience routines (Figure 7.1) help your clients build the capacity to meet challenges without being pulled into and held captive by a survival response. Encourage your clients to take time finding two or three core daily resilience practices. These should be simple practices that they find easy to use and lead to an increased sense of actively regulating and resourcing. Have your clients share their resilience routines with you. During sessions you can use their core practices to support working at the edges of regulation.

CHAPTER 7 **SUMMARY**

> *If light is in your heart you will find your way home.*
>
> —RUMI

The word *integrate* comes from the Latin to make whole. When your clients integrate new autonomic rhythms, they make their systems whole in new ways. They move from a pattern of rigid responses to an autonomic platform that supports flexibility. Integration of new autonomic patterns happens over time and can be explicitly encouraged.

The exercises in Chapter 7 help your clients incorporate the skills they explored in Befriending, Attending, and Shaping. You can think about the process of integration through the four "D's": discover, disrupt, develop, deepen.

Discover. Your clients begin their journey to integration by discovering their patterns of protection and connection.

Disrupt. The next step toward integration is to disrupt familiar autonomic survival responses and the stories of mobilization and disconnection that accompany them.

Develop. Having interrupted old patterns, opportunities open for clients to develop new ways of responding that are grounded in ventral vagal safety.

Deepen. The final step is to bring together new responses and new stories.

Integration takes time, happens incrementally, and is a lifelong endeavor.

CHAPTER 8

CONNECTING
TO OTHERS

We were all hungry, but it was Elizabeth who realized our true starvation was for connection, the company of other people . . . for fellowship.

—ANNIE BARROWS, THE GUERNSEY LITERARY

AND POTATO PEEL SOCIETY

Through the process of evolution, anatomy and biology have been shaped to enable social engagement and reciprocal connection (Carter & Porges, 2012). Experiences of social relationships and loneliness significantly predict wellness, illness, and mortality. "There are perhaps no other factors that can have such a large impact on both length and quality of life" (Holt-Lunstad, Robles, & Sbarra, 2017, p. 527). The social environment effects biology. It has become apparent that social connections and physiology enter into a reciprocal relationship that impacts the ways genes are expressed (Cole, 2014). When people feel socially disconnected, they seem to have an increased inflammation response coupled with an impaired immune response (Cole, 2009). Applying this understanding of the interconnection of physiology and psychology, the British town of Frome developed a project focused on building networks of social support and connection and found hospital admissions reduced by over 30% (Abel & Clarke, 2018). Your biology responds to being out of connection and your happiness is interwoven with the happiness of people with whom you are connected. Community can be a cure for illness.

"Life on Earth is fundamentally social" (Carter & Porges, 2012 p. 12). Connecting invites your clients into exploration of social connections, reciprocity, and co-regulation. Your clients connect with people whose autonomic patterns fit with theirs and feel familiar. Their relationships are often with people who are similarly dysregulated or whose autonomic responses mimic their childhood experiences. As a result of engaging in polyvagal exercises, your clients' autonomic patterns begin to change, and they are drawn to look for other people who attune to their new patterns. Looking at relationships through the lens of a reshaped system brings clarity to what is autonomically draining and filling. Autonomic resonance is a powerful guide for your clients to use in evaluating current relationships, shaping old relationships in new ways, and looking for new connections with people whose rhythms are similar.

Chapter 8 offers two categories of exercises that help your clients embrace the human longing and biological need to create community: Belonging, and Connecting to Something Greater than Self. Each of these offers ways to engage the autonomic nervous system in deepening pathways to connection. Belonging begins the process with three exercises that use the experience of reciprocity to help your clients understand their personal needs for connection and create ways to meet those needs. Connection to Something Greater than Self offers clients ways to connect to the autonomic experiences of gratitude, compassion, and awe and build connections beyond their immediate personal relationships.

BELONGING

Every heart sings a song, incomplete, until another heart whispers back.

—PLATO

We come into the world wired for connection, one autonomic nervous system reaching out to another. Connection is a biological imperative—essential to survival. Being predictably cared about creates a sense of belongingness (Baumeister & Leary, 1995). The autonomic nervous system requires reciprocity to regulate states and to feel safe (Porges, 2012). In fact, the quality of your clients' relationships has more impact on their health and well-being than the quantity (Ozbay et al., 2007). Although your clients may interact with lots of people in the course of a day, they can still feel profoundly lonely. They can be "alone together" (Turkle, 2011).

A sense of belonging to a group and having things in common with fellow group members brings satisfaction with life (Wakefield et al., 2016). In an ever-increasing feedback loop, when your clients are embedded in connections with friends, they are more likely to experience life satisfaction and when they experience life satisfaction, they are more likely to have stronger and more intimate connections (Amati et al., 2018).

Your clients' individual sense of happiness is impacted by being part of a network of happy people (Fowler & Christakis, 2008).

─────── **EXERCISE** ───────────────────────

Rules of Reciprocity

This exercise helps clients look at experiences of intra- and interconnection in daily living and ways to create the right balance to meet their autonomic needs (Figure 8.1).

BACKGROUND

You don't require reciprocity, proximity, and face-to-face interactions all the time. In fact, well-being is found in a balance of time with others and time by yourself. You have your own reciprocity requirements, and when they aren't met, your body feels the absence. Without the right measure of reciprocity, your autonomic state begins to shift from readiness for connection to preparation for protection. Incorporating a therapeutic dose of reciprocity (the amount necessary to bring the desired effect) into your daily living means first knowing your needs and then building sustainable connections and opportunities to meet those needs.

STEPS

1. Fill in the following equations to find your reciprocity rhythms. Recognize the signals that you've been on your own for too long, you've spent too much time connected to others, or you're in a sweet spot of symmetry.

The amount of time I want to spend on my own today is: Today I'm going to spend time alone doing:	$=$ reciprocity balance	The amount of time I want to spend with friends today is: Today I'm going to connect with: And we're going to:
These work responsibilities mean that I work by myself: These things in my personal life mean that I'm on my own:	$>$ alone and out of balance	I've neglected being with the people in my life who are important to me by not paying attention to: and not making time for:
I've lost track of my: I've been so busy with others I haven't made time for:	$<$ with others and out of balance	I feel too involved in the life of: I feel over-saturated by doing things with others because I said yes to:

FIGURE 8.1. Reciprocity Equation Chart

2. Reciprocity is not a static experience. Return to this practice regularly to track when you are out of balance or in a resourcing relationship to yourself and others.

3. Take care of your connections.

   • Write reciprocity intentions that describe how you are going to pay attention each day to ways you are in and out of reciprocity. Examples might be, "I will track my reciprocity rhythms and take action when I'm out of balance" or "At the end of the day I'll reflect on my moments of reciprocity."

   • Create time and space for reciprocal interactions. Identify when, where, and with whom you can build predictable, sustainable opportunities for connection into your life.

TIPS

In beginning therapy it is expected that your clients' equations will be out of balance. Often one of the things that brings clients to treatment is the experience of autonomic dysregulation that is an outcome of focusing too much on others or on themselves. Help your clients understand that there is no one single formula for balance; rather, each person creates their own formulas based on their personal autonomic needs. This is a process of finding and maintaining a balance between tending to self and connecting with others.

——— EXERCISE ———

Personal Connection Plan

This exercise helps clients identify what they are doing to feel connected, decide what they would like to try, and use that awareness to create a connection plan (Figure 8.2).

BACKGROUND

What does a map of your pathways to connection look like? Your personal plan brings a dual focus: what's working (the things that are already in place) and what's wanted (things to explore and invite in). The questions in this exercise reference people, but feel free to add pets to your exploration.

STEPS

1. Identify what's working.

- Who are the people in your life with whom you feel a connection?
- What are the things you do together that foster that connection?
- What are the things you do to nourish your sense of connection to self?

2. Identify what you want.
   - Who would you like to invite into connection?
   - What might you do to explore new connections?

People I want to continue to connect with:	People I would like to get to know:
Things I want to continue to do with my friends:	Things I'd like to explore doing with others:
Things I want to keep doing to connect to my own experience:	New things I'd like to try on my own:

FIGURE 8.2. Personal Connection Plan

- What would you like to explore on your own?
- How does interacting with others in a playful way fit into your connection plan?
- How do moments of shared stillness fit in your connection plan?

3. Fill in the boxes to create your personal connection plan. Update your plan as you try new things and make new connections.

TIPS

Clients may feel the absence of connection as they work on this exercise. Moving into sympathetic or dorsal vagal reactions shuts down their ability to explore what they want. Help your clients anchor in the energy of their ventral vagal state so they stay in self-compassion when looking at what is present and have access to curiosity when considering what they want.

——— **EXERCISE** ———

Clusters of Connection

Connecting with others is a universally beneficial experience, but the ways people benefit from connection are individually created experiences. This exercise uses the categories of who, how, and how often to help clients look at the ways they connect with people in their networks.

BACKGROUND

There are many ways to reach for reciprocity. There are many pathways to connection. Who you connect with and how you connect is an individual experience. Find the ways your autonomic nervous system feels nourished and create relationships with people (and pets) that nurture your sense of being woven into a resilient network.

STEPS

1. Look at people in your life.
   - Make a list of the people to whom you are connected.
   - Listen to your autonomic response as you think about each person. Using a scale of 1–3, loosely connected; 4–7, pretty connected; or 8–10, very connected, identify how close you feel to these people. You may find that you have several people in the 4–7 pretty connected range or one person in the 8–10 very connected range and feel very safe and supported with either configuration. It isn't a particular number of connections that matters, it's the ways your personal autonomic needs are met by those connections.
2. Look at how often you connect with people in your network. A match with others feels resourcing while a mismatch between your wish for connection and your experience of connection is painful.
3. Look at the ways you connect.
   - Create a pie chart to map your kinds of connection. Use the communication categories that fit for you.

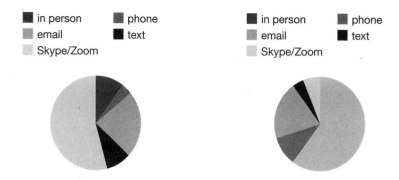

FIGURE 8.3. Types of Connection

The two examples in Figure 8.3 show very different connection profiles, but each person identified feeling deeply connected to their network.

4. Look at what you do when you connect.
   - quiet moments
   - physically active adventures
   - go out or stay in
   - favorite activities you love to return to
   - new things you want to try

TIPS

Your clients each have their own connection needs and ways of connecting and often judge their patterns in comparison to what they think is the right or normal way to connect. Help your clients change from thinking about ways of connecting as right or wrong and instead stay curious as they look at the different kinds of connection that are personally autonomically satisfying.

CONNECTING TO SOMETHING GREATER THAN SELF

*The world is full of magic things, patiently waiting for
our senses to grow sharper.*

—W. B. YEATS

Gratitude, compassion, and awe—called self-transcendent emotions—are experiences that bind people together. They bring benefits beyond individual experiences and create relationships that extend outside the family system. These experiences are associated with ventral vagal activity, bring physiological and psychological health, and may even be connected to your molecular well-being (Cole, 2014).

Gratitude is a universal experience, offered and received by people in cultures around the world (Emmons & Stern, 2013). "Whether it stems from the acceptance of another's kindness, an appreciation for the majesty of nature, or a recognition of the gifts in one's own life, gratitude enhances nearly all spheres of human experience" (Emmons & Stern, 2013, p. 846). Individual moments of gratitude weave together to create a more general sense of being grateful in daily life (McCullough, Tsang, & Emmons, 2004). Just as compassion can be deepened through practice, practice strengthens the gratitude response.

The ventral vagal state of safety creates a platform for compassion (Porges, 2017b). When you feel held in the safety of a regulated nervous system, you can look out into the world and see the ways other people are suffering and respond with compassion. Increased ventral vagal activity is linked to compassion and self-compassion and both are strengthened with regular practice (Neff & Germer, 2017; Stellar, Cohen, Oveis, & Keltner, 2015).

Awe is defined by two features: vastness (experiencing something larger than yourself or beyond your ordinary experience) and accommodation (a reorganization of your ways of thinking to adjust to the new experience) (Keltner & Haidt, 2003). Awe is an information-rich experience that pulls your attention outside yourself toward something greater than your individual experience and expands your frame of reference (Shiota, Keltner, Mossman, 2007). Awe reminds you that you are part of humankind, inextricably connected to the world.

———— EXERCISE ————
With Gratitude

This exercise brings attention to everyday experiences of gratitude that clients often miss. These experiences of gratitude are in the family of ventral vagal micro-moments that, when brought to conscious awareness, strengthen the pathways to regulation.

BACKGROUND

Sometimes gratitude comes in the form of life-giving or life-saving events (a stranger donating a kidney, someone not leaving your side when you are in the depths of despair) that irrevocably change the way you think about and move through the world. More often the gifts of gratitude come through ordinary, everyday experiences. Simple interactions with people (holding a door open, offering a smile, recognizing someone's contribution), pets (your dog greeting you at the door, your cat nuzzling you awake in the morning), or in nature (the return of the sun after a stretch of rain or the rain after a period of drought, the first hint of spring) are opportunities for gratitude. Gratitude is good for your body and brain (fewer physical complaints, better heart health, less depression and anxiety, more happiness). A gratitude practice helps you see the small, everyday experiences of goodness that might otherwise pass by unnoticed.

STEPS

1. Keep a gratitude list. Make a practice of noticing what you might otherwise take for granted.
2. Find ways to express your gratitude. Say thank you. Return the favor.
3. Use a breath practice to deepen into appreciation.
   - Imagine breathing into the beginnings of your ventral vagus at the base of your skull. Follow the pathway as it makes its way to your heart, and then breathe out of your heart. Follow this cycle of breath and imagine your autonomic nervous system supporting your experience of gratitude.
   - Breathe in with a word that acknowledges a moment to be grateful for. Breath out with a word that expresses your gratitude.

TIPS

Gratitude is often an easier experience for your clients to recognize and resource than compassion or self-compassion and builds the foundation for moving into those experiences. Because gratitude grows over time and seems to have lasting effects in increased ventral vagal experiences, changes in personal stories, and increased connections with others, an ongoing gratitude practice is a simple way for your clients to shape their intra- and interpersonal connections.

EXERCISE

Compassionate Connections

This exercise helps clients connect to their ventral vagal state and use the language of the autonomic nervous system with three small practices that build the capacity for compassion and self-compassion.

BACKGROUND

Through the eyes of compassion, from your own regulated nervous system, you can see another person's dysregulated system, respond with regulation, and connect with kindness. From the energy of your ventral vagal system, you can also connect inside and be with your own suffering in an act of self-compassion. Ongoing experiences build the capacity for connecting with compassion. Find the combination of practices that brings your ventral vagal system alive. Create your own compassionate connections.

STEPS

1. Create a compassion statement using the language of the autonomic nervous system.
   - Use language that recognizes another person's dysregulated state and names the ways your ventral vagal state helps you see them with compassion.
   - Decide on a timeframe for using your statement. You might choose to create a new statement each week or each day.
   - Notice people in need of compassion and use your statement to send a message either in silent thought or in spoken words.

2. Make this three-step compassion practice a routine part of your day.
   - Find your ventral vagal anchor.
   - Look through the energy of your ventral vagal system. See the other person not as bad or unworthy but as dysregulated, pulled into sympathetic or dorsal vagal protection, and unable to regulate.
   - Hold the other person in your ventral vagal energy. Let your nervous system send cues of safety toward theirs.

3. Create a self-compassion statement using the language of the autonomic nervous system.
   - Use language that acknowledges your own dysregulated state, identifies that dysregulation is a nor-

mal human experience, and reminds you that your autonomic nervous system knows the way back to regulation.

- Decide on a timeframe for using your statement. You might choose to create a new statement each week or each day.
- Notice when you are in need of compassion and say your statement to yourself either silently or out loud.

TIPS

It is only from a state of being anchored in ventral vagal that your clients have access to compassion and self-compassion. Remind your clients that their ventral vagal state and compassion form a feedback loop that deepens both experiences. When they are anchored in ventral, they build their capacity for compassion; likewise, more moments of compassion strengthen their ventral vagal capacities. The ability for compassion and self-compassion is built over time. Understanding that compassion and self-compassion emerge from an autonomic state offers your clients a way to think about, talk about, and work with these practices and bring patience to the process.

Create your own examples or use these samples to illustrate autonomically guided language.

Sample statements for compassion:

- I see the suffering your dysregulation brings.
- I can hold you in my ventral vagal energy.

Sample statements for self-compassion:
- Even as I feel myself losing my anchor in ventral, I remember my system knows the way back.
- It's natural to move in and out of regulation.

—— **EXERCISE** ————————————————

Awe Inspiring

For many clients, the experience of being alone and disconnected is one of the things that brings them to treatment. This exercise gives clients ways to bring the autonomic state of awe alive and feel connected to something larger than their individual experience.

BACKGROUND

You feel moved when you are awe-filled and motionless when you are awestruck. Awe lives along a continuum of ordinary to extraordinary. Some moments stop you in your tracks and demand your attention. Other everyday moments pass by without being recognized. People, nature, architecture, the arts, spiritual experiences, and inexplicable events each have the potential to elicit feelings of awe. Where are your moments of awe each day that are waiting to be discovered?

STEPS

1. Build a reservoir of awe memories.
   - Remember a moment of awe.

- Replay it in your mind and bring the richness of it back into full awareness.
- Revisit it in writing to deepen the experience.

2. Notice where in your life you find awe.
   - Certain people inspire awe. Who are those people for you? They may be people you know and have a relationship with or people you know of and admire.
   - Places, the architecture of a particular structure, and natural formations in the outside world routinely bring experiences of awe.
   - Art and music predictably activate awe.
   - Spiritual experiences are awe-filled.

3. Either physically or through a memory, return to the awe-inspiring people, places, and events you identified in step two. Returning in person or revisiting in memory brings the experience and your ventral vagal response alive again.

4. Be open to the inexplicable events that unexpectedly appear. Let go of the need to understand and explain those moments and let in the experience of awe.

TIPS

Awe is an experience that is accessible to everyone. While an awe experience often leads to a desire to share the experience with others, it is first an individual experience that happens when people are by themselves. Although the state of awe is often unexpected, it can also be intentionally inspired. Help your clients find small moments of awe that are easily repeatable.

Here is an example of revisiting an experience and bringing the richness of the memory alive through writing an awe story:

I was visiting the medieval city of Bruges in Belgium a few years ago when I found a church. I was drawn into the church by its commanding Gothic architecture and the stillness I knew I would find within. As I entered the church, I went from being curious to something more, something palpable I could not explain. I walked along the nave toward the altar and came upon a series of paintings depicting the Passion of the Christ. As I walked from painting to painting, I could feel the pain and sadness of all humanity, and yet I could also feel a deep and abiding love. Tears streamed down my face as a force larger than myself flowed through me. I was everything at once: grief and joy, love and pain, anger and peace. When I left the silence of the sanctuary and climbed the stone stairs into the sunshine of the medieval town square, it was as if I was entering an entirely new world. I couldn't put words to what had just happened, but I knew I had touched a holy place, both inside and outside of myself. I am forever changed by my experience that day in Bruges when I knew that all was broken and all was right in precisely the same moment.

CHAPTER 8 **SUMMARY**

*You discover that your longings are universal longings, that
you're not lonely and isolated from anyone. You belong.*

—F. SCOTT FITZGERALD

Connecting invites your clients to explore the questions,
"Where are the places, what are the experiences, and who are
the people that nourish my nervous system now?" Through this
process of inquiry, your clients bring their implicit experience
into explicit awareness in order to discover their new rhythms
of regulation and experiment with creating daily living experiences that fit their changing autonomic profiles. Recognizing
the combination of newly established and still emerging autonomic pathways now available to guide their choices is often
both exciting and alarming for clients. As they begin to connect to self, others, the world, and spirit in new ways, your
clients may feel sad about the things they are letting go of,
anxious about all the changes new perspective brings, or confident in connecting to their autonomic nervous system and
ready for the adventure. Learning how to move through the
world with new rhythms can be daunting. Help your clients
hold on to the ventral vagal pathways they've built and tend to
the new patterns that are taking root.

The exercises in this chapter support your clients in building inward and outward connections by engaging the power
of their ventral vagal pathways. Simple awareness practices
that lead to the creation of safe and sustaining connections are
offered in combination with exercises to engage with the tran-

scendent experiences that evoke a sense of being woven into a network much bigger than self.

SECTION II   SUMMARY

Little by little, one travels far.

—J. R. R. TOLKIEN

Everyday life is filled with challenges. To safely navigate throughout the day, the autonomic nervous system quickly responds to both actual and perceived demands in order to assure survival in moments of danger and the ability to thrive in times of safety. With a flexible autonomic nervous system, your clients have the ability to meet those challenges with equanimity—to stand in the middle, anchored in a ventral vagal state. With a nervous system that has been shaped away from connection toward protection, a system that can neither self-regulate nor co-regulate with ease, a cascade of events is set in motion that ends in suffering. When your clients are stuck in old patterns that use the mobilizing energy of the sympathetic nervous system or the shutdown response of the dorsal vagal system, they are separated from the biological resource of their ventral vagal system. These adaptive responses, once necessary for survival, now keep them from connecting to themselves, to others, and to the world around them.

With a foundation of understanding Polyvagal Theory, your clients can look at daily life and explore how to connect to the world through the lens of the autonomic nervous system. When you and your clients speak the language of the autonomic nervous system, you share a language—a kind of shorthand—that creates clarity and facilitates communication. With Polyvagal Theory as a guide, you can help your clients shape their autonomic nervous systems toward safety, regulation, and relationship. The steps presented in the BASIC sequence empower your clients to listen to their embodied stories, find cues of safety, and create new patterns that bring the possibility of health, growth, and restoration.

CONCLUSION

To live will be an awfully big adventure.

—PETER PAN

Science continues to demonstrate that your brain and body systems are in a constant state of change. The concept of neuroplasticity (the way brain networks reorganize) has been incorporated into mainstream thinking. In an explosion of interest in the past several years, Polyvagal Theory has not only been embraced by therapists but is finding its way into the legal system, medical settings, the business world, and schools. We are drawn to want to know more as we recognize the profound changes evoked in individuals, families, groups, systems, and even society when we are held in the safety of ventral vagal energy.

The autonomic nervous system is at the heart of daily living. The three circuits of the autonomic nervous system "co-arise, co-exist, and co-mingle to create the array of complex human physiological, emotional and behavioral states" (Sullivan et al., 2018, p. 5). These autonomic circuits continually assess safety and risk and initiate actions to help your clients navigate the demands of the day. With the evolutionary emergence of the ventral vagal system, clients have the ability to regulate their autonomic nervous systems through connection with others in face-to-face interactions (Flores & Porges, 2017). Through a polyvagal lens, social engagement is the "go-to default activity" that people use to regulate (Lucas et al., 2016, p. 6). With a system shaped in safety, your clients are able to embody these patterns of connection. With a system shaped by trauma, their pathways to regulation through connection are disrupted and they are guided instead by patterns of protection.

Your clients' stories begin in their bodies. Science has shown that behind the scenes, the autonomic nervous system, through habitual patterns of response, generates stories. With awareness and practice, you can help your clients reshape their responses and rewrite their stories. With a map of their autonomic circuits, you can help your clients use autonomic exercises to create new patterns, move out of adaptive survival responses, and begin to meet the ordinary, and perhaps even the extraordinary, challenges of daily life from an autonomically regulated state of safety.

"The capacity for affect regulation is not biologically guaranteed or innately hard-wired into our nervous system at birth" (Flores & Porges, 2017, p. 6). How often your clients are met with attunement or misattunement, how they are seen, heard, and held, and the ways they are offered the safety of co-regulation all combine to organize a personal autonomic profile. While their early life experiences establish their autonomic profile, ongoing experiences can modify it. Exercising neural circuits supports the essential ability to "immobilize without fear, mobilize without rage or anger, and socially engage with others" (Williamson et al., 2015, p. 2). Regularly exercising circuits of connection promotes flexibility and shapes a system that can respond and not simply react.

Helping your clients engage with their autonomic nervous systems through polyvagal exercising is an invitation for them to become students of their systems. Repatterning the autonomic nervous system happens over time, not only in therapy but in the time between therapy. The following two vignettes offer a look at what is possible when clients engage in exercises to shape their systems and is a reminder that polyvagal exercises have impact when they are practiced over time.

Autonomic Exercising

Before I started using polyvagal exercises, I was stuck in a state of dysregulation. Although back then I didn't have words for it, I know now that my system was moving between dorsal vagal collapse and sympathetic activation in an endless, enduring loop. I was living a story of survival and suffering. Like most complex trauma survivors, I couldn't imagine feeling relaxed and present in the moment. I couldn't imagine feeling safe.

When I was introduced to Polyvagal Theory, I didn't know there was anything except a survival state and even when I learned about ventral vagal safety and connection, I rarely found myself in that place and couldn't hold on to the moments when I did. Now, after many months of practice, I find my way to ventral with relative ease and I've learned from experience that it's only when I have enough ventral energy on board that a positive outcome is possible. Over the time I've been using polyvagal exercises, I've become much less reactive. I'm more tolerant, compassionate, and even self-compassionate. I experience moments of calm, curiosity, humor, and gratitude and worry less about what might happen to overwhelm me. Even my longing for co-regulation is no longer shameful. Now I know it's a normal, autonomic experience. My daily challenge is to tune in to what I need and then find ways to safely and wisely meet my needs both on my own and in connection with others.

An essential part of my autonomic exercising is to notice and name. In the beginning I had to physically stop and ask myself what state I was in and for a long time I could name dorsal, sympathetic, and ventral but naming the nuances of those states was difficult. Now I feel the flow of big and small changes in my system and noticing and naming has become second nature to me.

When I'm not regulated, I find a ventral vagal anchor. I've created many anchors since I first learned about them, but my go-to one is still my breath. And recently I've discovered that the more I notice, name, and anchor in ventral, the more I can look at other people and see their states. While I'm still improving, tracking my states and seeing other people's states is incredibly helpful in learning to set boundaries and the biggest gift is that other people's dysregulation no longer automatically triggers me.

My favorite practice of all the exercises is finding glimmers. Life before polyvagal exercising was mostly black and white and finding a glimmer felt as impossible as finding a four-leaf clover. Now there are colors and, while I faithfully do the "find three glimmers a day practice," most of my days bring many more than three glimmers.

I have a regular autonomic exercise plan and am committed to daily practice. I know I am building new wiring and resilience. I feel it in my body, see it in the way I move through my day, and hear it in my stories.

An Expert State Detector

The notice-and-name practice is the foundation of my polyvagal exercise program. I'm skilled at putting myself on my autonomic map and sensitive to recognizing even subtle state shifts. I can tell when I'm in a ventral vagal state and things are emotionally difficult but manageable. I know when I'm getting close to slipping into sympathetic fight or flight. And I can track when I'm in a sympathetic mobilization, becoming overwhelmed, and heading toward shutdown. Noticing shifts and being able to tune in to the feeling that I'm just about to move into a different state gives me the moment I need to interrupt my familiar habitual response and attempt something different. When I am able to name my state, that awareness translates into having some choice in my reaction. If I notice I'm heading toward sympathetic, which would normally bring an angry outburst, I try to use the energy in a different way, to use flight in a healthier way. I might end a conversation or leave a situation in a way that isn't aggressive. And if I'm sinking into dorsal, I've discovered that moving (shifting my body, standing up, moving to a different place) and looking for just a moment of social connection can stop the free fall.

There are still times when the shift happens so suddenly that I don't notice until it's already happened. Even then, if I can name the change, the experience feels less scary and I can move out of it more quickly. I'm trying to build a community of people who speak "polyvagal" because I don't feel so alone when there are people around who know the language. Sharing my state with someone who understands my autonomic shorthand can help me return to regulation quickly. I use the smile experiment when I notice the beginning pull toward dorsal. I head out to the places around me where I know there will be people and make a point of looking at the faces of clerks, customers, and people around me and smile. I've found with just a bit of feedback from another face, I can begin to move away from the dorsal vagal hole I'm in danger of falling in.

Noticing and naming is now built into my daily life and I find I not only attend to my own states but I'm also able to think about what's happening for others. When coworkers or family members direct their anger at me, I find myself wondering why their system is reacting in that way and I consider the underlying need. It used to be impossible for me to not get sympathetically triggered or retreat into dorsal vagal disconnection when someone was yelling at me or accusing me of something. Now I can usually see they are having an autonomic response of their own and most of the time I stay regulated and even look at them with compassion.

Since beginning to use polyvagal exercises, I understand more about my autonomic nervous system. I know that while dorsal shutdown is my familiar pathway of protection and still feels more livable and less damaging than the anger of sympathetic, I also recognize the huge cost I pay in the way it limits having the connections I long for in my life. Seeing small changes add up to more regulation makes each day a bit easier even with the ongoing challenges in my life. I can often move through the day without my old survival responses taking control. I'm beginning to trust that my ventral vagal state will help me meet whatever the day brings.

I alone cannot change the world, but I can cast a stone across the waters to create many ripples.
—MOTHER THERESA

Polyvagal exercises are one way to bring William James' century old invitation to befriend our nervous systems into practical application. Polyvagal exercises are designed to engage the power of the autonomic nervous system and help clients (and therapists) move out of automatic survival responses into the possibilities held in the ventral vagal state. It's my hope that you will experiment with the practices yourself and feel the benefits both in your personal life and in your professional practice. Then, with a polyvagal exercise savvy therapist as a guide, your clients can explore practices and create an ongoing autonomic exercise plan that leads to shaping their systems in new ways and writing stories of well-being.

Through a polyvagal lens, benevolence is the active, ongoing use of ventral vagal energy in service of healing. Benevolence can be the stone we cast across the water. If we each are a regulated and regulating force in the world, we will change the world one autonomic nervous system at a time.

APPENDIX

PERSONAL PROGRESS TRACKERS

Hope is an essential ingredient in change. Clients come to treatment with long-standing autonomic patterns that bring ongoing experiences of physical and psychological suffering and often carry a flavor of hopelessness. Tracking the nuances of autonomic reorganization is an important part of the therapy process. Bringing explicit attention to the subtle beginnings of change is a hope-filled action. Personal Progress Trackers offer concrete ways to note early successes, track small shifts, and identify the steps that are moving the autonomic nervous system in the direction of change.

Chapter 4: Befriending Personal Progress Tracker

Use the following questions to explore your deepening befriending capacities. Check in each week to see how you are becoming more able to tune in and turn toward your autonomic nervous system with the befriending qualities of curiosity and compassion.

- I notice my autonomic nervous system and the state I am in. (seldom, sometimes, usually)
- I can find my place on the autonomic hierarchy. (seldom, sometimes, usually)
- I have a variety of ways to connect to my autonomic nervous system. (a few, would like more, enough)
- I am able to be curious about where I find myself. (seldom, sometimes, usually)
- I am able to be self-compassionate and not self-critical about where I find myself. (seldom, sometimes, usually)

Chapter 5: Attending Personal Progress Tracker
Use the following questions to explore your deepening capacity to attend. Check in each week to see the ways you are becoming more able to track the autonomic path of your day and mark your moments of ventral vagal regulation.

- I am able to track my movement through changing states of activation. (seldom, sometimes, usually)
- I'm comfortable identifying cues of safety from another social engagement system. (seldom, sometimes, usually)
- I'm comfortable identifying cues of danger from another social engagement system. (seldom, sometimes, usually)
- I feel playful. (seldom, sometimes, usually)
- I find moments to savor. (seldom, sometimes, usually)

- I understand my personal needs around solitude. (seldom, sometimes, usually)
- I take care of my personal needs around solitude. (seldom, sometimes, usually)
- I find regulation in connection with art and nature. (seldom, sometimes, usually)

Chapter 6: Shaping Personal Progress Tracker

Use the following questions to explore your deepening capacity to nourish new pathways. Check in each week to see the practices that are shaping your system in new ways.

- I can identify shaping options that work for me. (one, several, many)
- I engage regularly with practices to shape my system. (seldom, sometimes, usually)
- I use shaping practices from multiple sources.

Sound	Seldom	Sometimes	Usually
Movement	Seldom	Sometimes	Usually
Environment	Seldom	Sometimes	Usually
Breath	Seldom	Sometimes	Usually
Touch	Seldom	Sometimes	Usually
Reflection	Seldom	Sometimes	Usually

- I have places in my home that nourish my nervous system. (not yet, working on it, yes)
- I have places at work that nourish my nervous system. (not yet, working on it, yes)

Chapter 7: Integrating Personal Progress Tracker

Use the following questions to explore the ways your new patterns are beginning to integrate and support you in navigating the world in new ways. Check in each week to notice the places where integration is taking root and the places that are calling for your attention.

- I see more than one option when making decisions. (seldom, sometimes, usually)
- I trust the choices I make. (seldom, sometimes, usually)
- I listen to my body. (seldom, sometimes, usually)
- I understand the messages my body is sending. (seldom, sometimwes, usually)
- I move through my daily activities with ease. (seldom, sometimes, usually)
- I recognize old response patterns as they happen. (seldom, sometimes, usually)
- I have ways to interrupt patterns that are no longer necessary. (one, several, many)
- I have ways to deepen new patterns. (one, several, many)
- I can restore my sense of regulation. (seldom, sometimes, usually)

Chapter 8: Connecting Personal Progress Tracker

Use the following questions to explore the ways you are feeling more connected to your own experience, to others, and to the world around you. Check in each week to bring awareness to your personal pathways to connection.

- I feel safe with other people. (seldom, sometimes, usually)
- I keep my social engagement system alive and online. (seldom, sometimes, usually)
- I know when my connection with others is out of balance. (seldom, sometimes, usually)
- I take action to come back into balance. (seldom, sometimes, usually)
- I know the kinds of connections I need to feel regulated. (seldom, sometimes, usually)
- I feel compassion for others. (seldom, sometimes, usually)
- I am self-compassionate. (seldom, sometimes, usually)
- I have experiences of gratitude and awe. (seldom, sometimes, usually)

EXERCISE WORKSHEETS

CHAPTER 4: BEFRIENDING EXERCISES

——— **EXERCISE** ————————————————

Autonomic Landmarks—
Stories of Landmark Moments

BACKGROUND

Landmarks give structure to our environments, forming cognitive anchors, marking points of orientation, and becoming references for communication. Autonomic landmarks are the internal reference points that mark the experience of states. We have personal landmarks that represent the embodied experience of a state and are stored in our memory. This is a moment that stands out from all the others, a moment you can look back on as a defining experience of an autonomic response. Identifying the landmark moment for each state is a way to quickly bring the properties that personify the state to mind.

STEPS

1. What are the stories of your dorsal vagal (collapse or shutdown), sympathetic (fight or flight), and ventral vagal (safe and connected) landmark moments? To make it easier to think about your states, you can give them descriptive names in addition to the physiological ones. Take time to look back and locate the moments in your memory. Find the times that stand out and become the archetype for each state.

2. Landmarks are recognizable by their names and characteristics. Write a story describing the landmark moment. Make sure to identify the concrete details of what happened, how you responded, what your body felt like, and what you thought.

3. When you are done, read through the story and identify the crucial moment. Use this to give the story a name.

———— EXERCISE ————————————

Ventral Vagal Anchors—Anchoring in Safety

BACKGROUND

The Merriam-Webster dictionary defines an anchor as "something that serves to hold an object firmly; a reliable support." A ventral vagal anchor holds the connection to the energy of your ventral vagal system when experiences threaten to pull you into a sympathetic or dorsal vagal state. Your ventral vagal anchors help you find the way back to regulation and stay there. These are autonomic cues of safety that can be found in the categories of who, what, where, and when. You can use your anchors by reconnecting to the anchor or by activating the memory of the anchor. With regular practice, ventral vagal anchors strengthen your capacity to return to regulation.

STEPS

1. **Who.** Reflect on the people in your life and make a list of the ones who bring you a feeling of being safe and welcome. You might also have a pet who fills that role. First identify a person or pet who is present in your life. Then, if you wish, you can expand your search to also include people who are no longer living, people you haven't met but who bring your ventral vagal state alive, and spiritual figures.

2. **What.** Think about what you do that brings your ventral vagal state alive. Look for small actions that feel nourishing and inviting of connection. Keep track of

the things that bring moments, or micro-moments, of ventral vagal regulation.

3. **Where.** Take a tour of your world and find the physical places that bring you cues of safety. Look around your home, your neighborhood, your community, your workplace, a place you feel a spiritual connection. Bring to mind the everyday places you move through. Take note of the environments and name the ones that activate your ventral vagal state.

4. **When.** Identify the moments in time when you feel anchored in your ventral vagal energy. Take a moment to go back and revisit those experiences. Bring them into conscious awareness and write them down.

5. **Create a portfolio of your ventral vagal anchors.** Decide how you want to gather your anchors together in one place: write them in a notebook, illustrate them in a journal, make a list and hang it in a prominent place, write on sticky notes and put them around your home and at work in places that are easy to see. Experiment and find the way that works for you, making sure you have easy access to your anchors.

——— **EXERCISE** ———————————————

Befriending the Hierarchy

BACKGROUND

With the ability to name your states and recognize the shifts that happen between states, you can represent your experience of moving along the hierarchy. Portraying these movements in different ways expands that connection. As you engage in the process of designing hierarchies, you are engaging in an act of befriending.

STEPS

1. Draw a vertical line, divide it in thirds, and mark the three states (ventral, sympathetic, dorsal, or the words you choose to name your states).

2. Imagine moving along that line and feel the autonomic state shifts.

3. Illustrate the small increments of change that happen as you travel down and up the hierarchy using:

   • color to represent your states and transitions from state to state, blending shades to illustrate the full range of the autonomic hierarchy

   • words to label the continuum of your experience from dorsal through sympathetic to ventral

   • photos of faces to show how the many ways your states are expressed

   • images of animals to represent states

   • pictures of places that bring the points along the continuum to life

- nature scenes that portray the many stops you make along the hierarchy
- names of songs that carry the energy of states

4. Create a few illustrated hierarchies to get a sense of how different designs work for you. See if you resonate with one particular way of representing the hierarchy or if you connect with several different styles.

5. Choose one or more hierarchies and create an ongoing practice of using it (or them) to find your place and name your state.

--------- **EXERCISE** --

Autonomic Trees

BACKGROUND

A tree is a commonly used metaphor. The tree of life is often used to illustrate both evolutionionary processes and patterns of relationships. Using a tree metaphor, you can investigate your autonomic experiences: with trees representing regulated responses and ones representing reactive systems. There are many ways to dive into discovering the qualities of autonomic trees, and each brings its own pathways to befriending the embodied experience of your autonomic nervous system.

Art: Making art is a safe way to explore autonomic states. Creating images of regulated and reactive trees invites you to bring your autonomic states to life and befriend them through color and design.

Writing: Sitting down to write the stories of regulated and reactive autonomic trees requires a stance of curiosity that lends itself to befriending.

Movement: Imagined or enacted movement is a way to feel the rhythms of your regulated and reactive trees. Autonomic trees can feel as if they are stomping and swaying, their trunks bending or twisting, their branches reaching up and out, and their spring buds emerging or autumn leaves falling.

STEPS FOR AUTONOMIC TREE ART

1. Set up your creative space. Gather various-sized papers and other art materials.

2. There are thousands of species of trees, many living only in one specific place in the world. Your regulated and reactive trees live in your personal world and have their own unique characteristics. Visualize their roots, branches, and leaves. See their forms, shapes, and colors.

3. Create your trees. You might design a tree that illustrates all three states, one regulated and one reactive tree, or a family of regulated and reactive trees.

4. Reflect on your designs. What autonomic experiences do they represent?

5. Periodically return to your trees and connect to your personal tree kingdom.

STEPS FOR WRITING TREE STORIES

1. If you have created your tree maps, you can use those as an entry point for listening. Otherwise, bring your regulated and reactive trees to life by focusing on an internal image.

2. Use the following prompts to begin to write a story for each of your trees:
   - The (roots, trunk, branches) of my tree bring . . .
   - When I sit under my tree, I . . .
   - When I put my arms around my tree, I . . .
   - When I listen to my tree, I hear . . .

3. Read your story and add any other information you want to complete it.

4. Give your story a title.

STEPS FOR MOVING TREES

1. Visualize your tree and feel its movement inside your body.

2. Either see the movement in your mind's eye or let the movement come into physical expression. Choose the way that brings a neuroception of safety.

3. Explore the ways your tree moves. Ventral vagal regulation is experienced in many different ways along the continuum of stillness to joy-filled passion. Reactivity includes both the intensity of sympathetic mobilization with fight and flight and the absence of energy in dorsal vagal disappearance, disconnection, and collapse.

4. Repeat the process with all of your trees.

5. Build an ongoing practice of moving with your trees.

─── **EXERCISE** ───────────────────────

Body Language

BACKGROUND

With an ability to safely connect to your autonomic states and bring that embodied experience into explicit awareness, you have access to the important autonomic information that is guiding your daily experience.

STEPS

1. Find the place in your body where you feel most connected to your ventral vagal state. Bring the qualities of that experience into explicit awareness and add language to describe it.

2. Find the place in your body where you feel most connected to your sympathetic state. Bring the qualities of that experience into explicit awareness and add language to describe it.

3. Find the place in your body where you feel most connected to your dorsal vagal state. Bring the qualities of that experience into explicit awareness and add language to describe it.

4. Connect to the three places in your body where you identified feeling each state most fully. Move from one place to another. Feel the ways your experience changes as you shift your focus.

5. Connect to your ventral vagal state of safety and connection. Tune in to how this is expressed in your body. Identify the qualities of your breath, muscle

tone, and posture. Track the flow of energy throughout your body and notice any movements connected
with this state.

6. Move to your sympathetic nervous system and consider the activation of the mobilizing energy of fight
and flight. Tune in to how this is expressed in your
body. Identify the qualities of your breath, muscle
tone, and posture. Track the flow of energy throughout your body and notice any movements associated
with this state.

7. Move to your dorsal vagal state and consider the ways
collapse and shutdown are experienced. Tune in to
how this state is expressed in your body. Identify the
qualities of your breath, muscle tone, and posture.
Track the flow of energy throughout your body and
notice any movements associated with this state.

8. Move from state to state and notice the changes that
happen. Become familiar with the ways your body
moves through states.

—— **EXERCISE** ————————————————

The Continuum Between Survival
and Social Engagement

BACKGROUND

Between the two ends of autonomic responses, there are many points along the way. Some bring a nuanced experience of an autonomic shift while other points are where you make a bigger step from one state to another. Using a continuum is a way for you to map the progression of small steps that connect two opposite end points. To create this continuum, bring focused attention to the particular ways you move between protection and connection.

STEPS

1. Draw a horizontal line and name the two ends of your continuum. What is your label for engagement? What is your label for disconnection?
2. Start at either end. Identify the first small step out of that state toward the other end. Repeat this, marking small steps along the way until you reach the other end.
3. Mark the midpoint where you feel the larger shift from connection to protection. The midpoint is a good way to identify this moment of change.
4. Remember you are always moving along this continuum, sometimes firmly planted in one place and other times pulled from one end to the other. Stop and see where you are. Use the midpoint to first see if you are on the side of protection or closer to the state of con-

nection. Then identify more precisely where you are on your range of responses.

5. Return to your continuum and practice placing yourself on it until it becomes second nature for you to know where you are and in which direction your autonomic nervous system is taking you.

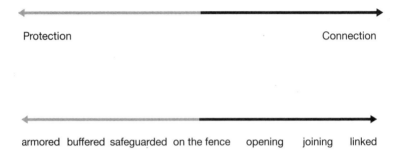

FIGURE 4.2. Between Protection and Connection Continuum and Example

————— **EXERCISE** —————————————————————

The Social Engagement Scale

BACKGROUND

Rather than a straightforward on or off mode, the social engagement system can be online and bring a range of responses. Sometimes you may feel a pull to enter into conversations and at other times feel a deep contentment in sitting back and listening. One moment you may be moving in synchrony with another person, while the next brings the joy of being an observer. Between the two ends of engagement there are a variety of experiences. In addition to the expected everyday fluctuations, the capacity for social engagement is impacted by illness and wellness. In a state of illness, the social engagement system retracts, responding to the physiological demand to attend to internal conditions. In a state of wellness, the social engagement system is at work in the external environment, seeking and signaling readiness for connection.

STEPS

1. Use the scale to fill in your personal experience of the points between "open and engaged" and "internal and engaged." Start by naming each end and then label the points between.

2. Consider where you are right now. Stop and find your place on your scale.

3. Reflect on recent experiences and see where you were on your scale.

4. Look at when your place on the scale fits with the environmental and relational demands of the moment and when there is a mismatch.

5. Recognize any patterns to your placement on the scale. Look for people, places, and experiences that predictably take you to a certain point along the scale. Become curious about the characteristics of the interactions that activate that response. Get to know your personal social engagement profile.

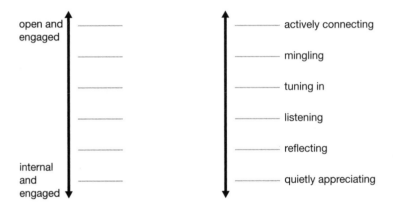

FIGURE 4.3. Social Engagement Scale and Example

——— EXERCISE ———
A Neuroception Notebook

BACKGROUND

Neuroception, the messages the autonomic nervous system receives and records from inside your body, in the environment around you, and between you and other people, provides a valuable stream of information when brought to conscious awareness. When you bring perception to neuroception, you can find reminders of ventral vagal possibilities and identify moments of messiness and distress. Keeping a neuroception notebook is one way to bring explicit awareness to the ways the autonomic nervous system is working in the background shaping your life.

STEPS

1. Divide a notebook in sections for the three categories of neuroception: ventral vagal safety, sympathetic danger, and dorsal vagal life-threat. Use your own words to name the sections.
2. Carry the notebook with you and write in it as you feel your state shifting. Or create time at the end of the day to look back and reflect on your experiences.
3. Look for the specific cues that activated your state changes. Write down the cues of safety, danger, or life-threat you have identified.
4. Find any predictable patterns in the cues that move you toward connection or into protection.

CHAPTER 5: ATTENDING EXERCISES

———— **EXERCISE** ————————————————

Autonomic Alphabets

BACKGROUND

Looking beyond the primary description of a state creates an expanded understanding of the ways each of your states can be experienced. Finding the variety of flavors of each state encourages you to become aware of the subtle ways your states shift.

STEPS TO CREATING YOUR ALPHABET:

1. Find a word that begins with each letter of the alphabet to describe qualities of your autonomic three states. (You may have to get creative with the letter X.)
2. Begin by creating your dorsal vagal alphabet.
3. Move up the hierarchy and create your sympathetic alphabet.
4. Continue to the top of the hierarchy and create your ventral vagal alphabet.
5. Use your alphabets. When you notice a familiar feeling, a quality you identified in one of your alphabets, stop and name the state. When you notice you are in a state, go to your alphabet and find the quality.

—— EXERCISE ——

Autonomic Names

BACKGROUND

In Shakespeare's *Romeo and Juliet*, Juliet asks "What's in a name?" In fact, your name is often the first label you are given, and is an important way you identify who you are. Looking at your name through the qualities of autonomic states invites you to experience who you are in different ways.

STEPS TO WRITING YOUR NAME:

1. Use the letters of your name to describe who you are in a dorsal, sympathetic, and ventral state.
2. Create several autonomic name descriptions for each state and compare the effects.

—— **EXERCISE** ————————————

Autonomic Short Stories

BACKGROUND

Adding language to autonomic events is a way to become acquainted with states and state changes. The plots of your short stories illustrate a slice of an autonomic experience. This is a quick writing exercise designed to bring attention to a specific autonomic point in time and spend a moment getting to know it.

STEPS

1. Use these five prompts to write your autonomic short story. Spend no more than a minute or so on each.
    *   My autonomic state is . . .
    *   My system is responding to . . .
    *   My body wants to . . .
    *   My brain makes up the story that . . .
    *   When I review my short story, I notice . . .
2. When you feel a state change, take a couple of minutes to listen in and follow the five prompts.
3. When you want to appreciate where your autonomic nervous system has taken you, follow the prompts and write a short story.
4. Track how your stories change as your autonomic responses begin to reshape.

——— EXERCISE ———

Attending over Time

BACKGROUND

While atomic clocks measure time with precision and accuracy, it seems your personal experience of time is changed by your state of engagement with it. Time sometimes seems to stand still and other times fly by. You can feel stuck in a state of dysregulation or unable to hold onto a state of regulation. Using increments of time to attend to state changes adds chronology to your understanding of how you move through daily experiences. Attending over time, both in short and long intervals, invites you to see the ongoing ebb and flow of your autonomic nervous system and the ways it responds both in moment-to-moment shifts and in patterns over time.

SHORT-DURATION ATTENDING STEPS:

1. Decide on a 5- or 10-minute increment as your measure of time. Use the following series of prompts to check in three times over that span of time.
   - In this moment my autonomic state is . . .
   - And I am feeling . . .
   - Now my autonomic state is . . .
   - And I am feeling . . .
   - And now my autonomic state is . . .
   - And I am feeling . . .
2. Repeat this exercise a few times a day for several weeks.

3. Look for any patterns that emerge. When are the times you respond flexibly and when are the times you get stuck? Are any changes happening over the course of tracking?

LONG-DURATION ATTENDING STEPS:

1. Longer time periods offer an expanded, bird's eye view of your experience. Decide on a timeframe to use. You can experiment with doing the exercise in the morning, at the end of the day, or even once a week.

2. Answer the following four questions.

   • *Where am I?* The starting point is where you are right now. Begin with noticing your current state.

   • *Where have I been?* From your present reference point, reflect back and notice any state changes.

   • *What does this mean for where I might be heading?* With an understanding of your movement from past to present, bring curiosity to the trajectory you have found. Is there a pattern? Does it make sense to you when you see it clearly?

   • *What do I want to do now?* Is this a path you want to follow or a pattern you want to interrupt?

3. Repeat this exercise over successive days or weeks and track emerging patterns.

—— EXERCISE ——————————————

Daily Pie Charts

BACKGROUND

We tend to give our days a label—this was a good day or a difficult day, a quiet day or a busy day—based on one particularly intense moment or on a string of related experiences. When you name your days in this way, you often miss the moments that didn't fit the pattern. When considering the day through an autonomic lens, looking at the relationship between states and the relative amount of time spent in each gives a more complete picture of your daily experience. With a pie chart, ventral vagal, sympathetic, and dorsal vagal experiences are seen as part of an integrated autonomic system. The global flavor of your day is a result of the contributions of each. The design of a pie chart (Figure 5.1) offers an uncomplicated image of the overall sense of a day and brings the feeling of the day alive in shape and color. What name would you use to describe each of the days illustrated here?

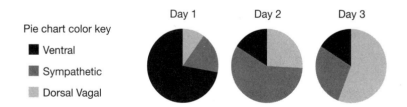

FIGURE 5.1. Daily Pie Charts

STEPS

1. What does your autonomic pie chart look like? Use a blank circle each evening to review your day.

2. Choose the colors you want to represent each state and divide your pie into ventral vagal, sympathetic, and dorsal vagal pieces.

3. Name your day.

4. Make a collection of your daily charts. Use your collection of daily charts to get a sense of your autonomic experience over a period of time. With a series of charts, you can look at the ebb and flow of states and the impact on your general autonomic experience.

   • Is there a day of the week that repeatedly brings the same autonomic responses?

   • What is the overall tone of a week?

   • Is there a pattern to your weekends?

   • If you are in a time of transition, use your pie chart to see how your autonomic nervous system is responding.

---- **EXERCISE** ----------------------------------

Daily Tracker—Three Different Things

BACKGROUND

An end-of-the-day reflection during which you listen to the subtleties of autonomic change is a good way to look back at the autonomic path you've traveled. With a habit of autonomic reflection, implicit knowing and explicit awareness combine to bring you into a deeper understanding of the ways the autonomic nervous system shapes your days. Remembering that the autonomic response is always considered an adaptive one, don't look for what is better, but instead look for what is different. A regular tracking practice brings attention to the small shifts in patterns that highlight the ways your system is reorganizing.

STEPS

1. Review the day and identify three different ways your autonomic nervous system responded.
2. Bring attention to what happened. You might notice a slightly less intense response to an event or an easier recovery into regulation. Or maybe you recognize a different kind of response—sympathetic mobilization in place of a dorsal vagal collapse or a moment of ventral vagal connection instead fight or flight.
3. It's equally important to attend to what didn't happen. The absence of a reaction is also a good measure that a response pattern is changing and that your system is moving toward regulation.

4. Keep a journal of your daily "three different things" experiences. As small changes begin to add up, new autonomic patterns take root.

5. Review your daily journal periodically to see how your responses are changing. Look back over the range of autonomic responses and consider the larger picture of change that is happening. Is there a shift? If so, in what direction? Consider the intensity, frequency, and duration of your states and state changes in your reflection.

——— **EXERCISE** ———————————————

The Autonomic Request for Connection

BACKGROUND

The autonomic nervous system is a relational system. Through your biology you are wired for connection. Eyes, voices, faces, and gestures telegraph cues that it is safe to explore a relationship. The elements of the social engagement system are essential to assessing safety and danger. Yet, through the ways the nervous system has been shaped by your personal experiences, you might miss or misread those invitations.

An ongoing stream of signals of welcome and warning are received and sent through the pathways of the social engagement system. The muscle around the eyes (the orbiculares oculi) opens and closes the eyelid and contributes to the wrinkles around the eyes that express emotions. This is where the nervous system looks for signs of warmth and an invitation to connect. Prosody (patterns of rhythm, tone, frequency in the voice) is an important nonverbal signal and sends messages of welcome or warning to another nervous system. Facial expressions convey social information. An unmoving face is seen as a sign of danger, while a mobile face is experienced as alive and sending social information. Finally, turning and tilting the head signals availability and interest.

You can begin to understand the conversation that is taking place between two nervous systems when you are aware of the cues you are sending and can accurately interpret the cues you are receiving. As you become familiar with this way of listening, you'll find you are able to navigate relationships more skillfully.

STEPS

1. Make a practice of looking at eyes, listening to voices, seeing facial expressions, and watching for social gestures. Bring explicit awareness to your present-moment experiences with another social engagement system. Use the following prompts to build skill in noticing:

   - Their eyes are signaling . . .
   - Their tone of voice sounds . . .
   - Their face is expressing . . .
   - Their gestures convey . . .

2. Identify the specific characteristics that invite connection or prompt a move into disconnection. Exactly what is it about the other person's eyes, voice, face, and movements that sends cues of safety or danger to your nervous system?

3. Ask yourself if your response is a match for the present-moment situation or linked to a prior experience.

4. As you get to know your responses to another social engagement system, bring attention to your own end of the interaction using the same questions.

   - My eyes are signaling . . .
   - My tone of voice sounds . . .
   - My face is expressing . . .
   - My gestures convey . . .

───── **EXERCISE** ─────────────────────
Pathways to Playfulness

BACKGROUND

You can be playful both by yourself and with others. Playfulness and a sense of well-being go together. A playful attitude supports seeing new perspectives and being able to cope with adversity. As Dr. Seuss (1960) said, fun is good.

STEPS

1. Get to know yourself as a playful person. Look at the conditions that support your sense of playfulness:
   - Identify where, when, and with whom you feel your sense of playfulness emerge.
   - Identify where, when, and with whom you feel your sense of playfulness disappear.
2. Track your experiences of the different kinds of playfulness. Identify where you find yourself on your autonomic hierarchy when you engage in, or think about engaging in, these kinds of playfulness:
   - playing with others
   - playing with thoughts and ideas
   - spontaneous play
   - daydreaming

——— **EXERCISE** ———

Playful Moments

BACKGROUND

Playfulness is an important quality that contributes to well-being. As you find ways to create opportunities for moments of playfulness, you can become a more playful person and experience the joy and creativity that accompanies play.

STEPS

1. Notice how often, easily, and intensely you engage in a playful experience.

2. Increase your playful experiences. Find the ones that bring a smile and the ones that bring energy and play in those ways a little bit more.

3. Expand your playfulness. Experiment with experiences in the kinds of play that aren't in your play repertoire.

——— **EXERCISE** ——————————————————————

Personal Preferences Around Solitude

BACKGROUND

Distinct from loneliness, which has been shown to have a multitude of negative physical and psychological outcomes, entering into moments of solitude has positive benefits for well-being. Practicing a moment of solitude is an autonomic exercise that creates an experience of feeling centered and peaceful.

STEPS

1. Locate the experiences of solitude and loneliness on your autonomic hierarchy. Feel the difference between them.

2. Explore where in your daily environment you find solitude.

3. Nature is often where people go to find a private place to escape to when they are surrounded by the demands of the day and the autonomic nervous system is needing room to breathe.

   • Reflect on your daily experiences to discover where you choose to find solitude.

   • Identify what kind of natural habitat are you drawn to.

   • Notice where in your everyday natural environment are the places you can predictably visit and feel the benefits of solitude.

4. Solitude is a state of being and doesn't have to take

234 CHAPTER 5: ATTENDING EXERCISES

place in isolation. Solitude is also found in spaces where there are other people.

- Identify the places and spaces you visit every day that include other people and also offer you an opportunity for a moment of solitude.

5. Notice when you reach for solitude.

Consider what is happening in your life that prompts you to seek quiet.

- Look at your physical environment.
- Consider the actions of people around you.
- Reflect on the number, frequency, and kinds of requests for your time and attention.

6. Identify how much solitude you need.

Focus on your moments of solitude and the length of time that brings a sense of nourishment.

- Consider when a few moments of solitude meet your need.
- Compare that to when you need a longer experience of solitude to feel nurtured.
- Notice how you know when your system has taken in enough solitude and you're ready to rejoin the world outside yourself.

——— EXERCISE ———

Attending to Stillness

BACKGROUND

Over the course of evolution, humans developed the ability to become still as a way to rest and renew. Sometimes, instead of feeling nurtured by stillness, the beginning of calm can bring cues of danger and a sense of vulnerability. As your autonomic nervous system begins to move from action to quiet, you might feel your sympathetic nervous system reacting with mobilizing energy or you might feel pulled into dorsal vagal collapse. Bring curiosity to identifying the elements that add safety to your experiences of rest so you can find your way to the places where you can receive the benefits of moments of quiet.

STEPS

1. Identify restful and restless environments.
   - Many people label environments with lots of people, activity, sound, and movement as restless. Workplaces and the daily commute are two environments that are often cited as mobilizing and not restorative. In comparison, the natural environment and at home are often identified as places to rest and renew.
   - Find the environments at the two ends of your experience—places that bring you a feeling of restlessness and places that offer you the opportunity to rest.

2. Attend to the qualities of the spaces that bring you a rhythm of rest
   - location
   - size and shape of the space
   - colors, sounds, and textures
3. Consider when you want to be by yourself and when you want to be with others (people or pets).
4. Make a list of the combination of qualities you've identified. Go out and find places that offer those.
5. Create a plan to regularly visit the places you identified as offering the opportunity for rest.
6. Create your own space, incorporating qualities you identified that support you in resting in a moment of stillness.

——— **EXERCISE** ————————————————————————

Savoring Snapshots

BACKGROUND

To savor is to take a moment of ventral vagal regulation and the feeling of a sense of safety and experience a story of connection to self, to another, or to nature. Savoring is a quick practice whereby you capture a ventral vagal moment and hold it in your conscious attention for just a short time. Moments to savor routinely happen in the course of every-day living. Because a 20- to 30-second snapshot is all that is needed to benefit from the practice, it is easy to do during the natural flow of your day.

STEPS

1. Look for a ventral vagal moment to savor, bring it into conscious awareness, and place your attention on it for 20–30 seconds. In the beginning, if the experience of savoring is challenging, start with micro-moments of savoring (5–10 seconds). Each micro-moment shapes your system. Over time, your ability to savor will build to the 20–30 second maximum that defines a savoring experience.

2. Practice savoring each day. Begin with finding one moment to savor each day. As savoring becomes eas-ier, increase the number.

3. Track your savoring moments.
   • Keep a savoring notebook or a joy journal.

- Reflect at the end of the day to find and savor moments you may have missed.
- Create an agreement to share savoring moments with a friend using technology or in person.
- Organize a savoring circle—online, in person, or a combination of the two.
- Create a savoring album using simple illustrations of your savoring moments and adding captions.

4. Establish a habit of savoring.

- Remind yourself that moments to savor are common occurrences in everyday life.
- Be on the lookout for the small moments that bring you into a ventral vagal state.
- Set a goal to see and savor a certain number of moments each day.
- Invite a friend to savor with you.

——— EXERCISE ———————————————

Attending Through Art

BACKGROUND

Art comes in many forms and no special training is necessary to benefit from seeing it. Art speaks to the body through your autonomic pathways and brings responses that can lead to new ways of thinking about yourself and the world. Finding ways to invite art into your life is an act of listening to your autonomic nervous system and discovering the particular ways you connect.

STEPS

1. Explore the ways that are easily available to you to see and be with art. Museums, artists' workshops, public art spaces, arts festivals, and an illustrated art book are just some of the options.

2. Identify the kinds of art you are drawn to. View different kinds of artwork (photography, sculpture, drawing, painting, ceramic, mosaic, textiles, and other forms of art) and notice how you respond.

3. Decide how and how often you need to connect to art in order to feel as if you have enough art in your life.

——— EXERCISE ————————————————

Attending in Nature

BACKGROUND

Nature, both in real life and through viewing images, offers relaxing and restorative opportunities. Abundant in the natural world are fractals, simple patterns that repeat over and over creating increasing complexity (the nautilus shell, a leaf, a pinecone, broccoli buds, dandelions, ice crystals, clouds). Viewing fractals for just a few moments brings a regulating autonomic response. Find the particular places and ways to connect with nature that bring your ventral vagal system alive.

STEPS

1. Attend to the natural environment around you and track your responses. Identify the places that bring you into ventral vagal regulation, sympathetic mobilization, and dorsal vagal disconnection.
2. Visit the places that are regulating for you either in person, through images, or in a combination of both.
3. Look for fractals as you move through your day. Stop for a just a few seconds to take them in.
4. Find images of fractals or objects that have the characteristics of fractals and notice the ones that bring an intense ventral vagal response. An internet search will bring up a wealth of images, and the plants and trees around you offer living examples.
5. Display fractal images or objects in a way that you can

easily return to them. (A screen saver, photos on your phone, or a flowering plant or cactus in your home or office are some suggestions.)

CHAPTER 6: SHAPING EXERCISES

────── **EXERCISE** ──────────────────────────

Energy and Actions Map

BACKGROUND

Activities that shape the autonomic nervous system fall along a scale of passive to active. There are times when thinking about moving, remembering a connection with a friend, or simply looking up toward the sky is the right choice and other times when you need to take action, put your body in motion, or head out into the world and seek social connection. Choose an experience that brings a return of energy when the dorsal vagal immobilizing collapse is present, a way to safely discharge energy when feeling the frenetic activity of the sympathetic state, and an action that deepens the feeling of regulation when anchored in the safety of ventral vagal.

STEPS

1. Label your state in the box at the top of the Energy and Actions map. Identify your state through its biological name (dorsal, sympathetic, ventral) or name it in a way that has meaning for you.
2. For sympathetic and dorsal vagal states, move along the line between passive and active and identify actions that take you in the direction of a return to the ventral vagal state of regulation. Use the left side

to identify self-regulating actions and the right side to identify co-regulating actions.

3. For your ventral vagal state, move along the line between passive and active and identify actions that deepen your experience of safety and connection. Use the left side to identify self-regulating actions and the right side to identify co-regulating actions.

4. Complete a map for each state.

5. Use your maps to find a resource that is in the range of energy that fits your needs in the moment.

6. Update your maps as you create additional resources.

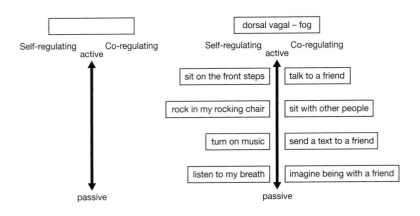

FIGURE 6.1. Energy and Actions Map and Example

——— EXERCISE ———

Finding Glimmers

BACKGROUND

Glimmers are the micro-moments of ventral vagal experience that routinely appear in everyday life yet frequently go unnoticed. To ensure survival, human beings are built with a negativity bias. This means you are biologically wired to pay more attention to negative events than positive ones and can often miss the ventral vagal moments that coexist with moments of dysregulation. Things like seeing a friendly face, hearing a soothing sound, or noticing something enjoyable in the environment go unnoticed. A fundamental step in shaping your system is seeing a glimmer, pausing to take it in, and then beginning to look for more.

STEPS

1. Set an intention to look for a certain number of glimmers each day. Choose a number that feels doable to begin. If glimmers are an unfamiliar experience, watch for a single glimmer. As finding glimmers becomes easier, set a new goal.

2. Notice when you feel a spark of ventral vagal energy. Look for glimmers in your daily activities. Glimmers happen regularly, but because they are micro-moments you need to be on the lookout for them.

3. See, stop, and appreciate your glimmers. Create an easy way to acknowledge a glimmer when it happens. You might bring attention to the moment by simply

saying "glimmer" or with a small movement (perhaps your hand on your heart).

4. Track your glimmers. Create a daily glimmers notebook or keep a running list.

5. Look for glimmers in specific places, with particular people, at certain times. Find the ways your glimmers routinely appear.

6. Share your glimmers. You might text your glimmers to a friend, make talking about daily glimmers a family nighttime ritual, or share your list of weekly glimmers with your therapist. Find the way that works for you.

—————— **EXERCISE** ——————————————————

From Glimmer to Glow

BACKGROUND

When you recognize the micro-moment of a glimmer, you feel the spark of your ventral vagal system. Just as sparks can be used to ignite a fire, glimmers can be turned into the deeper experience of a glow. With a glimmer, you pause just long enough to acknowledge that a ventral vagal moment is happening in the flow of your day. With a glow, stop and celebrate the glimmer. Take time to soak it in and give it deeper meaning.

STEPS

1. Notice a glimmer and stop and let the experience fill you. Move beyond a few seconds and stay with the experience for a half a minute or more. Give the glimmer time to become a glow.

2. Feel what happens as you move from connecting for a micro-moment to a longer experience of taking in.

3. Listen to the story that accompanies the glow.

4. Describe your experience of the glimmer and the glow. Notice how the experience changes. For example, a particular glimmer moment might be described as a quick hit of happiness that brings a smile, and when you turn it into a glow, the experience feels like basking in the warmth of the sun while breathing a sigh of contentment.

—— **EXERCISE** ————————————————————————

The Sound of Your Voice

BACKGROUND

The autonomic nervous system uses tone of voice as a way to discern safety. You respond to intonation before you take in information. The way you speak changes the way you feel, the story you tell, and changes the way people around you hear what you are saying.

STEPS

1. Experiment with the ways your voice impacts the way you feel. Tell, or record, a short story in different tones of voice. Notice where the different tones of your voice take you on your autonomic map.

2. Track the way the same word spoken in different tones of voice elicits a different state and feeling. Choose a word, speak it in different ways, and follow the ways your states and feelings shift. Try out a variety of words and notice the specific ways of speaking that elicit certain states and feelings.

3. Talk about a difficult experience using different tones of voice. Track what happens to your autonomic state. Find the way of speaking that brings you into a ventral vagal state. Notice the way of speaking that helps you see options and take regulated actions.

4. Find a friend and experiment with sound. Talk in different tones of voice and get feedback on their response. Ask your friend to do the same and track your own responses.

——— EXERCISE ———

The Music in Your Life

BACKGROUND

Music is all around you, affecting your physiology and your feelings. Along with activating a ventral vagal response, music has a paradoxical effect that allows you to safely connect to, and even enjoy, your sympathetic and dorsal vagal states.

STEPS

1. Take an inventory of the way music is a part of your life.
   - Music listening: Do you regularly listen to music? Have a favorite radio station? Favorite songs or artists? Do you go to hear live music?
   - Music making: Do you make music? Do you play an instrument or sing by yourself or with others?
2. Assess how much music is in your everyday life.
   - Is there enough music in your daily experience?
   - Do you miss music and want to hear more?
3. If your everyday experience is already filled with music, acknowledge the role of music in your life and identify the ways music is a regulating resource.
4. If your inventory brings a recognition that you have a desire for more musical moments, begin to look for ways to add music to your daily experience.
5. Identify the particular pieces of music that take you to different places on the autonomic hierarchy. Sing along, play along, or move along with the music. Use

different selections to safely join with your sympathetic and dorsal vagal states and dive into all the flavors of ventral vagal.

—— EXERCISE ——
Moments of Movement

BACKGROUND

Movement occurs along a continuum of expression: simple through complex, micro-movements to full body motions. Each autonomic state has different levels of energy that you can connect with and use to shape your experience. Intentional use of movement is a way to engage your dorsal vagal and sympathetic states, making them less intense and persistent, and it's also a way to deepen your ventral vagal capacities.

FIGURE 6.2. Movement Continuums

STEPS

1. Choose an autonomic state. Using a line to represent ways you move, identify movements at either end. Look for movements that engage the least and most energy available to you in the state.

2. Identify movements that happen between the ends. In dorsal vagal, look for movements that begin to gently energize you. In sympathetic, look for movements that use the activated energy in organized and safe ways. In ventral vagal, look for movements that prolong the experience.

3. Design a series of movement lines to bring awareness to the range of movements that are possible in each autonomic state.

—— **EXERCISE** ————————————————

Imagined Action

BACKGROUND

Motor imagery is a way for you to be in motion when the environment you're in doesn't support moving, when physical challenges make moving difficult, or when making a movement doesn't feel safe and instead activates a protective survival response. Imagined movement practices, either as a replacement for or as a complement to movement, are another way to get the benefits of moving and experience safely moving through space.

STEPS

1. Identify a movement you are drawn to but haven't brought into action yet. Play with it. Imagine yourself safely bringing the action to life. See yourself doing it. Sense your body moving on the inside. Feel the emotions that accompany your moving. Hear the story of who you are as you move.

2. Once you get the feel for imagined movement, create a series of movements. Use your imagination to move in ways you have always wanted.

3. Make time each day to bring one of your movements to life on the inside.

4. Notice if, over time, using motor imagery invites bringing the movement out of your imagination into the world or if it is autonomically nourishing when it remains an imagined experience.

——— EXERCISE ———

Labyrinth Walking

BACKGROUND

People have been walking labyrinths for centuries. Unlike a maze, a labyrinth has one path and no dead ends. Often thought of as a path to transformation, when you enter a labyrinth, there is a release of connection to the everyday world, a sense of receiving wisdom when you reach the center, and a subtle shift in your sense of yourself and the world when the circuit is completed. When walking a labyrinth there is first a slight increase in mobilization followed by a return to calm making this a gentle autonomic exercise.

STEPS

1. Investigate labyrinth-walking options. The location of thousands of labyrinths around the world as well as access to virtual and printed ones are available at https://labyrinthsociety.org
   - Walk a full-size labyrinth.
   - Navigate a virtual labyrinth on your computer.
   - Trace a printed labyrinth.
   - Walk a labyrinth with your fingers using a finger-walking guide.
2. Identify your physiological response to each of the different labyrinth-walking options. Which ones feel the most regulating?
3. Notice any ways your thinking shifts over the course of your labyrinth walk.

4. Keep track of the stories about yourself and the world that you connect with on your labyrinth walks.

5. Find an easily accessible form of labyrinth-walking you can use to return to regulation when you notice a rise in stress.

6. Combine different forms of labyrinth-walking to create a regular practice.

—— **EXERCISE** ————————————

Find Your Breath

BACKGROUND

There are many ways of breathing. Sometimes breath comes in a quiet and rhythmic cycle and other times it arrives in an erratic and stressed way. Different rhythms of breathing change your physiology, making breath a direct route to shaping your autonomic responses. Use the autonomic hierarchy to map the many kinds of breaths you breathe each day.

STEPS

1. Begin by bringing awareness to what kind of breathing happens in your ventral vagal, sympathetic, and dorsal vagal states.
2. Experiment with different kinds of breath. Notice how each impacts your autonomic state. Identify breaths that are mobilizing, calming, disconnecting, and connecting.
3. Create a breath map.
   - Using a line to depict the autonomic hierarchy, come into connection with each state and feel the ways of breathing that happen there.
   - Breathe in different ways and see where the breath takes you. Place those breaths on your breath map.

4. Use your breath map to find your place on the hierarchy.

ventral vagal	full, deep, easy, steady, slow, long, calming, filling, even, regular, flow between heart and belly, healthy, sustaining
sympthetic	sharp, short, fast, loud, forced, irregular, tight, restricting, fiery, gasping
dorsalvagal	shallow, silent, unfulfilling, flat, empty, weak, depleting

FIGURE 6.3. Sample Breath Map

─────── **EXERCISE** ────────────────────────────

Understand Your Breath

BACKGROUND

The diaphragm is the most important muscle in the process of breathing. The diaphragm divides your torso into two parts: the chest cavity inside the ribcage where the lungs and heart reside and the abdominal cavity where the stomach, liver, intestines, and adrenal glands are found. With each breath cycle, the diaphragm changes shape. On an inhalation the muscles of the diaphragm contract and the diaphragm flattens, stretching the lungs to make room for more air. On the exhalation the muscles of the diaphragm relax, restoring the natural curve of the diaphragm to help push air out. When you need extra strength to lift things, during exercise, or in a sympathetically charged state of fight or flight, your breath moves up from your belly to your chest. While this is necessary in the moment, if used for prolonged periods, chest breathing brings anxiety and fatigue. Belly breathing on the other hand emphasizes moving the abdomen, letting it fill and expand on the inhale, empty and contract with each exhale. Belly breathing engages the diaphragm, deepens the breath, and activates the ventral vagal system, inviting a return to regulation.

STEPS

1. Get a feel for the way your diaphragm works.
   - Hold your hands in front of you, fingers interlaced,

elbows at your side. In this position, your hands take on the shape of the curve of the diaphragm.

- Inhale, raising your elbows pointing them outward and let your fingers flatten.
- Exhale, relaxing your arms letting your elbows fall to your side as your fingers return to the shape of the curve.
- Follow this cycle, letting your motion reflect the rhythm of your breath as you imagine the action of your diaphragm.

2. Play with changing the rhythm of the motion and synchronizing your breath. Speed the motion up and slow it down. Track the ways your autonomic state shifts with different breath rhythms.

3. Listen to the stories that accompany state shifts.
- Practice connecting the action of your diaphragm with your breath and listening to the story.
- Breathe into your chest and track the way your autonomic state changes. Bring awareness to the stories that accompany the change.
- Breathe into your belly and track the way your autonomic state changes. Bring awareness to the stories that accompany the change.

——— **EXERCISE** ———————————————

Follow Your Breath

BACKGROUND

Some of the ways to follow your breath are to attend to each cycle, track the ways your breath moves in your body, add movement to your breath cycle, and create a mantra to tie intention to inhalation and exhalation.

STEPS

1. Count your breaths. Breath counting (counting each exhalation) has been a part of mindfulness training for over 1500 years.
   - Begin with short sets—between 3 and 10 exhalations. Experiment until you find the number that brings you into the ventral vagal place on your breath map.
   - Count to that number of exhalations and begin again. Experiment with repeating the cycle two or three times to find the number of repetitions that brings a balance between challenge and nourishment.
2. Find the places you feel breath moving in your body.
   - Some of the common places to find your breath are the abdomen, chest, heart, throat, just under the breastbone, in the side ribs, and in your lower back.
   - Choose two places and put one hand on each. As you inhale and exhale, feel your breath moving between your hands. Find places that offer an easy pathway to feel the breath flowing between your two hands.

3. Create a mantra. The use of mantras is common in mindfulness practice and is a way to bring focused intention to your breath.

   - Find a word or a phrase for each inhalation and exhalation that brings awareness to:
     - the feeling of energy rising and falling (mobilize, calm)
     - sensing inward and outward connection (tune in, reach out)
     - moving between action and rest (attentive, peaceful).
   - Honor the ways your autonomic nervous system and breath are interconnected. Let your breath and body guide you in finding your own words and phrases.

4. Take breath outside your body and add movement.

   - There is a strong connection between breath and posture. Experiment with changing postures (lying down, sitting, or standing; posture slumped, straight, or slightly curved) and listen to the story that accompanies each shift.
   - Integrating breath and arm movements strengthens the muscles used in breathing and increases lung capacity. Experiment with adding arm movements to your breath cycle. Try it both seated and standing. Let your body lead the way. Invite your arms to illustrate your inhalation and exhalation. Notice how your movements change when the quality of your breath changes. Find a pattern that feels restor-

ative and create a daily practice of moving with your breath.

5. Add a sigh. Sighing resets the respiratory system, affects your physiological state, and impacts the story that emerges. Humans sigh many times an hour and those spontaneous sighs are a sign your autonomic nervous system is looking for regulation. You can intentionally sigh to engage your system in that process.

- Become aware of the times you spontaneously sigh as your system looks for regulation. Make a practice of noticing. Spend a moment actively appreciating the wisdom of your biology.

- Intentionally sigh. Experiment with a sigh to interrupt a sympathetically activated moment or to bring some energy into a dorsal vagal moment of collapse. Create a habit of bringing a sigh to a difficult situation. Breathe a sigh of relief or sink into a sigh of contentment to deepen a state of regulation and nourish a story of well-being.

——— **EXERCISE** ——————————————————

Green, Blue, and Flowering

BACKGROUND

It is a generally accepted that the *green effect* (the impact of being in green spaces) is a powerful contributor to physical and psychological well-being and that being in a *blue environment* (around or in the water) reduces stress and enhances well-being. Even the simple act of directly connecting to the earth's surface, known as grounding, is an autonomically regulating experience. Drawing on the power of the environment and feeling nurtured by nature is a natural way to shape your system toward well-being.

STEPS

1. Head outside into the natural world.
   - Walk in the woods. Forest bathing, a term coined in Japan in the 1980s denoting the benefits of being in a forest environment, is regulating and restorative.
   - Find the green spaces around your home and work. Regularly return to the places that bring you into a ventral vagal state.
2. Find your way to water.
   - Being by the water is an autonomically regulating and restorative experience. Locate the places around you that offer you the opportunity to be in a *blue environment*. Look toward the ocean, rivers, lakes, ponds, streams, and fountains in city parks.
   - Being in the water brings its own benefits. Cool

water experiences have been shown to bring a sympathetic nervous system response, and immersion in warm water lowers sympathetic activation and increases ventral vagal influence. Find a way to immerse yourself in the temperature of water that fits your autonomic need in the moment.

3. Make a physical connection to the earth's surfaces.
   - Walk barefoot in the grass, on the ground, or in the sand.
   - Dig your hands in the dirt or in the sand.

4. Bring the outside in.
   - Add flowers and plants to your home and work environments and benefit from their autonomically regulating effects.
   - The smell of clean air and wet earth is something all animals and especially humans are sensitive to. Track what happens in your body and where your autonomic nervous system takes you when you encounter those smells.
   - Experiment with scent. The smells found in nature are powerful activators of autonomic states. Juniper, lavender, rose oil, and bergamot are some of the scents that have been shown to bring relaxation and regulation. Rosemary, grapefruit, and fennel increase alertness.
   - Discover the fragrances that your autonomic nervous system finds renewing. Experiment with different ways to use them. Living or dried objects from the natural world, candles, essential oils, and body

creams are some possibilities. Incorporate your chosen fragrances into your everyday experience.

5. View nature.

- Looking out a window at the natural world for as little as 5 minutes facilitates the return to regulation following a distressing experience.

- Images can be used to complement your time in nature or as a stand-in for spending time in nature when opportunities in real time are limited. Find pictures of nature that are autonomically regulating for you.

---- **EXERCISE** ————————————————————

A Ventral Vagal Space of Your Own

BACKGROUND

Danish people have one all-encompassing word for a life-style that brings well-being. *Hygge* describes a way of living that is cozy, caring, content, friendly, and safe. This speaks to our longing to create and inhabit environments that are filled with cues of safety and inspire an enlivening of ventral vagal energy. Bringing these qualities into your home and workplace in small and simple ways is an act of autonomic shaping.

STEPS

1. Listen to your autonomic nervous system and become aware of what is present in your environment.
   - Look around your home and see where your sympathetic and dorsal vagal systems begin to activate. Identify what brings those states alive.
   - Consider the objects around you that bring a flavor of dissatisfaction or unease.
   - Look around your home and find the places that feel cozy, comforting, and connecting. Identify what makes them feel that way.
   - Notice the objects around you that inspire safety, contentment, and warmth.
   - Do the same with your workplace.
2. Make a list of the places and things in your home and work environments that bring a feeling of safety and

connection. Identify the specific qualities that feel regulating and nourishing to your nervous system.

3. Bring curiosity to what might be possible. Look for spaces at home and at work (a room, a corner, or even a shelf) that could become a place of ventral vagal inspiration for you.

4. Find objects that bring your ventral vagal system alive and bring them into your space. Make small changes and track your autonomic response to each. Remember, small moments add up to a tipping point. Look for the moment when a space feels welcoming. Stop and take that in.

5. Ventral vagal spaces are filled with abundance, but abundance does not mean that your spaces are filled with lots of things. Abundance and scarcity are felt not in the presence of absence of objects but in your autonomic states. Find the balance of open and filled spaces that brings you an autonomic feeling of abundance.

——— EXERCISE ———

Writing Your Reflections

BACKGROUND

Your autonomic states carry a wealth of information. Adding words brings a different kind of awareness to your autonomic stories. Even if you don't think of yourself as a writer, your autonomic nervous system benefits as you listen to your state and begin to put words on paper.

STEPS

1. Think of a time when you experienced a dysregulated response. Take just a few minutes to write about it. Listen to your sympathetic or dorsal vagal survival state and write what you hear.
2. Think of a time when you felt the flow of ventral vagal energy. Turn toward that experience. Listen and write what your ventral vagal state wants you to know.
3. Choose a period of time and set an intention to write about an experience from each autonomic state. A suggested timeframe is once a week over the course of 6 weeks. After the initial writing period, if it feels like a positive experience, set the next intention.
4. Find someone to share your writing with or bring your writing to your therapy sessions. You hear your stories in a new way when you tell them to someone. In the telling, deeper awareness and different insights often emerge.

─── **EXERCISE** ─────────────────────

Reflecting with Compassion

BACKGROUND

Compassion emerges from a ventral vagal state and then shapes your system toward experiencing more ventral vagal energy. Loving-kindness meditation is an ancient practice that focuses on self-generated feelings of love, compassion, and goodwill toward oneself and others. Loving-kindness meditation engages the power of the ventral vagal system first through self-compassion and then by offering compassion to others.

The traditional four phrases of loving-kindness meditation are, "May I be happy. May I be healthy. May I be safe. May I live with ease." Some variation of these four phrases has been used for centuries. Jack Kornfield and Sharon Salzberg, two giants in the field of meditation, note that it's okay to adjust the words to find the phrases that are most personally meaningful. What words bring these statements alive for you? Let your ventral vagal state guide you.

STEPS

1. Look at the four categories (happy, healthy, safe, and living with ease) through the language of the autonomic nervous system.

   • Find the words that you would use and write your own four phrases. Here is one example of the four phrases:

     – May I find glimmers every day.

- May I be nourished by the flow of ventral vagal energy.
- May I be filled with a neuroception of safety.
- May I live in the rhythm of a regulated nervous system.

2. Say your phrases out loud. Listen to the words and feel how they land in your system. You'll know you've found the right words when you feel a deep connection to your ventral vagal system.

3. Say the phrases to yourself ("May I"). Then send the phrases to others ("May you") beginning with someone you feel safe and connected to, then a neutral person, then someone you may have an unrepaired rupture with, and finally to all living beings.

4. Share your four phrases with someone else. This might be a friend, a family member, or your therapist. Say the phrases to the other person and also have them read your phrases back to you. Notice what happens when you offer and receive your unique phrases. Track your autonomic response to the experience of first offering compassion and then of receiving compassion.

CHAPTER 7: INTEGRATING EXERCISES

—— **EXERCISE** ———————————————

Recognize

BACKGROUND

Autonomic awareness is a protective factor. Without the ability to recognize states and state changes, you are at risk for remaining stuck in dysregulation. The question, "Where am I on my autonomic map?" is a simple way to build autonomic awareness.

STEPS

1. Notice. Bring awareness to your autonomic state. Use what you learned about your autonomic states from the exercises in Chapters 4 and 5 to tune in.
2. Name. Stay out of your story and identify your state. Where are you on your autonomic map?
3. Repeat these two steps often. Create ease with this practice until you can quickly and accurately place yourself on your autonomic map.

——— EXERCISE ————————————
Reflect

BACKGROUND

Once the notice-and-name practice becomes easy and automatic, add the next step of turning toward your autonomic nervous system to listen for just a quick moment to what it is telling you. Don't spend a long time hearing the full story. Just take long enough to get the general idea of what is happening.

STEPS

1. Be curious about what just prompted a mobilization of your sympathetic system, a descent into dorsal vagal conservation mode, or an experience of ventral vagal regulation.
2. Listen to what your state wants you to know.
   - My sympathetic mobilization is telling me . . .
   - My dorsal vagal state is letting me know . . .
   - My ventral vagal system is inviting me to . . .
3. Listen for just a brief moment with curiosity and without judgment. Don't spend more than a minute or so listening. This practice is a quick experience of listening to the outlines of your story and not diving deeply into the details.

EXERCISE
Regulate

BACKGROUND

Everyday navigation of daily living involves setting goals and then acting to make your goals a reality. Goals are helpful in identifying what you want to achieve and are often stated in the form of an intention.

STEPS

1. Consider the autonomic goals you want to set. Ask yourself:
   - Where do I want my autonomic patterns to take me?
   - What do I want to change?
   - What do I want to deepen?
2. Write goals that address what you discovered. Begin each statement with the words "I intend to." For example: I intend to not get stuck in dorsal vagal collapse. I intend to more quickly manage my sympathetic response. I intend to find moments of ventral vagal happiness to savor. Find the words that express your autonomic goals and write your personal intentions.

——— **EXERCISE** ———————————————

Create "If-Then" Statements

BACKGROUND

Once you identify your autonomic goals, the next step is to translate your intention into action by adding what is called an implementation intention. An implementation intention is an if-then statement that identifies when, where, and how you plan to respond to a situation. Writing implementation intentions brings awareness to experiences by creating a link between cues and responses, making it easier for you to recognize situations and take action.

STEPS

1. Set goals for responding to cues of safety and danger in new ways. Set goals for all three states. Make sure your goals aren't too big (unrealistic as a starting point), too broad (undefined and hard to put into action), or too bland (uninteresting and don't keep your attention). Set goals that begin with small steps and lead to a larger change, are well defined with tangible ways to measure, and entice you to want to see what happens when you follow through.

2. Use the beginning statement, "If this happens then I will" to write if-then statements for each of your identified goals.

3. Write statements for external cues (response to certain people, places, or events).

4. Write statements for internal cues (response to autonomic state changes).

5. Read your if-then statements and check your autonomic response. Make sure each statement brings a neuroception of safety. Rewrite any statements that trigger a move into a sympathetic or dorsal vagal response.

6. Use your statements and track what happens. As your responses shift you may want to add new goals and write new if-then statements.

—— **EXERCISE** ————————————————————————

Re-Story

BACKGROUND

Humans are meaning-making beings, automatically pulled toward story. Working with the skills of recognizing, reflecting, and regulating brings you to the important step of re-storying. As you integrate new patterns, you move out of your old stories and head toward new ones. This transition often brings with it discomfort and you can easily be pulled back into old familiar stories about yourself and the world. The re-storying process disrupts the habit of listening to an old story and encourages the development of a new one. Re-storying invites you to become an active author of your own autonomic adventure.

STEPS

1. What are the ways your autonomic nervous system is responding differently? Fill in the following sentences to bring awareness to the shifts that are happening.
   - Instead of my expected sympathetic mobilization I . . .
   - Instead of my familiar dorsal vagal disconnection I . . .
   - I notice I am more . . .
   - I notice I am less . . .
2. Write a story that speaks to your new pattern. Choose words that come from your ventral vagal state and keep that state online and active. For example, "I'm

strong when I interact with other people" might bring sympathetic mobilization while "I have inner strength that serves me when I'm interacting with others" could keep you anchored in ventral.

3. Write about qualities and not behaviors. Use sentences that begin with "I am" (a quality) rather than "I do" (a behavior). *I am kind* is a different story than *I do kind things*.

4. Create a story that illustrates your new autonomic responses.

   • Use *I am beginning to* or *It is possible that* as the opening line to the new story.

   • Write in small increments. In the re-storying process, a short story is more effective than a long essay.

—— **EXERCISE** ———————————————

Exercise the Vagal Brake

BACKGROUND

The vagal brake is responsible for speeding up and slowing down your heart rate. The vagal brake allows you to feel more sympathetic nervous system energy while keeping your ventral vagal system online and in charge. As the vagal brake begins to release, the mobilizing energy of the sympathetic nervous system that is in the background begins to move into the foreground. Then as the vagal brake reengages, the process is reversed, sympathetic energy moving to the background and ventral vagal back to the foreground. Think about the vagal brake working similarly to the brakes on a bicycle. Imagine you are riding a bike down a hill and you want to go a little faster. Release the brakes a bit and feel the wheels spin faster. Gently squeeze the brakes to slow down.

When your vagal brake relaxes but doesn't fully release, you have access to a range of responses, including feeling calm, engaged, joyful, excited, passionate, playful, attentive, alert, or watchful, while still safely anchored in the ventral vagal system. You can bring the energy necessary to respond to what is needed in the moment. When working well, the vagal brake supports flexibility in your responses and a creates sense of ease to transitions.

Using metaphor and imagery you can experiment with relaxing and reengaging the vagal brake and experience the ways this part of the ventral vagal system helps you safely navigate everyday challenges. With ongoing practice, you create more flexibility in your responses and feel the benefits of a resilient autonomic nervous system.

STEPS

1. Find an image of your vagal brake that brings to life your sense of regulating the increase and decrease of energy in your ventral vagal pathways. Look for an image that gives you the feeling of controlling the dimensions of something. Some commonly used images include bicycle brakes, a door, a bridge, a gate, a water faucet, a volume control knob, and a dimmer switch. Let your imagination guide you as you find an image that you can manipulate and measure the changes.

2. Write a simple story about your vagal brake using the image. Describe your image and how you use it to increase energy and return to calm.

3. Use a movement. Not everyone creates imagery to come into connection with inner experience. For some people movement is the preferred method. Find a movement that changes shape to illustrate the increase and decrease of energy.

4. Connect your vagal brake image and/or movement to your breath cycle. A subtle pattern of relaxation and reengagement happens with every breath cycle. With each inhalation, the brake relaxes just a bit, allowing a slight speeding up of the heart, and then reengages on the exhalation to bring a return of the slower beat. Take a moment and play with these two pathways.

Feel your vagal brake relax, then reengage with each breath in an ongoing cycle. Move through several breath cycles until it begins to feel natural.

5. Use the image and/or movement to intentionally engage, relax, and reengage the brake.

   • See yourself as an active operator of your vagal brake, shaping the rise and fall of energy. Bring the image to life—see it, hear it, feel yourself adjusting it, and feel your energy moving in synchrony with the changing image.

   • Bring the movement connected to your vagal brake into awareness either in outward action or inward experience. Change the movement and feel the increase and decrease of sympathetic energy in your system.

6. Play with the experience of intentionally exercising your vagal brake.

   • Start with a small challenge, perhaps something that is commonly experienced in your day-to-day life. On a scale of intensity from 1–10, choose something in the 1–3 range.

   • Use your image and/or movement to relax the brake to meet your chosen challenge and reengage the brake when the challenge is over. Feel the influence you have over the ways your vagal brake works in service of managing the challenge.

7. Experiment with a variety of challenges. Build confidence in using your vagal brake to meet everyday challenges.

- Once you feel confident in successfully meeting small challenges, choose a slightly stronger challenge. Notice how your vagal brake relaxes, allowing your energy to rise to more intense challenges while maintaining the ventral vagal state of safety. Then reengage the brake and return to your ventral vagal starting point.
- Practice using your vagal brake with environmental experiences.
- Practice using your vagal brake with relationship stressors.

───── **EXERCISE** ───────────────────────────

Resilience Routines

BACKGROUND

Resilience is an emergent property of a ventral vagal state. As you build resilience, instead of responding to a challenge with an automatic move into a survival response, you are able to respond with more flexibility. And in the times when you are pulled into a survival response, rather than getting stuck there, you're able to return to the state of ventral vagal regulation. As resilience builds, your capacity for flexibility of response deepens.

STEPS

1. Create resilience routines that draw from practices that engage your body and brain in a variety of ways. Revisit Chapter 6 and see if there are shaping exercises from the different categories that fit into your resilience routine.

2. Experiment with actions that bring moments of ventral vagal experience.
   - Look inward to breath and reflection practices.
   - Look outward into the environment of your home and nature.
   - Look at the way you move in the world and the people who accompany you.

3. Choose experiences that feel nourishing and ones that feel a bit challenging. You want a mix of practices that feel comfortable and are easy to engage with and

ones that take concerted effort. Building resilience is about both deepening into ongoing practices that feel sustaining and inviting in new practices that bring the right degree of neural challenge for your system.

4. Find a few core practices that will remain constant in your resilience routine.

5. Create a second category of practices that routinely change.

   • Decide on the length of time you want to use. The time period can be anywhere from 1 week to 6 months.

   • Choose a few new practices to experiment with over your chosen time period. At the end of that time some practices may become core practices while you let others go. As you try out new practices, your resilience routines continue to develop.

6. Regularly review and revise your resilience routines. Some practices will become lifelong, while others will serve you for a time and then be replaced with new ones.

My Core Practices	Changing Practices This month I will . . .
vagal brake image with breathing	use breath counting once a day
intentional sighing	find a place I feel safe to be quiet
glimmers with my hand on my heart	try a different yoga class each week

FIGURE 7.1. Sample Resilience Routines

CHAPTER 8: CONNECTING EXERCISES

——— EXERCISE ————————————————
Rules of Reciprocity

BACKGROUND

You don't require reciprocity, proximity, and face-to-face interactions all the time. In fact, well-being is found in a balance of time with others and time by yourself. You have your own reciprocity requirements, and when they aren't met, your body feels the absence. Without the right measure of reciprocity, your autonomic state begins to shift from readiness for connection to preparation for protection. Incorporating a therapeutic dose of reciprocity (the amount necessary to bring the desired effect) into your daily living means first knowing your needs and then building sustainable connections and opportunities to meet those needs.

STEPS

1. Fill in the following equations to find your reciprocity rhythms. Recognize the signals that you've been on your own for too long, you've spent too much time connected with others, or you're in a sweet spot of symmetry.
2. Reciprocity is not a static experience. Return to this practice regularly to track when you are out of balance or in a resourcing relationship to yourself and others.
3. Take care of your connections.

- Write reciprocity intentions that describe how you are going to pay attention each day to ways you are in and out of reciprocity. Examples might be, "I will track my reciprocity rhythms and take action when I'm out of balance" or "At the end of the day I'll reflect on my moments of reciprocity."
- Create time and space for reciprocal interactions. Identify when, where, and with whom you can build predictable, sustainable opportunities for connection into your life.

The amount of time I want to spend on my own today is: Today I'm going to spend time alone doing:	= reciprocity balance	The amount of time I want to spend with friends today is: Today I'm going to connect with: And we're going to:
These work responsibilities mean that I work by myself: These things in my personal life mean that I'm on my own:	> alone and out of balance	I've neglected being with the people in my life who are important to me by not paying attention to: and not making time for:
I've lost track of my: I've been so busy with others I haven't made time for:	< with others and out of balance	I feel too involved in the life of: I feel over-saturated by doing things with others because I said yes to:

FIGURE 8.1. Reciprocity Equation Chart

——— **EXERCISE** ———————————————————
Personal Connection Plan

BACKGROUND

What does a map of your pathways to connection look like? Your personal plan brings a dual focus: what's working (the things that are already in place) and what's wanted (things to explore and invite in). The questions in this exercise reference people, but feel free to add pets to your exploration.

STEPS

1. Identify what's working.
   - Who are the people in your life with whom you feel a connection?
   - What are the things you do together that foster that connection?
   - What are the things you do to nourish your sense of connection to self?
2. Identify what you want.
   - Who would you like to invite into connection?
   - What might you do to explore new connections?
   - What would you like to explore on your own?
   - How does interacting with others in a playful way fit into your connection plan?
   - How do moments of shared stillness fit in your connection plan?
3. Fill in the boxes to create your personal connection plan. Update your plan as you try new things and make new connections.

People I want to continue to connect with:	People I would like to get to know:
Things I want to continue to do with my friends:	Things I'd like to explore doing with others:
Things I want to keep doing to connect to my own experience:	New things I'd like to try on my own:

FIGURE 8.2. Personal Connection Plan

———— **EXERCISE** ————————————————

Clusters of Connection

BACKGROUND

There are many ways to reach for reciprocity. There are many pathways to connection. Who you connect with and how you connect is an individual experience. Find the ways your autonomic nervous system feels nourished and create relationships with people (and pets) that nurture your sense of being woven into a resilient network.

STEPS

1. Look at the people in your life.

   • Make a list of the people to whom you are connected. Listen to your autonomic response as you think about each person. Using a scale of 1-3, loosely connected; 4-7, pretty connected; or 8-10, very connected, identify how close you feel to these people. You may find that you have several people in the 4-7 pretty connected range or one person in the 8-10 very connected range and feel very safe and supported with either configuration. It isn't a particular number of connections that matters, it's the ways your personal autonomic needs are met by those connections.

2. Look at how often you connect with people in your network. A match with others feels resourcing while a mismatch between your wish for connection and your experience of connection is painful.

3. Look at the ways you connect.

   • Create a pie chart to map your kinds of connection. Use the communication categories that fit for you. The two examples in Figure 8. 3 show very different connection profiles, but each person identified feeling deeply connected to their network.

4. Look at what you do when you connect.

   • quiet moments

   • physically active adventures

   • go out or stay in

   • favorite activities you love to return to

   • new things you want to try

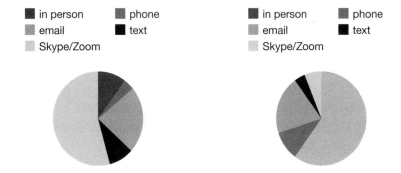

FIGURE 8.3. Types of Connection

——— **EXERCISE** ———————————————————————
With Gratitude

BACKGROUND

Sometimes gratitude comes in the form of life-giving or life-saving events (a stranger donating a kidney, someone not leaving your side when you are in the depths of despair) that irrevocably change the way you think about and move through the world. More often the gifts of gratitude come through ordinary, everyday experiences. Simple interactions with people (holding a door open, offering a smile, recognizing someone's contribution), pets (your dog greeting you at the door, your cat nuzzling you awake in the morning), or in nature (the return of the sun after a stretch of rain or the rain after a period of drought, the first hint of spring) are opportunities for gratitude. Gratitude is good for your body and brain (fewer physical complaints, better heart health, less depression and anxiety, more happiness). A gratitude practice helps you see the small, everyday experiences of goodness that might otherwise pass by unnoticed.

STEPS

1. Keep a gratitude list. Make a practice of noticing what you might otherwise take for granted.
2. Find ways to express your gratitude. Say thank you. Return the favor.
3. Use a breath practice to deepen into appreciation.
   • Imagine breathing into the beginnings of your ventral vagus at the base of your skull. Follow the

pathway as it makes its way to your heart, and then breathe out of your heart. Follow this cycle of breath and imagine your autonomic nervous system supporting your experience of gratitude.

• Breathe in with a word that acknowledges a moment to be grateful for. Breath out with a word that expresses your gratitude.

——— **EXERCISE** ———————————————————————

Compassionate Connections

BACKGROUND

Through the eyes of compassion, from your own regulated nervous system, you can see another person's dysregulated system, respond with regulation, and connect with kindness. From the energy of your ventral vagal system, you can also connect inside and be with your own suffering in an act of self-compassion. Ongoing experiences build the capacity for connecting with compassion. Find the combination of practices that brings your ventral vagal system alive. Create your own compassionate connections.

STEPS

1. Create a compassion statement using the language of the autonomic nervous system.

    •   Use language that recognizes another person's dysregulated state and names the ways your ventral vagal state helps you see them with compassion.

    •   Decide on a timeframe for using your statement. You might choose to create a new statement each week or each day.

    •   Notice people in need of compassion and use your statement to send a message either in silent thought or in spoken words.

2. Make this three-step compassion practice a routine part of your day.

    •   Find your ventral vagal anchor.

- Look through the energy of your ventral vagal system. See the other person not as bad or unworthy but as dysregulated, pulled into sympathetic or dorsal vagal protection, and unable to regulate.
- Hold the other person in your ventral vagal energy. Let your nervous system send cues of safety toward theirs.

3. Create a self-compassion statement using the language of the autonomic nervous system.

- Use language that acknowledges your own dysregulated state, identifies that dysregulation is a normal human experience, and reminds you that your autonomic nervous system knows the way back to regulation.
- Decide on a timeframe for using your statement. You might choose to create a new statement each week or each day.
- Notice when you are in need of compassion and say your statement to yourself either silently or out loud.

──── EXERCISE ────

Awe Inspiring

BACKGROUND

You feel moved when you are awe-filled and motionless when you are awestruck. Awe lives along a continuum of ordinary to extraordinary. Some moments stop you in your tracks and demand your attention. Other everyday moments pass by without being recognized. People, nature, architecture, the arts, spiritual experiences, and inexplicable events each have the potential to elicit feelings of awe. Where are your moments of awe each day that are waiting to be discovered?

STEPS

1. Build a reservoir of awe memories.
   - Remember a moment of awe.
   - Replay it in your mind and bring the richness of it back into full awareness.
   - Revisit it in writing to deepen the experience.
2. Notice where in your life you find awe.
   - Certain people inspire awe. Who are those people for you? They may be people you know and have a relationship with or people you know of and admire.
   - Places, the architecture of a particular structure, and natural formations in the outside world routinely bring experiences of awe.
   - Art and music predictably activate awe.
   - Spiritual experiences are awe-filled.
3. Either physically or through a memory, return to the

awe-inspiring people, places, and events you identi-fied in step two. Returning in person or revisiting in memory brings the experience and your ventral vagal response alive again.

4. Be open to the inexplicable events that unexpectedly appear. Let go of the need to understand and explain those moments and let in the experience of awe.

REFERENCES

Abel, J., & Clarke, L. (2018). Compassion is the best medicine. *Resurgence and Ecologist,* March/April. Retrieved from https://www.resurgence .org/magazine/article5050-compassion-is-the-best-medicine.html

Achtziger, A., Gollwitzer, P. M., & Sheeran, P. (2008). Implementation intentions and shielding goal striving from unwanted thoughts and feelings. *Personality and Social Psychology Bulletin, 34*(3), 381–393. doi:10.1177/0146167207311201

Alkon, A., Boyce, W. T., Tran, L., Harley, K. G., Neuhaus, J., & Eskenazi, B. (2014). Prenatal adversities and Latino children's autonomic nervous system reactivity trajectories from 6 months to 5 years of age. *PloS ONE, 9*(1), e86283. doi:10.1371/journal.pone.0086283

Amati, V., Meggiolaro, S., Rivellini, G., & Zaccarin, S. (2018). Social relations and lifesatisfaction: the role of friends. *Genus, 74*(1), 7. doi :10.1186/s41118-018-0032-z

American Psychiatric Association. (2013). *Diagnostic and statistical manual of mental disorders* (5th ed.). Arlington, VA: Author.

Andersson, U., & Tracey, K. J. (2012). A new approach to rheumatoid arthritis: Treating inflammation with computerized nerve stimulation. *Cerebrum,* 2012, 3.

Aucouturier, J. J., Johansson, P., Hall, L., Segnini, R., Mercadié, L., & Watanabe, K. (2016). Covert digital manipulation of vocal emotion alter speakers' emotional states in a congruent direction. *Proceedings of the National Academy of Sciences, 113*(4), 948–953. doi:10.1073/pnas.1506552113

Bateson, Patrick. (2014). Play, playfulness, creativity and innovation. *Animal Behavior and Cognition, 2*, 99–112. doi:10.12966/abc.05.02.2014

Baumeister, R. F., & Leary, M. R. (1995). The need to belong: Desire for interpersonal attachments as a fundamental human motivation. *Psychological Bulletin, 117*(3), 497–529. http://dx.doi.org/10.1037/0033-2909.117.3.497

Beckwith McGuire, K. M., Greenberg, M. A., & Gevirtz, R. (2005). Autonomic effects of expressive writing in individuals with elevated blood pressure. *Health Psychology, 10*(2), 197–209. https://doi.org/10.1177/1359105305049767

Bell, S., Phoenix, C., Lovell, R., & Wheeler, B. (2015). Seeking everyday wellbeing: The coast as a therapeutic landscape. *Social Science & Medicine, 142.* doi:10.1016/j.socscimed.2015.08.011

Bhullar, N., Schutte, N. S., & Malouff, J. M. (2011). Writing about satisfaction processes increases well-being. *Individual Differences Research, 9*, 22–32.

Blanco C. A. (2014). The principal sources of William James' idea of habit. *Frontiers in Human Neuroscience, 8*, 274. doi:10.3389/fnhum.2014.00274

Bolwerk, A., Mack-Andrick, J., Lang, F. R., Dörfler, A., & Maihöfner, C. (2014). How art changes your brain: Differential effects of visual art production and cognitive art evaluation on functional brain connectivity. *PLoS ONE, 9*(7). e101035. doi:10.1371/journal.pone.0101035

Brieber, D., Nadal, M., Leder, H., & Rosenberg, R. (2014). Art in time and space: Context modulates the relation between art experience and viewing time. *PloS ONE, 9*(6), e99019. doi:10.1371/journal.pone.0099019

Brown, D. K., Barton, J. L., & Gladwell, V. F. (2013). Viewing nature scenes positively affects recovery or autonomic function following acute-mental stress. *Environmental Science & Technology, 47*(11). doi:10.1021/es305019p

Buchanan, M. (July 4, 2007). Why we are all creatures of habit. Retrieved from http://cdn2.hubspot.net/hub/41475/file-14044534-pdf/pdf%20downloads/new.scientist._being_human.pdf

Bush, N. R., Jones-Mason, K., Coccia, M., Caron, Z., Alkon, A., Thomas, M., Coleman-Phox, K., Wadhwa, P. D., Laraia, B. A., Adler, N. E., . . . Epel, E. S. (2017). Effects of pre- and postnatal maternal stress on infant temperament and autonomic nervous system reactivity and regulation in a diverse, low-income population. *Development and Psychopathology, 29*(5), 1553–1571. doi:10.1017/S0954579417001237

Cacioppo, J. T., & Cacioppo, S. (2014). Social relationships and health: The toxic effects of perceived social isolation. *Social and Personality Psychology Compass, 8*(2), 58–72. http://doi.org/10.1111/spc3.12087

Carnevali, L., Koenig, J., Sgoifo, A., & Ottaviani, C. (2018). Autonomic and brain morphological predictors of stress resilience. *Frontiers in Neuroscience, 12*, 228. doi:10.3389/fnins.2018.00228

Carter, C. S., & Porges, S. W. (2012). The biochemistry of love: An oxytocin hypothesis. *EMBO Reports, 14*(1), 12–6. doi:10.1038/embor.2012.191

Chanda, M. L., & Levitin, D. J. (2013). The neruochemistry of music. *Trends in Cognitive Sciences, 17*(4),179–93. doi:10.1016/j.tics.2013.02.007

Cigna. (2018). U. S. Loneliness Index retrieved from https://www.cigna.com/assets/docs/newsroom/loneliness-survey-2018-fact-sheet.pdf

Cole, S. W. (2009). Social regulation of human gene expression. *Current Directions in Psychological Science, 18*(3), 132–137. doi:10.1111/j.1467-8721.2009.01623.x

Cole, S. W. (2014). Human social genomics. *PLoS Genetics*, 10(8), e1004601. doi:10.1371/journal.pgen.1004601

Cole, S. W., Levine, M. E., Arevalo, J. M., Ma, J., Weir, D. R., & Crimmins, E. M. (2015). Loneliness, eudaimonia, and the human conserved transcriptional response to adversity. *Psychoneuroendocrinology, 62*, 11–7. doi:10.1016/j.psyneuen.2015.07.001

Collet, C., Di Rienzo, F., El Hoyek, N., & Guillot, A. (2013). Autonomic nervous system correlates in movement observation and motor imagery. *Frontiers in Human Neuroscience, 7*, 415. doi:10.3389/fnhum.2013.00415

Costa, J. M., Jung, M. F., Czerwinski, M., Guimbretière, F., Le, T., & Choudhury, T. (2018). Regulating feelings during interpersonal conflicts by changing voice self-perception. *CHI 2018. CHI '18 Proceedings of the 2018 CHI Conference on Human Factors in Computing Systems Paper No. 631.* doi:10.1145/3173574.3174205

Critchley, H., & Harrison, N. (2013). Visceral influences on brain and behavior. *Neuron, 77*(4), 624–38. doi:10.1016/j.neuron.2013.02.008.

Dana, D. (2018). *The polyvagal theory in therapy: Engaging the rhythm of regulation.* New York: Norton.

Darwin, C. (1873). *The expression of the emotions in man and animals.* New York: D. Appleton.

De Jong Gierveld, J., & Van Tilburg, T. (2010). The De Jong Gierveld short scales for emotional and social loneliness: Tested on data from 7 countries in the UN generations and gender surveys. *European Journal of Ageing, 7*(2), 121–130. doi:10.1007/s10433-010-0144-6

DePierro, J. M., D'Andrea, W., & Frewen, P. (2014). Anhedonia in trauma related disorders: The good, the bad, and the shut-down. In M. S. Ritsner (Ed.), *Anhedonia: A comprehensive handbook: Neuropsychiatric and physical disorders* (pp. 175–189). New York, NY, US: Springer Science + Business Media. doi: 10.1007/978-94-017-8610-2_7

de Vries, S., Ten Have, M., van Dorsselaer, S., van Wezep, M., Hermans, T., & de Graaf, R. (2016). Local availability of green and blue space and prevalence of common mental disorders in the Netherlands. *BJPsych Open, 2*(6), 366–372. doi:10.1192/bjpo.bp.115.002469

Demougeot, L., Normand, H., Denise, P., & Papaxanthis, C. (2009). Discrete and effortful imagined movements do not specifically activate the autonomic nervous system. *PloS ONE, 4*(8), e6769. doi:10.1371/journal.pone.0006769

DiMenichi, B. C., Lempert, K. M., Bejjani, C., & Tricomi, E. (2018). Writing about past failures attenuates cortisol responses and sustained attention deficits following psychosocial stress. *Frontiers in Behavioral Neuroscience, 12,* 45. doi:10.3389/fnbeh.2018.00045

Doidge, N. (2015). *The brain's way of healing.* New York: Penguin Books.

Dorrance, A., & Fink, G. (2015). Effects of stroke on the autonomic nervous system. *Comprehensive Physiology, 5*, 1241–1263. doi:10.1002/cphy .c140016.

Duros, P., & Crowley, D. (2014). The body comes to therapy too. *Clinical Social Work J, 42*, 237. doi:10.1007/s10615-014-0486-1

Emmons, R. A., & Stern, R. (2013) Gratitude as a psychotherapeutic intervention. *Clinical Psychology, 69*, 846–855. doi:10.1002/jclp.22020

Evans, S., Seidman, L. C., Tsao, J. C., Lung, K. C., Zeltzer, L. K., & Naliboff, B. D. (2013). Heart rate variability as a biomarker for autonomic nervous system response differences between children with chronic pain and healthy control children. *Pain Research, 6*, 449–57. doi:10.2147/JPR.S43849

Fifer, W. P., Fingers, S. T., Youngman, M., Gomez-Gribben, E., & Myers, M. M. (2009). Effects of alcohol and smoking during pregnancy on infant autonomic control. *Developmental Psychobiology, 51*(3), 234–42. doi:10.1002/dev.20366

Fisher, S. (2014). *Neurofeedback in the treatment of developmental trauma.* New York: Norton.

Flores, P., & Porges, S. (2017). Group psychotherapy as a neural exercise: Bridging polyvagal theory and attachment theory. *International Journal of Group Psychotherapy, 67*, 202–222. doi:10.1080/00207284.2016.1263544

Furman, D. J., Waugh, C. E., Bhattacharjee, K., Thompson, R. J., & Gotlib, I. H. (2013). Interoceptive awareness, positive affect, and decision making in major depressive disorder. *Journal of affective disorders, 151*(2), 780–5. doi: 10.1016/j.jad.2013.06.044

Füstös, J., Gramann, K., Herbert, B. M., & Pollatos, O. (2012). On the embodiment of emotion regulation: Interoceptive awareness facilitates reappraisal. *Social cognitive and affective neuroscience, 8*(8), 911–7. doi: 10.1093/scan/nss089

Fowler, J. H., & Christakis, N. A. (2008). Dynamic spread of happiness in a large social network: Longitudinal analysis over 20 years in the Framingham Heart Study. *BMJ (Clinical Research Ed.), 337*, a2338. doi:10.1136/bmj.a2338

Franz, E. A., & Gillett, G. (2011). John Hughlings Jackson's evolutionary neurology: A unifying framework for cognitive neuroscience, *Brain*, *134*(Pt 10), 3114–20. doi:10.1093/brain/awr218

Friis, A. M., Consedine, N. S., & Johnson, M. H. (2015). Does kindness matter? Diabetes, depression, and self-compassion: A selective review and research agenda. *Diabetes Spectrum*, *28*(4), 252–7. doi:10.2337/diaspect.28.4.252

Fukushima, A., Nakai, K., Kanasugi, T., Terata, M., & Sugiyama, T. (2011). Assessment of fetal autonomic nervous system activity by fetal magnetocardiography: Comparison of normal pregnancy and intrauterine growth restriction. *Pregnancy*, *2011*, 218162.

Geiger, P. J., Morey, J. N., & Segerstrom, S. C. (2016). Beliefs about savoring in older adulthood: Aging and perceived health affect temporal components of perceived savoring ability. *Personality and Individual Differences*, *105*, 164–169. doi:0.1016/j.paid.2016.09.049

Georgiou, K., Larentzakis, A. V., Khamis, N. N., Alsuhaibani, G. I., Alaska, Y. A., & Giallafos, E. J. (2018). Can wearable devices accurately measure heart rate variability? A systematic review. *Folia Medica*, *60*(1), 7–20. doi:10.2478/folmed-2018-0012

Gerbarg, P. L., & Brown, R. P. (2016, November 30). Neurobiology and neurophysiology of breath practices in psychiatric care. *Psychiatric Times*. Retrieved from http://www.psychiatrictimes.com/special-reports/neurobiology-and-neurophysiology-breath-practices-psychiatric-care

Gladwell, M. (2000). *The tipping point: How little things can make a big difference.* New York: Little, Brown and Company.

Gollwitzer, P., & Sheeran, P. (2006). Implementation intentions and goal achievement: A meta-analysis of effects and processes. *Advances in Experimental Social Psychology, 38,* 69–119. doi:10.1016/S0065-2601(06)38002-1

Gopnik, A. (Jan 16, 2005). How we learn. Retrieved from https://www.nytimes.com/2005/01/16/education/edlife/how-we-learn.html

Gould van Praag, C. D., Garfinkel, S. N., Sparasci, O., Mees, A., Philippides, A. O., Ware, M., Ottaviani, C., . . . Critchley, H. D. (2017). Mind-wandering and alterations to default mode network connectivity when listening to naturalistic versus artificial sounds. *Scientific Reports, 7,* 45273. doi:10.1038/srep45273

Graham, L. (2018). *Resilience: Powerful practices for bouncing back from disappointment, difficulty, and even disaster.* Novato, CA: New World Library.

Gray, A. (2018). Roots, rhythm, reciprocity: Polyvagal-informed dance movement therapy for survivors of trauma. In S. W. Porges & D. Dana (Eds.), *Clinical application of the polyvagal theory: The emergence of polyvagal-informed therapies.* New York: Norton.

Grippo, A. J., Lamb, D. G., Carter, C. S., & Porges, S. W. (2007). Social isolation disrupts autonomic regulation of the heart and influences negative affective behaviors. *Biological Psychiatry, 62*(10), 1162–1170. doi:10.1016/j.biopsych.2007.04.011

Haase, L., Stewart, J., Youssef, B., May, A., Isakovic, S., Simmons, A., Johnson, D., Potterat, E., & Paulus, M. (2015). When the brain does not adequately feel the body: Links between low resilience and interoception. *Biological Psychology, 113,* 37–45. doi:10.1016/j.biopsycho.2015.11.004

Halifax, J. (2012). A heuristic model of enactive compassion. *Current Opinion in Supportive and Palliative Care, 6*(2), 228–235. doi:10.1097/spc.0b013e3283530fbe

Hall, S. E., Schubert, E., & Wilson, S. J. (2016). The role of trait and state absorption in the enjoyment of music. *PLoS ONE, 11*(11), e0164029. doi:10.1371/journal.pone.0164029

Hambleton, M. T., Reynolds, E. W., Sithisarn, T., Traxel, S. J., Patwardhan, A. R., Crawford, T. N., Mendiondo, M. S., . . . Bada, H. S. (2013). Autonomic nervous system function following prenatal opiate exposure. *Frontiers in Pediatrics, 1,* 27. doi:10.3389/fped 2013.00027

Haviland-Jones, J., Rosario, H. H., Wilson, P., & McGuire, T. R. (2005). An environmental approach to positive emotion: Flowers. *Evolutionary Psychology, 3*(1). doi:10.1177/147470490500300109

Hawkley, L., & Cacioppo, J. (2010). Loneliness matters: A theoretical and empirical review of consequences and mechanisms. *Annals of Behavioral Medicine, 40*(2), 218–27. doi:10.1007/s12160-010-9210-8

Herbert, R. (2011). An empirical study of normative dissociation in musical and non-musical everyday life experiences. *Psychology of Music*, *41*(3), 372–394. doi:10.1177/0305735611430080

Herbert, C., Sfärlea, A., & Blumenthal, T. (2013). Your emotion or mine: Labeling feelings alters emotional face perception—an ERP study on automatic and intentional affect labeling. *Frontiers in Human Neuroscience*, *7*, 378. doi:10.3389/fnhum.2013.00378

Holt-Lunstad, J., Robles, T. F., & Sbarra, D. A. (2017). Advancing social connection as a public health priority in the United States. *American Psychologist*, *72*(6), 517–530. doi:10.1037/amp0000103

Homan, K. J., & Sirois, F. M. (2017). Self-compassion and physical health: Exploring the roles of perceived stress and health-promoting behaviors. *Health Psychology Open*, *4*(2), 2055102917729542. doi:10.1177/2055102917729542

Ikei, H., Komatsu, M., Song, C., Himoro, E., & Miyazaki, Y. (2014). The physiological and psychological relaxing effects of viewing rose flowers in office workers. *Physiological Anthropology*, *33*(1), 6. doi:10.1186/1880-6805-33-6

Ijzerman, H., Gallucci, M., Pouw, W. T., Weißgerber, S. C., Van Doesum, N. J., & Williams, K. D. (2012). Cold-blooded loneliness: Social exclusion leads to lower skin temperatures. *Acta Psychologica*, *140*(3),283–8. doi:10.1016/j.actpsy.2012.05.002

James, W. (1890). *Habit*. New York: Henry Holt.

Jamieson, J. P., Nock, M. K., & Mendes, W. B. (2011). Mind over matter: Reappraising arousal improves cardiovascular and cognitive responses to stress. *Journal of Experimental Psychology. General*, *141*(3), 417–22. doi:10.1037/a0025719.

Jefferies, A. L., Canadian Paediatric Society, Fetus and Newborn Committee (2012). Kangaroo care for the preterm infant and family. *Paediatrics & Child Health*, *17*(3), 141–6.

Jerath, R., Edry, J. W, Barnes, V. A., & Jerath, V. (2006). Physiology of long pranayamic breathing: Neural respiratory elements may provide a mechanism that explains how slow deep breathing shifts the autonomic nervous system. *Medical Hypotheses, 67,* 566–71. doi:10.1016/j .mehy.2006.02.042

Jo Cox Loneliness (n.d.). Retrieved from https://www.redcross.org.uk › *media › documents › about-us › combatting-loneliness.*

Jose, P. E., Lim, B. T., & Bryant, F. B. (2012). Does savoring increase happiness? A daily diary study. *Positive Psychology, 7*(3), 176–187. doi:10.1080/17439760.2012.671345

Joung, D., Kim, G., Choi, Y., Lim, H., Park, S., Woo, J. M., & Park, B. J. (2015). The prefrontal cortex activity and psychological effects of viewing forest landscapes in autumn season. *International Journal of Environmental Research and Public Health, 12*(7), 7235–43. doi:10.3390/ijerph120707235

Kahn, P. H., Severson, R. L., & Ruckert, J. H. (2009). The human relation with nature and technological nature. *Current Directions in Psychological Science, 18*(1), 37–42. doi:10.1111/j.1467-8721.2009.01602.x

Kanbara, K., & Fukunaga, M. (2016). Links among emotional awareness, somatic awareness and autonomic homeostatic processing. *Biopsychosocial Medicine, 10,* 16. doi:10.1186/s13030-016-0059-3

Kang, S. H. (2016). Spaced repetition promotes efficient and effective learning: Policy implications for instruction. *Policy Insights from the Behavioral and Brain Sciences, 3*(1), 12–19. doi:10.1177/2372732215624708

Keltner, D., & Haidt, J. (2003). Approaching awe, a moral, spiritual, and aesthetic emotion. *Cognition and Emotion, 17*(2), 297–314. doi:10.1080 /02699930302297

Kim, J. H., Bae, H. S., & Park, S. S. (2016). The effects of breath-counting meditation and deep breathing on heart rate variability. *Korean Medicine, 37,* 36–44. doi:10.13048/jkm.16019

Kinsella, M. T., & Monk, C. (2009). Impact of maternal stress, depression and anxiety on fetal neurobehavioral development. *Clinical Obstetrics and Gynecology, 52*(3), 425–40. doi:10.1097/GRF.0b013e3181b52df1

Kirby, J. N., Doty, J. R., Petrocchi, N., & Gilbert, P. (2017). The current and future role of heart rate variability for assessing and training compassion. *Frontiers in Public Health, 5,* 40. doi:10.3389/fpubh.2017.00040

Kobayashi, H., Song, C., Ikei, H., Park, B. J., Lee, J., Kagawa, T., & Miyazaki, Y. (2018). Forest walking affects autonomic nervous activity: A population-based study. *Frontiers in Public Health, 6,* 278. doi:10.3389/fpubh.2018.00278

Kok, B. E., & Fredrickson, B. L. (2011). Upward spirals of the heart: Autonomic flexibility, as indexed by vagal tone, reciprocally and prospectively predicts positive emotions and social connectedness. *Biological Psychology, 85*(3), 432–436. doi:10.1016/j.biopsycho.2010.09.005

Kok, B. E., Coffey, K. A., Cohn, M. A., Catalino, L. I., Vacharkulksemsuk, T., Algoe, S. B., . . . Fredrickson, B. L. (2013). How positive emotions build physical health: Perceived positive social connections account for the upward spiral between positive emotions and vagal tone. *Psychological Science, 24*(7),1123–32. doi:10.1177/0956797612470827

Laborde, S., Mosley, E., & Thayer, J. F. (2017). Heart rate variability and cardiac vagal tone in psychophysiological research—Recommendations for experiment planning, data analysis, and data reporting. *Frontiers in Psychology, 8,* Article ID 213. doi:10.3389/fpsyg.2017.00213

Lally, P., Wardle, J., & Gardner, B. (2011). Experiences of habit formation: A qualitative study. *Psychology, Health & Medicine, 16,* 484–9. doi:10.1080/13548506.2011.555774

Lally, P., van Jaarsveld, C. H., Potts, H. W. & Wardle, J. (2010), How are habits formed: Modelling habit formation in the real world. *European Journal of Social Psychology, 40,* 998–1009. doi:10.1002/ejsp.674

Lee, M. S., Lee, J., Park, B. J., & Miyazaki, Y. (2015). Interaction with indoor plants may reduce psychological and physiological stress by suppressing autonomic nervous system activity in young adults: A randomized crossover study. *Physiological Anthropology, 34*(1), 21. doi:10.1186/s40101-015-0060-8

Lepecki, André. (2001). Undoing the fantasy of the (dancing) subject: 'Still Acts' in Jérôme Bel's the last performance. In Steven de Belder and Koen Tachelet (Eds.) *The Salt of the Earth. On dance, politics and reality.* Brussels: Vlaams Theater Instituut.

Long, C.R., & Averill, J.R. (2003). Solitude: An exploration of benefits of being alone. *Journal for the Theory of Social Behavior, 33, 21–44.*

Lucardie, Dorothy. (2014). The impact of fun and enjoyment on adult's learning. *Procedia - Social and Behavioral Sciences, 142,* 439–446. doi:10.1016 /j.sbspro.2014.07.696

Lucas, A. R., Klepin, H. D., Porges, S. W., & Rejeski, W. J. (2018). Mindfulness-based movement: A polyvagal perspective. *Integrative Cancer Therapies, 17*(1), 5–15. doi:10.1177/1534735416682087

Luo, Xi & Qiao, Lei & Che, Xianwei. (2018). Self-compassion modulates heart rate variability and negative affect to experimentally induced stress. *Mindfulness, 9*(2). doi:10.1007/s12671-018-0900-9

Ma, X., Yue, Z. Q., Gong, Z. Q., Zhang, H., Duan, N. Y., Shi, Y. T., Wei, G. X., . . . Li, Y. F. (2017). The effect of diaphragmatic breathing on attention, negative affect and stress in healthy adults. *Frontiers in Psychology, 8,* 874. doi:10.3389/fpsyg.2017.00874

Maas, J., Spreeuwenberg, P., Winsum-Westra, M. van, Verheij, R. A., Vries, S., & Groenewegen, P. P. (2009). Is green space in the living environment associated with people's feelings of social safety? *Environment and Planning A: Economy and Space, 41*(7), 1763–1777. doi. org/10.1068/a4196

Manini, B., Cardone, D., Ebisch, S. J., Bafunno, D., Aureli, T., & Merla, A. (2013). Mom feels what her child feels: Thermal signatures of vicarious autonomic response while watching children in a stressful situation. *Frontiers in Human Neuroscience, 7,* 299. doi:10.3389/fnhum .2013.00299

Maran, T., Sachse, P., Martini, M., Weber, B., Pinggera, J., Zuggal, S., & Furtner, M. (2017). Lost in time and space: States of high arousal disrupt implicit acquisition of spatial and sequential context information. *Frontiers in Behavioral Neuroscience, 11,* 206. doi:10.3389/fnbeh .2017.00206

Mazur, M., Furgała, A., Jabłoński, K., Mach, T., & Thor, P. (2012). Autonomic nervous system activity in constipation-predominant irritable bowel syndrome patients. *Medical Science Monitor, 18*(8), CR493–499. doi:10.12659/MSM.883269

McCraty, R., & Zayas, M. A. (2014). Cardiac coherence, self-regulation, autonomic stability, and psychosocial well-being. *Frontiers in Psychology, 5,* 1090. doi:10.3389/fpsyg.2014.01090

McCullough, M., Tsang, J. A., & Emmons, R. A. (2004). Gratitude in intermediate affective terrain: Links of grateful moods to individual differences and daily emotional experience. *Personality and Social Psychology, 86*(2), 295–309. doi:10.1037/0022-3514.86.2.295

McPherson, M. J., Barrett, F., Lopez-Gonzalez, M., Jiradejvong, P., & Limb, C. J. (2016). Emotional intent modulates the neural substrates of creativity: An fMRI study of emotionally targeted improvisation in jazz musicians. *Scientific Reports, 6,* 18460. doi:10.1038/srep18460

Merz, C. N., Elboudwarej, O., & Mehta, P. K. (2015). The autonomic nervous system and cardiovascular health and disease: A complex balancing act. *JACC: Heart Failure, 3*(5), 383–385. doi:10.1016/j.jchf.2015.01.008

Milne, S., Orbell, S., & Sheeran, P. (2002). Combining motivational and volitional interventions to promote exercise participation: Protection motivation theory and implementation intentions. *British Journal of Health Psychology, 7,* 163–84. doi:10.1348/135910702169420

Mojet, J., Köster, E. P., Holthuysen, N. T. E., Van Veggel, R. J. F. M., De Wijk, R. A., Schepers, H. E., & Vermeer, F. (2016). The emotional influence of flowers on social perception and memory: An exploratory study. *Food Quality and Preference, 53,* 143–150. doi:10.1016/j.foodqual.2016.06.003

More, T. A., Long, C., Averill, J.. (2004). Solitude, nature, and cities. In: Murdy, James, comp., ed. Proceedings of the 2003 Northeastern Recreation Research Symposium; 2003 April 6–8; Bolton Landing, NY. Gen. Tech. Rep. NE-317. Newtown Square, PA: U.S. Department of Agriculture, Forest Service, Northeastern Research Station: 224–229.

Neal, D. T., Wood, W., Wu, M., & Kurlander, D. (2011). The pull of the past: When do habits persist despite conflict with motives? *Personality and Social Psychology Bulletin, 37*(11), 1428–1437. doi.org/10.1177/0146167211419863

Neff, K. D., & Germer, C. (2017). Self-compassion and psychological wellbeing. In J. Doty (Ed.) *Oxford Handbook of Compassion Science,* Chap. 27. Oxford University Press.

Neyfakh, L. (July 20, 2014). What playfulness can do for you. Retrieved from https://www.bostonglobe.com/ideas/2014/07/19/what-playfulness-can -for-you/Cxd7Et4igTLkwpkUXSr3cO/story.html

Nguyen, T. T., Ryan, R. M., & Deci, E. L. (2018). Solitude as an approach to affective self-regulation. *Personality & Social Psychology Bulletin, 44*(1), 92–106. doi:10.1177/0146167217733073

Ostlund, B. D., Measelle, J. R., Laurent, H. K., Conradt, E., & Ablow, J. C. (2017). Shaping emotion regulation: Attunement, symptomatology, and stress recovery within mother-infant dyads. *Developmental Psychobiology, 59*(1), 15–25. doi:10.1002/dev.21448

Ozbay, F., Johnson, D. C., Dimoulas, E., Morgan, C. A., Charney, D., & Southwick, S. (2007). Social support and resilience to stress: From neurobiology to clinical practice. *Psychiatry (Edgmont), 4*(5), 35–40.

Park, G., & Thayer, J. (2014). From the heart to the mind: Cardiac vagal tone modulates top-down and bottom-up visual perception and attention to emotional stimuli. *Frontiers in Psychology, 5,* 278. doi:10.3389/fpsyg.2014.00278

Pelowski, M., Markey, P. S., Lauring, J. O., & Leder, H. (2016). Visualizing the impact of art: An update and comparison of current psychological models of art experience. *Frontiers in Human Neuroscience, 10,* 160. doi:10.3389/fnhum.2016.00160

Pennebaker, J. W. (2018). Expressive writing in psychological science. *Perspectives on Psychological Science, 13*(2), 226–229. doi:10.1177/1745691617707315

Petersen, S., Schroijen, M., Mölders, C., Zenker, S., & den Bergh, O. V. (2014). Categorical interoception: Perceptual organization of sensations from inside. *Psychological Science, 25*(5), 1059–1066. doi:10.1177/0956797613519110

Philippe, F. L., Lecours, S. & Beaulieu-Pelletier, G. (2009). Resilience and positive emotions: Examining the role of emotional memories. *Journal of Personality, 77,* 139–176. doi:10.1111/j.1467-6494.2008.00541.x

Porges, S. W. (2003). Social engagement and attachment. *Annals of the New York Academy of Sciences, 1008*, 31–47. doi:10.1196/annals.1301.004

Porges, S. W. (2004). Neuroception: A subconscious system for detecting threats and safety. *Zero to Three, 24*(5), 19–24.

Porges S. W. (2006). The polyvagal perspective. *Biological Psychology, 74*(2), 116–43. doi:10.1016/j.biopsycho.2006.06.009

Porges, S. W. (2009). Reciprocal influences between body and brain in the perception and expression of affect: A polyvagal perspective. In D. Fosha, D. J. Siegel, & M. F. Solomon (Eds.), *The power of emotion: Affective neuroscience, development, clinical practice.* New York: Norton.

Porges, S. W. (2010). Music therapy and trauma: Insights from the polyvagal theory. In Stewart, K. (Ed.), *Symposium on music therapy and trauma: Bridging theory and clinical practice.* New York: Satchnote Press.

Porges, S. W. (2011). *The polyvagal theory: Neurophysiological foundations of emotions, attachment, communication, self-regulation.* New York: Norton.

Porges, S. W. (2012). Polyvagal theory: Why this changes everything [Webinar]. In NICABM Trauma Therapy Series.

Porges, S.W. (2014). Talk presented at meeting of New England Society for Trauma and Dissociation, Lexington, MA.

Porges, S. W. (2015a). Making the world safe for our children: Down-regulating defence and up-regulating social engagement to 'optimise' the human experience. *Children Australia, 40*(2), 114–123. doi:10.1017 /cha.2015.12

Porges, S. W. (2015b). Play as a neural exercise: Insights from the polyvagal theory. In D. Pearce-McCall (Ed.), *The power of play for mind-brain health* (pp. 3–7). Available from: http://mindgains.org/

Porges, S. W. (2016). Mindfulness & co-regulation. (Serge Prengel, Interviewer) (Transcript) Retrieved from https://somaticperspectives.com /zug/transcripts/Porges-2016-09.pdf

Porges, S. W. (2017a). *The pocket guide to the polyvagal theory: The transformative power of feeling safe.* New York: Norton.

Porges, S. W. (2017b). Vagal pathways: Portals to compassion. In E. M. Seppälä, E. Simon-Thomas, S. L. Brown, M. C. Worline, C. D. Cameron, & J. R. Doty (Eds.). *Oxford Handbook of Compassion Science*. New York: Oxford University Press.

Porges, S. W. (2017c). The significance of stillness. *Human Givens Journal, 24*(2), 28–35. Retrieved from http://stephenporges.com/images/stillness.pdf

Porges, S. W., & Carter, C. S. (2017). Polyvagal theory and the social engagement system: Neurophysiological bridge between connectedness and breath. In P. L. Gerbarg, P. R. Muskin, & R. P. Brown (Eds.), *Complementary and integrative treatments in psychiatric practice*. Arlington, VA: American Psychiatric Association.

Porges, S. W., & Furman, S. A. (2011). The early development of the autonomic nervous system provides a neural platform for social behaviour: A polyvagal perspective. *Infant and Child Development, 20*(1), 106–118. doi:10.1002/icd.68

Porges, S. W. & Lewis, G. F. (2009). The polyvagal hypothesis: Common mechanisms mediating autonomic regulation, vocalizations and listening. *Handbook of Behavioral Neuroscience, 19*, 255–264. doi:10.1016/B978-0-12-374593-4.00025-5

Rabellino, D., D'Andrea, W., Siegle, G., Frewen, P., Minshew, R., Densmore, M., Neufeld, R., Théberge, J., & Lanius, R.. (2017). Neural correlates of heart rate variability in PTSD during sub- and supraliminal processing of trauma-related cues. *Biological Psychiatry, 81*, S149–S150. doi:10.1016/j.biopsych.2017.02.382

Reger, J., Lind, M., Robinson, M., & Beckerman, A. (2017). Predation drives local adaptation of phenotypic plasticity. *Nature Ecology & Evolution, 2*, 100–107. doi:10.1038/s41559-017-0373-6

Rejeski, W. J., & Gauvin, L. (2013). The embodied and relational nature of the mind: Implications for clinical interventions in aging individuals and populations. *Clinical Interventions in Aging, 8*, 657–65. doi:10.2147/CIA.S44797

Ruini, C., Offidani, E., & Vescovelli, F. (2015). Life stressors, allostatic overload, and their impact on posttraumatic growth. *Loss and Trauma, 20*(2). doi:10.1080/15325024.2013.830530

Sahar, T., Shalev, A., & Porges, S. (2001). Vagal modulation of responses to mental challenge in posttraumatic stress disorder. *Biological Psychiatry, 49,* 637–43. doi:10.1016/S0006-3223(00)01045-3

Schwartz, R. (2001). *Introduction to the internal family systems model.* Oak Park, IL: Trailheads Publications.

Segerstrom, S. C., & Sephton, S. E. (2010). Optimistic expectancies and cell-mediated immunity: The role of positive affect. *Psychological Science, 21*(3), 448–55. doi:10.1177/0956797610362061

Seppälä, E., Rossomando, T., & Doty, J. (2013). Social connection and compassion: Important predictors of health and well-being. *Social Research, 80*(2), 411–430. doi:10.1353/sor.2013.0027

Seuss, Dr. (1960). *One fish, two fish, red fish, blue fish.* New York: Random House.

Shiota, M. N., Keltner, D., & Mossman, A. (2007). The nature of awe: Elicitors, appraisals, and effects on self-concept. *Cognition and Emotion, 21*(5), 944–963. doi:10.1080/02699930600923668

Siegel, D. J. (2007). Mindfulness training and neural integration: Differentiation of distinct streams of awareness and the cultivation of well-being. *Social Cognitive and Affective Neuroscience, 2*(4), 259–263. doi:10.1093/scan/nsm034

Song, C., Ikei, H., & Miyazaki, Y. (2018). Physiological effects of visual stimulation with forest imagery. *International Journal of Environmental Research and Public Health, 15*(2), 213. doi:10.3390/ijerph15020213

Song, C., Ikei, H., & Miyazaki, Y. (2017). Sustained effects of a forest therapy program on the blood pressure of office workers. *Urban Forestry & Urban Greening, 27,* 246–252. doi:10.1016/j.ufug.2017.08.015

Speer, M. E., Bhanji, J. P., & Delgado, M. R. (2014). Savoring the past: Positive memories evoke value representations in the striatum. *Neuron, 84*(4), 847–856. doi:10.1016/j.neuron.2014.09.028

Stellar, J. E., Cohen, A., Oveis, C., & Keltner, D. (2015). Affective and physiological responses to the suffering of others: Compassion and vagal activity. *Personality and Social Psychology, 108*(4), 572–585. doi:10.1037/pspi0000010

Stillman, T. F., Baumeister, R. F., Lambert, N. M., Crescioni, A. W., Dewall, C. N., & Fincham, F. D. (2009). Alone and without purpose: Life loses meaning following social exclusion. *Experimental Social Psychology, 45*(4), 686–694. doi:10.1016/j.jesp.2009.03.007

Stuckey, H. L., & Nobel, J. (2010). The connection between art, healing, and public health: A review of current literature. *American Journal of Public Health, 100*(2), 254–63. doi:10.2105/AJPH.2008.156497

Sullivan, M. B., Erb, M., Schmalzl, L., Moonaz, S., Noggle Taylor, J., & Porges, S. W. (2018). Yoga therapy and polyvagal theory: The convergence of traditional wisdom and contemporary neuroscience for self-regulation and resilience. *Frontiers in Human Neuroscience, 12,* 67. doi:10.3389/fnhum.2018.00067

Taylor, R. P. (2006). Reduction of physiological stress using fractal art and architecture. *Leonardo, 39,* 245–251. doi:10.1162/leon.2006.39.3.245

Taylor R. P., & Spehar, B. (2016) Fractal fluency: An intimate relationship between the brain and processing of fractal stimuli. In A. Di Ieva (Ed.), *The fractal geometry of the brain.* Springer Series in Computational Neuroscience. New York: Springer.

Thayer, J. F., & Sternberg, E. (2006), Beyond heart rate variability. *Annals of the New York Academy of Sciences, 1088,* 361–372. doi:10.1196/annals.1366.014

Tillich, P. (1963). *The eternal now.* New York: Charles Scribner's Sons.

Tronick, E. Z., & Gianino, A. (1986). Interactive mismatch and repair: Challenges to the coping infant. *Zero to Three, 6*(3), 1–6.

Turkle, S. (2011). *Alone together: Why we expect more from technology and less from each other.* New York: Basic Books.

Utz, S., & Breuer, J. (2017). The relationship between use of social network sites, online social support, and well-being: Results from a six-wave longitudinal study. *Media Psychology, 29*(3), 115–125. doi:10.1027 /1864-1105/a000222.

Vaillancourt, M., Chia, P., Sarji, S., Nguyen, J., Hoftman, N., Ruffenach, G., Eghbali, M., Mahajan, A., . . . Umar, S. (2017). Autonomic nervous system involvement in pulmonary arterial hypertension. *Respiratory Research, 18*(1), 201. doi:10.1186/s12931-017-0679-6

Van Cauwenbergh, D., Nijs, J., Kos, D., Van Weijnen, L., Struyf, F., & Meeus, M. (2014). Malfunctioning of the autonomic nervous system in patients with chronic fatigue syndrome: A systematic literature review. *European Journal of Clinical Investigation, 44*(5), 516–26. doi:10.1111/eci.12256

van den Berg, M. M., Maas, J., Muller, R., Braun, A., Kaandorp, W., van Lien, R., van Poppel, M. N., van Mechelen, W., . . . van den Berg, A. E. (2015). Autonomic nervous system responses to viewing green and built settings: Differentiating between sympathetic and parasympathetic activity. *International Journal of Environmental Research and Public Health, 12*(12), 15860–74. doi:10.3390/ijerph121215026

van der Kolk, B. (2014). *The body keeps the score: Brain, mind, and body in the healing of trauma.* New York: Penguin Books.

Wakefield, J., Sani, F., Madhok, V., Norbury, M., Dugard, P., Gabbanelli, C., . . . Poggesi, F. (2016). The relationship between group identification and satisfaction with life in a cross-cultural community sample. *Journal of Happiness Studies.* 10.1007/s10902-016-9735-z.

Webb, T. W. L, Chang, B. P. I., & Benn, Y. (2013) "The Ostrich Problem": Motivated avoidance or rejection of information about goal progress. *Social and Personality Psychology Compass, 11*(7), 794–807. doi:10.1111/spc3.12071

Wells, N. M., & Evans, G. W. (2003). Nearby nature: A buffer of life stress among rural children. *Environment and Behavior, 35*(3), 311–330. doi:10.1177/0013916503035003001

White, M., Smith, A., Humphryes, K., Pahl, S., Cracknell, D., & Depledge, M. (2010). Blue space: The importance of water for preferences, affect and restorativeness ratings of natural and built scenes. *Environmental Psychology, 30,* 482–493. doi:10.1016/j.jenvp.2010.04.004

Wieber, F., Thürmer, J. L., & Gollwitzer, P. M. (2015). Promoting the translation of intentions into action by implementation intentions: Behavioral effects and physiological correlates. *Frontiers in Human Neuroscience, 9,* 395. doi:10.3389/fnhum.2015.00395

Williamson, J. B., Porges, E. C., Lamb, D. G., & Porges, S. W. (2015). Maladaptive autonomic regulation in PTSD accelerates physiological aging. *Frontiers in Psychology*, *5*, 1571. doi:10.3389/fpsyg.2014.01571

Wilson, T., Reinhard, D., Westgate, E., Gilbert, D., Ellerbeck, N., Hahn, C., Brown, C., & Shaked, A. (2014). Just think: The challenges of the disengaged mind. *Science*, *345*, 75–7. doi:10.1126/science.1250830

York III, G., & Steinberg, D. (2011). Hughlings Jackson's neurological ideas, *Brain*, *134*(10), 3106–3113. doi:10.1093/brain/awr219

INDEX

ABOUT THE AUTHOR

Deb Dana, LCSW, is a clinician and consultant specializing in helping people safely explore and resolve the consequences of trauma. She is a consultant to the Traumatic Stress Research Consortium in the Kinsey Institute, lectures internationally on ways Polyvagal Theory informs therapy, and works with organizations wanting to bring a polyvagal-informed approach to working with clients. She developed the Rhythm of Regulation Clinical Training Series and teaches this polyvagal-informed approach to therapy to clinicians around the world.

Deb is the author of *The Polyvagal Theory in Therapy: Engaging the Rhythm of Regulation*, *Polyvagal Exercises for Safety and Connection: 50 Client Centered Exercises*, creator of the *Polyvagal Flip Chart*, and coeditor, with Stephen Porges, *Clinical Applications of the Polyvagal Theory: The Emergence of Polyvagal-Informed Therapies*.

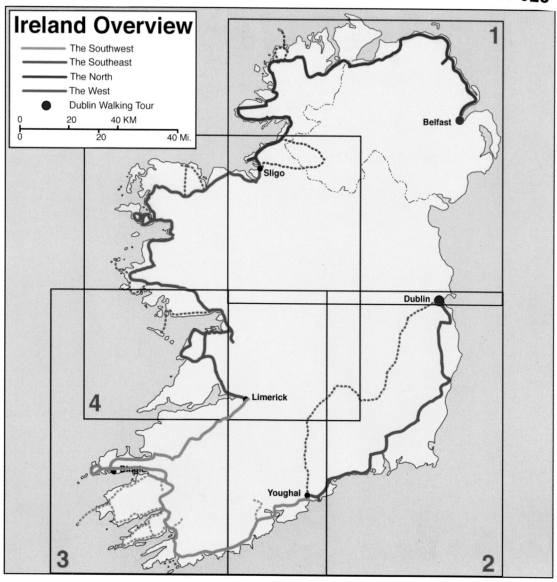

Ireland Overview

- The Southwest
- The Southeast
- The North
- The West
- ● Dublin Walking Tour

0   20   40 KM
0   20   40 Mi.

1

Belfast

Sligo

Dublin

4

Limerick

Dingle

Youghal

3

2

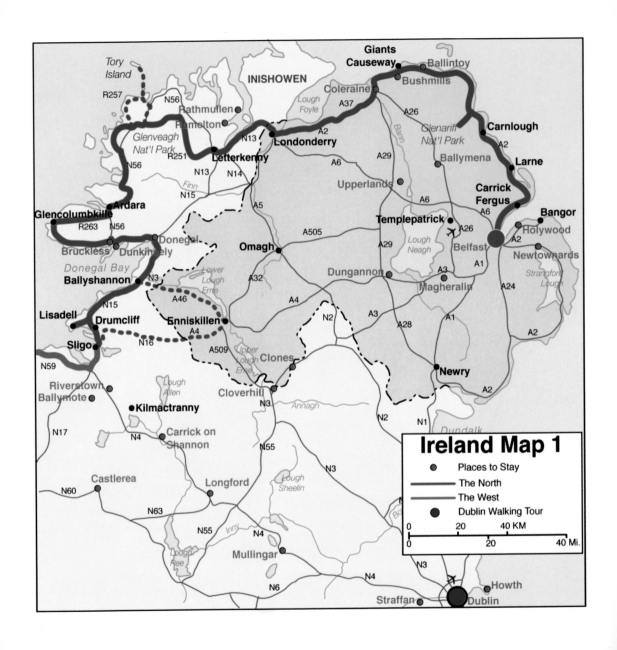

Tory Island

R257

INISHOWEN

Giants Causeway
Ballintoy
Bushmills
Coleraine
A37
A26

N56
Rathmullen
Ramelton
Glenveagh Nat'l Park
R251
N13
Letterkenny
Londonderry
A2
Glenariff Nat'l Park
Carnlough
A2
Larne

N56
N13
N14
N15
Finn

Lough Foyle
A6
A29
Upperlands
A6
Ballymena

Carrick Fergus
A6

Bangor
Holywood

Ardara
A5

Glencolumbkille
R263 N56
Bruckless
Dunkineely
Donegal

Omagh
A505

Templepatrick
A26
Belfast
A2
Newtownards
Strangford Lough

Donegal Bay

Ballyshannon
N3
Lower Lough Erne
A46
A32
A4

Dungannon
A3
Magheralin
A1

A24

N15
Enniskillen
A4
N2
A3
A28
A1
A2

Lisadell
Drumcliff
N16
A509
Upper Lough Erne
Clones

Sligo
N59

Newry
A2

Riverstown
Ballymote
N17
Lough Allen
Kilmactranny
Cloverhill
N3
Annagh
N2
N1
Dundalk

N4
Carrick on Shannon
N55
N3

Castlerea
N60
Longford
Lough Sheelin

N63
N55
Inny

Lough Ree
Mullingar
N4
N6

N3
Howth

Straffan
Dublin

Ireland Map 1

- ● Places to Stay
- —— The North
- —— The West
- ● Dublin Walking Tour

0   20   40 KM

0   20   40 Mi.

Ireland Map 2

- Places to Stay
- The Southwest
- The Southeast
- The West
- Dublin Walking Tour

0   20   40 KM

0   20   40 Mi.

Irish Sea

St. George's Channel

Howth
Dublin
Straffan
Naas
R115
Powerscourt
N4
N7
Dunlavin
Ashford
Rathnew
Glendalough
R755
N11
Wicklow
Aughrim
R752
Carlow
R747
Arklow
N6
N62
N52
N80
Portlaoise
N7
N9
Abbeyleix
Freshford
Bagenalstown
N80
N11
Gorey
Ferns
N65
Shannon
Terryglass
Lough Derg
N52
N18
Thor Balee
Kilkenny
Maddoxstown
Borris
N10
Thomastown
N30
Enniscorthy
Ballymurn
Bunratty
Limerick
N7
Thurles
N8
N62
Suir
N76
Callan
Callan
New Ross
N25
Wexford
Adare
N24
Tipperary
Cashel
Clonmel
N24
R733
Campile
Rosslare
Ballingarry
Cahir
Newcastle
Suir
Nire Valley
Waterford
Arthurstown
Tagoat
Kilmallock
Clogheen
N8
R668
Ballymacarbry
N25
N20
Doneraile
Blackwater
Cappoquin
R675
Mallow
Fermoy
N72
Milstreet
Dungarvan
N20
Castlelyons
Blarney
Youghal
Lee
Cork
Killeagh
Ardmore
Farran
N27
Midleton
Cobh
Shanagarry
N71
Kinsale
R600
Ballinspittle
Killbrittain
Timoleage

Ireland Map 3

- ● Places to Stay
- The Southwest
- The Southeast
- The West

0   20   40 KM
0   20   40 Mi.

ATLANTIC OCEAN

Cashel
Oughterard
Lough Corrib
N17
N59
R388
Galway
Kilconnell
N6
N62
N52
Craughwell
Galway Bay
Shannon
New Qual
Dunguaire
N65
Terryglass
Ballyvaughan
Cliffs of Moher
BURREN
Thor Balee
N67
R478
R480
N18
Lough Derg
N52
N7
Corofin
Lahinch
Ennis
N85
Aran Islands
Miltown Malbay
N68
Newmarket-on-Fergus
N7
N62
Suir
N18 Bunratty
Thurles
N8
River Shannon
Limerick
Adare
Ballingarry
Tipperary
Cashel
N24
Glin
N69
Listowel
N21
Kilmallock
Clonmel
Cahir
Newcastle
N20
Clogheen
N8
Ballynacarbry
R668
Tralee
Doneraile
N70 N23
Kanturk
Mallow
Blackwater
Cappoquin
Millstreet
Ballydavid
DINGLE
R561
N72
Fermoy
N72
R559
Dingle
Beaufort
Killarney
Castlelyons
Youghal
Blasket Islands
Dingle Bay
Lough Leane
Blarney
Killeagh
Ardmore
N70
RING OF KERRY
N71
Kenmare
Macroom
Lee
Cork
Midleton
Sneem
N22
Farran
N27
Cobh
Shanagarry
Gougane Barra
Caherdaniel
Kenmare River
BEARA
Glengarriff
Kinsale
Youghal
Great Skellig
R571
R572
Ballylickey
Bantry
N71
R600
Ballinspittle
Kilbrittain
Dursey Island
Bantry Bay
Schull
N71
Clonakilty
Timoleage
Butlerstown
Goleen
Toormore

Ireland Map 4

● Places to Stay

— The Southwest
— The Southeast
— The North
— The West

0   20   40 KM
0   20   40 Mi.

Ballyshannon N3

N15 A46 Lower Lough Erne A32

Lisadell **Drumcliff** **Enniskillen** A4

Sligo A4

N16 A509 Upper Lough Erne **Clones**

Ceide Fields

Ballycastle R314

R315 N59 Riverstown **Kilmactranny** Lough Allen Cloverhill

Crossmolina Ballymote N3

N59 Lough Conn N26 N5 Carrick on Shannon N3

Achill Island N59 Rosturk R319 N4 N55

Clew Bay **Castlebar** N5 Castlerea Lough Sheelin

Westport N60 N60 Longford

Croagh/Patrick N59 N63 Inny N4

Killary Harbour R335 Leenane Lough Mask N55 **Mullingar**

Inishbofin **CONNEMARA** N17 Lough Ree N6

Letterfrack Leenane Caherlistrane Lough Corrib Kilconnell N62

Clifden Ballynahinch Cashel N59 N6 N52 N80

Roundstone R341 Oughterard **Galway** Shannon

R336 Galway Bay Craughwell N65 N52 Portlaoise

Aran Islands Ballyvaughan **Dunguaire** Terryglass N7

Cliffs of Moher N67 **BURREN** **Thor Balee** Lough Derg N52

R478 R480 N18 Corofin

Lahinch N85 **Ennis** **Abbeyleix**

Miltown Malbay Newmarket-on-Fergus N62 **Freshford**

N68 N18 **Bunratty** N7 Thurles N8 **Kilkenny**

River Shannon **Limerick** N24 N76

Adare

Glin

ATLANTIC OCEAN

Karen Brown's

IRELAND

2008

Rathsallagh House, Dunlavin

Contents

Beneta
you live on in the hearts of everyone
you touched and loved while you were here

Cover painting: Rathsallagh House, Dunlavin.

Author: June Eveleigh Brown.

Editors: Anthony Brown, Clare Brown, Karen Brown, June Eveleigh Brown, Iris Sandilands, Debbie Tokumoto, Melissa Jaworski.

Illustrations: Barbara Maclurcan Tapp.

Cover painting: Jann Pollard.

Front photos: Cottage adjacent to Drumcliff Churchyard, Co Sligo.

Maps: Michael Fiegel, Rachael Kircher-Randolph.

Technical assistance: Andrew Harris

Distributed by National Book Network, 15200 NBN Way, Blue Ridge Summit, PA 17214, USA. Tel: 717-794-3800 or 1-800-462-6420, Fax: 1-800-338-4500, Email: custserv@nbnbooks.com

A catalog record for this book is available from the British Library.

ISSN 1535-7341

Introduction

Writers wax lyrical about Ireland's spectacular scenery: ever-changing landscapes, splendid seascapes, purple moorlands, monastic ruins, enchanting lakes, towering fortresses, and vast, spreading patchworks of fields in every shade of green. Believe every word they say, but realize that it's the people with their open friendliness and warmth of welcome that make a visit to Ireland special. This guide is all about Irish hospitality and staying in places where you are a houseguest rather than a customer. Ireland is not conducive to rushing: the narrow country roads lend themselves to exploration at a leisurely pace where you return the smile and wave of greeting of those you pass. Take time to stop at a pub and be drawn into conversation, and when you get lost, ask directions and learn a bit of history or folklore as a bonus, along with the directions.

About This Guide

Karen Brown's Ireland is written specifically for independent travelers who want to experience a slice of Irish life staying as guests in country houses, farms, and family-run hotels. Our guide is not written for those who want the symmetry of worldwide, hotel chains with their identical bathrooms and mini-bars. The fondest memories of a visit to the Emerald Isle are those of its warm-hearted, friendly people, and there can be no better way to meet the Irish than to stay with them in their homes.

The guide includes all types of lodgings ranging from a simple farmhouse bed & breakfast to a luxurious country estate, owned and run by a welcoming family. These are often the kinds of places where you are expected to carry your own bags. Service may not be the most efficient and occasionally the owners have their eccentricities, which all adds to the allure. There are enough recommendations in every price category to enable you to tailor your trip to your budget. We have recommended accommodation in the widest of price ranges, so please do not expect the same standard of luxury at, for example, Foxmount Farm, as The Park Hotel Kenmare—there is no comparison—yet each is outstanding in what it offers. Rates are quoted in euros in the Republic of Ireland and pounds sterling in Northern Ireland.

To keep you on the right track, we have formed itineraries linking the most interesting sightseeing, enabling you to spend from a few weeks to a month exploring this fascinating island. In addition, we have designed a walking tour of Dublin's fair city that blends culture, history, shopping, and Guinness.

Please supplement this book with the Karen Brown website (*www.karenbrown.com*). Our site contains not only a wealth of information for planning your vacation, but also post-press updates on our guides, and is a handy source for Michelin maps. A great many of the properties in this guide are featured there (their web addresses are on their description pages) with photos and direct links to their email and their own website.

About Ireland

The following pointers are given in alphabetical order, not in order of importance.

AIRFARE

Karen Brown's Guides have long recommended Auto Europe for their excellent car rental services. Their air travel division, Destination Europe, an airline broker working with major American and European carriers, offers deeply discounted coach- and business-class fares to over 200 European gateway cities. It also gives Karen Brown travelers an additional 5% discount off its already highly competitive prices (cannot be combined with any other offers or promotions). We recommend making reservations by phone at (800) 835-1555. When phoning, be sure to use the Karen Brown ID number 99006187 to secure your discount.

CLIMATE

It has been said that there is no such thing as climate in Ireland—only weather, and no such thing as bad weather—only the wrong clothes. This is because the changes in conditions from day to day, and even from hour to hour, seem greater than the changes from one season to the next. The Atlantic Ocean and the air masses moving east give Ireland very little seasonal variation in temperature, producing mild winters and cool summers. The ocean's influence is strongest near the coast, especially in winter when areas bordering the sea are milder than those inland. Coastal areas, particularly in the west, also have less variation in temperature between day and night. Even when it rains, and it does, it never pours—it's just soft Irish rain that keeps the isle emerald. The best thing is to be prepared for sun and sudden squalls at all times.

CLOTHING

Ireland is an easygoing place and casual clothes are acceptable everywhere, even at the fanciest restaurants. Because the weather is changeable, layers of sweaters and shirts that can be added to and removed are recommended. A lightweight, waterproof jacket with a hood is indispensable. Do not haul huge suitcases into bed & breakfasts; rather, we suggest that you have a small suitcase (the size that fits under your airline seat) that you take into the places you stay, leaving larger luggage in the car.

CURRENCY

The unit of currency in Northern Ireland is the pound sterling, while in the Republic of Ireland it is the euro. The two currencies do not have equal value. Visit our website (*www.karenbrown.com/news/currency.html*) for an online currency converter.

An increasingly popular and convenient way to obtain foreign currency is simply to use your bankcard at an ATM machine. You pay a fixed fee for this but, depending on the amount you withdraw, it is usually less than the percentage-based fee charged to exchange currency or travelers' checks. Be sure to check with your bank or credit card company about fees and necessary pin numbers prior to departure.

DRIVING

It is to the countryside that you must go, for to visit Ireland without driving through the country areas is to miss the best she has to offer. Driving is on the left-hand side of the road, which may take a little getting used to if you drive on the right at home, so avoid driving in cities until you feel comfortable with the system. If your arrival city is Dublin, do not pick your car up until you are ready to leave for the countryside. A valid driver's license from your home country is required. Your car will not be an automatic unless you specifically reserve one. Petrol (gasoline) is extremely expensive.

In the Republic, people often do not use road numbers when giving directions: they refer to roads as where they might lead to (e.g., the Cork road). To add to the confusion, new

4   *Introduction: About Ireland*

road signs quote distances in kilometers, while old signs are in miles. The Irish seem to use neither, always quoting distances in the number of hours it takes them to drive.

The distances in Ireland are not great, but often the roads are not great either—though they are getting a lot better. Plan on being in a traffic jam every time a road goes through a town. Roads and motorways around Dublin are nearly always congested. Estimate your journey on the basis of an average of 30 miles (about 50 kilometers) per hour.

The types of roads found in Ireland are as follows:

MOTORWAYS: The letter "M" precedes these fast roads, which have two or three lanes of traffic either side of a central divider. Motorways are more prevalent in Northern Ireland though they are becoming more common between larger towns in the Republic.

NATIONAL ROADS: The letter "N" precedes the road number in the Republic, while in Northern Ireland, the road number is preceded by the letter "A." They are the straightest and most direct routes you can take when motorways are not available.

REGIONAL ROADS: The letter "R" precedes the road number on maps, but their numbers rarely, if ever, appear on signposts. They are usually wide enough for two cars or one tractor.

Off the major routes, road signs are not posted as often as you might wish, so when you drive it's best to plan some extra time for asking the way. Asking the way does have its advantages—you get to experience Irish directions from natives always ready to assure you that you cannot miss your destination—which gives you the opportunity of asking another friendly local the way when you do. One of the joys of meandering along less traveled country roads is rounding a bend to find that cows and sheep take precedence over cars as they saunter up the middle of the road.

DRIVING–CAR RENTAL

Readers frequently ask our advice on car rental companies. We always use Auto Europe—a car rental broker that works with the major car rental companies to find the lowest possible price. They also offer motor homes and chauffeur services. Auto Europe's toll-free phone service, from every European country, connects you to their U.S.-based, 24-hour reservation center (ask for the Europe Phone Numbers Card to be mailed to you). Auto Europe offers our readers a 5% discount (cannot be combined with any other offers or promotions) and, occasionally, free upgrades. Be sure to use the Karen Brown ID number 99006187 to receive your discount and any special offers. You can make your own reservations online via our website, *www.karenbrown.com* (select *Auto Europe* from the home page), or by phone (800-223-5555).

INFORMATION

The Irish Tourist Board (*bord failte*) and Northern Ireland Tourist Board are invaluable sources of information. Outside Ireland, they have combined their organizations under the auspices of "Tourism Ireland." They can supply you with details on all of Ireland and, on request, specific information on accommodation in homes, farmhouses, and manors; and information on festivals, fishing, and the like. The easiest way to contact them is via *www.tourismireland.com.* You can also reach them by phone as follows:

Australia: (0)2 9299 6177
Canada: (800) 223 6470
Great Britain: 0800 0397000
New Zealand: 0 9 977 2255
USA: (800) 669 9967

MAPS

Each of our driving itineraries is preceded by a map showing the route, and each hotel listing is referenced to a map at the front of the book. These are an artist's renderings and, although we have tried to include as much information as possible, you will need a more detailed map to plan your travels. Our preference is for the Michelin Map of Ireland, Map 712, where the scale is 1 centimeter to 4 kilometers (i.e. 1 inch to 6.3 miles), available in our website store at *www.karenbrown.com*.

PUBS

Ireland's pubs will not disappoint—if you do not expect sophisticated establishments. Most of the 12,000 pubs, where the Irish share ideas over frothing pints of ale and porter, have a contagious spirit and charm. Stop at a pub and you'll soon be drawn into conversation. At local pubs, musicians and dancers perform for their own enjoyment, their audience being those who stop by for a drink. If this kind of entertainment appeals to you, ask someone wherever you are staying to recommend a local pub that will have live music that night.

ROOTS

The Potato Famine of the 1840s cut population by a fourth. Through the lean decades that followed, the Irish left by the thousands to make new lives, primarily in the United States, Canada, Australia, and New Zealand. The first step in tracing your Irish roots is to collect together as much information on your Irish antecedent as possible, and to find out from relatives or documents (death or marriage certificates) just where he or she came from in Ireland. Armed with this information, your choices are several:

DO IT YOURSELF: If your ancestors hailed from Southern Ireland, visit the genealogical office on Kildare Street in Dublin. If your ancestors came from Northern Ireland, visit the Public Record Office of Northern Ireland, 66 Balmoral Avenue, Belfast BT9 6NY, which is open for visitors to do their own research.

HAVE SOMEONE DO IT FOR YOU: The Republic's genealogical office charges a small fee, but often has a backlog, so it takes time to do a general search. Write to Chief Herald, General Office of Ireland, 2 Kildare Street, Dublin 2, tel: (01) 603 0200, enclosing whatever information you have on your ancestors.

If your ancestors came from Northern Ireland, send information about them, along with a letter, to one of the following: General Register Office, Oxford House, 49 Chichester Street, Belfast BT1 4HL; Presbyterian Historical Society, Church House, Fisherwick Place, Belfast BT1 6DU.

The major tourist offices have brochures on tracing your ancestors that give more detailed information and provide information on publications that may be of interest to those of Irish descent.

SHOPPING

Prices of goods are fairly standard throughout Ireland, so make your purchases as you find items you like, since it is doubtful that you will find them again at a less expensive price. The most popular items to buy are hand-knitted sweaters, tweeds, crystal, china, and hand-embroidered linens.

Value Added Tax (VAT) is included in the price of your purchases. There is usually a minimum purchase requirement, but it is possible for visitors from non-EU countries to get a refund of the VAT on the goods they buy in one of two ways:

1. If the goods are shipped overseas direct from the point of purchase, the store can deduct the VAT at the time of sale.

2. Visitors taking the goods with them should ask the store to issue a VAT refund receipt. A passport is needed for identification. On departure, **before** you check in for your flight, go to the refund office at Shannon or Dublin airport. Your receipts will be stamped and they may ask to see your purchases. You will be given a cash refund in the currency of your choice.

About Itineraries

To keep you on the right track, we have created driving itineraries covering the most interesting sightseeing. If time allows, you can link the four itineraries together and travel all around Ireland. Each itinerary explores a region's scenic beauty, history, and culture, and avoids its large cities. Along the way, we suggest alternative routes and side trips (indicated in italics). At the beginning of each itinerary, we suggest our recommended pacing to help you decide the amount of time to allocate to each region. Do not try to see all of Ireland in a week—this is frankly impossible. You will enjoy yourself much more if you concentrate on a smaller number of destinations and stay for at least a couple of nights in each, rather than spending most of your precious vacation rushing from place to place. The capricious changes in the weather mean that often what appears sparkling and romantic in sunshine, appears dull and depressing under gathering storm clouds. If the weather is stormy, find a nice place to stay with good company. Once the rain clears, there is much to see. Each itinerary is preceded by an artist's rendering of the proposed route, and outlined on the color maps at the front of the book. We suggest that you outline this on a commercial map: our preference is the Michelin Map of Ireland where the scale is 1 centimeter to 4 kilometers (1/400,000).

Overview Map: Driving Itineraries

The North

Rosgull Peninsula

Tory Island

Giant's Causeway

Glencolumbkille

Donegal

Belfast

The West

Céide Fields

Sligo

Achill
Island

Crossmolina

Lough Gill

Inishbofin
Island

Connemara

Clifden

Galway

Dublin

Dublin
Walking
Tour

Burren

Aran
Islands

Kilkenny

Limerick

Dingle Peninsula

Cashel

Waterford

The Southeast

Killarney

Ring
of Kerry

Kenmare

Blarney

Skellig Michael

Cork

Youghal

Kinsale

Beara Peninsula

The Southwest

- - - - Itinerary Route
········ Alternative Routes
& Sidetrips

About Places to Stay

This book does not cover the many, modern hotels in Ireland with their look-alike bedrooms, televisions, and direct-dial phones. Rather, it offers a selection of personally recommended lodgings that cover the widest range, from a very basic, clean room in a simple farmhouse to a sumptuous suite in an elegant, castle hotel. In some, the decor is less than perfect, but the one thing they all have in common is that their owners offer wholehearted hospitality. We have inspected each and every one, and have stayed in a great many. The accommodations selected are the kind of places that we enjoy. We have tried to be candid and honest in our appraisals and to convey each listing's special flavor so that you know what to expect and will not be disappointed. To help you appreciate and understand what to expect when staying at listings in this guide, the following pointers are given in alphabetical order, not in order of importance.

CHILDREN

The majority of listings in this guide welcome children. A great many places offer family rooms with a double and one or two single beds in a room. If you want to tuck your children up in bed and enjoy a leisurely dinner, many of the listings will—with advance notice—provide an early supper for children.

CHRISTMAS

If the information section indicates that the listing is open during the Christmas holiday season, there is a very good chance that it offers a festive Christmas package.

CREDIT CARDS

Whether or not an establishment accepts credit cards is indicated in the list of icons at the bottom of each description by the symbol ▭CREDIT. We have also specified in the accommodation description which cards are accepted as follows: none, AX–American Express, MC–MasterCard, VS–Visa, or simply, all major.

DIRECTIONS

We give concise driving directions to guide you to the listing, which is often in a more out-of-the-way place than the town or village in the address. We would be very grateful if you would let us know of cases where our directions have proven inadequate.

ELECTRICITY

The voltage is 240. Most hotels, guesthouses, and farmhouses have American-style razor points for 110 volts. If you are coming from overseas, it is recommended that you take only dual-voltage appliances and a kit of electrical plugs. Your host can usually loan you a hairdryer or an iron.

HANDICAP FACILITIES

If there is *at least* one guestroom that is accessible by wheelchair, it is noted with the symbol ♿. This is not the same as saying it meets full disability standards. In reality, it can be anything from a basic ground-floor room to a fully equipped facility. Please discuss your requirements when you call your chosen place to stay to see if they have accommodation that is suitable for you.

HIDDEN IRELAND

Several of the listings are members of Hidden Ireland, a consortium of private houses that open their doors to a handful of guests at a time. All houses are of architectural merit and character with owners to match. These are the kinds of houses where you can indulge yourself by staying with people who have mile-long driveways, grand dining rooms watched over by redoubtable ancestors, four-poster beds that you have to climb into, and vast billiard rooms. The kinds of places most of us can only dream of living in, but where you are very welcome as guests because you are the ones who help the owners pay their central heating bills, school fees, and gardeners. Guests become a part of the household and family life carries on around you—you are not expected to scuttle up to your room. Everyone usually dines together round a polished table and, unless you make special requests, you eat what is served to you. The conversation flows and you meet people you might never have met elsewhere. Early or late in the season, you may find that you are the only guests and you can enjoy a romantic, candlelit dinner in a house full of character and charm. There are lakes full of salmon and stylish modern bedrooms at Delphi, gigantic old-fashioned bedrooms at Temple House, homey friendliness at Lorum Old Rectory, and delightful thematically decorated bedrooms at Quay House. When a property is a member of this group, we note it at the bottom of the description.

Introduction: About Places to Stay   13

ICONS

We have these icons in the guidebooks and more on our website, *www.karenbrown.com.* ❄ Air conditioning in bedrooms, ▬ Breakfast included in room rate, ⚸ Children welcome (age given on website), ♨ Cooking classes offered, ▭ Credit cards accepted, ☎ Direct-dial telephone in room, ▲ Dinner served upon request, ⌂ Dogs by special request, ▦ Elevator, 'Ⴟ' Exercise room, @ Internet or Wireless access available for guests ⊗ Some non-smoking rooms, P Parking available (free or paid), ¶ Restaurant, ⍦ Room Service, ✿ Spa, ≈ Swimming pool, ⌁ Tennis, ▣ TV with English channels in bedrooms, ♥ Wedding facilities, ♿ Wheelchair friendly bedrooms, ⏆ Beach nearby, ⌁ Golf course nearby, ⋀ Hiking trails nearby, ⛐ Horseback riding nearby, ⛷ Skiing nearby, ⚓ Water sports nearby.

Icons allow us to provide additional information about our recommended properties. When using our website to supplement the guides, positioning the cursor over an icon will give you further details.

IRELAND'S BLUE BOOK

Several of our listings are members of the Irish Country Houses Association, usually referred to as The Blue Book because of the distinctive blue color of its brochure. This is an association of owner-managed country houses, hotels, and restaurants. The majority are country house hotels offering accommodation in charming surroundings with restaurants, bars, and room service. However, there are several members who welcome guests to their ancestral homes on house-party lines (much as members of Hidden Ireland) with no bar and a set dinner menu. When a property is a member of this group, we note it at the bottom of the description.

MAPS

At the front of the book are four regional maps showing each recommended place to stay's location. The pertinent regional map number is given at the right on the top line of each accommodation's description.

MEALS

Owners of guesthouses, farmhouses, and bed & breakfasts are often happy to serve an evening meal, if you make arrangements 24 hours in advance. Country houses offer a set menu of more elaborate fare and most offer interesting wines—again, arrangements to dine must be made 24 hours in advance. Whether or not an establishment offers dinner is indicated in the list of icons at the bottom of each description by the symbol ♠. **You cannot just arrive and expect dinner.** Hotels and restaurants offer menus and wine lists, giving you more dining choices. If an establishment has a restaurant we indicate it with a ¶. Our suggestion is that you make arrangements for dinner on the night of your arrival at the same time as you make reservations for accommodation.

RATES

Rates are those quoted to us, either verbally or by correspondence, for the 2008 high season (June, July, and August). The rates given generally cover the least expensive to the most expensive double room (two people sharing a room) inclusive of taxes and, in most cases, breakfast. We do not quote rates for a single person occupying a room. When a listing does not include breakfast in its rates, we mention this in the description. We feel a great deal of resentment when an obligatory service charge of 10–15% is added to the bill, and feel that establishments often use this as a way of padding their rates. Forewarned is forearmed, so we have indicated if an establishment adds a service charge. Please **always check** prices and terms when making a reservation. Rates are quoted in euros in the Republic of Ireland and pounds sterling in Northern Ireland. Prices vary considerably and, on the whole, reflect the type of house in which you will be staying.

From the charm of a simple farmhouse to the special ambiance of a vast sporting estate, each listing reflects the Irish way of life.

RESERVATIONS

When making your reservations, be sure to identify yourself as a "Karen Brown Traveler." The hotels appreciate your visit, value their inclusion in our guide, frequently tell us they take special care of our readers, and many offer special rates to Karen Brown members (visit our website at *www.karenbrown.com*). We hear over and over again that the people who use our guides are such wonderful guests!

It is important to understand that once reservations for accommodation are confirmed, whether verbally by phone or in writing, you are under contract. This means that the proprietor is obligated to provide the accommodation that was promised, and that you are obligated to pay for it. If you cannot, you are liable for a portion of the accommodation charges plus your deposit. Although some proprietors do not strictly enforce a cancellation policy many, particularly the smaller properties in our book, simply cannot afford not to do so. Similarly, many airline tickets cannot be changed or refunded without penalty. We recommend insurance to cover these types of additional expenses arising from cancellation due to unforeseen circumstances. A link on our website (*www.karenbrown.com*) will connect you to a variety of insurance policies that can be purchased online.

Reservations should always be made in advance for Dublin accommodation. In the countryside, space is not so tight and a room can often be had simply by calling in the morning. July and August are the busiest times and if you are traveling to a popular spot, you should make advance reservations. Be specific as to what your needs are, such as a ground-floor room, en suite shower, twin beds, family room. Check the prices, which may well have changed from those given in the book (summer 2008). Ask what deposit to send or give your credit card number. Tell them about what time you intend to arrive and request dinner if you want it. There are several options for making reservations.

EMAIL: This is our preferred way of making a reservation. If the hotel/bed & breakfast is on our website and has email, its web page contains a link to its email. (Always spell out the month as the Irish reverse the American month/day numbering system.)

FAX: If you have access to a fax machine, this is a very quick way to reach a hotel/bed & breakfast. If the place to stay has a fax, we have included the number in the listing. (See EMAIL above about spelling out the month.)

LETTER: If you write for reservations, you will usually receive your confirmation and a map. You should then send your deposit. (See comment on EMAIL about spelling out month.)

TELEPHONE: By telephoning you have your answer immediately, so if space is not available, you can then decide on an alternative. If calling from the United States, allow for the time difference (Ireland is five hours ahead of New York) so that you can call during their business day. Dial 011 (the international code), 353 (Republic of Ireland's code) **or** 44 (Northern Ireland's code), then the city code (dropping the 0), and the telephone number.

SELF-CATERING ACCOMMODATION

An excellent way to explore an area is to rent self-catering accommodation on a weekly basis. You can unpack your bags, put your feet up and make yourself at home, come and go as you please, and eat what you like when you like. Tir Na Fiúise in Terryglass is our only exclusively self-catering properties. Several of the country houses that operate as bed & breakfasts can be rented in their entirety as luxurious homes. A great many listings have additional houses, cottages, and converted outbuildings that range from former coach houses to a one-time hen house. Because our primary focus is on beds, breakfasts, and evening meals, we often do not have space to discuss self-catering accommodation at length. We quote a range of rates: from the smallest unit in the low season to the largest unit in the high season, on a weekly or daily basis. Please discuss your requirements when contacting owners to see if they have accommodation that is suitable for you.

SIGHTSEEING

We have tried to mention sightseeing attractions near each lodging to encourage you to spend several nights in each location.

WEBSITE

Please visit the Karen Brown website (*www.karenbrown.com*) in conjunction with this book. Our website provides trip planning assistance, new discoveries, post-press updates, feedback from you, our readers, the opportunity to purchase goods and services that we recommend (rail tickets, car rental, travel insurance, etc.), and one-stop shopping for our guides, associated maps and watercolor prints. Most of our favorite places to stay are featured with color photos and direct website and email links. Also, we invite you to participate in the Karen Brown's Readers' Choice Awards. Be sure to visit our website and vote so your favorite properties will be honored.

Dublin Walking Tour

KEY

1. Belcamp Hutchinson
2. The Clarence
3. The Merrion
4. Shelbourne Hotel
5. Harrington Hall
6. Number 31
7. Mespil Hotel
8. Waterloo House
▪▪▪▪ Walking Tour

19

Dublin Walking Tour

"In Dublin's fair city, where the girls are so pretty . . ." goes the popular old ballad. The girls are certainly pretty and the city fair, if you can overlook the rash of modern office developments begun in the 1960s and the areas that have been razed and seemingly abandoned. Dublin now appears to have seen the error of its ways and efforts are being made to restore what the bulldozers have spared. A car is more trouble than it is worth in Dublin. If your visit here is at the outset of your trip, we suggest that you not get your car until you are ready to leave or—if Dublin is a stop on your trip—park it for the duration of your stay. Dublin is a walking town, so don comfortable shoes and set out to explore the buildings, streets, and shops of this bustling, friendly city. If you feel weary along the way, there is no shortage of pubs where you can revive yourself with a refreshing drink.

Recommended Pacing: If you select a few museums that appeal to you and simply skirt the exterior of the others, this walking tour can be accomplished in a day, which means that you will need two nights' accommodation in Dublin.

Make your first stop the **Dublin Tourism Centre**, in a sturdy, granite church on Suffolk Street. Here you can book sightseeing tours; purchase ferry, train, and bus tickets; arrange lodgings; find out what is in Dublin—and enjoy a cup of coffee. (*Tel: 01 605 7720, www.visitdublin.com.*) Dublin is easily explored on foot, but as an introduction take one of the double-decker sightseeing buses. The tours run every ten minutes and wind a circular route through the city with a commentary on the significance of the buildings along the route. Your ticket is valid for twenty-four hours. The bus makes frequent stops so you can take the entire tour for an overview of what there is to see and then later use it as transportation between the sights, hopping on and off to visit the places that interest you.

Our walking tour begins at the southern end of O'Connell Street where **O'Connell Bridge** spans the River Liffey dividing the north from the south of Dublin. (It is also just by the city center terminus for buses: those displaying "*An Lar,*" meaning city center, usually end up here.) Turn south into **Westmoreland Street** past the somber, windowless **Bank of Ireland**, which began life in 1729 as the seat of the Irish parliament. Cross the street and enter through the front arch of **Trinity College** into the cobbled square. Founded in 1591 by Elizabeth I, it contains a fine collection of buildings from the 18th to the 20th centuries. Cross the square to the library, where a display center houses the jewel of Trinity College, the ***Book of Kells***, a Latin text of the Four Gospels. A page of this magnificent, illuminated manuscript is turned every month and if you are not overly impressed by the page on display, return to the library bookshop and browse through a reproduction. (*Open daily.*) While at the college visit **The Dublin Experience**, a sophisticated audio-visual presentation that orients you to the main events of Irish history. (*Open end of May–Sep.*)

Retrace your steps to the front gate and turn south into pedestrians-only **Grafton Street**, teeming with people and enlivened by street musicians. Its large, department store, **Brown Thomas**, is popular with visitors.

At the end of Grafton Street, dodge the hurrying buses and cross into the peaceful tranquility of **St. Stephen's Green**, an island of flowers, trees, and grass surrounding small lakes dotted with ducks. On the far side of the square, at 85 and 86 St. Stephen's Green, is **Newman House**, once the home of the old Catholic University (later University College Dublin), which boasted James Joyce amongst its distinguished graduates. Number 85 is restored to its pristine, aristocratic years of the 1740s. On the ground floor are wall reliefs of the god Apollo and his nine muses, done elaborately in stucco. A staircase of Cuban mahogany leads to a reception room with more riotous plasterwork figures on the ceiling. Number 86 has some rooms with interesting associations with the Whaley family and Gerard Manley Hopkins, and the Bishop's Room has been restored to its Victorian splendor. (*Open Jun, Jul, Aug, tours on the hour from noon, tel: 01 706 7422.*)

Return to the north side of the square to the landmark **Shelbourne Hotel**, long recommended as the perfect place to enjoy afternoon tea. Follow **Merrion Row** and turn left into **Merrion Street** passing the back of **Leinster House**, the Irish Parliament. It consists of two chambers—the *Dáil*, the lower house, and the *Seanad*, the upper house or senate. You can tour the building when parliament is not in session. Adjacent to the parliament building is the **National Gallery of Ireland**, which is a Victorian building with about 3,000 works of art. There's a major collection of Ireland's greatest painter, Jack Yeats, and works by Canaletto, Goya, Titian, El Greco, Poussin, Manet, Picasso, and many others. (*Open daily, tel: 01 661 5133, website: www.nationalgallery.ie.*)

Merrion Square is one of Dublin's finest remaining Georgian squares and the onetime home of several famous personages—William Butler Yeats lived at 82 and earlier at 52, Daniel O'Connell at 51, and Oscar Wilde's parents occupied number 1. The jewel of Merrion Square is **Number 29** Lower Fitzwilliam Street (corner of Lower Fitzwilliam Street and Upper Mount Street), a magnificently restored, late 18th-century townhouse.

From the basement through living rooms to the nursery and playroom, the house is meticulously furnished in the style of the period 1790–1820. (*Closed Mon, tel: 01 702 6165.*)

Stroll into **Clare Street**, stopping to browse in **Greene's Bookstore** with its lovely, old façade and tables of books outside.

Detour into **Kildare Street**, where you find the **National Museum** displaying all the finest treasures of the country. There are marvelous examples of gold, bronze, and other ornaments, as well as relics of the Viking occupation of Dublin—the 8th-century Tara Brooch is perhaps the best-known item here.

Merrion Square

Follow the railings of Trinity College to the **Kilkenny Design Centre** and **Blarney Woolen Mills**, fine places to shop for Irish crafts and clothing.

With your back to the front gate of Trinity College, cross into **Dame Street**, where the statue of Henry Grattan, a famous orator, stands with arms outstretched outside the parliament building. Walk along Dame Street past Dublin's most famous 1960s "modern" building, the **Central Bank**, which looks like egg boxes on stilts. Go under the bank and you are in **Temple Bar**, with its narrow cobbled streets and little old buildings. In the daytime it's a place of coffee houses and little shops. At night its narrow streets become very vibrant as the clubs open with many good pubs and lots of restaurants—a favorite place for young people. Returning to Dame Street and a more sedate side of Dublin, you come to **Dublin Castle**, built in the early 13th century on the site of an earlier Danish fortification. The adjoining 18th-century **State Apartments** with their ornate furnishings are more impressive inside than out. (*Open daily, tel: 01 677 7129.*)

Returning to Dame Street, you pass **City Hall** and, on your right, the impressive **Christ Church Cathedral** comes into view. Dedicated in 1192, it has been rebuilt and restored many times. After the Reformation when the Protestant religion was imposed on the Irish people, it became a Protestant cathedral (Church of Ireland). The large crypt remained as a gathering spot and marketplace for the locals (Catholics) who used it for many years, until a rector expelled them because their rowdiness was interrupting church services. Another point of interest is **Strongbow's Tomb**: he was one of the most famous Norman lords of Ireland and, by tradition, debts were paid across his tomb. When a wall collapsed and crushed it, a replacement—an unknown crusader's tomb—was conscripted and named Strongbow's Tomb. (*Open daily, tel: 01 677 8099.*)

Joined to the cathedral by a covered bridge arching across the street is **Dublina**, where you learn the history of Dublin through an audio-visual display. You conclude your tour at the large-scale model of the city and the gift shop. (*Open daily, tel: 01 679 4611.*)

At the junction of High Street and Bridge Street, pause to climb the restored remains of a portion of **Dublin's Walls**. When they were built in 1240, the walls fronted onto the River Liffey.

Just down **Thomas Street** is that thriving Dublin institution, the **Guinness Brewery**, whence flows the national drink. As you near your goal, the smell of roasting grains permeates the air. The Guinness Storehouse, a 7-story glass atrium, is built on the site where Arthur Guinness first signed his 9000-year brewery lease in 1759. Journey through the history of the brewing process, learn the story of the Guinness family, and end your tour with a pint of the black stuff in the Gravity bar with its panoramic views of the city. Of course there are lots of opportunities to purchase souvenirs of all-things Guinness. (*Open daily, tel: 01 408 4800.*)

If you decide not to visit the Guinness Brewery, cross diagonally from the walls to the **Brazen Head** in **Bridge Street**, where you can enjoy that same brew in Dublin's oldest pub. There has been a tavern on this site since Viking times, though the present, rather dilapidated, premises date from 1688. It's always a crowded spot that comes alive late in the evening, when musicians gather for impromptu sessions of traditional music.

Cross the River Liffey and, strolling along the **Inns Quay**, you come to the **Four Courts**, the supreme and high courts of Ireland. You can look inside the fine, circular waiting hall under the beautiful green dome, which allows light through its apex.

Turn left up **Capel Street** and make the third right into **Mary Street** which leads to the busiest pedestrian shopping street in Dublin, **Henry Street**. A short detour down **Moore Street** takes you through Dublin's colorful open-air fruit, vegetable, and flower market.

On reaching **O'Connell Street**, turn left. O'Connell Street has its share of tourist traps and hamburger stores, but it's a lively bunch of Dubliners who walk its promenades—placard-carrying nuns, nurses collecting for charity, hawkers of fruit, flowers, and plastic trinkets—all are there for you to see as you stroll along this wide boulevard and continue past the **Gate Theatre** into **Parnell Square**. At the north end of the square in a restored

18th-century mansion, you find the **Dublin Writers Museum**, where you can view the paintings and memorabilia with an audio tape telling you all about them. Among those featured are George Bernard Shaw, William Butler Yeats, Oscar Wilde, James Joyce, and Samuel Beckett. (*Open daily, tel: 01 872 2077.*)

Retrace your steps down O'Connell Street to the **General Post Office**. The GPO, as it is affectionately known, is a national shrine known as the headquarters of the 1916 revolution. Pass the statue of Daniel O'Connell and the millennium "spike" and you are back at your starting point, O'Connell Bridge.

Four Courts

The Southeast

- ● Orientation/ Sightseeing
- ▬ ▬ Itinerary Route
- ▬ Roads
- • • • Alternative Route & Sidetrips
- ✈ Airport

Dublin
Howth
Powerscourt Gardens & Waterfall
N1
Sally Gap
Rathnew
Glendalough
Annamoe
Wicklow
Vale of Avoca
Avoca
N9
Arklow
Gorey
Kilkenny
N11
R693
Freshford
Ferns
N8
Enniscorthy
Cashel
New Ross
Cahir
N24
Wexford
Waterford
John F. Kennedy Park
Arthurstown
The Vee
Passage East
Lismore
N25
Tramore
N72
Dungarven
N25
Youghal
Cork
N25

Belfast
Dublin

The Southeast

All too often visitors rush from Dublin through Waterford and on to western Ireland, never realizing that they are missing some of the most ancient antiquities and lovely scenery along the seductive little byways that traverse the moorlands and wind through wooded glens. This itinerary travels from Dublin into the Wicklow Mountains, pausing to admire the lovely Powerscourt Gardens, lingering amongst the ancient monastic ruins of Glendalough, visiting the Avoca handweavers who capture the subtle hues of heather and field in their fabric, and admiring the skill of the Waterford crystal cutters.

Glendalough

Recommended Pacing: If you are not a leisurely sightseer, and leav[...] can follow this itinerary and be in Youghal by nightfall. But resist the temp[...] a base for two nights in two places and explore at leisure. If you are not c[...] westward and returning to Dublin via The Vee, Cashel, and Kilkenny, select a pla[...] stay near Cashel or Kilkenny.

Leave Dublin following the N11 in the direction of Wexford. (If you have difficulty finding the correct road, follow signs for the ferry at Dun Laoghaire and, from there, pick up signs for Wexford.) As soon as the city suburbs are behind you, the road becomes a dual carriageway. Watch for signs indicating an exit signposted **Enniskerry** and **Powerscourt Gardens**. Follow the winding, wooded lane to Enniskerry and bear left in the center of the village. This brings you to the main gates of Powerscourt Gardens. As you drive through the vast, parklike grounds, the mountains of Wicklow appear before you, decked in every shade of green. Powerscourt House was burnt to a ruin in 1974: a rook's nest blocked one of the chimneys, and when a fire was lit in the fireplace, the resultant blaze quickly engulfed this grand home. Restoration is under way and, while there are no grand rooms to visit, you can enjoy refreshments at the restaurant and shopping at the Avoca knitwear store. The gardens descend in grand tiers from the ruined house, as if descending into a bowl—a mirror-like lake sits at the bottom. Masses of roses adorn the walled garden and velvet, green, grassy walks lead through the woodlands. Many visitors are intrigued by the animal cemetery with its little headstones and inscriptions—not an uncommon sight in Irish stately homes. (*Open mid-Mar–Oct, tel: 01 204 6000, email: gardens@powerscourt.ie, website: www.powerscourt.ies.*) Leaving the car park, turn left for the 6-kilometer drive to the foot of **Powerscourt Waterfall**, the highest waterfall in Ireland and a favorite summer picnic place for many Dubliners.

Turn to the left as you leave the waterfall grounds to meander along narrow country lanes towards **Glencree**. As you come upon open moorland, take the first turn left for the 8-kilometer uphill drive to the summit of **Sally Gap**. This road is known as the "old military road" because it follows the path that the British built across these wild mountains to aid them in their attempts to suppress the feisty men of County Wicklow.

Dublin early, you
tation—select
continuing
ce to

Powerscourt Gardens

Neat stacks of turf are piled to dry in the sun. Grazing sheep seem to be the only occupants of this vast, rolling moorland. Below **Glenmacnass Waterfall**, the valley opens up to a patchwork of fields beckoning you to **Laragh** and Glendalough.

Glendalough, a monastic settlement of seven churches, was founded by St. Kevin in the 6th century. After St. Patrick, St. Kevin is Ireland's most popular saint. He certainly picked a stunning site in this wooded valley between two lakes to found his monastic order. Amidst the tilting stones of the graveyard, the round tower—still perfect after more than a thousand years—punctuates the skyline. The Interpretive Centre presents a 15-minute movie and display on the history of the area. (*Open all year, tel: 0404 45325.*) Take time to follow the track beyond Glendalough to the Upper Lake (you can also drive there). Tradition has it that St. Kevin lived a solitary life in a hut near here. Farther up on a cliff face is a cave known as St. Kevin's Bed. Here, so the story goes, Kathleen—a beautiful temptress—tried to seduce the saint who, to cool her advances, threw her into the lake.

Retrace the road to Laragh, turn right, and travel south through the village of Rathdrum where sturdy stone cottages line the street, and continue through the crossroad following signposts for **Avondale House**, the home of Charles Stewart Parnell. Parnell was born into the ruling Anglo-Irish gentry; but, due in part to the influence of his more open-minded mother, an American, he became the leading light in Ireland's political fight for independence. His downfall was his long-term affair with a married English lady. The house is sparsely furnished and takes just a few minutes to tour. You can also wander around the estate with its wonderful trees. (*Open mid-Mar–Oct, tel: 0404 46111.*)

Leave Avondale to the left and you soon join the main road that takes you through the **Vale of Avoca** to the "Meeting of the Waters" at the confluence of the rivers Avonmore and Avonbeg. Detour into **Avoca** to visit the **Avoca Handweavers**. You are welcome to wander amongst the skeins and bobbins of brightly hued wool to see the weavers at work and talk to them above the noise of the looms. An adjacent shop sells tweeds and woolens. (*Open daily all year, tel: 01 286 7466.*)

At **Arklow** join the N11, a broad, fast road taking you south through Gorey and Ferns to **Enniscorthy**. Amidst the gray stone houses, built on steeply sloping ground by the River Slaney, lies a Norman castle. Rebuilt in 1586, the castle houses a folk museum that includes exhibits from the Stone Age to the present day, with emphasis on the part played by local people in the 1798 rebellion against English rule. (*Open all year, tel: 054 35926.*)

Take the N30 towards Waterford and just before **New Ross**, turn left towards Arthurstown. After about 1 kilometer, turn right for the **Kennedy Homestead** in **Dunganstown**, where the great-grandfather of American President John F. Kennedy lived before being driven from Ireland by the terrible potato famine of the 1840s. His simple, family cottage has been rather overly restored, but the rural location has changed little since the American branch of the family left Ireland. Interestingly, the farm is still owned by a Kennedy. (*Tel: 051 388264, email info@kennedyhomestead.com.*) Leaving the homestead, continue along the country lane to the main road and the **John F. Kennedy Arboretum**, a memorial to the slain president of row upon row of trees. (*Open all year, tel: 051 388171.*)

Leave the arboretum towards Arthurstown and, at the first Y in the road, take the right-hand fork for the short drive to Great Island and **Kilmokea** at **Campile** with its 7 acres of lovely gardens. Around the house are the formal, walled gardens and a heavy, wooden door set into the stone wall leading you to the winding paths of the woodland garden. Enjoy an excellent lunch or afternoon tea in the conservatory tearoom, and ask for directions for the short cut down narrow lanes to **Arthurstown**, where the **Passage East ferry** takes you across the estuary to **Passage East**, the tiny village on the western shores of Waterford harbor. Arriving at the N25, you turn right to visit the town of **Waterford** fronting the River Suir, and left to arrive at the **Waterford Crystal Factory**. This is a very worthwhile excursion, as the tours give you an appreciation for why these hand-blown, hand-cut items are so expensive. It takes many years to become a master craftsman, and one little mistake in the intricate cutting means painstaking hours of work are wasted and the defective item is simply smashed and recycled—there are no seconds. (Waterford crystal items are uniformly priced throughout the country.) It is a very popular venue, the stopping place for seemingly every coach tour. Fortunately, separate transportation is provided to shuttle individual tourists to and from the factory. I thoroughly enjoyed touring with a guide who allowed plenty of time to watch the skilled workmen. The showroom displays the full line of Waterford's production, from shimmering chandeliers to sparkling stemware. The visitors' center also has a gift shop, tourist information center, and café. (*Open daily, tel: 051 332500, fax: 051 332716, www.waterfordvisitorscentre.com.*)

If the weather is inclement, stay on the N25 in the direction of Cork, but otherwise meander along the coast road by doubling back in the direction of Waterford for a **very short** distance, turning to the right to **Tramore**, a family holiday town, long a favorite of the "ice-cream-and-bucket-and-spade" brigade. Skirting the town, follow the beautiful coastal road through **Annestown** to **Dungarvan**.

Where the coastal road meets the N25, detour from your route, turning sharp left to **Shell House**. Like it or hate it, there is nothing quite like it on any suburban street in the world—a cottage where all available wall surfaces are decorated with colored shells in various patterns.

Returning to the main road after crossing Dungarvan harbor, the N25 winds up and away from the coast, presenting lovely views of the town and the coast. If you haven't eaten, try **Seanachie** (a restored, thatched farmhouse, now a traditional restaurant and bar), which sits atop the hill and serves good Irish and Continental food. After passing through several kilometers of forests, turn left on the R673 to **Ardmore**, following the coastline to the village. Beyond the neatly painted houses clustered together lies the **Ardmore Monastic Site**. The well-preserved round tower used to have six internal timber landings joined by ladders, and at the top was a bell to call the monks to prayer or warn of a hostile raid. The round tower is unique to Ireland, its entrance door placed well above the ground: entry was gained by means of a ladder, which could be drawn up whenever necessary. Early Christian monks built round towers as protection against Vikings and other raiders. Leaving the ruins, turn left in the village for **Youghal** where this itinerary ends. Sightseeing in Youghal is outlined in the following itinerary. From Youghal you can continue west to follow *The Southwest* itinerary, or take the following alternative route back to Dublin via The Vee, Cashel, and Kilkenny.

Youghal

ROUTE FROM YOUGHAL TO DUBLIN VIA THE VEE, CASHEL, AND KILKENNY

From Youghal, retrace your steps towards Waterford to the bridge that crosses the River Blackwater, and turn sharp left (before you cross the river) on **Blackwater Valley Drive**, a narrow road which follows the broad, muddy waters of the Blackwater through scenic wooded countryside. The "drive" is well-signposted as "Scenic Route." Quiet country roads bring you into **Lismore**. Turn left into town and right at the town square. Cross the river and take the second road to the left, following signs for **Clogheen** and **The Vee**. As the road climbs, woods give way to heathery moorlands climbing to the summit where the valley opens before you—a broad "V" shape framing an endless patchwork of fields in every shade of green.

Continue on to **Cahir Castle**, which has stood on guard to defend the surrounding town of **Cahir** since 1375. A guided tour explains the elaborate defensive system, making a visit here both interesting and informative. A separate audio-visual presentation provides information about the castle and other monuments in the area. (*Open Oct–May, closed Mon, tel: 052 41011.*)

Leaving the castle, continue through the town square for the 16-kilometer drive to **Cashel**. The **Rock of Cashel** seems to grow out of the landscape as you near the town and you can see why this easily defensible site was the capital for the kings of Munster as long ago as 370 A.D. In the course of converting Ireland to Christianity, St. Patrick reached the castle and, according to legend, jabbed his staff into the king's foot during the conversion ceremony. The king apparently took it all very stoically, thinking it was part of the ritual. Upon reaching the summit of the rock, you find a 10th-century round tower, a 13th-century cathedral, and a 15th-century entrance building or Hall of Vicars Choral—a building which was sensitively restored in the 1970s and now houses some exhibits including St. Patrick's Cross, an ancient Irish high cross of unusual design. (*Open all year, tel: 062 61437.*) If you overnight in or near Cashel, be sure to enjoy **Brú Ború**, a foot-tapping evening of traditional Irish entertainment in the theater below the Rock. (*Jun–Sep, Tue–Sat, 9 pm, tel: 062 61122, fax: 062 62700.*)

Rock of Cashel

Leave Cashel on the N8 for the 40-kilometer drive northeast to **Urlingford**, where you bear right through **Freshford** for the 27-kilometer drive to **Kilkenny** (see listings). Kilkenny is quite the loveliest of Irish towns and it is easy to spend a day here sightseeing and shopping. Entering the town, turn left at the first traffic lights along the main street and park your car outside the castle.

Kilkenny Castle was originally built between 1195 and 1207. The imposing building, as it now stands, is a mixture of Tudor and Gothic design and is definitely worth a visit. The east wing picture gallery is flooded by natural light from the skylights in the roof and displays a collection of portraits of the Ormonde family, the owners of Kilkenny Castle from 1391 until 1967. (*Open all year, tel: 056 21450.*)

Opposite the castle entrance, the stables now house the **Kilkenny Design Centre**, a retail outlet for goods of Irish design and production: silver jewelry, knits, textiles, furniture, and crafts.

Undoubtedly, the best way to see the medieval buildings of Kilkenny is on foot. A walking tour starts from the tourist office in the **Shee Alms House**, just a short distance from the castle. Stroll up High Street into Parliament Street to **Rothe House**. The house, built in 1594 as the home of Elizabethan merchant John Rothe, is now a museum depicting how such a merchant lived. You should also see **St. Canice's Cathedral** at the top of Parliament Street. The round tower dates from the 6th century, when St. Canice founded a monastic order here. Building began on the cathedral in 1251, though most of the lovely church you see today is an 1864 restoration.

Alleyways, with fanciful names such as The Butter Slip, lead you from the High Street to St. Kieran Street where you find **Kylters Inn**, the oldest building in town. This historic inn has a lurid history—supposedly a hostess of many centuries ago murdered four successive husbands, was then accused of witchcraft, and narrowly escaped being burnt at the stake by fleeing to the Continent.

This is an area noted for its craftspeople (leatherworkers, potters, painters) and culinary artists, resulting in a plethora of restaurants and craft shops in the surrounding villages, making this a very interesting area in which to spend several days. I always head for the **Nicholas Mosse Pottery** in Bennetsbridge where you can purchase quality seconds, as well as watch skilled potters making and decorating this classic spongewear. (*Open all year, tel: 056 27105, fax: 056 27491, website: www.nicholasmosse.com.*)

The Southwest

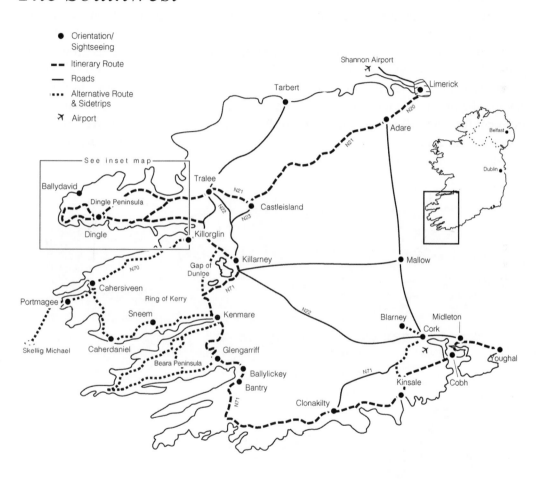

- ● Orientation/ Sightseeing
- ▬ ▬ Itinerary Route
- ▬ Roads
- ▪▪▪▪ Alternative Route & Sidetrips
- ✈ Airport

See inset map

Shannon Airport

Limerick

Tarbert

Belfast

Dublin

Adare

N20

N21

Tralee

N21

Castleisland

N22

N23

Ballydavid

Dingle Peninsula

Killorglin

Dingle

Gap of Dunloe

Killarney

Mallow

N70

Cahersiveen

Ring of Kerry

Portmagee

N71

Sneem

Kenmare

Blarney

Midleton

Skellig Michael

Caherdaniel

Beara Peninsula

Glengarriff

N22

Cork

Youghal

Ballylickey

Bantry

N71

Kinsale

Cobh

N71

Clonakilty

37

The Southwest

The scenery of the southwest is absolutely magnificent: the mellow charm of Kinsale Harbor, the rugged landscape that winds you towards Glengarriff and its island filled with subtropical vegetation, the pretty 19th-century town of Kenmare, the translucent lakes of Killarney, and the ever-changing light on spectacular seascapes on the Dingle Peninsula. Relish the fabled beauties of this lovely part of Ireland. Take time to detour to Blarney to take part in the tradition of climbing atop Blarney Castle to kiss the stone that is said to confer "the gift of the gab." Do not hurry: allow time to linger over breakfast, enjoy a chat over a glass of Guinness, sample fresh salmon and scallops, and join in an evening singsong in a local pub.

Kinsale

Recommended Pacing: For this itinerary, select two places to stay near the coast, one in either Kenmare or Killarney, and one in Dingle. Allow one or two nights in each spot.

Your journey to the southwest begins in **Youghal** (pronounced "yawl"). Sir Walter Raleigh, who introduced the potato and tobacco from the New World, was once its mayor. It's a pleasant, old town dominated by the clock tower, which was built in 1776 and served as the town's jail. The one-way traffic system makes it impossible to explore without parking the car and walking. Several of the Main Street shops have been refurbished, but the town still has an unspoiled look to it. Make your first stop the **Heritage Centre** with its displays on the town, where you can pick up a brochure that outlines a walking tour of the old buildings.

Traveling the N25, a 30-kilometer drive brings you to the heart of **Midleton** where you find the **Jameson Heritage Centre** in the old whiskey distillery. Marvel at the world's largest pot distillery in the courtyard (capacity 143,872 liters), learn about whiskey production, visit the huge waterwheel, and be rewarded by a sample of the golden liquor. There's also a shop and café. (*Open Mar–Oct, tel: 021 4631821.*)

Nearby **Cobh** (pronounced "cove") was renamed Queenstown to mark the visit of Queen Victoria in 1849 and reverted back to Cobh in 1922. There's a long tradition of naval operations here, as its large harbor is a safe anchorage. The **Cobh Experience**, an audio-visual display housed in the restored Victorian railway station, tells the story of this port. Cobh was the point of departure for many emigrants off to seek a better life in America and Australia. For many it was the last piece of Irish soil they stood on before taking a boat to a new life. The ill-fated *Lusitania* was torpedoed not far from Cobh and survivors were brought here. It was also the last port of call of the *Titanic*. There's an excellent shop and café—an enjoyable place to spend a couple of hours on a rainy day. (*Open May–Sep.*)

Retrace your steps a short distance to the **Carriagaloe-Glenbrook ferry**, which transports you across Cork harbor and eliminates the hassle of driving through Cork city. A short, countryside drive brings you to **Kinsale**, its harbor full of tall-masted boats.

Narrow, winding streets are lined with quaint and several sadly derelict houses lead up from the harbor. Kinsale has some attractive shops and a great variety of restaurants. For lunch, Fishy Fishy is an excellent choice. At all but the ethnic restaurants, reservations are needed for dinner. It's a pleasant pastime to check the menus on display as you inhale mouth-watering aromas and peek at happy people enjoying their food. A good way to orient yourself is to take the walking tour which leaves the tourist office at 11:15 am.

There has been a fortress in Kinsale since Norman times. A great battle nearby in 1601 precipitated the flight of the earls and sounded the death knell of the ancient Gaelic civilization. It was from Kinsale that James II left for exile after his defeat at Boyne Water.

About 3 kilometers east of Kinsale, the impressive, 17th-century **Charles Fort** stands guard over the entrance to its harbor. It takes several hours to tour the five bastions that make up the complex. The ordnance sheds are restored and hold a photographic and historical exhibition about the fort. (*Open mid-Mar–Oct, tel: 021 4772263.*)

Across the estuary, you see the 1603 **James Fort** where William Penn's father was governor of Kinsale, while William worked as a clerk of the Admiralty Court. Later, William was given a land grant in America on which he founded the state of Pennsylvania.

SIDE TRIP TO BLARNEY

*About a half-hour drive north of Kinsale lie **Blarney Castle** and its famous tourist attraction, the **Blarney Stone**. Kissing the Blarney Stone, by climbing atop the keep and hanging upside-down, is said to confer the "gift of the gab." Even if you are not inclined to join in this backbreaking, unhygienic pursuit, the castle is worth a visit. (Open all year, tel: 021 4385252.) The gardens are beautiful, there's several well-signposted walks, the village is adorable with its shops round the village green, and there's a great shopping opportunity at **Blarney Woolen Mills** for allthings Irish, particularly knitwear.*

Blarney Castle

Leave Kinsale along the harbor, cross the River Bandon, and follow country lanes to the sleepy, little village of **Ballinspittle**. As you drive through the village, it is hard to imagine that in 1985 it was overwhelmed by pilgrims. They came to the village shrine after a local girl reported seeing the statue of the Virgin Mary rocking back and forth. You pass the shrine on your right just before you come to the village. Follow country lanes to **Timoleague**, a very small coastal village watched over by the ruins of a Franciscan abbey, and on to the N71 and **Clonakilty** and **Skibbereen**. As you travel westwards, rolling fields in every shade of green present themselves.

Arriving at the waterfront in **Bantry**, you come to **Bantry House**. Like so many other Irish country houses, it has seen better days, but the present owner, Egerton Shelswell-White, makes visitors welcome and gives a typed information sheet—in the language of your choice—that guides you room-by-room through the house. The house has a wonderful collection of pictures, furniture, and works of art, brought together by the second Earl of Bantry during his European travels in the first half of the 19th century. In contrast to his ancestors' staid portraits, Egerton is shown playing his trombone. (*Open mid-Mar–Oct, tel: 027 50047.*)

Apart from furnishing the house, the second Earl, inspired by the gardens of Europe, laid out a formal Italian garden and a "staircase to the sky," the steep terraces rising up to the crest of the hill behind the house. There's a marvelous view of the house and Bantry Bay from the top. If you are not up to the climb, you can still enjoy a magnificent, though less lofty view across the boat-filled bay from the terrace in front of the house. A very pleasant cafe occupies the old kitchen. One wing of the house has been renovated and modernized to provide upmarket bed & breakfast accommodation.

In the stable block next to the house, the **1796 Bantry French Armada Centre** relates the story of the French Armada's attempt to invade Ireland in 1796. It failed and a model of one of the armada's ships that sank in Bantry Bay is on display—a very interesting look at a little-known piece of Irish history. (*Open Apr–Oct, tel: 027 50047.*)

Eight kilometers north lies **Ballylickey**.

SIDE TRIP TO GOUGANE BARRA LAKE

*From Ballylickey an inland excursion takes you to **Gougane Barra Lake**, a beautiful lake locked into a ring of mountains. Here you find a small hotel where you can stop for a snack or a warming drink, and a little church on an island in the lake, the oratory where St. Finbarr went to contemplate and pray. The road to and from the lake takes you over a high pass and through mountain tunnels.*

Continue along the N71 and just before you enter **Glengarriff**, turn left for the harbor to take a ferryboat for the ten-minute ride to Garinish Island, a most worthwhile trip. (*Harbour Queen Ferryboats, tel: 027 63116, fax: 027 63298.*) **Garinish Island**, once a barren rock where only gorse and heather grew, was transformed into a miniature botanical paradise at the beginning of this century by a Scottish politician, Arran Bryce. The sheltered site of the island provides perfect growing conditions for trees, shrubs, and flowers from all over the world. It took a hundred men over three years to sculpt this lovely spot with its formal Italian garden, caseta, and temple. (*Open Apr–Oct, closed Sat, tel: 027 63081.*)

From Glengarriff, the road winds upwards and, glancing behind, you have a spectacular view of **Bantry Bay** lying beyond a patchwork of green fields. Rounding the summit, the road tunnels through a large buttress of rock and you emerge to stunning views of sparse, rocky hillsides.

Cross the River Kenmare into **Kenmare**. This delightful town of gray stone houses, with gaily painted shopfronts lining two broad main streets, is a favorite with tourists who prefer its peace and charm to the hectic pace of Killarney. Kenmare is full of excellent shops: **Cleo's** has outstanding knitwear, **Quills** has vast quantities of woolens, **Brenmar Jon** sells top-of-the-line fine knitwear, **The Craft Shop** offers souvenirs and pottery, and **Nostalgia** offers antique and new linen and lace. The town also has some delightful restaurants: **The Purple Heather**, a daytime bistro; **Packies**, a lively restaurant; the charming **Lime Tree** restaurant in the Old Schoolhouse; and **The Park Hotel** with its opulent afternoon silver-service teas and superb restaurant. Visit the **Heritage Centre** with its displays of locally made lace (*tel: 064 41233*). Just a short walk from the Heritage Centre, the **Kenmare Stone Circle** is the largest in the southwest of Ireland. Walks abound, from strolling along the broad river estuary to strenuous hill hikes. Kenmare is a perfect base for exploring both the Iveragh (Ring of Kerry) and Beara peninsulas and for visiting Killarney. It also serves as a stepping-off point for a side trip to Skellig Michael.

SIDE TRIP TO THE BEARA PENINSULA

If you do not stop along the way, it will take you between two and three hours to drive the **Beara Peninsula***, where the scenery is wild, but gorgeous. From Kenmare, a minor road (R571) takes you along the north shore of the peninsula to* **Ardgroom***, a picturesque village nestled beside a little harbor at the foot of the mountains. Farther west,* **Eyeries** *village looks out over the Skellig Rocks and several rocky inlets. Behind the village, the mountain road rises up through the Pass of Boffickle for a fantastic view back over the bay. In the 19th century,* **Allihies** *was a center of the copper mining industry, but now it is a resort with a magnificent beach curving along the bay. At the most westerly point of the peninsula lies* **Garinish***, where a cable car takes visitors over to* **Dursey Island***.*

Dursey is a long, mountain island encircled by high cliffs. Offshore are several other islands, the most interesting of which is Bull Rock, a roosting place for gannets. A cave passes right through it, creating a massive rock arch.

Skirting the southern shore of the peninsula, the narrow road hugs the ocean through **Castletownbere** *and* **Adrigole***, from where you can follow the coastal road into Glengarriff or take the opportunity for a spectacular view by turning left and ascending the* **Healy Pass***. It's hard to turn and admire the vista of* **Bantry Bay** *as the road gently zigzags up the pass, so stop at the top to relish the view before continuing down to* **Lauraugh,** *where you turn right for Kenmare.*

The Southwest

SIDE TRIP TO IVERAGH PENINSULA—RING OF KERRY

Instead of following the itinerary, you can use the Ring of Kerry as a route to Dingle or Killarney, or as a daytrip, traveling the complete "Ring" from Kenmare to Kenmare.

*The drive round the **Iveragh Peninsula** is, in my opinion, somewhat overrated, but if you want to see the much-publicized **Ring of Kerry**, hope that the fickle Irish weather is at its best. For when mists wreathe the Ring, it takes a lot of imagination to conjure up seascapes as you drive down fog-shrouded lanes. Even if the weather is dull, do not lose heart because at any moment the sun could break through. Driving the Ring can be a trial during the busy summer months when the roads are choked with tourist coaches, but your trip will be more enjoyable if you take advantage of some local knowledge before starting your journey. The coaches leave Killarney between 10 and 11 am and travel around the Ring in a counterclockwise direction, arriving back in Killarney by 5 pm. I prefer to meet the coaches head on (see below) rather than inhale their exhaust fumes and suggest an early start to meet them later in the day. If you prefer to avoid them totally: make an early start, travel counterclockwise, and make certain that you are beyond Killarney before 9:30 am.*

*Beginning the Ring, a pleasant drive takes you along the Kenmare river estuary and you get tempting glimpses of water and the Beara Peninsula. Arriving at **Sneem**, enjoy the most picturesque village on the Ring, with its tiny, gaily painted houses bordering two village greens. (The most beautiful coastal scenery lies between Sneem and Waterville.)*

*Continuing your journey westward you come to **Caherdaniel** village where you turn left for **Derrynane House**, the home of Daniel O'Connell, "The Liberator," a title he earned for winning Catholic emancipation. If the weather is inclement, concentrate on the house with its furnished rooms, audio-visual presentation, museum, and tearooms. But if the weather is fine, spend your time outdoors walking along the sandy beach of Derrynane Bay and crossing the narrow strip of sand that separates the mainland from **Abbey Island** where St. Fionan founded a monastic order over 1,000 years ago. Just round the point lies **Iskeroon** and **Bunavalla** pier where boats leave for the Skellig Islands (see*

*"Side Trip to Skellig Michael"). A panoramic view of Derrynane Bay can be enjoyed form the **Scariff Inn**—you cannot miss the landmark bright-red pub sitting beside the road 3 kilometers above the seashore.*

*Cresting the Coomakesta Pass, you turn north for **Waterville**, an aptly named town surrounded by water. Its main street with several colorfully painted houses is built along the shore. From here a pleasant drive takes you to **Cahersiveen,** a classic Irish town with a long main street made up of shops and pubs. Onwards you go to **Killorglin** and then to **Killarney** and back to **Kenmare** (see Kenmare to Killarney drive on next page). However, our suggested route for your return to Kenmare is to take a right-hand turn to **Caragh Lake** (5 kilometers before your reach Killorglin) and follow the narrow lanes around this beautiful lake and across the rugged **Macgillycuddy's Reeks** (Ireland's highest mountains) to Blackwater Bridge (on the Ring) and Kenmare—a trip to be undertaken only on a clear day.*

SIDE TRIP TO SKELLIG MICHAEL

***Skellig Michael** is a very special place, a rocky island topped by the ruins of an ancient monastery lying 12 kilometers off the coast of the Ring of Kerry. Boats run daily between Easter and October, and you need to call at least two days in advance to make a reservation. However, the trip to the island cannot be counted upon until the actual day because it depends on calm seas. Boat service operates from several harbors on the Ring of Kerry—Bunavalla: Kenneth Roddy, www.skelligtrips.com, email: ken@skelligtrips.com; Seamus Shea, tel: 066 9475129; Portmagee: Des Lavelle, tel: 066 9476124, email: lavelles@indigo.ie; or Brendan O'Keefe, Fisherman's Bar, tel: 066 9477103. Remember to wear flat-heeled shoes and take a waterproof jacket, an extra sweater, and lunch. The morning departure for the island and the late afternoon return necessitate your spending two nights on the Ring of Kerry (see listings in Caherdaniel, and Kenmare).*

View to Little Skellig from Skellig Michael

After you arrive at the cove beneath the looming rock, the first part of your ascent follows the path to the abandoned lighthouse, past seabirds' nests clinging to tiny crevasses in the steep rock slopes. As you round a corner, the monks' stairway appears and you climb up hundreds and hundreds of hand-hewn stone steps to the monastery perched on a ledge, high above the pounding ocean. Pausing to catch your breath, you marvel at the monks who set out in fragile, little boats to establish this monastery and toiled with crude implements to build these steps up the sheer rock face.

At the summit, six little beehive huts, a slightly larger stone oratory, and the roofless walls of a small church nestle against the hillside, some poised at the edge—only a low stone wall between them and the churning ocean far below. The windowless interiors of the huts hardly seem large enough for a person to lie down. Remarkably, the monks' only water source was rainwater runoff stored in rock fissures. The Office of Public Works is maintaining and restoring the site and there might be someone there to impart information.

It is reputed that the monks arrived in 600 A.D. According to annals, the Vikings raided in 812 and 823 and found an established community. It is documented that the last monks departed in the 13th century. When it is time to leave this spot, you feel a sense of wonder for the men who toiled in this rocky place, enduring deprivation, hardship, and solitude to achieve a state of grace.

*As a complement (or alternative) to visiting Skellig Michael, visit the **Skellig Heritage Centre** on Valencia Island. The center is found where the road bridge meets the island, directly opposite Portmagee. An audio-visual presentation, "The Call of the Skelligs," takes you to the Skellig Michael monastery while displays show the bird and sea life of the islands. (Open Apr–mid-Nov, tel: 066 9476306.)*

From Kenmare travel over one of Ireland's most beautiful roads (N71) for the twisty 34-kilometer drive over mountains to Killarney, stopping at **Ladies' View** to admire a spectacular panorama with the lakes of Killarney spread at your feet.

In amongst the woodlands you find the car park for **Torc Waterfall**. Following the stream, a short uphill walk brings you to the celebrated 20-meter cascade of water.

Muckross House and Gardens are 5 kilometers out of Killarney on the Kenmare road. (Be sure to choose the entrance gate that enables you to take your car to the car park beside the house). Tudor-style Muckross was built in 1843 in an enviable position beside the lake. The main rooms are furnished in splendid Victorian style and the remainder of the house serves as a folk museum with various exhibits. There's also a bustling gift shop and tearoom. (*Open daily, Mar–Nov, tel: 064 31440, fax: 064 33926.*) The gardens surrounding the house are lovely, containing many subtropical plants, and there is no more delightful way to tour the grounds than by horse and trap. Take a step back in time and visit **Muckross Traditional Farms** (the entrance is on the opposite side of the car park to the house). Stroll up the lane (or ride the old bus) to visit three farms that demonstrate what Kerry farming was like in the 1930s before the advent of electricity and farming machinery. Chat with the farmers and their wives as they go about their daily work. Muckross House and its vast estate were given to the Irish nation by the Bourne family of California, who had a smaller, lakeside estate, Filoli, just south of San Francisco.

Believe everything you ever read about the magnificent beauty of the Killarney lakes, but realize that **Killarney**, not an attractive town, is absolutely packed with tourists during the summer season. If you would like additional views of the lakes, then a tour to Aghadoe Hill or a boat trip from Ross Castle should give you what you are looking for. Leave Killarney on the road to Tralee (N22) and turn left for the 5-kilometer drive to **Aghadoe**, where Killarney town, lakes, and mountains can all be seen from this vantage point. If you prefer a close look at the lake and its island, take the 90-minute boat tour of the lower lake, which leaves from the jetty alongside Ross Castle. Tickets for this trip can be purchased from the tourist office in town. **Ross Castle** has been restored and you can climb its steep, stone stairs to see what living in a castle was like.

SIDE TRIP UP THE GAP OF DUNLOE

*The road through the **Gap of Dunloe** (signposted from the Killorglin road just past the golf course) is a single-lane dirt track up a 6-kilometer ravine carved by glaciers. **Kate Kearney's Cottage** sits at the entrance to the ravine. Legend has it that Kate was a beautiful witch who drove men wild with desire—now her home is greatly enlarged as a coffee and souvenir shop. As you travel up the gap the dramatic setting is enhanced by the purple mountains on your left and **Macgillycuddy's Reeks** on your right.*

In the past I have recommended an evening drive up the gap to emerge on the N71, just west of Moll's Gap, and returning to Killarney with a quick stop at Ladies' View to admire the unparalleled views of the lakes of Killarney. Signs have been posted to discourage motor traffic. I recommend that you either park your car near Kate Kearney's cottage and walk, arrange for a jaunting car to take you up the gap or purchase a ticket at the tourist office for the Dero Tours day trip. This includes a shuttle service from your lodging to the gap, horse or jaunting car rides up the ravine, transportation by electric boat through the lakes of Killarney, and transportation back to your lodging.

Ladies' View, Killarney

The Southwest

The Dingle Peninsula

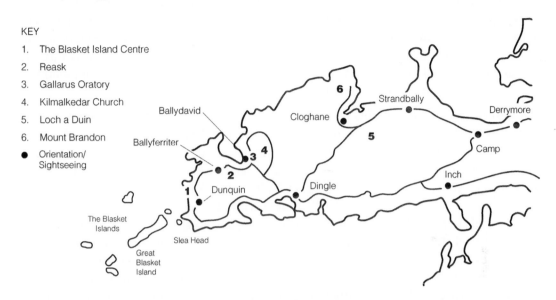

KEY

1. The Blasket Island Centre
2. Reask
3. Gallarus Oratory
4. Kilmalkedar Church
5. Loch a Duin
6. Mount Brandon
● Orientation/ Sightseeing

Leaving Killarney, a two-hour drive will bring you to Limerick, but rather than taking a direct route, take the time to explore the lovely **Dingle Peninsula**. It's a very special place, a narrow promontory of harshly beautiful land and seascapes where the people are especially friendly and welcoming to strangers. The road from Killarney to Dingle town takes you northwest to **Castlemaine** where you follow the coast road west through **Inch** to Dingle town, the largest settlement on the peninsula (it's only an hour-and-a-half drive from Killarney to Dingle).

Colorfully painted pubs, shops, and houses welcome you to **Dingle** (*An Daingean*) where fishing boats bob in the harbor unloading bountiful catches of fish and shellfish. It is not surprising that you find a great many excellent seafood restaurants here: **The Half Door** and adjacent **Doyle's** are two upmarket favorites. After dinner, ask where you can go to hear traditional Irish music. Dingle's population is under 2,000, yet it has over 50 pubs, some of which double as shops—like **Foxy John's**, where you can buy hardware while enjoying a drink, and **McCarthy's** with its poetry readings. There are several interesting shops—**Brian de Staic's** jewelry store contains exquisite gold and silver jewelry inspired by Dingle's flora and ancient Celtic motifs. The town's most famous resident is **Fungie**, a playful, bottle-nosed dolphin who took up residence in the harbor in 1985 and who loves to perform for visitors (tour boats leave from the harbor).

Plan to spend at least two nights on the peninsula to experience the beauty and tranquility offered by the unspoiled scenery of the spectacular beaches and rocky promontories that lie to the west of Dingle town. Take time to wander along the beaches or walk along the lanes, where fuchsia hedges divide the fields and friendly locals wave a salute of welcome, and to take the trip to the Blasket Islands. Because Irish is the official language of the peninsula, signposts are in Irish (though commercial maps are in English) so we give the Irish in parentheses to aid you in finding your way. We outline a route that will take you on a half-day drive around Slea Head. But for a real appreciation of the 2,000 archaeological sites of the Dingle Peninsula (peppered with lots of interesting stories), we recommend forsaking your car and taking one of **Sciuird's** minivan or walking tours. Michael and his dad, Timothy, offer tours that range from an hour's walk round Dingle town to visiting ancient, Ogham stones, wedge tombs, standing stones, and ring forts. (*Sciuird, Holyground, Dingle, Co Kerry, tel: 066 9151606, email: collinskirrary@eircom.net.*)

The road to Slea Head, signposted as **Slea Head Drive** (*Ceann Sléibhe*), twists and turns, following the contours of the increasingly rocky coast. Stunning seascapes present themselves, demanding that you pause just to admire the view. Several of the farms along the way have beehive stone huts and, for a small fee, the farmers will let you climb up to visit them. Conjecture has it that these small huts were used by early pilgrims traveling the St. Brendan's pilgrimage route. A large, white crucifix marks **Slea Head**, which affords the first view of the **Blasket Islands** (*Na Blascaodaí*), alternately sparkling like jewels in the blue ocean and disappearing under dark clouds a moment later.

Around the point, the scattered village of **Dunquin** (*Dún Chaoin*) and the **Blasket Island Centre** come into view. The building is impressive, with exhibits lining a long corridor that leads to an observatory overlooking the island's abandoned village. Remarkably, this tiny, isolated island abode produced an outpouring of music and writing. Three classics of Irish literature emerged with Peig Sayers' *Peig,* Thomas Crohan's *The Islandman*, and Maurice O'Sullivan's *Twenty Years a'Growing*. The islands have been uninhabited since 1953, when the last islanders evacuated their windswept homes. The center's large, airy dining room serves food and provides enticing island views. (*Open all year, tel: 066 9156444.*)

Before you visit the center, take a left turn, park on the cliff top (opposite the two yellow bungalows), and walk down to Dunquin's **pier**, which sits away from the scattered village and is reached by a steep path that zigzags down the cliff. As you round the last twist, you see curraghs turned upside-down looking like giant, black beetles stranded high above the water line. Curraghs are fragile boats made of tarred canvas stretched over a wooden skeleton. St. Brendan is reputed to have discovered America in such a boat. In clear weather a ferry takes day-trip visitors to and from **Great Blasket Island**. The little village on the island is mostly in ruins, and paths wander amongst the fields where the hardy islanders struggled to earn a living—a café offers the only shelter. (*Ferry sails every hour 10 am–6 pm in summer, tel: 066 9156444.*)

On the road to **Ballyferriter** (*Balle an Fheirtearaigh*), the pottery of **Louis Mulcahy** makes an interesting stop. During the summer you can try your hand at throwing a pot, and thus gain an appreciation for how difficult it is. (*Open all year 10 am–5:30 pm.*) One kilometer after driving through **Ballyferriter** (*Balle an Fheirtearaigh*), an attractive little village with a couple of pubs, pass Tig Bhric (a pub and shop) on your right and make a right-hand turn (small signpost) to **Reask** (*Riasc*), an ancient monastic settlement with its large slab cross and foundations of beehive huts.

Returning to the main road, a couple of kilometers' drive brings you to the **Gallarus Oratory** (*Séipéilín Ghallarais*). Over 1,000 years ago many of St. Brendan's contemporaries lived on the Dingle Peninsula in unmortared, beehive-shaped stone huts called clochans. The most famous example is the Gallarus Oratory, a tiny church built not as a circle, but in the shape of an upturned boat. It has a small window at one end, a small door at the other, and is as watertight today as when it was built over 900 years ago. A privately run enterprise offers a little visitors' center and a café, and charges a fee to cross their land to visit the monument. If you would rather not pay a fee, drive up the adjacent, public road and the monument is signed a short walk to your left.

Arriving in the nearby village of **Múirioch,** turn right at the Y for **Kilmalkedar Church** (*Séipéal Chill Mhaolcéadair*). This now-roofless place of worship was built in the 12th century on the site of a 7th-century church. However, it dates back even further, for within the graveyard is a magnificent, early Christian cross, an ancient Ogham stone, and an intricately decorated sundial. Within the church stands a rare alphabet stone, which the monks used for teaching the alphabet. Locals refer to the little slit east window as the eye of the needle and folklore has it that if you climb through the window, you will surely marry within a year and a day.

Continuing uphill, the field to your right contains the ruins of the Chancellor's House. Park your car by the gate on the right that follows the little lane (not signposted) and walk into the farmer's field to examine the waist-high foundations of the **Caher Dorgan** *(Cathar Dairgáin)* ring fort with its beehive huts. On a clear day, you get a magnificent view of the Three Sisters, a line of three mountains that tumble into the sea.

Cresting the rise, you travel 5 kilometers of the Dingle Peninsula's straightest road, known as *An Bóthar Fada*—The Long Road. It must have seemed a very long road for farmers walking to town. In the distance, the entrance to Dingle's harbor is guarded by **Esk Tower**, built in 1847 by an English landlord to give paid work to the men of Dingle. Its giant wooden hand serves as a marker for fishermen to the entrance to the protected harbor.

NOTE: If you get lost on the peninsula's little lanes, ask a friendly local or follow signposts for *An Daingean*, Dingle town.

There are lots of interesting walks on the Dingle Peninsula. Two of the more unusual ones are following the **Way of St. Brendan**, and exploring the **Loch a Duin Valley**. The Way of St. Brendan is laid out on a map that you obtain at **Cloghane's** tiny tourist office. The route begins in nearby Brandon and follows a well-marked route that the saint supposedly took to the top of **Mount Brandon** (about five hours of walking). Cloghane's tourist office also sells a booklet that takes you on a self-guided tour through the Loch a Duin Valley (Sciuird also leads a walking tour). Beginning at the hut beside the road at the bottom of Connor Pass, this route leads you on a well-marked, three-hour walk through the valley's boglands. Structures associated with prehistoric habitation (2,000 B.C.), ritual, and agriculture, along with several kilometers of prehistoric field wall, still survive. The valley is also of interest to bird watchers, botanists, and geologists.

Leaving the Dingle Peninsula (signposted Tralee), the **Connor Pass** twists you upward to the summit, where a backward glance gives you a magnificent view of Dingle and its harbor. The view is spectacular, but there is no guarantee that you will see it—all will be green fields, blue sea and sky, until the mists roll in and everything vanishes. Follow the coast road through **Ballyduff**, **Stradbally**, and **Camp** to **Tralee**. (If you are heading for the Cliffs of Moher, take the N69 to the **Tarbert ferry**, which takes you across the River Shannon.) At Tralee you join the main road (N21) for the drive to **Castleisland** and on to **Adare** with its charming row of thatched cottages and tree-lined streets. Less than an hour's drive will find you in **Limerick**, whose traffic-crowded streets can be avoided by taking the ring road signposted Ennis and Shannon Airport.

Dingle

The West

Céide Fields

Sligo

Bangor

N59

N59

Crossmolina   Ballina

Achill Island

Lough Conn   N17

Mulrany

Newport

Rosturk   N59   Castlebar

Westport

Louisburgh

Inishbofin Island   N59

Leenane

Lough Mask

Cleggan

Letterfrack

Lough Corrib

Clifden

Oughterard   Aughnanure Castle

Roundstone

N59

Rossaveel   Galway

Dunguaire Castle

Aran Islands

Kilronan

Dún Aengus

Lisdoonvarna   Ballyvaughan   Thoor Ballylee

The Burren   Kilfenora

N18

Corofin

Ennis

Shannon Airport

Limerick

Belfast

Dublin

●   Orientation/ Sightseeing

■ ■ ■   Itinerary Route

——   Roads

• • •   Alternative Route & Sidetrips

✈   Airport

The West

This itinerary takes you off the beaten tourist track through the wild, hauntingly beautiful scenery of Connemara, and County Mayo. Lying on the coast of County Clare, The Burren presents a vast landscape of smooth, limestone rocks—whose crevices are ablaze with rock roses, blue gentians, and all manner of Arctic and Alpine flowers in the spring and early summer. Otherwise, there are no trees, shrubs, rivers, or lakes—just bare "moonscapes" of rocks dotted with forts and ruined castles, tombs, and rock cairns. Traveling to Connemara, your route traces the vast, island-dotted Lough Corrib and traverses boglands and moorlands. Distant mountains fill the horizon and guide you to the coast, where gentle waves lap at rocky inlets sheltering scattered villages with whitewashed cottages dotting the landscape. Ireland's holy mountain, Croagh Patrick, and the windswept Achill Island leave a deep impression on the visitor.

Cliffs of Moher

Recommended Pacing: It is possible to tour the west in just a few days, but this beautiful area calls for you to linger. Our ideal would be one or two nights on or near The Burren, two or three nights in Connemara, and two or three nights near either Crossmolina or Sligo.

Leave **Limerick** in the direction of Ennis and Shannon airport and you soon arrive at **Bunratty Castle and Folk Park.** An interesting history and guide to the castle is available at the entrance. As the majority of castles in Ireland stand roofless and in ruins, it is a treat to visit a 15th-century castle that has been restored so beautifully. The authentic 14th- to 17th-century furniture in the rooms gives the castle a real lived-in feel. In the evenings, firelit banquets warmed with goblets of mead whisk visitors back to the days when the castle was young. In the castle grounds, a folk park contains several cottages, farmhouses, and a whole 19th-century village street of shops, houses, and buildings furnished appropriately for their era. The community is brought to life by costumed townspeople who bake, make butter, and tend the animals. (*Open daily, tel: 061 360788, fax: 061 472523.*) **Bunratty Cottage**, opposite the castle, offers a wide range of handmade Irish goods, and just at the entrance to the park is **Durty Nelly's**, one of Ireland's most popular pubs, dating from the 1600s.

Just to the northwest lies the strangest landscape in Ireland, **The Burren**. Burren means "a rocky place" and this is certainly the case for, as far as the eye can see, this is a wilderness—a wilderness that is rich in archaeological sites (megalithic tombs, ring forts, and the remains of ancient huts) and strange rock formations whose tiny crevices are a mass of Arctic, Mediterranean, and Alpine flowers in springtime. Ludlow, one of Cromwell's generals, passing through the area in 1649, wrote, "There is not enough wood to hang a man, nor water to drown him, nor earth enough to bury him in."

Base yourself at either **Corofin** or **Ballyvaughan** (see *Places to Stay*) to explore this unique area. One of the most photographed sights, the **Poulnabrone Portal Tomb,** is found alongside the road between Corofin and Ballyvaughan.

To help you appreciate this unusual landscape, first visit The **Burren Display Centre** at **Kilfenora**, which offers a film on the geology and rare flora and fauna of the area. Models explain the pattern of settlement and the geological makeup of the area, and show the non-botanist what to look for. Next to the Centre, the crumbling remains of Ladies Chapel has a glass roof sheltering three celtic crosses with symbolic carvings from the elements. A fourth cross is open to the elements in an adjacent field.

Turn right as you leave the interpretive center and left as you come to the main road to reach the **Cliffs of Moher**—the most spectacular section of the coastline—where towering cliffs rise above the pounding Atlantic Ocean. These majestic cliffs, stretching along 5 kilometers of the coast, are one of Ireland's most popular sights. The cliffs face due west, which means that the best time to see them is on a bright, summer evening. The visitors' center offers welcome shelter on cool and windy days. A short distance from the visitors' center, **O'Brien's Tower** (built in 1835 by Sir Cornelius O'Brien, Member of Parliament, for "strangers visiting the magnificent scenery of this neighborhood") marks the highest and most photographed point along the clifftops.

On leaving the cliffs, head north toward, but not into, Lisdoonvarna. Follow the coastal road around Black Head, where the rocky Burren spills into Galway Bay—to Ballyvaughan, where you turn right following signs for the **Aillwee Caves** on the bluff above. The visitors' center is so cleverly designed that it is hard to distinguish it from the surrounding gray landscape. Beneath the eerie "moonscape" of the Burren lie vast caves, streams, and lakes. You can take a tour through a small section of these underground caverns. The first is called Bear Haven because the bones of a brown bear that died long ago were found here. In other chambers, you see limestone cascades, stalactites, and stalagmites before the tour ends at the edge of an underground river. Remember to dress warmly, for it's cool in the caves. (*Open all year, www.aillweecave.ie, tel: 065 7077036.*)

Retrace your steps a short distance down the road towards Ballyvaughan and take the first turn left, passing Gregans Castle hotel and up Corkscrew Hill, a winding road that takes you from a lush, green valley to the gray, rocky landscape above. Take the first turn to the left and you come to **Cahermacnaghten**, a ring fort that was occupied until the 18th century. You enter via a medieval two-story gateway, and the foundations of buildings of similar date can be seen inside the stone wall.

Some 7 kilometers farther south, you come to another ring fort, **Ballykinvarga**. You have to walk several hundred meters before you see the Iron-Age fort surrounded by its defensive, pointed stones known as *chevaux de frise*, a term derived from a military expression describing how Dutch Frisians used spikes to impede attackers. Ireland has three other such forts, of which the two most impressive are found on the Aran Islands.

When you leave The Burren, head directly for the coast and follow it east (N67) to **Kinvarra**, a pretty village with boats bobbing in the harbor and small rocky islands separating it from the expanse of Galway Bay. On the outskirts of the village, the restored **Dunguaire Castle** has a craft shop and, on summer evenings, hosts medieval banquets. (*Open May–Oct, tel: 091 637108.*)

From the castle car park, turn towards the village and immediately take a left-hand turn (opposite the castle entrance) for the 5-kilometer drive to **Ardrahan**, where you turn right on the N18 and, after 6 kilometers, left for the 2-kilometer drive to **Thoor Ballylee**. William Butler Yeats bought this 13th-century tower house and cottage in 1917 and it was his summer home for 11 years. The cozy, thatched cottage is now a bookshop. An audio-visual presentation tells of Yeats's artistic and political achievements. Two floors of the tower are sparsely furnished as they were in his occupancy. By pressing a green button on each room's wall you receive information and hear excerpts of his poetry. (*Open May–Sep, tel: 091 631436.*) Leaving Thoor Ballylee, retrace your steps to the N18 for a 24-kilometer drive to **Galway**.

SIDE TRIP TO THE ARAN ISLANDS

*If you are planning to visit the **Aran Islands**, take the coastal route through Spiddal to **Rossaveel** where two ferry companies operate a shuttle service to **Kilronan** on **Inishmore**, the largest of the three Aran Islands. (Island Ferries, tel: 091 561767 and 091 568903.) Until a decade or so ago, time had stood still here and the way of life and the culture of the islanders had changed little. Now their traditional dress comes out only* *for TV cameras and special occasions, and their traditional way of life has been replaced by a more profitable one—tourism. In the summertime, more than double the population of the islands arrives on Inishmore as day-trippers. When you arrive, visit the Tourist Information Centre by the harbor to discuss the cost of horse and trap, bicycle (there are plenty of shops where you can rent bikes), and minibus transportation. The barren landscape is closely related to that of The Burren: sheer cliffs plunge into the pounding Atlantic Ocean along the southern coast, while the north coast flattens out with shallow, rock-ringed, sandy beaches. You will have no difficulty obtaining transportation to **Dún Aengus** (about 8 kilometers from the harbor), the best known of the island's stone forts, believed to date from the early Celtic period some two to three thousand years ago. It has sheer cliffs at its back and is surrounded by pointed boulders designed to twist ankles and skin shins. Despite the hordes of visitors scrambling over its walls and stones, Dún Aengus is remarkably well preserved. With four stone forts, remains of stone huts, high crosses, and ruined churches to examine, the archaeologically minded could spend many days with detailed map in hand exploring the islands.*

Those who are not island bound should follow signs for Clifden (N59) around Galway. Leaving the town behind, the road is straight and well paved, but a tad bouncy if you try to go too fast. Accommodation signs for nearby Oughterard alert you to watch for a right-hand turn to **Aughnanure Castle**. Approaching the castle, you may be greeted, as we were, by a friendly family of goats snoozing on the wooden footbridge before the castle gates. Aughnanure Castle was the stronghold of the ferocious O'Flahertys, who launched attacks on Galway town until their castle was destroyed by English forces in 1572. The clan regained their castle for a period of time until wars with Cromwell and William of Orange saw them expelled again. (*Open Jun–Sep, tel: 091 552214.*) Nearby **Oughterard** is a pleasant, bustling town, "the gateway to Connemara," whose main street has several, attractive shops. A stay here affords the opportunity for fishing and exploring the island-dotted Lough Corrib by boat.

Clifden

Beyond Oughterard, you plunge into Connemara past the **Twelve Bens** mountains, which dominate the wild, almost treeless landscape of bogs, lakes, and rivers; a landscape that is ever being changed by the dashing clouds that rush in from the Atlantic. Apart from the occasional craft shop, there are no houses until you reach **Clifden** (see listings) on the Atlantic coast (N59, 80 kilometers). Clifden is the major market town of Connemara and the home of the annual Connemara Pony Show (*third week in August*). The town presents a gay face with shopfronts painted in bright hues of red, blue, yellow, and green. Craft and tourist shops alternate with the butchers, the hardware store, pubs, and restaurants. On Market Street, you find the **Connemara Walking Centre** where you can buy booklets on the locale and sign up for one of the walking tours that vary from an interesting stroll through the Roundstone bogs—great walking amongst lakes full of otters and interesting plant life—to the demanding climb up one half of the great

Glanhoaghan Horseshoe in the stark Twelve Bens mountains. (*Contact Michael Gibbons, Connemara Walking Centre, Island House, Market Street, Clifden, Co Galway, tel: 095 21379, fax: 095 21845, email: walkwest@indigo.ie, website: www.walkingireland.com.*)

SIDE TRIP TO ROUNDSTONE

*To the south of Clifden, the road has more views of sea than land, as little boats bob in rocky inlets and cottages gaze westward across tiny islands. The road passes the marshy area where Alcock and Brown crash-landed after the first transatlantic flight in 1919 (commemorated by a monument about 500 meters from the main road). Via **Ballinaboy**, **Ballyconneely**, and **Roundstone**, the sweeping seascapes that this route presents are so compelling that it is difficult to concentrate on the driving.*

SIDE TRIP TO INISHBOFIN ISLAND

*If the weather is fine, a delightful day trip can be taken to **Inishbofin Island**. The Inishbofin boat leaves from Cleggan pier at 11:30 am, returning at 5 pm (the crossing takes less than an hour). Be at **Cleggan** pier half an hour before sailing time and buy your ticket at the Pier Bar. Sailings depend on weather conditions, so it's best to phone ahead to verify departure times. (Kings Ferries, Cleggan, tel: 095 21520 or The Inishbofin Experience, the O'Halloran family, tel: 095 45903/45806/45831.) The boat sails into the sheltered harbor presided over by the remains of a Cromwellian castle, and you wade ashore at a cluster of houses that make up the island's main settlement. Many islanders have left in search of greener pastures and their cottages have fallen into disrepair, but those who remain eke out a hard living from the land and the sea. As you walk down lanes edged with wild fuchsias and brightly colored wildflowers, whitewashed farmhouses appear and you see fields dotted with handmade haystacks. (Regrettably, the odd, long-abandoned, rusting car spoils the scene.) At the far side of the island, a row of cottages fronts the beach, one of them housing a welcoming little café, where you can have lunch or tea before walking back to the harbor to take the evening boat back to Cleggan.*

Clifden stands just outside the **Connemara National Park**, which covers 5,000 acres of mountain, heath, and bog—there are no pretty gardens or verdant woodlands. The video in the visitors' center gives a beautiful introduction to the park, which has wonderful hiking trails. If you want to tackle the smaller paths leading into the Twelve Bens mountains, consider joining one of the guided walks that begin at the visitors' center (four of the Twelve Bens, including Benbaum, the highest, are found in the park). Two signposted nature trails start at the center: one leads you through Ellis Wood while the other takes you into rougher terrain. (*Open Apr–Sep.*)

Leaving Clifden to the north, the N59 passes the much-photographed **Kylemore Abbey**. Originally built by a wealthy Englishman in the 19th century, this grand home, surrounded by greenery and fronting a lake, passed into the hands of Benedictine nuns who have a school here. You'll find ample parking (lots of coaches) and a large restaurant and gift shop. You can walk beside the lake to the abbey, where in summer the library is open to visitors. In the grounds, you can visit the restored Gothic chapel with its pretty, sandstone interior and different-colored, marble pillars. (*Open all year, tel: 095 41146.*) Follow the shore of **Killary Harbor**, the longest and most picturesque fjord in Ireland, to **Leenane**, a little village nestled at the head of the inlet. Continue along the shoreline and take the first turn to the left, signposted as a scenic route to Westport via Louisburgh. This interesting side road gently winds you along the sea lough to **Delphi**, an area of pools and loughs amongst some of the highest and wildest mountains in the west. Acres of woodlands offer shelter and there is not a bungalow in sight. The Marquis of Sligo built a lodge here in 1840 and called it "Delphi" because it reminded him of Delphi in Greece. After falling into dereliction, the house and estate were bought by the Mantles, who welcome guests to their restored home (see listing under Leenane).

Leaving Delphi, the isolated mountain road takes you along the shore of **Doo Lough** at the foot of **Mweelrea Mountain** and on through wild, remote scenery to **Louisburgh**; where, turning towards Westport, the summit of the conical-shaped **Croagh Patrick** (Ireland's most famous mountain) comes into view. Swirling mists substantiate its mystical place in Irish history. It was after St. Patrick spent the 40 days of Lent atop its rocky summit in 441 that the mountain became sacred to Christians. Every year thousands of penitential pilgrims begin their climb to the oratory at the summit at dawn on the last Sunday in July, several going barefoot up the stony track. The ritual involves stopping at three stations and reciting prayers. No climbing skills are needed as it's a well-worn path to the top and, on a clear day, a walk to the summit affords a panoramic view across Clew Bay to Achill Island.

Nearby **Westport** lies on the shore of Clew Bay and is unique amongst Irish towns because it was built following a pre-designed plan. The architect walled the river and lined the riverside malls with lime trees and austere Georgian homes, forming a most delightful thoroughfare. There's a buzz to the town and, on a sunny day, you can enjoy a drink at the tables and chairs outside **Geraghtey's Bar** and **Grand Central**, on the Octagon (the heart of the town with a granite pillar in the center of the square). At **Clew Bay Heritage Centre** on Westport Quay, postcards and old photographs show the town as it was at the turn of the last century. There is also a genealogical research center and a display on the maritime traditions of Westport. (*Open May–Sep, tel: 098 26852.*)

From Westport, the most direct route to Sligo is by way of the broad, well-paved, fast N5, and N17. However, if the weather is clear and bright, it is a delightful drive from Westport to Sligo via **Newport**, **Achill Island**, **Crossmolina,** and **Ballina**.

Achill Island is Ireland's largest offshore island. Traditionally, the Achill islanders traveled to Scotland as migrant farmworkers during the summer; but now the population that has not been enticed away by emigration, remains to garner a meager living from a harsh land. This was the home of the infamous British Captain Boycott; who gave his name to the English language when tenants "boycotted" him for his excessive rents during the potato famine. Today, this island holds the allure that belongs to wild and lonely places: in sunshine it is glorious; but in torrential rain, it is a grim and depressing place. On the island, take the first turn to your left, signposted for the windswept **Atlantic Drive**, where you drive along the tops of rugged cliffs carved by the pounding Atlantic Ocean far below. The "drive" ends at **Knockmore** where scattered houses shelter from the biting winds.

Returning to Mulrany, turn north on the N59 for the 32-kilometer drive across boglands, where vast quantities of turf are harvested by mechanical means, to **Bangor** and on to **Crossmolina, Ballina,** and **Sligo**. The many sightseeing opportunities in the Sligo area are outlined in the following itinerary.

Croagh Patrick

SIDE TRIP TO CÉIDE FIELDS

*From Ballina, you can detour north 20 kilometers to Ballycastle and drive another 8 kilometers east to the great cliffs of **Downpatrick Head**, where the Stone-Age settlements at **Céide Fields** (pronounced "kay-jeh") are being excavated. Under the peat has been unearthed the most extensive Stone-Age settlement in the world, with walls older than the pyramids, a vast site which once supported a community of over 10,000 people. Wander round a portion of the archaeological dig, and enjoy an audio-visual presentation and a cup of tea in the pyramid-shaped visitors' center. (Open mid-Mar–Nov, tel: 096 43325.)*

*The surrounding cliffs are amongst the most magnificent you will see in Ireland. Retrace your steps to Ballycastle, and take the R314 through **Killala** (a workaday village whose skyline is punctuated by an ancient, round tower) to **Ballina** where you turn left for* **Sligo**.

From the Sligo area—you can go into Northern Ireland, continue north on the following itinerary, or return south. If you travel south, consider visiting either **Ballintubber Abbey**, a beautifully restored church dating back to 1216, or the village of **Knock**. A religious apparition seen on the gable of the village church in 1879, and some hearty promotion, has led to the development of Knock as a religious pilgrimage site and a tourist venue. A giant basilica stands next to the little church, a large complex of religious souvenir shops sits across the road, and nearby Knock airport has a runway capable of providing landing facilities for large jets. Surrounded as it is by narrow country lanes, this sophisticated complex seems very out of place in rural Ireland.

The North

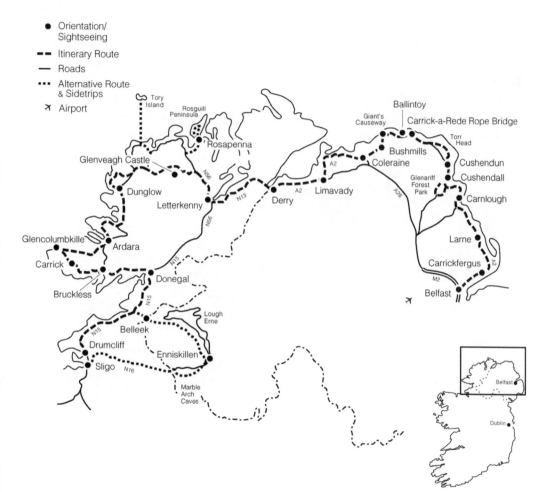

- ● Orientation/ Sightseeing
- ▬ ▬ Itinerary Route
- ▬ Roads
- • • • Alternative Route & Sidetrips
- ✈ Airport

Tory Island

Rosguill Peninsula

Rosapenna

Glenveagh Castle

Dunglow

Letterkenny

N56

N13

Derry

A2

Limavady

Giant's Causeway

Ballintoy

Carrick-a-Rede Rope Bridge

Torr Head

Bushmills

Coleraine

A26

Glenariff Forest Park

Cushendun

Cushendall

Carnlough

Larne

Glencolumbkille

Ardara

Carrick

Bruckless

N15

N56

Donegal

N15

Lough Erne

Belleek

Drumcliff

Enniskillen

Sligo

N16

Marble Arch Caves

Carrickfergus

M2

Belfast

✈

A2

Belfast

Dublin

The North

The northernmost reaches of Ireland hold special appeal. Herein lies the countryside that inspired the moving poetry of William Butler Yeats. Beyond Donegal, narrow roads twist and turn around the wild, rugged coastline of County Donegal, where villagers weave their tweeds and Irish is often the spoken language and that written on the signposts. The Folk Village Museum at Glencolumbkille, with its authentically furnished, thatch-topped cottages, demonstrates the harsh living conditions of the far north. Crossing into Northern Ireland, the honeycomb columns of the Giant's Causeway signpost the Antrim coast full of cliffs, lush green headlands, and beautiful views.

Dunluce Castle

The North

Recommended Pacing: Two or three nights around Sligo and Donegal, a night near Glenveagh National Park (to permit a leisurely visit), and two nights along the Antrim coast will give you time to explore this lovely area.

The county and town of **Sligo** are ever mindful of William Butler Yeats, and the whole area is promoted as being Yeats country. If you are an ardent admirer of the poet, you will want to visit the **County Museum**, which has a special section about his poetry and writing. Base yourself near the town for several days—**Ballymote** and **Riverstown** are our accommodation choices in the *Places to Stay* section. The countryside is very pretty and there is enough sightseeing to keep you busy for a week.

SIDE TRIP TO CARROWMORE AND CARROWKEEL

*Seven kilometers to the southwest of Sligo town, sitting in fields on either side of a narrow country lane, are the megalithic tombs of **Carrowmore**. Wander amongst the cows and explore the little stone circles and larger dolmens which make up what is reputed to be the largest Bronze-Age cemetery in Europe. Farther inland take the Boyle road (N4) 30 kilometers south of Sligo to Castlebaldwin, where you turn right following signposts for Carrowkeel. At the end of a mountain track, you come to **Carrowkeel**, a 4,000-year-old passage tomb cemetery. There are 13 cairns covering passage tombs, while the 14th is a long cairn. One of the tombs can be entered (backwards) and it is claimed that, on the summer solstice, the setting sun lights up the main chamber.*

SIDE TRIP AROUND LOUGH GILL

*A half-day sightseeing trip from Sligo can be taken by driving around Lough Gill, visiting Parke's Castle, and enjoying a meal at Markree Castle. Leave Sligo to the north and follow signposts for Enniskillen, Lough Derg, and Dromohair, which bring you to the northerly shore of **Lough Gill**. Glimpses of the lough through the trees give way to stunning lough views as the road hugs the shore and arrives at **Parke's Castle**, a fortified manor house whose ramparts and cottages (tearooms) have been restored. (Open Easter–Oct, tel: 071 64149.) In summer, you can take a boat trip on the lake which takes you around **Inishfree Island**. Leaving the castle, follow the lough into **Dromohair** where you pick up the Sligo road. After 5 kilometers, when the road divides, take a single-track lane to the right, which leads you down to the lakeside where John O'Connel's rowboat is tied to the pier. He lives by the lake and is sometimes available to row you to Inishfree Island. Returning to the main road, it's a short drive to **Collooney**, where you can partake of lunch or afternoon tea at **Markree Castle**.*

Leaving Sligo, travel north along the N15 to **Drumcliff Churchyard**, which has to be the most visited graveyard in Ireland. Handily there's an excellent café. William Butler Yeats is buried here under the epitaph he composed, "Cast a cold eye on life, on death. Horseman, pass by!" In the background is the imposing **Benbulben Mountain**. Beyond the village, a left turn leads to **Lissadell,** home of the Gore-Booth sisters with whom Yeats was friendly. The 1830s Greek Revival-style house is full of curiosities and quite a sight to behold, but in need of an injection of capital to prevent its decay. While the sisters belonged to the landed gentry, Eva went on to become a poet and an important member of the suffragette movement. Constance was a commander in the 1916 uprising and the first elected female Labour Party M.P. Sir Henry Gore-Booth went off with his butler to explore the Antarctic in the 1880s. The bear that the butler shot is on the stairs. (*Open intermittently, usually Jun–Sep, closed Sun, tel: 071 63150.*)

Leaving Lissadell, continue north on the N15 for the 60-kilometer drive to Donegal, or follow a more circuitous route through Northern Ireland.

ALTERNATIVE ROUTE TO DONEGAL

*From Drumcliff churchyard, return towards Sligo and, at **Rathcormack**, turn left through the village of **Drum** to join the N16 as it travels east towards **Enniskillen**. Cross into Northern Ireland and take the first turn to your right following signposts to **Marble Arch Caves**. This extensive network of limestone chambers (billed as "over 300 million years of history") is most impressive. The tour includes an underground boat journey, walks through large illuminated chambers, galleries hung with remarkable stalactites, and a "Moses Walk" along a man-made passage through a lake where your feet are at the bottom of the pool and your head is at the same level as the water. Remember to dress warmly and take a sweater. It is best to telephone in advance because, if there has been a lot of rain, the caves are closed. (Open Mar–Oct, tel: 02866 348855.)*

*Leaving the hilltop cave complex, follow signposts for Enniskillen for 7 kilometers to **Florence Court**, an 18th-century mansion that was once the home of the Earls of Enniskillen. The opulent mansion is elegantly furnished and famous for the impressive rococo plasterwork on the ceilings. (Open Apr–Oct, tel: 01365 348249.) On leaving Florence Court, do **not** go into Enniskillen, but turn left onto the A46, following the scenic southern shore of **Lough Erne** for the 38-kilometer drive to Belleek.*

***Belleek**, on the far north shore of the lough, is famous for its ornate, creamy pottery: porcelain festooned with shamrocks or delicate, spaghetti-like strands woven into trellis-like plates. You can tour the visitors' center and then browse at the factory shop. (Open May–Sep.) Crossing back into the Republic, head for **Ballyshannon** and follow the wide N15 north for 23 kilometers to Donegal.*

Glencolumbkille

Donegal is a busy, bustling place, laid out around a diamond-shaped area surrounded by shops. Donegal is one of the best places to buy tweed goods—**Magees** sells a variety. The **Four Masters Bookshop** is a handy place to stock up on reading material. The ruins of **Donegal Castle** (open to the public), built in the 16th century by Hugh O'Donell, stand beside the Diamond.

Take the N56 west, hugging the coast, through **Dunkineely** and **Bruckless** to **Killybegs**, Ireland's major fishing port. Large trawlers from all over the world have replaced family fishing boats in the working harbor of this most enjoyable town. As you move west from Killybegs, the roads become more difficult, the landscape more rugged, the signposts less frequent, and—to complicate things—they are often written in Irish (Irish names are referenced in parentheses).

If the weather is fine, you can enjoy some spectacular scenery by following the brown signs that indicate a coastal route from **Kilcar** to **Carrick** (*An Charraig*), where you turn left (in the center of the village opposite the pub) for **Telin** (*Teilean*) and follow the brown signs for **Bunglar** and The Cliffs. As the narrow road winds up, down, and around the rocky, rolling landscape; you see several examples of traditional Irish cottages with small, thatched, pony-cart barns huddled next to them. The road narrows to a single track taking you along the very edge of the headlands to a viewpoint that overlooks the spot where the **Slieve League Cliffs** plummet into the sea. Walkers will love the magnificent walks along the headlands. This is not a trip to be taken in inclement weather.

Retrace your steps to Carrick and turn left towards **Glencolumbkille** (*Gleann Cholaim Cille*). The road enters the Owenwee Valley where you climb before descending into the glen. Drive through the scattered village to **Glencolumbkille Folk Village Museum** at the water's edge. Glencolumbkille is a place that gives one an appreciation of the survival of a people who endured hardship, famine, and debilitating emigration. By the 1960s, emigration was threatening to turn Glencolumbkille into a ghost town. In an effort to create some jobs, the parish priest, Father McDyer, formed a cooperative of the remaining local residents to develop a tourist industry by building a folk museum and holiday homes, and by encouraging local crafts. Tucked against a rocky hillside, the cottages that comprise the folk museum are grouped to form a traditional, tiny, village (*clachan*). Each cottage is a replica of those lived in by local people in each of three successive centuries. The thick, thatched roofs are tied down with heavy rope and anchored with stones, securing them from the harsh Atlantic winds. Inside, the little homes are furnished with period furniture and utensils. Locals guide you through the houses and give you snippets of local history. A handicraft shop sells Irish cottage crafts and the adjacent tearoom serves scones and piping hot tea. (*Open Easter–Oct, tours every half hour, tel: 073 30017.*)

Leaving Glencolumbkille, the narrow road climbs and dips through seemingly uninhabited, rugged countryside, where the views are often obscured by swirling mists as you climb the Glengesh Pass before dropping down into **Ardara**.

The road skirts the coast and brings you to the twin fishing villages of **Portnoo** and **Nairn**, set amongst isolated beaches that truly have an "end-of-the-earth" quality about them. A short drive brings you to **Maas**, where you travel an extremely twisty road to the Gweebarra bridge taking you to **Lettermacaward** (*Leitir Mhic An Bhaird*) and on to **Dungloe** (*An Globhan Liath*). Nearby in **Burtonport** (*Ailt An Chorain*) more salmon and lobster are landed than at any other port. From here you drive north to **Kincasslagh**, and then it's on to **Annagary**, both tiny little communities that pride themselves on speaking the Irish language. A combination of wild, untamed scenery, villages that seem untouched by the 20th century, and narrow, curving roads in general disrepair, gives the feeling that the passage of time stopped many years ago in this isolated corner of Ireland.

Rejoin the N56 just south of **Gweedore** (*Gaoth Dobhair*) and follow it for a short distance as it swings inland paralleling a sea loch. As the main road swings to the right, continue straight up the mountain, following a narrow, winding road that brings you across peat bogs and purple, heather-covered moorlands inhabited only by sheep—to **Glenveagh National Park**, Ireland's largest, most natural, and most beautiful park. At its center lies a sheltered glen with a lake and mighty castle. The **Glenveagh Visitors' Centre** is well signposted and well disguised, being sunk into the ground with its roof camouflaged by peat and heather. There are displays, an audio-visual program, and a café (there's another at the castle), and it is here that you leave your car to take the minibus around the lake to **Glenveagh Castle** and its gardens. The heather and rose gardens, the rhododendrons, the laurels and pines, and busts and statues are all lovingly maintained, but the walled kitchen garden is especially memorable, with its profusion of flowers and tidy rows of vegetables divided by narrow, grass walkways. Surrounding this oasis of cultivated beauty are thousands of acres of wild countryside, where the largest herd of red deer in Ireland roam. Glenveagh Castle was built in 1870 by John Adair, using his American wife's money, in a fanciful gothic design that was popular in the later part of the century. The rooms have been beautifully restored and, for a small fee, you can tour the house (arrive by 2 pm if you're traveling in July and August). The Glenveagh estate was sold to the nation by the castle's second owner, Henry McIlhenny, who is largely responsible for the design of the gardens. (*Open Apr–Oct, tel: 074 37090.*)

Leaving the national park, turn right across the desolate boglands and heather-clad hills—your destination is **Glebe House and Gallery** (6 kilometers away) near the village of **Churchhill**. Derek Hill gave his home, Glebe House, and his art collection to the state, which remodeled the outbuildings to display his fine collection of paintings. Among the 300 paintings are works by Picasso, Bonnard, Yeats, Annigoni, and Pasmore. The decoration in the house includes William Morris papers and textiles, Victoriana, Donegal folk art, and Japanese and Islamic art. There is a tearoom in the courtyard. (*Open May–Sep, closed Fri, tel: 074 37071.*)

SIDE TRIP TO THE ROSGUILL PENINSULA AND TORY ISLAND

If you would like to experience more Donegal coastal landscape, you can do no better than tour the **Rosguill Peninsula**, *whose 25-kilometer Atlantic drive traces a wild, coastal route from* **Rosapenna** *through* **Downies** *and* **Doagh** *to* **Tranarossan Bay** *and back to Rosapenna. The road goes up and down, most of the time high above the ocean, then sweeps down to white, sandy beaches.*

If you follow the coastal road west through **Gortahawk**, *you come to* **Meenlaragh** *where you take the ferry to* **Tory Island**, *a windswept island where the inhabitants eke out a hard life farming and fishing. Sailing times of the ferryboat depend on the weather. If you want to visit the island, contact the Post Office in Meenlaragh. (Tel: 074 35165.)*

Giant's Causeway

From Glebe House, it is a 16-kilometer drive to **Letterkenny**. From the town, your route into Northern Ireland is well signposted to **Derry**. The N13 becomes the A2 as you cross the border and the pound sterling becomes the currency. Skirt Derry city on the **Foyle Bridge**, then follow the A2 to **Limavady** and the A37 for 21 kilometers to **Coleraine**.

Bushmills and the Giant's Causeway are well signposted from the outskirts of Coleraine. (One of the delights of traveling in Northern Ireland is that the roads are well paved and the signposting frequent and accurate.) **Bushmills** (see listings) is famous for its whiskey—a whiskey spelled with an "e"—of which Special Old Black Bush is the best. A tour of the factory demonstrates how they turn barley and water into whiskey and rewards you with a sample of the classic drink to fortify you for your visit to the nearby Giant's Causeway. (*Open daily, tel: 028 2073 1521.*)

In the last century, the **Giant's Causeway** was thought to be one of the wonders of the world. Formed from basaltic rock, which cooled and split into regular, prismatic shapes, it stepped out to sea to build an irregular honeycomb of columns some 70,000,000 years ago. More romantic than scientific fact is the legend that claims the causeway was built by the Irish giant, Finn MacCool, to get at his rival in Scotland. Do not expect the columns to be tall, for they are not—it is their patterns that make them interesting, not their size.

The first stop on a visit to the causeway is the **Giant's Causeway Centre**, where the facts and legends about the causeway are well presented in an audio-visual theater. (*Open all year, tel: 028 2073 1159, email: unavsm@smtp.ntrust.org.uk.*) A minibus takes you to the head of the causeway, where you follow the path past formations called "Honeycomb," "Wishing Well," "Giant's Granny," "King and his Nobles," "Port na Spaniagh" (where gold and silver treasure from the Spanish Armada ship, *Girona,* was found in 1967), and "Lovers' Leap" and then up the wooden staircase to the headlands, where you walk back to the visitors' center along the clifftops. (It's a 5-kilometer walk and you can truly say you have seen the causeway, if you complete the circuit.)

Leaving the causeway, turn right along the coast to visit the ruins of the nearby **Dunluce Castle**, a romantic ruin clinging to a wave-lashed cliff with a great cave right underneath. This was the main fort of the Irish MacDonnells, chiefs of Antrim. It fell into ruin after the kitchen (and cooks!) fell into the sea during a storm. (*Open Apr–Sep.*)

Retrace your route down the B146 and, at the causeway gates, turn left along the coast road. Watch carefully for a small plaque at the side of the road pointing out the very meager ruins of **Dunseverick Castle**. Dunseverick was at the northernmost end of the Celtic road where the Celts crossed to and from Scotland.

Shortly after joining the A2, turn left for **Port Braddon**. The road winds down to the sea where a hamlet of gaily painted houses and a church nestles around a sheltered harbor. As you stand in front of the smallest church in Ireland, the long, sandy beaches of **Whitepark Bay** stretch before you.

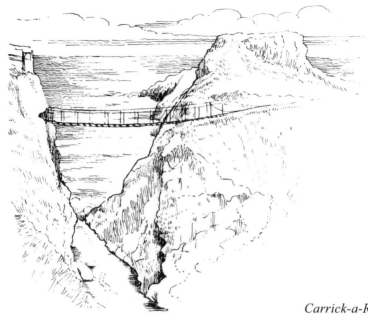

Carrick-a-Rede Rope Bridge

Farther along the coast, a narrow road winds down to the very picturesque **Ballintoy Harbour**, a sheltered haven for boats surrounded by small, jagged, rocky islands. At the first road bend after leaving Ballintoy village, turn sharp left for the **Carrick-a-Rede Rope Bridge**. This is one of the famous things to do in Ireland: walk high above the sea across a narrow, swinging bridge of planks and ropes that joins a precipitous cliff to a rocky island. Hardy fishermen, whose cottages and nets nestle in a sheltered cleft on the island and whose fragile wooden boats bob in the ocean below, still use the bridge. (*Open mid-Apr–mid-Sep.*)

Life in the nearby holiday town of **Ballycastle** centers around the beach, fishing, and golf. Cross the river and turn onto the A2 to **Ballyvoy**. If the weather is clear, turn left for the scenic drive to Cushendun around **Torr Head**. The narrow road, barely wide enough for two cars to pass, switches back across the headlands and corkscrews down the cliffside, offering spectacular views of the rugged coastline and the distant Mull of Kintyre in Scotland.

Nestled by the seashore, the pretty village of **Cushendun** has a National Trust Shop, an excellent place to buy high-quality souvenirs. When you leave Cushendun, the landscape softens and the road, thankfully, returns to a more manageable width. You are now entering the **Glens of Antrim**, where lush, green fields and a succession of beautiful views present themselves. At **Cushendall** you can detour into **Glenariff Forest Park**, the queen of the glens with a series of waterfalls plunging down a gorge traversed by a scenic path crossing rustic bridges. Thackeray described this glen as "Switzerland in miniature." (*Open all year.*)

After your return to the coast road, **Carnlough**, a pretty seaside and fishing town, soon comes into view, its little white harbor full of bobbing boats. The **Londonderry Arms** was once a coaching inn and now is a hotel and restaurant.

Nearby **Glenarm** is the oldest of the coastal villages, dating back to the time of King John. The pseudo-gothic castle is the home of the Earl of Antrim, part of whose demesne, **Glenarm Forest**, climbs up from the glen and is open to the public. (*Open all year.*)

Limestone cliffs present themselves as you approach **Larne**, a sizable seaport whose Viking origins are lost amongst more modern commercial developments. Wend your way through this busy port town, following the A2 to **Whitehead**. Nearby **Carrickfergus** is the oldest town in Northern Ireland. **Carrickfergus Castle**, a sturdy Norman castle overlooking the boat-filled harbor, was built as a stronghold in 1178 by John de Courcy after his invasion of Ulster; then taken by King John after a siege in 1210; fell to the Scots in 1316; and was captured by the French in 1760. Life-sized models and a film recreate the castle's turbulent past. (*Open all year.*)

Leaving Carrickfergus, a 12-kilometer drive along the A2 and M2/M1 whisks you through, or into, **Belfast** (see listings), where the A1 will take you south through **Newry** and into the Republic. Or, if you are staying near the Antrim coast for several days of leisurely sightseeing, take the M2 to the A26, which quickly returns you to that area.

Carrickfergus Castle

Places to Stay

The Dunraven Arms stands on the broad main street of this attractive town. With its sharply dressed staff, check-in desk, and lovely bedrooms it is has more the feel of a country house than a hostelry. Smartly decorated throughout, its attractive antique furniture adds to the old-world feeling. The large, informal bar is a gathering place for locals and residents alike, but if you want a few quiet moments, there are several quiet lounges with comfortable chairs overlooking the garden. While the bedrooms in the old hostelry have lots of character we also enjoy the luxurious rooms in the new wings that stretches down long corridors behind the inn into the garden. We love their spaciousness, large bathrooms and garden views. There's a good few of them that have antique four poster beds and fireplaces as well. The brasserie style dining room serves well priced food. There's always a traditional roast on the trolley to be carved at your table. For more casual dining visit the hotel's cozy restaurant, The Inn Between, in a quaint thatched cottage across the street. Enjoy the health center with its swimming pool, gymnasium and array of spa treatment rooms. The hotel specializes in making golfing, equestrian, and fishing arrangements for guests. *Directions:* Adare is on the N21, 40 km from Shannon airport, which makes it an ideal first or last stop in Ireland if you are traveling in the southwest.

DUNRAVEN ARMS
Owners: Louis & Bryan Murphy
Adare, Co Limerick, Ireland
Tel: (061) 605900, Fax: (061) 396541
90 Rooms, Double: €190–€335*
*Breakfast not included: €20, Service: 12.5%
Dinner: €45
Open: all year, Credit cards: all major
Inn
www.karenbrown.com/dunravenarms.html

Just down a country lane from the charming little ferry that plies its way to Waterford across the Barrow estuary, Dunbrody House was the onetime home of the Marquis of Donegal. Catherine and Kevin Dundon have transformed it from a private house to stylish top-class hotel complete with spa and cookery school. Kevin and his team produce food that is as exquisite to look at as it is gorgeous to eat. The house is a delightful blend of contemporary and country house—lots of scrumptious public rooms and some particularly spacious bedrooms, such as 300 with it's French windows opening up to the garden. Top of the line bathrooms are the order of the day and the house is wheelchair friendly. A resident corgi and labrador are on hand to escort you on invigorating walks that encompass terrific views of the Barrow Estuary. Be sure to visit the hens and stroll around the large organic fruit and vegetable gardens. Explore the wild and beautiful Hook Peninsula, visiting Europe's oldest lighthouse, and take the ferry to Waterford and its famous crystal factory. *Directions:* From Wexford take the R733 to Arthurstown. Dunbrody House is on your left as you approach the village. If arriving from Waterford, take the Passage East Ferry to Ballyhack. Turn right off the ferry and go 2 km (through Arthurstown) to Dunbrody House, which is on your right as you go up the hill.

DUNBRODY HOUSE
Owners: Catherine & Kevin Dundon
Arthurstown, Co Wexford, Ireland
Tel: (051) 389600, Fax: (051) 389601
20 Rooms, Double: €245–€395
Dinner: €65
Open: all year, Credit cards: all major
Ireland's Blue Book
Country house hotel
www.karenbrown.com/dunbrody.html

The Wicklow Mountains offer some of the finest walks in Ireland and there is no finer place to stay in the area than Ballyknocken House. Hospitality is Catherine Fulvio's keynote, with good baking and cooking providing the backbone for fine evening meals and decadent breakfasts. The house has been completely renovated and returned it to its original 1850s style so that it has all the charm of days gone by along with 21st-century plumbing. Five bedrooms have Victorian tubs with showers. All rooms are named after local places, the pronunciation of which may prove challenging! My favorites are Knocknaphrumpha and Aghowle at the front of the house with views over the garden. Catherine has a cooking school in the adjacent renovated milking sheds and guests often book one of her hour long classes on the baking of brown bread, scones and soda bread. If you want to stay for several days consider renting the two bedroom apartment over the cookery school. The Wicklow Way, Ireland's famous hill-walking route, is close by. If you are not up to long walks, the dogs will accompany you through the hills behind the farm—but be sure to have directions with you as they have a habit of depositing you at a neighbor's farm! *Directions:* Take the N11 south from Dublin towards Wicklow for 42 km to Ashford (just before Rathnew). Turn right immediately after the Petrol station up a steep hill and follow this road for almost 5 km to Ballyknocken House on your right.

BALLYKNOCKEN HOUSE
Owners: Catherine & Claudio Fulvio
Ashford, Glenealy, Co Wicklow, Ireland
Tel: (040) 444627, Fax: (040) 444696
7 Rooms, Double: €120–€130
1 Apartment: €600–€750 weekly
Dinner: €43 (not Sun or Mon)
Open: Feb to Dec, Credit cards: MC, VS
B&B
www.karenbrown.com/ballyknocken.html

Clone House was originally built in the 1650s and rebuilt around 1805 after burning down in the 1798 Rebellion. Now it's the home of Carla and Jeff Watson and their 3 children, with plenty of room for both family and guests. Make yourself at home in the drawing room, try your hand at the piano in the cozy music room, browse Carla's cookbooks in the parlor, or work out in the well-equipped gym. Carla uses fresh local produce cooked in Italian Tuscan style with lots of tomatoes, wine, porcini mushrooms and extra virgin olive oil. Fresh baked foccacia bread is always served with dinner. For breakfast, as well as the traditional Irish fry and soda breads, there are scones and a variety of sweet breads. Vale of Avoca is the largest bedroom with a skylight above the bed, a peat-burning fireplace, shower in the bathroom, and beautiful views of the garden. I also liked the coziness of Clara Vale with its rustic brick wall, red velvet drapes, bed hangings, fireplace, and view of the garden. Folks who admire what Jeff has done with his 5 acres of garden often head for Powerscourt Gardens. Nearby Avoca village is the Ballykissangel of the television series. The monastic settlement of Glendalough is interesting to visit, as are the beaches along Brittas Bay. *Directions:* In Aughrim, take the R4747 towards Tinahely. While in the village turn left at the low black and yellow-striped wall, then follow signs to the house. The entrance is on the right.

CLONE HOUSE
Owners: Carla & Jeff Watson
Aughrim, Co Wicklow, Ireland
Tel: (040) 236121, Fax: (040) 236029
7 Rooms, Double: €140–€200
Dinner: €55-€65
Open: all year, Credit cards: MC, VS
Hidden Ireland
Country house
www.karenbrown.com/clone.html

Bagenalstown is sometimes signposted Muine Bheag, which can lead to a certain amount of confusion in reaching Kilgraney House. But the effort put into finding it is worthwhile, for this is not your run-of-the-mill Irish country house—it's more like "Architectural Digest" than "Country Life." With its crisp lines and whimsical touches, the decor is the brainchild of your hosts, designers Bryan Leech and Martin Marley. After working abroad, Bryan and Martin returned to Ireland. Kilgraney House was put together with a touch of whimsy and artistic flair, traditional Irish antiques being added to their overseas treasures. The same attention to detail was lavished on the spotless modern bathrooms. The cooking is modern and imaginative and incorporates seasonal fruits, vegetables and herbs from the enclosed kitchen garden. In another courtyard there's a medicinal herb garden with nine raised beds in Irish oak timber, each planted with herbs suitable for treating a specific part of the body. In a converted apple house, there's an aromatherapy centre offering an all-encompassing selection of massages, facials and herbal wraps. *Directions:* Take the N9 from Dublin to Royal Oak (south of Carlow), turn left into Bagenalstown (Muine Bheag), and right in the village for the 6-km drive to Kilgraney crossroads. Turn right (signposted) and Kilgraney House is the first entrance on the left (a 2-hour drive).

KILGRANEY HOUSE
Owners: Bryan Leech & Martin Marley
Bagenalstown, Co Carlow, Ireland
Tel: (059) 9775283, Fax: (059) 9775595
6 Rooms, Double: €130–€240
2 Apartments: €400–€450 weekly
Dinner: €50 (not Mon or Tue)
Closed: Dec & Jan, Credit cards: all major
Country house & self-catering
www.karenbrown.com/kilgraneyhouse.html

A stay at Echo Lodge is all about eating fabulous food in the Mustard Seed Restaurant. Head chef David Rice's four-course table d'hote menu leaves you spoilt for choice. Owner Dan Mullane is usually on hand to explain your choices in delicious detail. Much of the produce is home grown—the organic fruit and vegetable gardens are in terraces behind the hotel and the hens in the kitchen garden provide fresh free-range eggs for breakfast. The atmosphere is convivial, Dan and his staff really go the extra mile to make you welcome. Outside diners give a real buzz to the place in an evening. Bedrooms range from quirky country house to elegant suites. There's a specially designed wheelchair-friendly room. A cute little sauna and a small exercise room are also available. A Thai masseur is on hand so indulge yourself. The quiet village location is well suited for touring the southwest and playing the several surrounding golf courses. The delightful town of Adare is a 15-minute drive away and the surrounding peaceful countryside offers lots of opportunities for horse riding, fishing, clay pigeon shooting, and antique hunting. *Directions:* From Adare take the N21, Killarney road for 2 km and turn left for Ballingarry. In the village take the Newcastle West road for 500 meters and Echo Lodge is on your right.

THE MUSTARD SEED AT ECHO LODGE
Owner: Dan Mullane
Ballingarry, Co Limerick, Ireland
Tel: (069) 68508, Fax: (069) 68511
14 Rooms, Double: €190–€310
Dinner: €60
Closed: first two weeks of Feb, Credit cards: all major
Ireland's Blue Book
Country house hotel
www.karenbrown.com/echolodge.html

Whitepark House has a perfect location on the prettiest part of the north Antrim coast between the famed Giant's Causeway and the precarious Carrick-a-Rede rope bridge. A narrow pathway leads down to the cluster of white cottages and tiny church that make up the much-photographed village of Portbraddan (on a sunny day one could easily imagine oneself in Greece). In clear weather views extend to Rathlin Island lighthouse and the distant Scottish islands of Islay and Jura. Small wonder that Siobhan and Bob love the area and are keen for guests to enjoy it and their home. Whitepark House was built in 1735, extended in the early 1900s and totally remodeled in 2007 to add spacious bedrooms, luxurious bathrooms and a lovely conservatory, where breakfast is served overlooking the garden. Bob and Siobhan are inveterate travelers—India, Japan, Sri Lanka, Thailand, Africa. Fascinating mementos of their travels are artfully displayed alongside masses of leafy green houseplants, which flourish under Bob's tender care. Bob is happy to drive walkers to the Giant's Causeway and welcomes them home after a 13-kilometer coastal walk with homemade biscuits and tea. *Directions:* Whitepark House is on the coast road 6.5 km east of the Giant's Causeway and just over 1.5 km west of Ballintoy.

WHITEPARK HOUSE
Owners: Siobhan & Bob Isles
Ballintoy
Co Antrim, BT45 6NH, Northern Ireland
Tel: (028) 2073 1482
3 Rooms, Double: £90
Open: all year, Credit cards: MC, VS
B&B
www.karenbrown.com/whitepark.html

Stella Maris has a fabulous location on the shores of Bunatrahir Bay where white topped waves cascade across the rocks and windswept sandy beaches stretch towards the rugged cliffs of Downpatrick Head. Built in 1853 as coastguard headquarters it later served as a convent and then as a school. Most recently new life, as a boutique hotel, has been breathed into these sturdy buildings by Frances Kelly and Terence McSweeney. It's a stylish place with a pleasing blend of traditional and modern décor. Quite the best place to enjoy the ever-changing seascape is from the conservatory built all along the front of the building to maximize the panoramic ocean views. Dinner is cooked by Frances and enjoyed in the dining room made up of four intimate little cottage rooms—then it's back to the conservatory for coffee and drinks. Almost all of the bedrooms are ocean facing and come in queens and kings/twins all named after local and famous golf courses. The many miles of wild County Mayo coastline are yours to explore. Be sure to visit nearby Ceide Fields, an excavated Stone-Age settlement with walls older than the pyramids. *Directions:* Stella Maris is located on the ocean, 25 km west of Ballina and 2 km west of Ballycastle.

STELLA MARIS COUNTRY HOUSE HOTEL
Owners: Frances Kelly & Terry McSweeney
Ballycastle, Co Mayo, Ireland
Tel: (096) 43322, Fax: (096) 43965
11 Rooms, Double: €200–€250
Dinner: €45
Open: Easter to mid-Oct, Credit cards: MC, VS
Ireland's Blue Book
Country house hotel
www.karenbrown.com/stellamarisire.html

We visited Gorman's at the insistence of Peter Haden, of Gregans Castle. We completely agree with everything he stated in his email to us: "…(This property) has a spectacular location out on the remotest part of the Dingle Peninsula overlooking Smerwick Harbour and out to the Atlantic—wild, savage scenery surrounds. The building is quite new and certainly not quaint, but the moment you step inside, there is a wonderful feeling of warmth generated by the most genuine greeting, open fires, sunny color schemes, and very comfortable furnishings. The tea and homemade biscuits make you immediately relax and feel at home. There are nine large, well-furnished bedrooms, all with fabulous views and good bathrooms with buckets of hot water and all the little extras. The dining room is designed to take advantage of the views, and we had dinner watching the sun set on the Atlantic horizon. Food is fine without being famous, and service is very friendly. Rarely before have I stayed in a place where I had such a good feeling of genuine friendliness and warmth from the owners, who are dedicated to providing the best for everyone. What more can I say?" Not a thing! *Directions:* Go through Dingle town keeping the harbor on your left. At the roundabout west of town, go straight (signpost An Fheothanach)—Gorman's is 13 km on. After about 8 km the road forks: stay left and you come back to the coast—the sea is on your right and Gorman's is on your left.

GORMAN'S CLIFFTOP HOUSE
Owners: Sile & Vincent Gorman
Glaise Bheag
Ballydavid, (Baile na nGall) Dingle Peninsula
Co Kerry, Ireland
Tel & Fax: (066) 9155 162
9 Rooms, Double: €130–€190
Dinner: €40 (not Sun)
Closed: Christmas, Credit cards: MC, VS
Guesthouse
www.karenbrown.com/gormans.html

This tall, bright-white Victorian house set amidst lush gardens rimming the shores of Bantry Bay is a most hospitable welcoming hotel. Run by Kathleen O'Sullivan and her gracious long time staff the atmosphere is friendly and informal, which accounts, I am sure, for the large number of guests who return here year after year. Enjoy a pre-dinner drink in the sitting room bar and select your dinner from the tempting menu which usually includes fresh seafood—we particularly enjoyed out selections of locally raised duck and fresh lemon sole. For those in search of peace and quiet there is an old-fashioned parlor/TV room. The dining room is cleverly divided into several areas which creates a most enjoyable experience. Be sure to request a room at the front of the house for a great many these rooms have tempting glimpses of the bay across the gardens and through the trees. Two garden view rooms have been especially equipped for the handicapped. The scenery hereabouts is absolutetely spectacular. If you have time, wander off the main roads to explore the Beara Peninsula with its views of barren, rocky mountains tumbling into the sea. A "must visit" is nearby Garinish Island, a spectacular garden with trees, shrubs, and plants from every part of the world. Just down the road is Bantry House, a grand mansion that is well worth a visit. *Directions:* Seaview House Hotel is located in Ballylickey on the N71 between Bantry and Glengarriff.

SEAVIEW HOUSE HOTEL
Owner: Kathleen O'Sullivan
Ballylickey, Co Cork, Ireland
Tel: (027) 50462/50073, Fax: (027) 51555
26 Rooms, Double: €160–€200
Dinner: €40
Open: mid-Mar to mid-Nov, Credit cards: all major
Country house hotel
www.karenbrown.com/seaviewhouse.html

Olive and Paddy O`Gorman have a relaxed, easygoing attitude to life. They welcome guests to the wing of their commodious farmhouse nestled in the pretty Nire Valley, an area of Ireland off the beaten tourist path and noted for its beautiful scenery. Knowing that you deserve the best, request one of Olive`s premier rooms with Jacuzzi tub and shower. Olive takes great pride in her bedrooms not only matching the bedspread and drapes with the wallpaper but taking it so far to see that each room has cups and saucers that match the room`s colorful decor. Olive finds it no problem at all to juggle her family and a houseful of guests, chatting with them over tea and cake when they arrive, feeding them copious breakfasts, packing tempting lunches, arranging for them to go walking and feeding them dinner in the conservatory on their return. Guests come to this quiet corner of County Waterford to walk the Comeragh Mountains and experience Irish farmhouse hospitality. If the outdoor pursuits of fishing, pony-trekking, and walking are not your cup of tea, you can drive to Lismore, Cashel, or over The Vee, returning in time for a visit to one of the nearby pubs for a late-night Irish music session. *Directions:* From Clonmel or Dungarven follow the R671 to Ballymacarbry. Glasha is signposted to your right just before you reach Ballymacarbry if you are coming from Clonmel or just after to your left if you are coming from Dungarven.

GLASHA
Owners: Olive & Paddy O'Gorman
Ballymacarbry, Via Clonmel
Co Waterford, Ireland
Tel & Fax: (052) 36108
8 Rooms, Double: €100–€120
Dinner: €25-€40 (not Sun)
Closed: Christmas, Credit cards: MC, VS
Farmhouse B&B
www.karenbrown.com/glasha.html

Marlagh Lodge dates back to 1853. It was originally built for Henry Hutchinson Hamilton O'Hara, son of local landholders and residents of nearby Crebilly Castle. Now a listed building it is described as an interesting Victorian mix of picturesque and Georgian elements, gabled bays and roof overhangs. Standing in its own grounds adjacent to the A3 secondary glazing helps to keep the high ceilinged bedrooms warm and reduces traffic noise to a minimum. Current owners Robert and Rachel Thompson have brought the property back to its former glory with the careful eye of experienced practitioners, a four poster here, a brass bed there, antiques and collectibles, black iron and tile fireplaces. The piano in the study attests to the Thompsons' musical talents. A hearty breakfast is served in the dining room, home made bread, local produce, porridge or a traditional Ulster Fry. A twenty minute drive finds you at Belfast International airport. Marlagh Lodge is ideal for visiting Belfast but the great draw lies in the opposite directions where you find the Giants Causeway and the lovely Antrim coast. *Directions:* Exit the M2 at Antrim and take the A26 to Ballymena. At the first roundabout take the A36 Larne and at the second the A36 Larne. After 1km you see the house on the right, turn right into Rankinstown Road and immediate left into the driveway.

MARLAGH LODGE   New
Owners: Rachel & Robert Thompson
71 Moorfields Road
Ballymena, Co Antrim, BT42 3BU, Northern Ireland
Tel: (028) 2563 1505, Fax: (028) 2564 1590
3 Rooms, Double: £80
Dinner: £32.50
Closed: Christmas & New Year, Credit cards: MC, VS
Hidden Ireland
Country house
www.karenbrown.com/marlagh.html

When I travel I'm always in search of something that is completely different from home and this is the case here as most of my house would fit itnot the entrance hall where Roderick and Helena Perceval keep the "wellies", fishing paraphernalia, and inclement weather gear. And that's just the tip of the iceberg for beyond lie rooms of enormous proportions. One bedroom is aptly named the half acre. Another is the twins' room because it has two of everything—all pleasingly idiosyncratic and just bursting with character. Furniture made for the house is still here along with a grand array of family portraits. Roderick makes certain guests are introduced to one another when they gather fro pre-dinner drinks round the fire in the snug little sitting room. Whenever I have stayed there have always been the most interesting of dinner conversations with my fellow guests around the polished dining room table and, of course, the food is always excellent. As for what to do during the day—some folks never leave the estate: there's a vast lake for fishing (a boat is available for pike fishing), a lakeside castle built by the Knights Templar in 1200, a huge walled garden, and miles of walking paths (Roderick will give you a map). The Percevals have lived here since 1665 and there are some wonderful stories of ancestors' exploits. *Directions:* From Sligo take the N4 to the N17 (Galway road). The house is signpost to the left 0.5km south of Ballinacarrow.

TEMPLE HOUSE
Owners: Roderick & Helena Perceval
Ballinacarrow, Ballymote
Co Sligo, Ireland
Tel: (071) 9183329, Fax: (071) 9183808
6 Rooms, Double: €160–€180
1 Cottage: €625-€995 weekly
Dinner: €42 (not Sun)
Open: Apr to Nov, Credit cards: MC, VS
Hidden Ireland, Country house
www.karenbrown.com/templehouse.html

Ballinkeele House was built for the Maher family in 1840, and Margaret and John are the fourth generation of Mahers to call this heritage house home. Set amidst 350 acres of parklike grounds, the house has all the solid quality of a grand home built in the early Victorian period: big rooms, fine ceilings, decorative doors, quality in every detail. Apart from the addition of heating and modern bathrooms, the house has not changed over the years. Soft Oriental rugs dress the flagstone entry, which is warmed by a huge, old-fashioned stove, and grand oil paintings and family portraits adorn the walls. Antique furniture graces the cozy drawing room and enormous dining room where guests enjoy delicious candlelit dinners. The Master Bedroom is a particularly large room decorated in soft red and beiges with an impressive four-poster bed sitting center stage. For recreation there are walks through the estate and croquet on the lawn. Settle in for several nights and enjoy County Wexford—historic Wexford's Georgian theater, home to the October Opera Festival; the Wexford Wildlife Reserve, famous for its wintering wildfowl; and the National Heritage Park with its old Irish buildings. The Mahers have bicycles for guests. The port of Rosslare is a 40-minute drive away. *Directions:* From Dublin take the N11, Wexford road, to Gorey. Turn left at the traffic lights for Wexford (R741) for 30 km and the 5-km drive to Ballinkeele House is signposted on your right.

BALLINKEELE HOUSE
Owners: Margaret & John Maher
Ballymurn, Enniscorthy
Co Wexford, Ireland
Tel: (053) 9138105, Fax: (053) 9138468
5 Rooms, Double: €160–€180
Dinner: €45 (not Tue)
Open: Feb to Nov, Credit cards: all major
Hidden Ireland
Country house
www.karenbrown.com/ballinkeelehouse.html

Ballynahinch Castle, former home of the O'Flaherty chieftains, a pirate queen and a maharajah, has enjoyed a long and colorful history. The heart of this friendly hotel is the bar with its old brick floor and little tables surrounded by Windsor chairs. Here a long table displays the "catch of the day" and fisherfolk hang the keys that give them access to the little huts on their fishing beats—no need to stand out in the rain when fishing here. The beats are so close to the house that folks return to the bar for lunch (packed lunches are also available). Bar food is served in the evening for those who are not inclined to partake of a more formal meal in the dining room whose windows overlook the river. Bedrooms come in three varieties: standard, superior, and luxury, which at Ballynahinch Castle means large, larger, and largest. On a recent visit I was particularly impressed by rooms on the top floor with their lovely décor and top of the line bathrroms. Plans are moving ahead to add an all things outdoors store to the courtyard along with a workout room and the opportunity to enjoy a massage. The beauty of Connemara is on your doorstep, Helpful staff assist you in planning daytrips. Often guests never leave the hotel's property, spending their days wandering through the 450 acres of grounds or by the fire with a book. *Directions:* From Galway take the N59 Clifden for 68 km and turn left for Roundstone. The hotel is on your right after 4 km.

BALLYNAHINCH CASTLE
Manager: Patrick O'Flaherty
Ballynahinch, Connemara
Co Galway, Ireland
Tel: (095) 31006, Fax: (095) 31085
40 Rooms, Double: €220–€420*
*Service: 10%
Dinner: €55
Closed: Feb, Credit cards: all major
Country house hotel
www.karenbrown.com/ballynahinch.html

With The Burren sheltering its back and a panoramic view of Ballyvaughan Bay to the towering cliffs of Black Head in front, Drumcreehy House commands an location just outside the picturesque village of Ballyvaughan. Bernadette and Armin designed this house to look as old as possible while including all modern amenities. To add to the traditional feel, they have furnished the sitting room and dining room with antiques, and all the bedrooms with old pine. Spring Gentian and Dog Violet are especially spacious with larger shower rooms, and along with Cowslip and Primrose enjoy spectacular views across the bay to Black Head. If you are not up to stairs request a room in the adjacent two bedroom cottage—perfect for families. Coffee, tea and an honesty bar are available in a cozy little room off the sitting room. Enjoy a cooked breakfast in the sunny yellow breakfast room where a vast sidebarard laden with fruit, cereal, cheeses, smoked salmon and meats caused me to cancel my cooked breakfast (ordered the night before). Shannon is an hour's drive away, making this an ideal first or last night on your trip, but stay longer and explore the beautiful Burren and beyond. *Directions:* From Shannon take the N18 to Ennis, the N85 towards Ennistymon, and the first right through Corofin and on towards Kilfenora. At the ruined castle turn right for Ballyvaughan and go about 10 km to the village. At Hylands Hotel, turn right and the house is on the righ after 1 km.

DRUMCREEHY HOUSE
Owners: Bernadette & Armin Grefkes
Ballyvaughan, Co Clare, Ireland
Tel: (065) 7077377, Fax: (065) 7077379
10 Rooms, Double: €80–€120
Open: all year, Credit cards: MC, VS
Guesthouse
www.karenbrown.com/drumcreehy.html

Gregans Castle is only 57 kilometers from Shannon airport, so if you are heading north or west, this is the perfect spot to begin your stay in Ireland. This is not an imposing castle, but a sprawling manor house set in lovely gardens in a lush green valley completely surrounded by The Burren, with its "moonscapes" of gray limestone and scattered alpine and arctic plants. While there are several comfortable lounges to congregate in, my preference is the beamed Corkscrew bar with its blazing turf fire. Lunch is served here, and in the evening guests gather for a drink and a chat. From the dining room, where tables are reserved for all guests for dinner each night, windows frame outstanding views of The Burren sweeping down to the edge of Galway Bay. On a recent visit I really liked Gleninagh—a standard twin room with a particularly nice bathroom, Mina's room—a superior king-bedded room in the oldest part of the house facing Galway Bay, and the three garden suites with their private patios and brand new bathrooms. Local attractions include the Ailwee Caves, full of stalactites and stalagmites, and the Cliffs of Moher. *Directions:* From Shannon take the N18 to Ennis, the N85 towards Ennistymon, the first right (R476) through Corofin, and on towards Kilfenora. At the ruined castle turn right onto the R480 towards Ballyvaughan and, as you crest The Burren, you see the hotel in the valley below.

GREGANS CASTLE
Owners: Frederieke & Simon Haden
Ballyvaughan, Co Clare, Ireland
Tel: (065) 7077 005, Fax: (065) 7077 111
21 Rooms, Double: €190–€230
Dinner: from €36
Open: Feb 4 to Nov 30, Credit cards: all major
Ireland's Blue Book
Country house hotel
www.karenbrown.com/gregans.html

Dating back to 1750 this stately home sits in an elevated position with magnificent views across Bantry Bay. The current owner, descendant of the Earls of Bantry, Egerton Shelswell-White opens the house and gardens to the public who, with information sheets in hand, tour its lofty rooms and admire its elegant furniture, tapestries and paintings, retiring afterwards to the tearoom in the old refectory. Yet this is a stately home with a difference for one entire wing of the house has been renovated to provide six large airy guestrooms, each with a top of the line bathroom. I was particularly impressed with room 25, its curving wall of windows and window seats overlooking the bay. Breakfast is prepared for you in the smartly decorated dining room in what used to be one of the old cellars. At night toast your toes by the fire in the little lounge, help yourself to drinks from the honesty bar, play billiards in the enormous billiard room or, if you wish, slip through the concealed door into the long gallery to wander at leisure through the museum like rooms of this grand old home. In addition two spacious, more simply decorated, family rooms are found above the tearoom. Dinner can be arranged for parties that rent the entire wing. There are several restaurants that you can walk to in town. *Directions:* Bantry is on the N71 between Skibereen and Kenmare. Turn through the arched gatehouse (beside the large white hotel on the waterfront) and drive up to the house.

BANTRY HOUSE   *New*
Owners: Egerton & Brigitte Shelswell-White
Manager: Cathy McCarter
Bantry, Co Cork, Ireland
Tel: (027) 50047, Fax: (027) 50795
8 Rooms, Double: €200–€300
Open: mid-Mar to Nov, Credit cards: MC, VS
Hidden Ireland
Country house
www.karenbrown.com/bantry.html

Rosemary and Brian McAuley had Dunauley designed to take advantage of the spectacular view of the island-dotted Bantry Bay, aptly framed by a wall of windows in the living/dining room. Three double-bedded bedrooms, each with en suite shower room, are found on the same level as the living room. Downstairs is an additional bedroom with a magnificent view. A snug one bedroom apartment (queen plus single bed) has its own entrance and can be rented on a weekly basis. Guests enjoy both the living room and its particularly fine view as they sit round the fire in the evening and while tucking into an ample breakfast before setting out on a day's sightseeing. Breakfast is the only meal Rosemary serves, and guests usually drive into town for dinner. The drive from Bantry to Glengarriff gives a taste of the rugged landscape and exotic flora that you find in this part of Ireland. From the town you can take a boat to Garinish Island, a lush collection of interesting shrubs, trees, and flowers from all over the world. For over three years a hundred men worked to make Arran Bryce's garden, caseta, and temple; but financial hardships precluded the building of his home. *Directions:* From the center of Bantry follow white signs for the hospital through the one-way system and up the hill. Pass a church on the right and continue on this road till you see Dunauley signposted to the right—keep going uphill to the house.

☕ P 🚭 🧍 👫 🐎 ⛵

DUNAULEY
Owners: Rosemary & Brian McAuley
Seskin
Bantry, Co Cork, Ireland
Tel & Fax: (027) 50290
4 Rooms, Double: €80–€90
1 apartment: €350–€450 weekly
Open: May to Sep, Credit cards: none
B&B & self-catering
www.karenbrown.com/dunauley.html

This impressive building with its façade of carved stonework columns and statuary dates back to 1860. Originally constructed as the grand headquarters of the Ulster Bank, it has been extensively remodeled and renovated prior to opening as a five-star hotel. Guestrooms feature dramatically high ceilings, custom furniture, antiques, original artwork and sumptuous soft furnishings. Splendid en-suite bathrooms with brown marble, white porcelain, sparkling chrome and glass are no less than would be expected. All the electronic needs of today's traveler, large flat- screen TV's, wireless internet and CD/DVD players complete the picture. Suites, with their splendid hip-bath soaking tubs, are located in the original bank management living quarters. Vaults, with their massive steel doors intact, have been converted to wine cellars and a snooker room. "The Bar", which specializes in cocktails, is to be found adjacent to the appropriately named "Great Room" Restaurant. The latter, created in what was the original public banking area is the epitome of elegance. The Restaurant, which features intricate plasterwork, an antique Clevi harp, a huge Tyrone Crystal chandelier, discreetly separated tables and rich décor, serves breakfast, lunch and dinner, and afternoon teas. *Directions:* From the M3 take the A2 south, turn left at Ann Street, turn right at Victoria Street and left at Waring Street to the hotel. Double park to unload and you will be directed to nearby parking.

THE MERCHANT HOTEL   New
Owner: Bill Wolsley
Manager: Adrian Mclaughlan
35-39 Waring Street
Belfast, BT1 2DY, Northern Ireland
Tel: (028) 9023 4888, Fax: (028) 9024 7775
26 Rooms, Double: £240–£640
Open: all year, Credit cards: all major
Ireland's Blue Book
City hotel
www.karenbrown.com/themerchanthotel.html

Ash-Rowan is the relaxed, very friendly, unpretentious home of Sam and Evelyn Hazlett—an excellent choice for a bed and breakfast while staying in the northern capital. A varied choice of breakfasts sets you up for the day—opt for organic porridge flavored with Drambuie and cream served with pancakes; Irish scramble with eggs, chopped bacon, and mushrooms, or the Ulster Fry, the ultimate cooked breakfast which the menu warns is not for the faint hearted. Vegetarians should try the flambéed mushrooms or vegetarian omlette. It's a climb to the top of the house (no large cases!) but worth it to secure one of the choice rooms (7 and 8) that offer more spacious quarters. All the rooms have TVs, phones, bathrobes, and hospitality trays with biscuits, teas, coffee, and instant soups. Beds are made with crisply starched linen sheets and pillowcases. The location, near the university, is perfect for strolling into the city and taxis are inexpensive for a night out on the town. Peruse the papers and the tourist literature in the wonderfully cluttered conservatory then seek out Sam or Evelyn to set you up with sightseeing venues for the day. *Directions:* From central Belfast take Dublin Road to Shaftesbury Square. Go through Bradbury Place onto University Road. Pass Queen's University on the left and go straight through the traffic lights into Malone Road. Windsor Avenue is the fifth avenue on your right.

ASH-ROWAN
Owners: Evelyn & Sam Hazlett
12 Windsor Avenue
Belfast, BT9 6EE, Northern Ireland
Tel: (028) 9066 1758, Fax: (028) 9066 3227
5 Rooms, Double: £89–£96
Closed: Christmas & New Year, Credit cards: MC, VS
Guesthouse
www.karenbrown.com/ashrowan.html

Set just across the street from Belfast's historic City Hall, Ten Square is a contemporary up-market town house hotel, built on the site of the old Post Office. A welcoming fire warms the seating area in the reception hall. On the ground floor the bustling public bar with its wooden columns, brick faced walls, leather cushioned seats and raffia lanterns is a lively meeting place for young and old alike. The equally stylish adjacent Grill Room restaurant with its leather benches, hardback chairs, dark wooden floors and tables, sparkling glass and silverware serves a typical bistro style menu supported by a very reasonably priced international wine list. Stylish bedrooms are to be found on the two floors above; pale earthtones are offset with splashed of color. Furnishings border on minimalist, but the work of local artist Terry Bradley is prominently displayed. King sized beds, high ceilings, all modern electronic conveniences and sparkling black and white tile bathrooms complete the picture. Ten Square is handy for walking to everything in central Belfast. *Directions:* Arriving in Belfast take the M2 and follow signs for city centre. Take the 1st right and 1st left in front and beside City Hall and you find Ten Square behind city hall on the corner of Linen Hall Street. Park in front to unload and be directed to an overnight stay car park.

*TEN SQUARE   **New***
Owners: Nicholas & Paul Hill
10 Donegal Square South
Belfast, BT1 5JD, Northern Ireland
Tel: (028) 9024 1001, Fax: (028) 9024 3210
22 Rooms, Double: £175–£250
Open: all year, Credit cards: all major
City hotel
www.karenbrown.com/tensquare.html

John and Ann are particularly gregarious hosts, perhaps influenced by their close proximity to the Blarney stone, said to confer the "gift of the gab." John would have you believe that you can tour the entire south of Ireland from their guesthouse. While this is somewhat of an exaggeration, it certainly is an ideal base for visiting Cork, Cobh, Kinsale, as well as enjoying a day in Blarney where the castle's lovely grounds and Blarney woolen mills are great attractions. While Ashlee Lodge may seem unremarkable from the road, the place is full of surprises. Comfortable bedrooms can all be either twin or king, with large TVs and CD players. They come in three sizes: executive—good size rooms with shower over the tub, garden—larger rooms with Jacuzzi bathtubs, or master—very large rooms with sitting area and Jacuzzi bathtubs. One bedroom is totally wheelchair friendly. There's also an upstairs deck with a hot tub. Drinks are served from the honesty bar in the evening and the light and airy breakfast room (lots of choices as well as a cooked Irish breakfast) doubles as the restaurant in the evening. Golf is endemic hereabouts and John will gladly arrange tee times and transportation. If you want to travel without a car, airport pickup can be arranged. Handily the bus to Blarney and Cork runs by the front door. *Directions:* Ashlee Lodge is located in Tower, 2 km west of Blarney. The house is on the R617—the Blarney to Killarney Road.

❄ ☕ ✗ 💳 ☎ 🐕 @ P ⑪ 🚭 ❀ 🖼 ♿ ⚓ 🚶 🎣

ASHLEE LODGE
Owners: John & Anne O'Leary
Blarney, Co Cork, Ireland
Tel: (021) 4385346, Fax: (021) 4385726
10 Rooms, Double: €120–€250
Dinner: €35 (not Sun or Mon)
Closed: Christmas & New Year, Credit cards: MC, VS
Guesthouse
www.karenbrown.com/ashlee.html

Bobbie Smith's home reflects her welcoming, easygoing personality. Filled with mellow old furniture, books, pictures, and family mementos, the Old Rectory is very much a lived-in, comfortable family home for Bobbie and her three daughters. Guests are welcomed with a reviving pot of tea in the homey drawing room, and it is here that they chat with fellow guests before dinner, which is taken by candlelight round the long, gleaming dining room table. Bedrooms have the same traditional family feel and range from a snug twin to two spacious rooms, one with a carved four-poster and the other with a splendid Victorian bed with turned posts decorating the foot and headboard. All have en suite shower rooms and there's an extra "bath" so that those who love to soak can do so in a claw-foot tub. The area is perfect for cycling; and holidays that include cycle hire, airport pickup, and baggage transportation can be arranged. Those who prefer to stick to their car will find Kilkenny with its castle, fine old shops, and lovely buildings just a 20-minute drive away. Day trips can be taken to Wexford, Kildare, and Glendalough. *Directions:* Take the N9 from Dublin to Royal Oak (south of Carlow), turn left into Bagenalstown, and right in the village for the 6-km drive to Lorum Old Rectory.

LORUM OLD RECTORY
Owner: Bobbie Smith
Kilgreaney, Bagenalstown, Borris
Co Carlow, Ireland
Tel: (059) 9775282, Fax: (059) 9775455
5 Rooms, Double: €150–€170
Dinner: €45
Closed: Nov to Feb, Credit cards: MC, VS
Hidden Ireland
Country house
www.karenbrown.com/lorumoldrectory.html

Bruckless House was built in the mid-18th century and lived in by the Cassidy brothers, traders and merchants who sold guns to Napoleon and pickled herrings to Wellington in Portugal. Later the house was owned by a passionate Communist, Commander Fforde, who is remembered for his many good works in the area. Continuing the tradition of colorful owners, Clive and Joan Evans moved here after spending many years in Hong Kong. This lovely home has the most marvelous location, set in wooded acres with garden paths leading down to the rocky shoreline of Bruckless Bay. Colorful Oriental rugs warm the flagstone entryway and mementos of the Evans' years abroad blend with comfortable family antiques. A log fire warms the dining room on chilly mornings as guests breakfast together round the long polished table. Bedrooms are found in what was once the children's wing up the back staircase. Nanny's Room is a delightful twin-bedded room with an en suite bathroom with a power shower over the tub, and a double-bedded room also has an en suite bathroom. Both rooms have single rooms adjacent to them for children. At the top of the driveway, an adorable two-bedroom lodge is perfect for families who wish to stay for several days (in summer it is let on a weekly basis). Bruckless is ideally placed for exploring Donegal. *Directions:* From Donegal take the N56 towards Killybegs. The house is on the left in Bruckless village.

BRUCKLESS HOUSE
Owners: Clive & Joan Evans
Bruckless, Co Donegal, Ireland
Tel: (074) 9737071, Fax: (074) 9737070
4 Rooms, Double: €110–€130
1 Cottage: €230–€500 weekly
Open: Apr to Sep, Credit cards: all major
Country house & self-catering
www.karenbrown.com/bruckless.html

This onetime coaching inn was in a sad and sorry state before it was rescued by the present owner, Roy Bolton, and transformed into the delightful hotel you see today. A rocking chair sits before an enormous fireplace and displays of old plates adorn the mantle. The ambiance of an old coaching inn continues to the restaurant with its whitewashed stone walls and tall pine settles dividing the room into intimate little areas. The inn's original kitchen, with its flagstone floor and open fire, links the hotel to the Victorian-style bar still illuminated by flickering gas light. Try a Black Bush whiskey from the distillery up the road—Bushmills is the home of the world's oldest licensed distillery and you can take a tour around it. There is a broad range of bedrooms. The most desirable are definitely the Superior Rooms of the Mill House, where you can expect to be pampered up to best 5-star standards. However, all the Mill House rooms are spacious with a small sitting area and ample room for luggage and golf clubs (lots of excellent courses nearby, including Royal Portrush). Small budget price rooms are also available in the original Coaching Inn overlooking the village. Just up the road are the picturesque ruins of 13th-century Dunluce Castle and the Giant's Causeway. *Directions:* From Coleraine take the B19 to Bushmills. As you cross the River Bush, the main entrance to the hotel is on your left.

BUSHMILLS INN HOTEL
Managers: Stella Minogue & Alan Dunlop
9 Dunluce Road
Bushmills,
Co Antrim, BT57 8QG, Northern Ireland
Tel: (028) 2073 3000, Fax: (028) 2073 2048
32 Rooms, Double: £98–£268
Dinner: from £30
Open: all year, Credit cards: MC, VS
Ireland's Blue Book, Inn
www.karenbrown.com/bushmillsinn.html

Even though it is only just over 4 kilometers from the Ring of Kerry, Iskeroon is one of the most hidden and secluded properties in Ireland. Reached by a precipitous lane that tumbles down to the sea and a narrow farm track, Iskeroon boasts the most spectacular view in Ireland—truly a hidden gem. Geraldine and David are the first family to call this home, for while the house was built in the '30s, it was previously used as holiday home. Snuggling into a sheltered spot, the long, low-lying house captures the sea view from every room, a view so enchanting that it takes you a while to realize that the house is also delightful with its three spacious bedrooms, living room, and dining room decorated in Mediterranean shades of yellow, blue, red, and green—furnished in a most attractive, unfussy way. Robes are provided for nipping across the hall to your private bathrooms. A lovely, two-person, self-catering apartment is found in the stables. The nearby town of Waterville has a good selection of restaurants for dinner—David and Geraldine are happy to advise. The garden tumbles down to a private jetty. Guests often take the boat from Bunavalla pier to the Skelligs. *Directions:* Derrynane is between Waterville and Caherdaniel. Find the Scarriff Inn (a large red building) between these villages and take the road signposted Bunavalla Pier all the way to the bottom. At the pier turn left over the track beside the beach to Iskeroon.

ISKEROON
Owners: Geraldine & David Hare
Caherdaniel, Derrynane, Co Kerry, Ireland
Tel: (066) 9475119, Fax: (066) 9475488
3 Rooms, Double: €150–€175
1 Apartment: €450–€550 weekly
Open: May to Sep, Credit cards: all major
Country house & self-catering
www.karenbrown.com/iskeroon.html

Lisdonagh House's last owner, Valda Palmer, discouraged visitors and frequently shot at them on sight. Thankfully a very different welcome is offered today by Finola and John Cooke. A smile, warm handshake, and a restorative cup of tea in the drawing room is their standard prescription for those of us who have wandered around seemingly identical lanes looking for the place (though it's certainly worth getting lost to stay here deep in the countryside). A striking feature of the house is the oval entrance hall with its 1790 murals depicting the virtues of valor, chastity, beauty, and justice. This leads to a grand staircase, which arches up to bedrooms and down to further bedrooms and a stone-faced lounge-cum-bar at the base of the tower. The house has been totally restored. Walk down to Lough Hackett and take the rowing boat out to the crannóg, a man-made island reputedly the home of the High Kings of Connaught over 2,000 years ago. Farther afield lie Galway and Cong. Lisdonagh can be rented as a whole on a self-catering basis or complete with chef and housekeeping staff. There are also two Victorian villas which can be rented for the night or on a weekly basis. *Directions:* From the N18 (Galway road) follow signposts for Sligo through Claregalway and keep on the N17 towards Tuam (about 18 km). Turn left on the R333 towards Headford to Caherlistrane. At Quealey's pub turn right towards Shrule and after 2 km turn left to Lisdonagh House.

LISDONAGH HOUSE
Owners: Finola & John Cooke
Caherlistrane, Headford, Co Galway, Ireland
Tel: (093) 31163, Fax: (093) 31528
10 Rooms, Double: €180–€280
2 Cottages: €850–€980 weekly
Dinner: €49
Open: May to Oct, Credit cards: all major
Ireland's Blue Book
Country house hotel & self-catering
www.karenbrown.com/lisdonagh.html

Ballaghtobin has everything: a beautifully decorated and furnished interior; acres of scenic parkland with a ruined Norman church just steps from the front door; an excellent location for exploring the Counties of Waterford and Kilkenny; and the most welcoming of owners in Mickey and Catherine Gabbett. Catherine's flair for interior design is evident in every elegant, informal room—soft, warm pastel walls, beautiful paintings, lovely antiques—it's very easy to settle in here. Bedrooms are absolutely gorgeous and have sparkling modern bathrooms. My favorite is the spacious Barrack Room—in years gone by, guests who drank too much at parties were sent here to sleep. Breakfast is the only meal served and for dinner guests often go to the Hunter Yard at Mount Juliet. You could really spend a week doing something totally different each day. There is medieval Kilkenny city with its wealth of historical sights; the craft trail that combines potters, leather makers, and glass blowers; golf courses from local to championship; Waterford with its historic harbor and famous crystal; and Cashel with its rock and historic abbey. *Directions:* From the main crossroads in the center of Callan take the road signed "Callan Garden Centre" (Mill Street). Go straight for 5 km (past Callan golf Club) and follow a sharp bend to the left. Take the left fork at the Y-junction (house is signposted) and after about .5 km Ballaghtobin's entrance is on your left opposite a pink gate lodge.

BALLAGHTOBIN
Owners: Catherine & Mickey Gabbett
Callan, Co Kilkenny, Ireland
Tel: (056) 7725227, Fax: (056) 7725712
3 Rooms, Double: €100
Closed: Dec & Jan, Credit cards: MC, VS
Country house
www.karenbrown.com/ballaghtobin.html

This is the place to stay if you are a garden buff for this lovely Georgian house, built in 1794, is surrounded by 7 acres of glorious gardens. Started in 1947, the gardens extend from walled formality with trim lawns and herbaceous borders to a magical informal woodland garden complete with millpond and literary corner where you can curl up with a good book. It's home to Mark and Emma Hewlett and their three young boys who Emma fervently hopes will be keen gardeners too. It's a lovely place to base yourself for explorations along the southeast coast. An ideal place to relax and enjoy the spectacular gardens, tennis court, heated indoor pool, exercise room or indulge yourself with a massage and aromatherapy session. Dinner in the peacock dining room is a real treat there's always fresh fish on the menu and most of the vegetables and fruit comes from the extensive kitchen garden. Breakfast and lunch are enjoyed in the airy conservatory which doubles as the Pink Teacup café for daytime garden visitors. Two interconnecting courtyard bedrooms are especially handy for families and friends traveling together. In the house Magnolia is an particularly inviting room with its large four-poster bed and clawfoot-tub with garden view. The Coach House and the Garden Suite are two lovely, self-catering apartments. *Directions:* From New Ross take the R733 signposted Campile and follow signposts to Kilmokea Gardens.

KILMOKEA
Owners: Emma & Mark Hewlett
Campile, Great Island, Co Wexford, Ireland
Tel: (051) 388109, Fax: (051) 388766
6 Rooms, Double: €180–€300
2 Apartments: €750–€1,250 weekly
Dinner: from €50
Open: Feb to Oct, Credit cards: MC, VS
Hidden Ireland
Country house hotel & self-catering
www.karenbrown.com/kilmokea.html

Paul's parents bought this huge home when he was a child and quickly discovered that it was far too large to maintain as a family home without an army of staff, so they opened it up to guests. His mum, Jean, while claiming to be retired still enthusiastically advises guests on where to go and what to see between breakfast and dinner—she has enough sightseeing venues to occupy a fortnight. Wife Clare does the front of house in an evening while Paul is in the kitchen. Up the grand staircase there are some very spacious, well equipped and comfortable bedrooms—be sure to discuss the size of bed, several are large zip-and-link beds while others are smaller with lovely old head and footboards. Do not miss the opportunity to visit Lismore Castle, Swiss Cottage, and Waterford Crystal, or to take a drive over The Vee. You need to keep busy to work off the delicious dinners that Paul prepares (a set four-course menu with choices or the flexibility of being able to order à la carte). Old and new guests alike revel in the relaxed idiosyncrasy of the place. *Directions:* From Waterford take the N72 (Killarney road) for about a one-hour drive to Cappoquin. Richmond House is on the left just before you enter town.

RICHMOND HOUSE
Owner: The Deevy family
Cappoquin, Co Waterford, Ireland
Tel: (058) 54278, Fax: (058) 54988
9 Rooms, Double: €160–€250
Dinner: €55 (not Sun)
Open: Feb to Dec, Credit cards: all major
Country house hotel
www.karenbrown.com/richmond.html

Hollywell is set in a large garden overlooking the River Shannon. It has a secluded riverside location, just a couple of minutes' walk to the heart of Carrick-on-Shannon, a lively riverside town. Tom and Rosaleen provide outstanding hospitality in their lovely old home. Guests have a large sitting room with comfy sofas, books, games, and TV where they gather round the fire in the evening. Breakfast is the only meal served at the little tables arranged round the grand piano in the dining room, but for dinner guests often go to the Oarsman on Bridge Street run by sons Conor and Ronan. Three grandfather clocks grace the hallways and a sofa and books are grouped at the head of the stairs to take advantage of the view over a broad stretch of the river. The two very large front bedrooms share the same lovely view, while the back bedrooms are small only in comparison to those at the front. You can fish without ever leaving Hollywell's grounds and there's an 18-hole golf club nearby. A few of the stately houses within reach are Strokestown House and Gardens, Clonalis, King House, Florence Court, Castle Coole, and Belvedere House and Gardens. Ask about the possibility of renting a launch for a day and take a little meander up the River Shannon. *Directions:* From Dublin take the N4 (Sligo road) to Carrick. Cross the river, turn up the hill by Gings pub, and Hollywell is on the left.

HOLLYWELL
Owners: Rosaleen & Tom Maher
Liberty Hill
Carrick-on-Shannon
Co Leitrim, Ireland
Tel & Fax: (071) 9621124
4 Rooms, Double: €110–€140
Closed: Christmas & New Year, Credit cards: all major
Country house
www.karenbrown.com/hollywell.html

The setting for Cashel House is spectacular: at the head of Cashel Bay with Cashel Hill standing guard behind, a solid white house nestles amongst acres and acres of woodland and gardens of exotic flowering shrubs. Kilometers of garden footpaths are yours to wander along, and the beautiful seashore is yours to explore. This is not the kind of hotel to spend just a night in—once you have settled into your lovely room and sampled the exquisite food in the splendid conservatory dining room, you will be glad that you have made Cashel House the base for your Connemara explorations. Graceful antiques, turf fires, and lovely arrangements of freshly picked flowers create a warm, country-house welcome. It feels particularly decadent to have breakfast served to you in bed on a prettily decorated tray. All the bedrooms are beautifully furnished and decorated, each accompanied by a sparkling bathroom. Thirteen exquisite suites occupy a wing and enjoy comfortable sitting areas overlooking the garden. Keen tennis players can enjoy the court bordering the bay. Be sure to visit the horses in the stables behind the hotel. The McEvillys can arrange for a car and driver to meet you at Galway airport. Day trips with a car and driver can also be arranged. Just down the road a small two bedroom cottage, with bay views, is let on a weekly basis. *Directions:* Take the N59 from Galway (towards Clifden) through Oughterard and turn left to the village of Cashel 2 km after Recess.

CASHEL HOUSE
Owners: Kay & Dermot McEvilly
Cashel, Co Galway, Ireland
Tel: (095) 31001, Fax: (095) 31077
32 Rooms, Double: €190–€270*
1 Cottage: €600 weekly
*Service: 12.5%, Dinner: from €55
Closed: mid-Jan to mid-Feb, Credit cards: all major
Relais & Châteaux
Country house hotel & self catering
www.karenbrown.com/cashelhouse.html

Cashel Palace was built as the Bishop of Cashel's sumptuous home in 1730. The bishop chose a prime location with an unparalleled view of the Rock of Cashel, which rises above the town topped by the ruins of a 13th-century cathedral. A grand staircase leads to the second-floor bedrooms where a lavish array of accommodation awaits. The grand Bishop's Bedroom (room 15) and room 11 with its grand four-poster bed and luxurious bathroom with tub and shower stand out as particular favorites. On the third floor, rooms are smaller with windows that peek out over the town or the gardens. An additional ten bedrooms are found in the adjacent mews house. The Bishop's Buttery, in the old vaulted palace cellars, offers the opportunity for fine dining. Casual by contrast, the adjacent bar reigns as the true "home" of Guinness, for it was first brewed here in 1740. The friendly staff are particularly helpful. Right in the town's center, the palace marks the perfect spot for browsing through the shops. Allow time to wander around the gardens, where the mulberry tree on the lawn was planted in 1702. Through the gate to the Bishop's Walk lies a private path that zigzags up the Rock of Cashel. *Directions:* If you are looking for the ocean and Connemara this is the wrong Cashel! Cashel is northeast of Cork on the N8, Dublin road. Find the tourist office, in the centre of town, and the entrance to Cashel Palace is adjacent to it, next to the large cross.

🍵 💳 ☎ 👪 @ P 🍽

*CASHEL PALACE   **New***
Owners: Susan & Patrick Murphy
Main Street
Cashel, Co Tipperary, Ireland
Tel: (062) 62707, Fax: (062) 61521
23 Rooms, Double: €185–€355
Dinner: €48
Open: all year, Credit cards: all major
Ireland's Blue Book
Country house hotel
www.karenbrown.com/cashelpalace.html

Ballyvolane is a great Irish country house. Set a few miles from Fermoy it's a perfect place for sightseeing between Waterford and Kinsale, Cashel to Lismore. It is beautiful at night when the long mahogany table is set with flickering candles and you enjoy drinks by the fire in the grand pillared hallway. It is lovely on a warm morning as you wander through the gardens. It's one of those houses that makes you feel happy just thinking about having stayed there. It's a friendly house where guests make themselves thoroughly at home. It is welcoming because Justin and Jenny Green suffuse it with their young energy, their charm and friendliness. Bedrooms in the house are roomy, stylish and furnished with antiques. One has a bath so deep that you have to step up to get into it. Want something different and totally private? Opt for one of the five cottages in the walled garden whose bedrooms, complete with sunken tub, overlooks the garden while the living room windows peer over the garden wall. Within a radius of a few kilometers there are 20 golf courses and within an hour's drive are Blarney with its famous castle, Cork city, and the bustling boating town of Kinsale. Ballyvolane has seven kilometers of privately managed salmon fishing on the renowned River Blackwater. A self-catering cottage is also available. *Directions:* From Fermoy take the N8 towards Cork to Rathcormac, and Ballyvolane House is 6 km further on down a signposted country lane.

BALLYVOLANE HOUSE
Owners: Jenny & Justin Green
Castlelyons, Co Cork, Ireland
Tel: (025) 36349, Fax: (025) 36781
6 Rooms, Double: €95–€150
1 Cottage: €380–€530 weekly
Dinner: €60
Open: all year, Credit cards: all major
Hidden Ireland
Country house & self-catering
www.karenbrown.com/ballyvolanehouse.html

I'm impressed that Pyers O'Connor Nash's home is built on land that has belonged to his family for over 2,000 years, the ancestral home of the O'Conors of Connaught, descendants of the last High Kings of Ireland and traditional Kings of Connaught. And what a home it is, a grand 45-room Victorian Italianate mansion full of fascinating heirlooms and lovely antique furnishings. There's the coronation stone of the Kings of Connaught by the front door, Carolan's harp, rare manuscripts, and a vast array of family portraits. It could be daunting, but Pyer's and Marguerite's way of sharing their home makes it entrancing: the tremendous dining room with its Sheffield silver from the Great Exhibition, the wondrous array of books in the library, the elegant drawing room. I loved room 13, huge with its historic four-poster bed, fabulous views, and large bathroom with bath and shower; but opted for the green room, my favorite, with its tall four-poster bed and large bathroom. The former billiard room displays interesting manuscripts, and there's a small museum of lace and costumes. When the house is open to the public (June to August) guests are welcome to tag along on the 4 pm tour. On the grounds are three cottages let on a weekly, self-catering basis. Galway and Sligo are an hours drive away. *Directions:* Clonalis House is situated on the west side of Castlerea on N60.

CLONALIS HOUSE
Owners: Marguerite & Pyers O'Connor Nash
Castlerea, Ireland
Tel & Fax: (094) 9620014
4 Rooms, Double: €190–€220
3 Cottages: €350–€550 weekly
Dinner: €45 (not Sun or Mon)
Open: mid-Apr to Sept, Credit cards: MC, VS
Hidden Ireland
Country house
www.karenbrown.com/clonalis.html

Byrne's Mal Dua House is a purpose-built guesthouse just outside Clifden. The sunny lobby doubles as a sitting room with sofas and chairs in deep-pink velour, which match the carpet and the balloon shades. An additional larger sitting room is decorated in shades of pink like the adjacent spacious dining room. All bedrooms are particularly spacious and come with different combinations of double and single beds. All have a bath or shower, hairdryer, TV, phone, trouser press, excellent reading lights, and tea- and coffee-makings. The decor is very attractive, with pastel-painted walls and coordinating drapes and bedspreads. Breakfast is the only meal served and Aideen and Peter are happy to recommend where to eat in town and arrange for a taxi to take you there. Having spent many years in the United States they are very in tune with American tastes. There's an absolute wealth of things to do in the area and Aideen and Peter will gladly help you plan your days activcities. During the third week in August, Clifden hosts the Connemara Pony Show and rooms are at a premium. *Directions:* Take the N59 from Galway to the outskirts of Clifden. Mal Dua is on your right as you enter the town.

BYRNE MAL DUA HOUSE
Owners: Peter & Aideen Byrne
Galway Road, Clifden, Connemara
Co Galway, Ireland
Tel: (095) 21171, Fax: (095) 21739
14 Rooms, Double: €90–€150*
*10% Service Charge
Dinner: €38
Open: all year, Credit cards: all major
Guesthouse
www.karenbrown.com/maldua.html

On a sunny day there is nowhere more magical than Dolphin Beach House, set on its own 35-acre headland at the head of Clifden Bay. The views across the water to Slyne Head and Ballconneely Bay are the best that wild, untamed places can supply. Billy and Barbara tell me that their headland offers views of dolphins, seals, otters, foxes, and all kinds of seabirds. The view changes by the minute with the vagaries of the Irish weather and you can sit for hours just watching the seascape unfold. Warm weather finds guests soaking up the sun on the most private of beaches. The house was built to give views not only from the dining room and sitting room but also from several of the bedrooms—be sure to request one of these. I particularly enjoyed Bay View, and The Cove Room both tall-ceilinged room with wooden floors, king-sized beds, and French windows framing sea views. The Garden Room (no sea view) also enjoys high ceilings and its king bed faces a private garden courtyard. There is no shortage of places to eat in town—dinner is sometimes available with advanced notice. It's very much a family operation and you may well find several of the Foyles' working here. *Directions:* Take the N59 from Galway to Clifden and follow the one-way system to the top of town where you take the upper fork at the Y-junction (in front of the Alcock and Brown hotel) onto the Sky Road. After 3 km take the first left for 1 km to Dolphin Beach House.

DOLPHIN BEACH HOUSE
Manager: Clodagh Foyle
Lower Sky Road, Clifden, Connemara
Co Galway, Ireland
Tel: (095) 21204, Fax: (095) 22935
Toll Free: (888) 497-4138 USA
8 Rooms, Double: €160–€190
Dinner: €43
Open: all year, Credit cards: MC, VS
B&B
www.karenbrown.com/dolphin.html

The harbormaster certainly picked a pretty site for his home on the quay, with its wide vista of the inlet of Ardbear Bay and the town of Clifden winding up the hillside. Since 1820, Quay House has served variously as the harbormaster's home, a convent, a monastery, and a hotel. Julia and Paddy have given them a new lease of life as a stylish hotel. They decorated the whole in a refreshingly eclectic style; blending old, modern, and unconventional in an idiosyncratic way with little jokes and quirks such as Vegetarian Alley, a corridor of hunting trophies. Breakfast in the conservatory is the only meal served. For dinner, a five-minute walk brings you into town where there are several good restaurants. There are seven spacious studios, of which six have small fitted kitchens and balconies, and seven bedrooms. All rooms have spacious bathrooms with separate showers and tubs. Several are "traditional country house" in their decor, others light, fresh, and more bohemian. Particular favorites are Napoleon, a tribute room to the famous Corsican which enjoys a sitting area with panoramic views of the harbor, Out of Africa, a safari-themed studio; and The Bird Room, a studio with a few wacky stuffed parrots and a couple of large pictures featuring parrots. *Directions:* Take the N59 from Galway to Clifden and follow the one-way system to the top of the town where you take the lower fork at the first Y-junction down onto the quay.

THE QUAY HOUSE
Owners: Julia & Paddy Foyle
Beach Road
Clifden, Connemara
Co Galway, Ireland
Tel: (095) 21369, Fax: (095) 21608
14 Rooms, Double: €140–€180
Open: mid-Mar to Nov, Credit cards: MC, VS
Hidden Ireland
Country house
www.karenbrown.com/quayhouse.html

How fortuitous that the storm of Christmas 1998 ripped off SeaMist's roof and caused such damage that only one room was habitable! This catapulted Sheila and her twin sister, whom she was visiting in California, into deciding to completely renovate this lovely old home with Sheila running it as a bed and breakfast. With her easy, friendly manner (not to mention talent at baking and jam-making), Sheila has proved a natural for the job. Add to this SeaMist's central location in Clifden and we have a real winner. Bedrooms are on the whole very spacious and accompanied by either a large bathroom or smaller shower room. Red-deal plank floors complement the warm pastel decor. For a sort of sea view, request a room at the top of the house and you'll catch a glimpse by standing on your tiptoes. Sheila's granddad was an auctioneer and some of his purchases have stayed at the house. I particularly admired the grand sideboard in the sitting room and the beautiful tall pine dresser purchased from Ballynahinch Castle. Walk out the front door and you are steps away from the main street of town with its shops, restaurants, and pubs. Drive a few yards in the other direction and you are in the lovely Connemara countryside. *Directions:* Take the N59 from Galway to Clifden and follow the one-way system to the top of town. Take a left at the square with the Alcock and Brown Hotel to the right. SeaMist is immediately on your right.

SEAMIST
Owner: Sheila Griffin
Clifden, Connemara, Co Galway, Ireland
Tel: (095) 21441
6 Rooms, Double: €80–€130
Closed: midweek in winter
Credit cards: MC, VS
B&B
www.karenbrown.com/seaview.html

Standing at the foot of the Knockmealdown mountains the Old Convent is a impressive building. Home to the Sisters of Mercy for over a hundred years Dermot and Christine Gannon have given it a complete new lease on life. Christine offers great hospitality and Dermot cooks. While the complete style of the place merits a stay THE reason to come is because of Dermot's spectacular cooking. Thursday through Sunday he presents a stunning eight course tasting menu with proper sized portions, all exquisitely cooked and beautifully presented, a divine evening long occasion. Guests are seated in the candlelit dining room, with its beautiful stained-glass windows, at around eight. o'clock. From the appetizers to the magnificent chocolate fondue we were enthralled. The same masterly talent goes into the preparation of breakfast dishes—consolation for those who are only able to stay the rest of the week. And stay you must for there is much to do in this wonderfully quiet corner of Ireland: climb the Rock of Cashel, scale the ramparts of Cahir castle, and ramble down country lanes to enjoy magnificent views from beauty spots such as the Vee. Perhaps you'll be lucky enough to come home to the room with a soaking tub perfectly placed to capture views of the mountains. *Directions:* From Cahir take the Cork road, pass the castle and take the next left for the 14km drive to Clogheen. Go through the village, turn left at the hospital sign and the convent is on your right.

THE OLD CONVENT   **New**
Owners: Christine & Dermot Gannon
Clogheen, Co Tipperary, Ireland
Tel: (052) 65565
7 Rooms, Double: €120–€170
Dinner: €58 (not Mon, Tue, Wed)
Open: all year, Credit cards: MC, VS
Country house
www.karenbrown.com/oldcovent.html

If you long to visit a spot off the beaten track and enjoy wonderful hospitality and divine food, you can do no better than to stay with Lucy and Johnny Madden on the Hilton Park estate. Lucy's passion is growing vegetables for the kitchen, Johnny's family home is so grand that it is hard to believe that it is a real home and not the kind where you pay a visitor's entrance fee and their son is the talented chef. It's a beautiful house of lovely rooms where guestrooms range from vast (the gorgeous Blue room and Parents room) with grand floor-to-ceiling beds, views of the lake and superb bathrooms with tubs and showers, to more modest in size, with regular-sized bathrooms containing old soaking tubs. Guests relax in the beautiful drawing room, enjoying pre-dinner drinks, conversation, and views across the terrace of formal gardens to the lake. The same enchanting view is enjoyed in the elegant dining room where guests dine at separate tables by the gentle flicker of candlelight. Breakfast is taken "below stairs" in the former servants' hall. Have your own house party by renting the entire place! Popular sightseeing includes Belleek with its pottery, Lough Erne, Castle Coole (a restored Palladian mansion), and Florence Court (a riot of rococo plasterwork). *Directions:* From the Cavan by-pass take the turnoff for Ballyhaise. Go through Ballyhaise and Scotshouse and the entrance to Hilton Park is on your left 1 km after the golf course.

HILTON PARK
Owners: Lucy & Johnny Madden
Clones, Scotshouse, Co Monaghan, Ireland
Tel: (047) 56007, Fax: (047) 56033
6 Rooms, Double: €250–€300
1 House: €550–€650 weekly
Dinner: €55
Open: Apr to Sept, Credit cards: MC, VS
Hidden Ireland
Country house
www.karenbrown.com/hilton.html

Guests stopping at Rockwood House on their way north have been known to go no farther, contenting themselves with whiling away the hours in this peaceful spot and enjoying the warm hospitality that Susan and James McCauley offer. Susan and James returned here after living in Dublin for many years, acquired a derelict rectory with trees growing through the roof, and replaced it with a well-appointed replica-Rockwood House. Enjoy breakfast in the conservatory overlooking the garden or just relax around the fire in the guests sitting room. For dinner guests have a choice of restaurants in Belturbert, to the Derragarra Inn just down the road in Butlersbridge or, for scrumptious more pricey fare, the adjacent Olde Post Restaurant. Upstairs, the spacious, very nicely decorated bedrooms are each accompanied by a snug bathroom. Beds are double, twin, or king if you request that the twin beds be zipped together. County Cavan is blessed with picture-postcard scenery—whichever way you turn you find waterways, rivers, and lakes set among gently rolling hills. Opportunities for fishing and walking abound. Popular sightseeing includes Belleek Pottery, Lough Erne, Castle Coole (a restored Palladian mansion), and Florence Court (a riot of rococo plaster). *Directions:* From Cavan follow signs for the N3 to Monaghan, then turn right at the sign for Monaghan/Butlersbridge (N54). Rockwood House is on your left, 3 km from the village of Butlersbridge.

ROCKWOOD HOUSE
Owners: Susan & James McCauley
Cloverhill, Belturbet, Co Cavan, Ireland
Tel: (047) 55351, Fax: (047) 55373
4 Rooms, Double: €64
Closed: Dec 10 to Feb 1, Credit cards: MC, VS
B&B
www.karenbrown.com/rockwood.html

Set high above the river surrounded by over three acres of grounds this grand 1840s Victorian commands an impressive position in Cobh—but the main point of interest is the fabulous interior as Pam and John spared no expense in revamping their longtime home into luxury guest accommodation. Their easy hospitality, as much as the comfort of their lovely home, is what makes Knockeven House special. Your stay often begins with tea and scones by the drawing room fire. Up the grand curving staircase you find the airy bedrooms—two have six foot beds (can also be twin), one has a queen, and the fourth has an adorable double bed (historic half tester) and gorgeous silk drapes. Showers are large, bedrooms are wired for internet access, and TVs are available. Scrambled eggs and smoked salmon is a breakfast specialty. Favorite activities are: visiting the cathedral and Queenstown Story a lively museum illustrating emigration to the US from 1845 to the 1950s; taking the ferry to Kinsale; going to Blarney to kiss the famous stone; and visiting the English market and shops in nearby Cork. John, an avid golfer, is a mine of information on local courses and happy to arranges tee times. *Directions:* Just before you arrive in Cork (from N25—Waterford to Cork Road) turn left on R624 to Cobh. On entering Cobh, pass the ferry on your right. At Satoil garage take a sharp left and an immediate right into the Knockeven House's driveway.

KNOCKEVEN HOUSE
Owners: Pam & John Mulhaire
Rushbrooke
Cobh, Co Cork, Ireland
Tel: (021) 4811778, Fax: (021) 4811719
4 Rooms, Double: €120–€130
Open: all year, Credit cards: MC, VS
B&B
www.karenbrown.com/knockeven.html

The charm of Greenhill House is that Elizabeth and James Hegarty are particularly sweet people who have been welcoming guests to their house for many years. They are particularly knowledgeable about the area and happy to direct guests on where to go and what to see—of course the nearby Antrim coast is particularly popular. Elizabeth makes sure you are always welcomed with tea and cakes and have everything that you need. The farmhouse is delightfully old-fashioned and lovingly decorated with antiques, with bouquets of fresh garden flowers adding the finishing touch. Bedrooms are well equipped with sightseeing information; a tray set with teapot, kettle, tea bags, coffee, and chocolate; hairdryer; television; and even a little box of After Eight mints by the bedside. Plump comforters top the beds and fluffy towels hang on the old-fashioned towel rail. One the main floor you find a double and twin room with their bathrooms cleverly popped into snug "fitted" cupboards: a shower in one and a sink and toilet in another. Bedrooms under the eaves have more spacious bathrooms. A bountiful breakfast is the only meal served and Elizabeth will suggest restaurants round and about for dinner. *Directions:* From Limavady take the A37 towards Coleraine, turn right on the A29 (Garvagh and Cookstown road) for 11 km. Turn left on the B66 (Greenhill Road) and Greenhill House is on the right.

GREENHILL HOUSE
Owners: Elizabeth & James Hegarty
24 Greenhill Road
Coleraine, Aghadowey
Co Londonderry, BT51 4EU, Northern Ireland
Tel: (028) 7086 8241, Fax: (028) 7086 8365
6 Rooms, Double: £60
Open: Mar to Oct, Credit cards: MC, VS
Farmhouse B&B
www.karenbrown.com/greenhill.html

Mary and Declan Kelleher like nothing more than to share their love of the Burren with visitors. They have gone so far as to compile a most interesting booklet on the district, which details its history and points of interest. To make sure you do not go wrong they will kit you out with maps and instructions on what to do each day. Fergus View was built as a teacher's residence at the turn of the last century and Declan's grandfather was its first occupant. Continuing in his grandfather's footsteps, Declan is the principal of Corofin's primary school. The next generation of teachers is in place with several of Mary and Declan's children training to be teachers. In an evening the fire is lit in the little parlor to encourage you to make yourself at home. A hearty breakfast is the only meal served but handily there's a restaurant in the village for dinner. Bedrooms are prettily decorated with matching drapes and bedspreads. All are of the leave-large-cases-in-the-car variety—facilities are not designed for persons of large proportions. The Kellehers also have a lovely self-catering cottage for week-long stays. The nearby Burren is fascinating, and the Cliffs of Moher are close at hand. *Directions:* From Shannon airport take the N18 to Ennis, the N85 towards Lisdoonvarna, turn first right to Corofin, go through the village, and the house is on your left after 3 km.

FERGUS VIEW
Owners: Mary & Declan Kelleher
Corofin, Kilnaboy, Co Clare, Ireland
Tel: (065) 6837606, Fax: (065) 6837192
6 Rooms, Double: €73–€75
1 Cottage: €440–€635 weekly
Open: mid Mar to mid-Oct, Credit cards: none
B&B & self-catering
www.karenbrown.com/fergusview.html

St. Clerans has had an impressive list of Irish owners but came into the limelight when John Huston (film director extraordinaire) called it home for over 20 years and spent an absolute mint on the place. More recently this impressive home prepared itself for the 21st century with another no-holds-barred face-lift from its current owner, former chat-show host Merv Griffin, and when he is not in residence you can enjoy a stay at his luxurious retreat. It's a treat to see an architectural gem coddled to the extent where everything is the absolute best that money can buy—the essence of pure indulgence. My personal favorite room is Merv's decadent suite—you can unpack into his very own closet and admire the artwork that Merv has places in the niches that once held John Houston's Oscars. The most private bedroom is the octagonal little building that was once Angelica Huston's playhouse. She would not recognize it today with its stenciled walls and opulent bathroom. Spend the day lounging on the premises soaking up the ambiance and being totally spoiled by the attentive Irish staff, play golf at Athenry and Loughrea, or go horseriding or clay pigeon shooting. The cliffs of Moher on the Burren and Galway city are within easy striking distance. *Directions:* From Galway take the N6 towards Dublin for 30 km to Craughwell. Go through the village and take the second left signposted St. Clerans and Athenry for the 8-km drive to St. Clerans.

ST. CLERANS
Owner: Merv Griffin
Craughwell, Co Galway, Ireland
Tel: (091) 846555, Fax: (091) 846752
12 Rooms, Double: €325–€475
Dinner: €65 (not Mon)
Open: all year when Merv's not there
Credit cards: all major
Country house hotel
www.karenbrown.com/stclerans.html

Enniscoe House is the home of Susan Kellett—a descendant of the original family who settled this estate in the 1670s—her son DJ, and their Labrador Frodo. Staying as her guest gives you a glimpse of what it was like to live in a grand country mansion—the old family furniture, portraits, books, and family memorabilia are yours to enjoy. The lofty rooms are decorated true to the Georgian period and all are in tiptop condition. The three front bedrooms, of grand proportions, are reached by a grand elliptical staircase. Those in the older part of the house are less grand but just as lovely. I particularly enjoyed the old nursery with half-tester and twin beds, and comfortable chintz chairs. Dinners by soft, flickering candlelight at little tables in the large dining room are a real treat. Tucked behind the house, the courtyard buildings house three delightful farmhouse-style self-catering apartments. The Victorian walled garden has been given a new lease of life and the barns display old farm machinery and artifacts. Fishery manager Gary Crossley offers help to anglers fishing Lough Conn (email: gary@cloonamoynefishery.com). Walk the trails that go through the woodlands past the forestry plantations and along the lake shore. There are great cliffs along the north coast, where the Stone-Age settlements at Céide Fields have been excavated. *Directions:* From Ballina take the N59 to Crossmolina, turn left in town for Castlebar, and the house is on the left after 3 km.

ENNISCOE HOUSE
Owners: Susan & DJ Kellett
Castlehill, Crossmolina, Co Mayo, Ireland
Tel: (096) 31112, Fax: (096) 31773
6 Rooms, Double: €180–€232
3 Cottages: €600–€850 weekly
Dinner: €50
Open: Apr to mid-Oct, Credit cards: MC, VS
Ireland's Blue Book, Hidden Ireland
Country house & self-catering
www.karenbrown.com/enniscoehouse.html

Doyle's Restaurant, owned and run by John, Charlotte and Clodagh Clusky, is famous the world over for the excellence of its seafood, fresh from the ocean. A small village shop and pub built in 1790 house the welcoming restaurant with its flagstone floor and cozy arrangements of tables and chairs, while the house next door offers the most delightful accommodation in Dingle. The two houses are interconnected yet self-contained, so that guests can come and go to the restaurant but will not have their peace disturbed when they are sleeping. You step from the street into the old-fashioned parlor with its pine floor, grandfather clock, and sofas drawn into seating areas. Large umbrellas are close at hand in case you should need them. The top-notch bedrooms have excellent bathrooms equipped with everything you might need. The two ground-floor rooms are ideal for anyone who has difficulty with stairs. After dinner inquire at the bar which of the many little pubs has traditional music that night and stroll along to join in the merriment. *Directions:* Dingle is a 2½-hour drive from Limerick. Turn right at the roundabout, right into John Street, and Doyle's is on your left.

DOYLE'S
Owners: John, Charlotte & Clodagh Clusky
John Street
Dingle, Co Kerry, Ireland
Tel: (066) 9151174, Fax: (066) 9151816
8 Rooms, Double: €100–€150
Dinner: à la carte (not Sun)
Closed: mid-Jan to mid-Feb, Credit cards: all major
Restaurant with rooms
www.karenbrown.com/doyles.html

Mary and John Curran are locals who built Greenmount House as a home for themselves and their small children then later cleverly expanded their bungalow adding a large sitting room, additional family accommodation, and large top-of-the-line guestrooms. Seven face the harbor and six have either French windows opening onto a patio or balcony (chairs provided for sitting out) and are large enough to accommodate a spacious sitting area—the kind of rooms you want to spend time in. Drift into the view in room 6 (Garran) whose bed and sofa face a breathtaking vista of Connor Pass soaring above the fields. A conservatory breakfast room, prettily furnished with painted pine furniture, has a panoramic view across fields and Dingle's rooftops to the harbor. Mary prepares the most bountiful of breakfasts and tries to offer at least two fruit dishes, delicious mueslis, and yogurts, as well as a cooked breakfast menu that includes not only the traditional breakfast but also fish and mushrooms in yogurt sauce. Breakfast is the only meal served. For dinner stroll down the hill into town where there are some particularly fine fish restaurants. Wander down to the harbor and watch the catch come in, window shop, and enjoy a pint in one of the many pubs. *Directions:* Turn right at the roundabout in Dingle, next right into John Street, and continue up the hill to Greenmount House.

GREENMOUNT HOUSE
Owners: Mary & John Curran
Gortonora
Dingle, Co Kerry, Ireland
Tel: (066) 9151414, Fax: (066) 9151974
9 Rooms, Double: €100–€180
Closed: Christmas, Credit cards: MC, VS
B&B
www.karenbrown.com/greenmounthouse.html

Heaton's, a purpose-built guesthouse, commands an enviable position at the head of Dingle Bay, with spectacular views across the water to Burnham Headlands. The mouth of the sheltered harbor is just a five-minute walk from the heart of this lively town. While the style outside is modern, the inside is more traditional with classic French furniture. The bedrooms are smartly decorated with beds coming in sizes from twin to king. Nuala is a stickler for quality when it comes to bedding and towels, so crisp white sheets adorn the beds and good-quality towels hang in the sparkling white bathrooms, which all have power showers over the tubs. Ten of the rooms have views to the bay and three are large enough to accommodate a second bed for a child (request a second-floor room for the best view). Rooms 14 and 16 are the most spacious of rooms, with a king-sized bed, roomy sitting area, and Jacuzzi tub and shower. Daughter Jackie, the breakfast chef, makes certain breakfast is a full Irish spread of local produce, with the fish and omelettes, made with free-range eggs, deserving a special mention. *Directions:* Arriving in Dingle, keep the harbor to your left and Heaton's is located 600 yards beyond the marina on your right, overlooking the bay.

HEATON'S
Owners: Nuala, Jackie & Cameron Heaton
The Wood
Dingle, Co Kerry, Ireland
Tel: (066) 9152288, Fax: (066) 9152324
16 Rooms, Double: €95–€190
Open: all year, Credit cards: MC, VS
Guesthouse
www.karenbrown.com/heatons.html

Set on a wooded, tidal island in Donegal Bay and joined to the mainland by a narrow causeway, St. Ernan's House was built in 1826 by John Hamilton, a nephew of the Duke of Wellington, for his wife. Over lunch here one day, Brian and Carmel O'Dowd decided that St. Ernan's was the kind of hotel they would like to own, so several years later when it came on the market they took the plunge and forsook their careers in banking and teaching to become hoteliers. From almost every one of the rooms you are treated to marvelous views across a mirrorlike span of water. In the lounge, window seats offer views across the water to the mainland and chairs are artfully arranged to provide numerous nooks for intimate after-dinner conversation. A four-course candlelit dinner, with choices for each course, is served in the dining room. The attractive bedrooms come in all shapes and sizes, and while almost all have delightful water views, the largest command the highest prices. Be sure to enjoy the walk around this delightful little island. You'll find some excellent shops in Donegal town, amongst them Magees, famous for its tweed. Beyond Donegal town lies the wild, rugged landscape that has made this county famous. *Directions:* From Sligo take the N15 towards Donegal as far as the village of Laghey (6.5 km before Donegal). Approximately 1.5 km past Laghey take the left-hand turn onto R267. Proceed for 1.6 km and St. Ernan's is signposted to your left.

ST. ERNAN'S HOUSE
Owners: Carmel & Brian O'Dowd
Donegal, Co Donegal, Ireland
Tel: (074) 9721065, Fax: (074) 9722098
10 Rooms, Double: €240–€330
Dinner: €54 (on Tue, Fri & Sat only)
Open: mid-Apr to Oct, Credit cards: MC, VS
Ireland's Blue Book
Country house hotel
www.karenbrown.com/sternans.html

"What a great place to have a party!" I exclaimed—and the thought had not escaped former owners, for there are tales in the town of grand parties long ago with guests dancing in the expansive drawing and dining rooms and a quartet in the back hallway. These aristocratic rooms have been restored to their former glory, with a wedding-cake icing of plasterwork ringing their lofty ceilings above sink-in sofas and chairs and a vast dining-room table. Upstairs has received the same sensitive treatment. The two premier rooms at the front of the house have vast bathrooms with large tubs and separate showers and enough room in the bedrooms to accommodate seating by the fire and a couple of beds. Between them stands an extra bedroom (without bath), ideal for an older child or traveling companion. The fourth bedroom overlooks the courtyard. For dinner guests usually drive to local restaurants. With advance notice Laura will prepare supper. Michael and Laura find that many guests are interested in their restoration and often give a tour of "behind the scenes" portions of the property. *Directions:* From Mallow take the N20 towards Limerick for 6.5 km to New Twopothouse. Turn right for the 6.5-km drive to Doneraile where you find Creagh House on your left at the far end of the main street.

CREAGH HOUSE
Owners: Laura O'Mahony & Michael O'Sullivan
Main Street
Doneraile, Co Cork, Ireland
Tel: (022) 24433, Fax: (022) 24715
4 Rooms, Double: €200–€240
Supper: €30
Open: Mar to Oct, Credit cards: all major
Hidden Ireland
Country house
www.karenbrown.com/creagh.html

Isolated by acres of fields and gardens, Belcamp Hutchinson is an oasis of country house elegance just 7 minutes` drive from Dublin airport. It is such an outstanding home and Doreen is such a gracious hostess that you will want to stay for several days and make this your base for Dublin and the surrounding area. On arrival you`ll doubtless be greeted by the dogs, Bullseye, and Dusty, who love to meet guests. A fire is lit in the drawing room in the evening; relax, help yourself to a drink from the honor bar and make yourself at home. There`s also a little TV room with "all" the channels—on the night I stayed guests were watching a sports match—however you also have a TV with local channels in your bedroom. Up the elegant staircase, spacious bedrooms are decorated in strong, dark, Georgian colors, each beautifully coordinated with lovely fabrics. Three further rooms are located atop the house with Gold being a particularly fun one. Large beds are the order of the day and there's always candies and interesting magazines by the bedside. Breakfast is a real treat with ham, an array of cheeses, fruit, cereal and yogurt in addition to a cooked breakfast. Be sure to explore the walled garden—the maze is a fun challenge. Leave your car and take the bus for the 30-minute ride to the heart of Dublin. *Directions:* Belcamp Hutchinson is just off the Malahide Road in Balgriffin. Doreen will fax or mail you detailed directions. See Dublin Walking Tour map for location.

BELCAMP HUTCHINSON
Owners: Doreen Gleson & Karl Waldburg
Carrs Lane, Malahide Road
Balgriffin, Dublin, Ireland
Tel: (01) 846 0843, Fax: (01) 848 5703
8 Rooms, Double: €150
Closed: Christmas, Credit cards: MC, VS
Country house
www.karenbrown.com/belcamphutchinson.html

The heart of Temple Bar with its trendy stores and vibrant nightlife is a most appropriate spot for a luxury boutique hotel. Originally built in 1852, the building was for many years a cleric's residence. The conversion to a hotel kept all the attractive architectural features such as oak paneling, wooden floors, and lovely old windows. The cleric colors of purple, brown, red, blue, and gold are subtly included in every room. Decor is uncluttered, with simple lines. Relax in the peace and quiet of the study with its open fire, writing table, and wood-paneled walls or enjoy conviviality and a cocktail in the Octagon Bar. The Tea Room, a onetime ballroom with magnificent art deco windows, is a grand place to eat dinner. Bedrooms and bathrooms have lots of lovely, mellow American White Oak, Egyptian cotton bedding and splashes of blue, brown, red or gold—all very serene—and double glazing ensures a quiet night's sleep. The handcrafted beds are king sized and rooms are equipped with interactive TV, entertainment systems, and wifi. There are seven balcony rooms, and several rooms that interconnect to make two bedroom family suites—children are made particularly welcome. The location, overlooking the River Liffey on Dublin's "left bank" is perfect for exploring Dublin on foot. The hotel has a small garage and valet parking is available. *Directions:* Wellington Quay is on the south bank of the River Liffey—see Dublin Walking Tour map.

THE CLARENCE
Manager: Olivier Sevestre
6–8 Wellington Quay
Dublin, Ireland
Tel: (01) 407 0800, Fax: (01) 407 0820
49 Rooms, Double: €350–€2,800*
*Breakfast not included: €27.5
Dinner: €60
Closed: Christmas, Credit cards: all major
City hotel
www.karenbrown.com/clarence.html

Just steps from St. Stephen's Green in the heart of Georgian Dublin, Harrington Hall is ideally located for walking to all the city's attractions. The tranquility of the spacious sitting room with its gold brocade sofas and comfortable armchairs drawn round a welcoming peat fire quickly convinced me that this was an enticing place to stay in central Dublin. Henry has taken great care with the design of the bedrooms—their size, amenities, and comfort—and the fitting out of the marble bathrooms. The result is that you will enjoy a quiet night's repose with the aid of double glazing and ceiling fans in a very comfortable room. Larger rooms can often accommodate an extra bed for a child. A ground-floor room is wheelchair-friendly. The two suites, Kitty O'Shea and Charles Parnell, provide the most spacious accommodation in large rooms with ceilings so lofty that the bed occupies a mezzanine level above the bathroom. Breakfast is the only meal served. Staff are often not familiar with local restaurants but there is a "King family dining guide" that gives some insight into local restaurants. *Directions:* Harcourt Street leads from the southwestern corner of St. Stephen's Green and Harrington Hall is on your left. The hotel will fax driving directions. At the rear is a secure, off-road car park—let them know if you are arriving by car as parking is limited. See Dublin Walking Tour map for location.

HARRINGTON HALL
Owner: Henry King
Manager: Kate Gallagher
70 Harcourt Street
Dublin, Ireland
Tel: (01) 475 3497, Fax: (01) 475 4544
28 Rooms, Double: €187–€290
Open: all year, Credit cards: all major
Guesthouse
www.karenbrown.com/harringtonhall.html

Grand as life in Georgian Dublin may have been, it is surpassed at The Merrion, a dream of a hotel found in the heart of the city opposite Leinster House, home of Ireland's parliament. A few steps from bustling city streets and you are in vast drawing rooms enjoying traditional afternoon tea overlooking a tranquil expanse of garden and watching the gardener manicure the box hedges. If you are in the mood for the most sophisticated of meals, adjourn to the two-Michelin-star restaurant Patrick Guilbaud or enjoy more traditional Irish cuisine in The Cellar Restaurant after letting your hair down over a few drinks in The Cellar Bar which lists over 50 wines by the glass on its menu. The Tethra Spa is an aptly named spot to assist guests in recovering from the revelry of the night before—swimming in the pool, working out in the gym, or enjoying a massage. It costs a good deal to stay in one of the elegant suites in the "old building" while more affordable accommodation is found in the deluxe garden wing whose most attractive rooms open up to views of the loveliest of gardens. The hotel has the largest collection of Irish art outside the National Gallery. A traditional hotel in the heart of this vibrant city—what more could you ask from a place to stay? *Directions:* The Merrion is adjacent to Merrion Square, opposite Leinster House. Park in front of the hotel and the porter will take care of your car. See Dublin Walking Tour map for location.

※ ✄ 🖃 ☎ ♨ ⛉ @ ☍ P ⑪ ⊘ ⚘ ≈ 🖼 ⚲ ♿ ⛱ ☂ ⚐ 🏃 🏇 ⚓

THE MERRION
Manager: Peter MacCann
Upper Merrion Street
Dublin, Ireland
Tel: (01) 603 0600, Fax: (01) 603 0700
142 Rooms, Double: €470–€2,695*
*Breakfast not included: €27
Dinner: €60
Open: all year, Credit cards: all major
City hotel
www.karenbrown.com/merrion.html

Modern hotels are not usually included in this guide, but I was so taken with the value for money and excellent location offered by the Mespil Hotel that I decided to stay there, and I was very pleased with the quality of the accommodation and the friendliness of the staff. Sitting beside the Grand Canal with its grassy verges and leafy trees, the Mespil sports a pleasing modern exterior that complements its attractive contemporary interior. Stylish sofas and chairs deck the lobby while the adjacent restaurant, all decked out in light wood, offers a bistro-style menu The bar with its clubby chairs and sofas offers a very popular carvery lunch. Bedrooms come in three varieties—front, back and side. Front rooms face the canal (opt for one of these as it's a treat to have a view room in Dublin), while back and side rooms offer complete peace and quiet. Nearly all of the bedrooms offer one queen and one single bed. From the hotel it is a 15 minute walk to St Stephens Green. *Directions:* Follow signs for South City to Baggot Street. Cross the canal, turn right, and the Mespil is on your left after 200 meters. The hotel has 50 parking spaces available on a first come first served basis. See Dublin Walking Tour map for location.

MESPIL HOTEL
Manager: Martin Holohan
Mespil Road
Dublin, Ballsbridge, Ireland
Tel: (01) 488 4600, Fax: (01) 667 1244
255 Rooms, Double: €155*
*Breakfast not included: €12
Dinner: from €25
Closed: December 24 to 26, Credit cards: all major
City hotel
www.karenbrown.com/mespil.html

A tall, creeper-covered wall and a discreet plaque are the only indications that you have arrived at 31 Leeson Close an absolutely top of the line bed and breakfast. Ring the buzzer, open the tall doors, and you enter an oasis of tranquility and greenery far from the clamor of the surrounding city. Number 31 was home to Ireland's famous 60s modern architect, Sam Stephenson, who fashioned it from two coach houses. Noel and Deirdre Comer, the present owners, have kept the cool, clean lines of this modern home. A contemporary painting hangs above the fireplace in the living room where the leather sofa, the only piece of furniture, hugs the wall of the conversation pit and stark, whitewashed brick walls contrast texturally with the mosaic tiled floor. Beautiful bedrooms and their accompanying luxury bathrooms are spread over two buildings—the décor is minimalist the quality of beds, bedding and toiletries luxurious. The main house has grand, high-ceilinged rooms, while the coach house naturally has lower-ceilinged rooms, several of which have their own private patio. Noel, Deirdre, and Homer (the Labrador) work hard to give a gracious welcome and (Homer excluded) provide you with all the information you need on what to see and where to go in Dublin. *Directions:* Lower Leeson Street runs off the southern end of St. Stephen's Green. Leeson Close is opposite 41 Lower Leeson Street. A secure, off-road car park is adjacent to Number 31.

NUMBER 31
Owners: Deirdre & Noel Comer
31 Leeson Close
Dublin, Ireland
Tel: (01) 676 5011, Fax: (01) 676 2929
21 Rooms, Double: €190–€220
Open: all year, Credit cards: all major
Hidden Ireland
Guesthouse
www.karenbrown.com/number31.html

When it first opened in the heart of Dublin in 1824, The Shelbourne offered a suitably handsome "home away from home" for Irish nobility and landed gentry. Today, this legendary grande dame welcomes a wider spectrum of guests–including the city's politicians and literati–but is still the place to stay, a luxurious, elegant hotel that easily lives up to its maxim as "the most distinguished address in Ireland." The comings and goings of Dublin socialites are reflected in the enormous mirror in the lobby as they pass on their way to the Lord Mayor's Lounge for afternoon tea, to the lively Horseshoe Bar for cocktails, to the contemporary Saddle Room for steak and seafood, or for a drink overlooking St. Stephen's Green in Number 27 Bar and Lounge. The beautifully appointed bedrooms include 19 suites, each named after a famous guest. You might consider treating yourself to the Princess Grace Suite, an opulent two-bedroom affair favored by the princess on her visits to Dublin. And be sure to visit the Constitution Room (known then as Room 112), which played an important role in the founding of the Irish nation), as it was here that the Irish Constitution was drafted in 1922. *Directions:* The Shelbourne is on the north side of St. Stephen's Green. Park in front to unload and your car will be taken to the hotel's garage. See Dublin Walking Tour map for location.

THE SHELBOURNE   *New*
Manager: Liam Doyle
27 St. Stephen's Green
Dublin, Ireland
Tel: (01) 663 4500, Fax: (01) 661 6006
265 Rooms, Double: €315–€2,500*
*Breakfast not included
Dinner: €60
Open: all year, Credit cards: all major
City hotel
www.karenbrown.com/shelbourne.html

Waterloo House is two tall Georgian townhomes cleverly combined to become a delightful guesthouse. Just a 15-minute walk to St. Stephen's Green and Trinity College, it is well set back from one of Dublin's quieter streets and has parking in front. Evelyn Corcoran and her friendly staff really try hard to look after their guests. Soft strains of classical music play in the lobby sitting room and there's an elevator for luggage and for those who do not want to climb as many as four flights of stairs. Whether your bedroom is on the garden level or at the top of the house, you'll be pleased with its smart décor. Rooms are cozy in size with king bedded rooms, overlooking the garden, being the most spacious. Breakfast is taken downstairs in the breakfast room that opens up to a sunny conservatory and gardens. Keycards give you access to the front door as well as your room so that you can come and go on your own timetable. There are lots of restaurants and bars within easy walking distance and Evelyn has comprised a "guide" giving useful eatery recommendations and pricing. *Directions:* Follow signs for South City. Cross the Baggot Street Bridge into Baggot Street. Pass a row of shops on your left and turn right into Waterloo Road—Waterloo House is on your left with a car park in front. See Dublin Walking Tour map for location.

WATERLOO HOUSE
Owner: Evelyn Corcoran
8–10 Waterloo Road
Dublin, Ballsbridge, Ireland
Tel: (01) 660 1888, Fax: (01) 667 1955
19 Rooms, Double: €114–€200
Open: all year, Credit cards: MC, VS
Guesthouse
www.karenbrown.com/waterloo.html

Dating back to 1698, Grange Lodge is one of those large, comfortable houses that have evolved as owners have added and altered over the years. Today it's the home of Norah and Ralph Brown, easygoing, friendly folk who offer guests the warmest of welcomes. Norah has won many awards for her outstandingly good food and runs regular cooking classes. Be sure to book dinner when you make your reservations. Norah serves coffee in the lovely drawing room or in the den, a cozy room where, on colder evenings, a log fire bids a cheery welcome. The Browns are inveterate collectors and as a consequence lovely furniture, old china, pewter, stoneware, and fascinating bygones fill every nook and cranny. Upstairs are the very comfortable, individually decorated bedrooms, all with their own pretty bathrooms full of little extras. Acres of gardens ensure peace and quiet though it's just a minute's drive to main roads, making this an ideal touring base for the northern counties. Tour the nearby Tyrone crystal factory and try your own hand at cutting the hand-blown sparkling crystal. Nearby are two National Trust properties: Ardress House, a 17th-century manor, and The Argory, an 1820s house with a lot of original furniture. *Directions:* Take the M1 from Belfast to junction 15, take the A29 towards Armagh for 2 km, turn left at the Grange Lodge sign. Turn almost immediately right and Grange Lodge is the first white-walled entrance on the right.

GRANGE LODGE
Owners: Norah & Ralph Brown
7 Grange Road
Dungannon,
Co Tyrone, BT71 7EJ, Northern Ireland
Tel: (028) 8778 4212, Fax: (028) 8778 4313
5 Rooms, Double: £85
Dinner: £32 (not Sun)
Open: Feb to mid-Dec, Credit cards: MC, VS
Country house
www.karenbrown.com/grangelodge.html

Ann and Jim Mulligan built An Bohreen high on a hill with fabulous views. From the outside, it looks like a conventional bungalow; but once you are inside the dining room, you are presented with a wall of windows overlooking the bay of Dungarvan. The sitting room windows frame the Comeragh Mountains. Bedrooms are fresh and pretty with antique dressers and attractive bed linen. Jim is quintessentially Irish with a gleam in his eye, and a natural friendliness. He carries your bag, plans sightseeing, and answers questions; while Ann has a reputation for excellent cooking. A dinner here may well be the highlight of your trip. The four-course dinner must be reserved 24 hours in advance and is often wild salmon or Waterford lamb. Breakfasts are a real treat with warm scones and fresh-squeezed juice preceding the cooked dish with choices such as crepes with sautéed apples or the traditional "full Irish." Main roads will whisk you off to Waterford for sightseeing. You can stay close to home, visit local potteries, go hill walking or riding. Of course, you must see the local fairy bush covered with ribbons and bits that folks decorate it with. You drive your car down the hill, stop at the fairy bush, and your car starts to reverse up the hill on its own. Jim assures me it happens every time. *Directions:* From Waterford take the N25 towards Cork. Make a right turn 5 km from the "Resume Speed" sign as you leave the hamlet of Lemybrien.

AN BOHREEN
Owners: Ann & Jim Mulligan
Killeneen West
Dungarvan
Co Waterford, Ireland
Tel: (051) 291010, Fax: (051) 291011
4 Rooms, Double: €90–€100
Dinner: €40 (not Tue, Wed, Thu)
Open: mid-Mar to Nov, Credit cards: MC, VS
B&B
www.karenbrown.com/anbohreen.html

You'll enjoy staying at Powersfield House on the outskirts of Dungarvan. Eunice has decorated her home with great style, she's a talented chef, and a warm, easy going person. When Eunice returned to Dungarvan to marry a local farmer they built this substantial neo-Georgian home large enough to provide plenty of space for their family on one side of the house and guests on the other. There are six most attractive bedrooms decorated with a modern flair in a traditional country house style. Downstairs guests have a comfortable sitting room adjacent to the dining room. Eunice is a talented chef who, until she had 3 young boys, ran a popular restaurant. Now she limits herself to dinner for guests though she is happy to give day-long cookery courses to parties of guests, demonstrating an arsenal of easy to prepare dishes for entertaining. Just down the road Dungarven is an attractive seaside town round a pretty bay. It's a particularly attractive coastal drive to Waterford and you can return by a faster, inland route. To the west is Ardmore, a 7th century monastic settlement. *Directions:* From Dungarvan take the Clonmel road. Powersfield House is the second turn to the left, and the first house on the right.

POWERSFIELD HOUSE
Owners: Eunice & Edmund Power
Ballinamuck
Dungarvan
Co Waterford, Ireland
Tel: (058) 45594, Fax: (058) 45550
6 Rooms, Double: €110–€120
Dinner: €27–€37
Open: all year, Credit cards: all major
Country house
www.karenbrown.com/powers.html

The summertime evening view from the dining room of Castle Murray House is simply staggering. As the night slowly draws in on green fields that tumble to the sea and scudding clouds dapple the reddening sky, the sun slowly sinks behind the distant Slieve League, the highest sea cliffs in Europe. The food, with lots of local seafood on the menu, is as outstanding as the view and served in portions that satisfy even the heartiest of Irish appetites. Chef Remy Dupuy's cooking attracts a large local following, so the best way to secure an often hard-to-come-by dinner reservation is to stay here. After an evening-long repast you can retire up the narrow pine staircase to one of the smartly decorated bedrooms with their sprightly contemporary decor and pleasing color schemes. Be sure to request a room with a view of the bay. If you want the most spacious of accommodation, opt for the "honeymoon room" found atop a narrow flight of stairs at the top of the house. While it does not have "the view" from its bedroom, it does from its spacious deck. Between breakfast and dinner the rugged Donegal landscape is yours to explore. *Directions:* From Donegal take the N56 towards Killybegs. The left-hand turn to Castle Murray House is after Dunkineely.

CASTLE MURRAY HOUSE
Owner: Marguerite Howley
Dunkineely, Co Donegal, Ireland
Tel: (074) 9737022, Fax: (074) 9737330
10 Rooms, Double: €130–€150
Dinner: €48-€60
Closed: Christmas & mid-Jan to mid-Feb
Credit cards: MC, VS
Restaurant with rooms
www.karenbrown.com/castlemurray.html

Joe and Kay O'Flynn bought Rathsallagh House, a converted Queen Anne stables with 530 acres of farmland, in 1978. Encouraged by the spaciousness of the house, Kay opened three rooms for bed and breakfast guests and thus began a venture that has evolved into the country house hotel and golf club that you see today. Tractor sheds and barns are gone, replaced by a parade of bedrooms, and fields that lined the driveway are now the groomed fairways of the championship golf course. The billiard room, tennis court, Jacuzzi, sauna and capacious gardens encourage total relaxation. While the size of the operation makes it all seem rather grand, Rathsallagh manages to keep the bonhomie of a friendly, relaxed country house hotel complete with homey touches like Joe still paying his bills at the old pine table in the breakfast room. Begin the day with a lavish breakfast, choosing from an array of savory dishes on the sideboard. Relax with a drink before dinner and enjoy the comfortable country house style of the place. Realize that you deserve the best and stay in one of the deluxe stable rooms. It's just a 45 minute drive to the K Club where the Ryder Cup was held in 2006. Sightseeing includes the Wicklow Mountains, Glendalough, and the National Stud. *Directions:* From Dublin airport take the M50 south the N7, which you exit for the M9 towards Carlow. After 9.5 km pass the Priory Inn on the left and just over 3 km later turn left for Rathsallagh.

❄ ☕ 💳 ☎ @ P ⏐⏐ ≈ 🏹 ⛷ 👤 🏇

RATHSALLAGH HOUSE   ***Cover painting***
Owner: The O'Flynn family
Dunlavin, Co Wicklow, Ireland
Tel: (045) 403112, Fax: (045) 403343
29 Rooms, Double: €270–€335
Dinner: €65
Open: all year, Credit cards: all major
Country house hotel
www.karenbrown.com/rathsallagh.html

Farran House is a large, elegant 18th century, Italianate style, manor house situated in the Lee valley, overlooking the medieval castle and abbey of Kilcrea. John and Patricia have completed a painstaking restoration and they now live in a wing while guests can rent the main house on a self-catering basis or choose dinner, bed, and breakfast country house-style. Relax round the fire in the sitting room, enjoy a game of billiards in the former music room, and chat with fellow guests round the dining-room table. Upstairs, you find four lovely, spacious bedrooms all enjoying south-facing views across the valley. Room One is extra special because of its bathroom—a super-sized affair with a claw-foot tub sitting center stage. Your hosts have collected a picture library of all things Ireland—they travel the length and breadth of the country taking photos, which gives them an intimate knowledge of every scenic spot in the country—very handy for advising guests where to go and what to see. Blarney is 16 kilometers away, Kinsale and the coast about 40 kilometers. If renting an estate is not within range of your pocketbook, Patricia and John also have a three-bedroom cottage available. *Directions:* From Cork take the N22 towards Killarney for 15 km. Go around Ballincollig on the ring road and, after Dan Sheanhan's pub on your right, take the second right. Take the next right up the hill and the first gate is on your left.

FARRAN HOUSE
Owners: Patricia Wiese & John Kehely
Farran, Co Cork, Ireland
Tel: (021) 7331215
4 Rooms, Double: €140–€200
1 Cottage: €500–€690 weekly
Dinner: €40 (not Sun or Mon)
Open: Apr to Oct, Credit cards: all major
Hidden Ireland
Country house & self-catering
www.karenbrown.com/farran.html

Catherine helped her mother in the antiques trade for many years and as her interest in furniture grew, so did her collection which is now large enough for her to theme her rooms depending on the period of the furniture: Art Nouveau, Victorian, Edwardian, Georgian and Regency. Having a fondness for Edwardian furniture I was particularly impressed by its spaciousness and the flat screen TV ideally placed for watching telly from the bed. A real prize is the Georgian room with its two beautiful commodes giving pride of place in this stately room with its V'Soske carpet and grand bathroom. If you want total peace and quiet opt for the garden suite, a large room decorated in vivid yellow and royal blue with a bay window large enough to accommodate two armchairs overlooking a sheltered corner of her vast garden. Catherine's style is ornate with grand gilded pieces and high-backed library chairs arranged before the fireplaces in each of the two sitting rooms. Her collecting is not limited to furniture, she has a whole array of silver and china which gives a great sense of occasion to breakfast in the dining room. Breakfast is the only meal served, which is no problem as there are several good restaurants close by. Guests often go the 6.5 kilometers into Galway city for city life and take day trips to the Aran Islands or to Connemara. *Directions:* From Galway take the N59 towards Clifden for 6.5 km and Killeen House is on your right.

KILLEEN HOUSE
Owner: Catherine Doyle
Bushypark
Galway, Ireland
Tel: (091) 524179, Fax: (091) 528065
6 Rooms, Double: €140–€190
Closed: Christmas, Credit cards: all major
B&B
www.karenbrown.com/killeen.html

Desmond, the 29th Knight of Glin's demesne is a 400-acre farm and late-18th-century castle stretching along the banks of the River Shannon. Staying here affords you the opportunity to live luxuriously—the house is an absolute beauty, full of exquisite furniture, family portraits, and beautiful artifacts. It is all very grand but not at all stuffy, for your host is Bob Duff, a gregarious New Zealander who ensures that you are well taken care of and well fed. He will give you a tour of the house with lots of suitably embellished stories. If you are passionate about art, literature, furniture, or books, be sure to ask if the Knight is in residence, for Desmond is happy to meet with guests when he is at home. Sip tea in the grand drawing room or curl up with a good book in the oh-so-comfortable sitting room. Bedrooms range from large and luxurious with extra-large bathrooms and dressing rooms to small and, by comparison, more ordinary. Ballybunion golf course is close at hand and the new Greg Norman-designed links course Doonbeg is an hour away via the Tarbert car ferry. *Directions:* From Limerick take the N69 towards Tralee for 50 km to Glin. At the end of the village turn left following the estate's wall to the castle entrance.

GLIN CASTLE
Owners: Olda & Desmond FitzGerald, Knight of Glin
Manager: Bob Duff
Glin, Co Limerick, Ireland
Tel: (068) 34173, Fax: (068) 34364
15 Rooms, Double: €310–€495
Dinner: €53
Closed: Nov to Mar, Credit cards: all major
Ireland's Blue Book
Country house hotel
www.karenbrown.com/glin.html

This dazzling, three-story Regency house, formerly the dower house of the Courtown estate, has an atmosphere of refined elegance created by vivacious hostess Mary Bowe and her delightful daughters Margaret and Laura. Mary has great charm and energy—during our stay she chatted with guests before dinner, made the rounds during dinner, and was back again at breakfast checking up to make certain that everything was perfect. The house is full of antiques, classic pieces that transport you back to the days of gracious living in grand houses. While we especially enjoyed our large, twin-bedded room with impressive, well-polished furniture, elegant decor, and a grand bathroom, I found the other bedrooms equally attractive. Six prized units are the ultra-luxurious, gorgeously decorated, extravagantly priced State Rooms tucked away in a separate ground-floor wing: request the Print Suite, Stopford, Georgian, or French. Dinner is served in the ornate Gothic conservatory dining room—all greenery and mirrors. The food is a delight—superb French and Irish dishes. *Directions:* Marlfield House is 88 km from Dublin. Take the N11 south to Gorey. As you enter the town turn left, before going under the railway bridge, onto the Courtown Road, straight across the roundabout, and the house is on your right after 2 km.

MARLFIELD HOUSE
Owners: Mary, Ray, Margaret & Laura Bowe
Courtown Road
Gorey, Co Wexford, Ireland
Tel: (053) 9421124, Fax: (053) 9421572
20 Rooms, Double: €275–€765
Dinner: €64
Closed: late Dec to Feb 1, Credit cards: all major
Relais & Châteaux
Country house hotel
www.karenbrown.com/marlfield.html

As newlyweds, Philomena and her husband John put in an exceedingly low bid on a very tumbledown Woodlands Farmhouse and it was many years before she found out why their offer had been accepted. To hear why and enjoy intriguing tales of gold sovereigns, cursed families, and arranged marriages, you will have to go and stay and ask Philomena for a story session with tea or coffee and scones upon arrival. What started out as a simple bed and breakfast has now grown into a very professional guesthouse. Guests have a cozily cluttered parlor with an eclectic assortment of sizeable Victorian chairs. The parlor opens up to an expansive dining room lit by two grand crystal chandeliers, which overlooks the lovely back garden. The front garden is even more impressive: a grand sweep of lawn with shrubs and trees going down to the river and the tennis court. All the smartly decorated bedrooms enjoy garden views and range in size from large family rooms to snug twins—all have electric blankets and small en suite shower or bathrooms with hairdryers. Room 6 is a particularly spacious room overlooking the back garden. In Wexford you can visit Wexford Heritage Park or Johnstown Castle Museum. To the north lies the Vale of Avoca. *Directions:* Woodlands Country House is signposted on the N11 between Arklow (10 km) and Gorey (6 km). It is just before the village of Killinierin, 2 km west of the N11.

WOODLANDS COUNTRY HOUSE
Owner: Philomena O'Sullivan
Gorey, Killinierin, Co Wexford, Ireland
Tel: (040) 237125, Fax: (040) 237133
6 Rooms, Double: €110–€130
Open: Apr to Oct, Credit cards: MC, VS
Guesthouse
www.karenbrown.com/woodlands.html

This is not your "Hollywood" of frantic freeways and homes of the rich and famous—this is the County Down version: a very nice town facing the sea backed by pastoral countryside. Here Beech Hill House, a Georgian-style dower house built for Victoria's grandmother, sits atop a little knoll. As we sat in the conservatory enjoying tea and fruitcake, I found it hard to believe that half an hour earlier I had been in the heart of Belfast. Victoria grew up just down the road on what is now the site of the Ulster Folk Museum so she is an expert on what to see and do in the area. She also has a real flair for decorating and her lovely home is filled with enviable family furniture. Bedrooms are on the ground floor and have all the right stuff: lovely furniture, books, hairdryers, TVs, goodies, firm beds (a zip-link twin/king, a double, and a queen), fine Irish linen, and well-proportioned bathrooms. We were up at dawn for a flight and Victoria insisted that we start our day with a "little" breakfast: the sideboard was groaning with bowls of fruit, yogurt, and fresh-baked bread accompanied by homemade jam...and then we moved on to the cooked items! For week long stays consider the Colonel's Lodge, a two-bedroom cottage in the garden. *Directions:* Leave Belfast on the A2 in the direction of Bangor. Bypass Holywood and about 2.5 km after going under the bridge at the Ulster Folk Museum turn right signed to Craigantlet. Beech Hill House is 3 km along on the left.

BEECH HILL COUNTRY HOUSE
Owner: Victoria Brann
23 Ballymoney Road, Craigantlet
Holywood, BT23 4TG, Northern Ireland
Tel & Fax: (028) 9042 5892
3 Rooms, Double: £80–£90
1 Cottage: £350–£400 weekly
Open: all year, Credit cards: all major
Country house
www.karenbrown.com/beechhill.html

The King Sitric is Ireland's premier fish restaurant, so here you can enjoy wonderful seafood then be lulled to sleep by the sea just 20 minutes from Dublin airport. Take an aperitif at the long tasting table in the wine cellar while perusing the menu, and then go upstairs to dine in the restaurant with its sweeping views over Dublin Bay. Aidan and Joan explain their food philosophy: "We have built up a network of suppliers of the finest Irish produce. Most of the fish is landed here at Howth. Our smoked salmon is smoked by McLoughlins on the West Pier and crab comes from John Sheridan who fishes Balscadden Bay a stone's throw from our door. Our Irish vegetables and meats are locally produced and mostly organic." After dinner enjoy a gentle stroll down the pier before retiring to bed in rooms named after Irish lighthouses. You'll find lots of polished wood and natural materials with subtle nautical touches. All bedrooms have sea views though Rockabill and Fastnet, the largest rooms at the top of the house, have the best. It's an excellent base for visiting Dublin—a 10-minute walk brings you to the Dart station for a 25-minute ride to Trinity College. Howth marina is just 3-minutes away by foot, while a more energetic hike takes you up to Howth Head. *Directions:* From Dublin airport take the M1 towards Dublin and leave at the first exit, N32, for Malahide Road and Howth. At Howth habor front you will find the King Sitric on your right.

≡ ✴ 💳 ☎ @ P ⑪ ⊘ ♨ ⊥ ⼂ ⼉ ♞ ⽕

KING SITRIC
Owners: Joan & Aidan MacManus
East Pier
Howth, Co Dublin, Ireland
Tel: (01) 832 5235, Fax: (01) 839 2442
8 Rooms, Double: €150–€210
Dinner: €55 (not Sun)
Open: all year, Credit cards: all major
Ireland's Blue Book
Restaurant with rooms
www.karenbrown.com/kingsitric.html

Glenlohane is a lovely Georgian home of spacious but not overly grand rooms, sitting in beautiful, parklike grounds. It is a comfortable house, full of attractive things—lovely antiques and furniture, fires, and rooms in cheerful colors. Hosts Desmond and Melanie—the tenth generation of the family who built the house—are most welcoming, as are their dogs. Enjoy tea by the fire in the drawing room, play a tune on the grand piano, and immerse yourself in the charm of it all. Alternatively, browse through Melanie's herbs or sit in the tranquility of the walled garden. For dinner there are two very nice restaurants a five minute drive away in Kanturk. A family, or small group of friends, can reserve the entire house. Garden lovers are directed to Anne's Grove gardens at Castletownroche and Garinish Island with its grand Italianate gardens. Glenlohane is a working farm of 200 acres with cattle, sheep, horses, and hens; as well as barley, wheat, and oats. Outdoor activities include fishing, golf, horse shows, and agricultural shows. *Directions:* From Kanturk take the R576 toward Mallow. Very soon, bear left at the religious monument towards Buttevant on the R580. Take the first right at Sally's Cross towards Ballyclough. Glenlohane is the first residential entrance on the left after 2.5 km—watch for Glenlohane bird sanctuary signs the house does not have a sign.

GLENLOHANE
Owners: Melanie & Desmond Sharp Bolster
Kanturk, Co Cork, Ireland
Tel: (029) 50014
4 Rooms, Double: €100
Open: all year, Credit cards: all major
Country house
www.karenbrown.com/glenlohane.html

The Irish name for Kenmare, An Neidin, means "the little nest" which is a good description of this attractive town nestling beside the River Kenmare at the foot of some of Ireland's most spectacular scenery. On the Cork road, out of the main bustle of town, The Lodge (purpose-built as a guesthouse and a substantial family home for the Quills and their four young sons) sits back from the road in 2 acres of grassy garden. Finbar works in the family's woollen shop in town, which has the largest selection of sweaters in Kenmare, if not all of Kerry, while Rosemary runs the bed and breakfast. She is exceedingly personable as is her staff of local ladies. Not a thing in the place (with the possible exception of two gigantic vases) is older than the house, from the traditional furniture to the portraits that line the staircase. Bedrooms are spacious and have large, top-of-the-line bathrooms. All have queen-size beds (one a grand four-poster) and nine are large enough to accommodate an additional single bed. One ground-floor bedroom is specially equipped for the handicapped. Kenmare is ideally placed for touring the Ring of Kerry and the prettier Beara Peninsula, as well as for visiting several historic houses and gardens including Muckross House and Derrynane House, home of Daniel O'Connell. *Directions:* Kenmare is about a three-hour drive from Shannon on the N71 between Killarney and Bantry. The Lodge is on the (Cork road) opposite the golf club.

❄ 🍽 🛒 💳 ☎ P ♿ ⛷ 🧍 🚶 🐎 🚣

THE LODGE
Owners: Rosemary & Finbar Quill
Killowen Road
Kenmare, Co Kerry, Ireland
Tel: (064) 41512, Fax: (064) 42724
11 Rooms, Double: €100–€120
Open: Mar to Nov, Credit cards: MC, VS
Guesthouse
www.karenbrown.com/lodge.html

The Park Hotel has come a long way since it began life in 1897 as the Great Southern Hotel Kenmare to provide a convenient overnight stop for railway travelers en route to or from the Ring of Kerry. Guests are greeted by a blazing coal fire, which casts its glow towards the cozy bar and lounge, and you sit down at a partners' desk to register before being shown to your room. Such touches give a small-hotel feeling to this larger establishment. Exquisite accommodations are provided in nine very luxurious suites with splendid views out over Kenmare Bay. Just as lovely are the superior bedrooms in the old house, many of which have bedrooms and an arch to the seating area—these also all have wonderful views of the bay. Rooms in the "newer" wing have balconies or patios to capture sideways bay views. The restaurant produces some of the finest food that you will find in Ireland. The Park provides programs for the Christmas and New Year holidays. Pamper yourself at the adjacent Sámas spa where you choose from over 40 holistic treatments. Use of the Thermal Suite (sauna, steam, aromatherapy mist and vitality pool with body, foot, and neck massage) is scheduled before your treatment and afterwards you relax on a day bed overlooking the woodlands. The spa has two couples private day suites. Beside the hotel is an 18-hole golf course. *Directions:* Kenmare is about a three-hour drive from Shannon on the N71 between Killarney and Bantry.

THE PARK HOTEL KENMARE
Owner: Francis Brennan
Manager: John Brennan
Kenmare, Co Kerry, Ireland
Tel: (064) 41200, Fax: (064) 41402
49 Rooms, Double: €346–€806
Dinner: €72
Open: Apr to Oct & Christmas, Credit cards: all major
Ireland's Blue Book
Luxury resort
www.karenbrown.com/parkhotel.html

Kenmare is one of my favorite Irish towns, and how appropriate that several of my favorite bed and breakfasts are located here, amongst them Sallyport House. Janie Arthur returned home after working for 15 years in California to help her brother, John, convert the family home into a luxurious bed and breakfast, decorating it in an uncluttered, sophisticated style. It's a family affair with John's wife Helen (who runs O'Sullivans pub at nearby Kilmakilogue) and sister Wanie and her children lending a hand. Return in the evening to chat round the fire in the drawing room or curl up in one of the comfortable chairs in the less formal sitting area with its exposed stone wall and old photographs of Kenmare. Breakfast is the only meal served—for dinner, it's a two-minute walk into town. The bedrooms are delightful, each furnished with antiques and accompanied by a large luxurious bathroom. Muxnaw has views of Muxnaw Mountain and deep window seats, Ring View looks out to the River Kenmare, Reen a Gross has an American king-sized four-poster bed, The Falls has a view of the pretty garden. It's delightful to stroll along the riverbank, through the park, and back through the town. You can spend several days exploring the Beara Peninsula, Ring of Kerry, and lakes of Killarney. *Directions:* From Killarney, follow Bantry signposts through Kenmare and Sallyport House is on your left before you come to the bridge.

SALLYPORT HOUSE
Owners: Janie & John Arthur
Kenmare, Co Kerry, Ireland
Tel: (064) 42066, Fax: (064) 42067
5 Rooms, Double: €140–€175
Open: Apr to Oct, Credit cards: none
B&B
www.karenbrown.com/sallyport.html

Sea Shore Farm, run by Mary and Owen O'Sullivan, is a particularly peaceful place to stay, no more than five minutes drive from Kenmare or a fifteen minute walk to town by a quiet side road. On arrival you are welcomed with a cup of tea or coffee "to settle you in" and given plenty of information on what to do in and around Kenmare. The lounge, overlooking the Kenmare Bay, has lots of literature on the area. The bedrooms look over the fields across the River Kenmare to the mountains of the Beara Peninsula where the roads are quieter and the scenery very similar to that on the Ring of Kerry. The two downstairs rooms have patios and are wheelchair compatible. It's a blissfully quiet and rural place to stay yet close to the bustle of Kenmare with its excellent restaurants, pubs, and shops. You are just off the Ring of Kerry. If you do not want to deal with coaches and lots of other traffic head for the Beara Peninsula where you get quieter roads and spectacular views. *Directions:* From Kenmare take the Killarney road (N71) for 300 meters. Pass the Esso petrol station on your right and take the next left onto the Ring of Kerry. Sea Shore Farm Guesthouse is signposted to your left after 300 meters.

SEA SHORE FARM GUESTHOUSE
Owners: Mary Patricia & Owen O'Sullivan
Kenmare, Tubrid, Co Kerry, Ireland
Tel & Fax: (064) 41270
6 Rooms, Double: €100–€130
Open: Mar to Nov, Credit cards: MC, VS
Guesthouse
www.karenbrown.com/seashore.html

We continue to receive rave reviews on Shelburne Lodge praising not only the high quality of the decor, but also the delicious breakfasts. The building, a Georgian farmhouse, is lovely and the grounds with their lawns, herb garden, and tennis court are very attractive, but it is the interior that is outstanding. The polished wooden floors gleam and lovely antiques grace the sitting room and hallway. Admire Maura's enviable art collection—all by local artists. Each lovely bedroom is accompanied by a luxurious bathroom, each with a different color scheme. Of course, the towel rails are heated and you'll find books of just the sort you want to read and browse through in your room. The same attention to detail goes into the scrumptious breakfast she prepares—even the compote of fresh fruits is artfully garnished. Husband Tom is helpful and friendly, always there with a map and pointing guests in the right direction. Kenmare has some excellent restaurants and Maura as former chef at one of the best (Packies) is happy to make recommendations (advance reservations are a must). Maura also helps her sister Grainne at The Purple Heather, a great venue for lunch or snacks. After dinner wander into one of Kenmare's many pubs—there's entertainment and music to suit all tastes. *Directions:* Shelburne Lodge is on the R569 (Cork road) opposite the golf club.

SHELBURNE LODGE
Owners: Maura & Tom Foley
Kenmare, Co Kerry, Ireland
Tel: (064) 41013, Fax: (064) 42135
9 Rooms, Double: €130–€170
Open: Mar to mid-Dec, Credit cards: MC, VS
Country house
www.karenbrown.com/shelburnelodge.html

An impressive tree lined gravel drive leads to Glen house and its gardens, surrounded by three hundred acres of farmland and with sweeping views down to Courtmacsherry Bay and the Atlantic Ocean beyond. Ten generations of the Scott family have farmed the land since the mid 1600's. The house dates back to 1860 but adjacent outbuildings are even older. Current owners Guy and Dianna have renovated and remodeled to provide four extremely comfortable bedrooms and a family suite, three of the rooms have ocean views, all have modern en-suite bathrooms. Guests can relax in front of the fire in the comfortable drawing room or, weather permitting, investigate the walled garden. Diana prides herself on the use of local produce, home grown fruits and vegetables and free range eggs from her own hens. The comprehensive breakfast menu is served on individual tables in the dining room under the watchful stare of John's predecessors, looking down from their framed photographs on the wall. Kinsale, with its shops and restaurants, is just a twenty minute drive away. *Directions:* Located just off the R600 Clonakilty to Kinsale Road. Take the Kilbrittain turnoff from beside the water (there are other Kilbrittain turns) and The Glen is the first house on the left.

THE GLEN   New
Owners: Diana & Guy Scott
Kilbrittain, Kinsale, Co Cork, Ireland
Tel & Fax: (023) 49862
5 Rooms, Double: €120–€130
Open: Apr to Oct, Credit cards: MC, VS
Country house
www.karenbrown.com/theglen.html

A gravel topped driveway curves through the woodland estate towards the early Georgian house, built on what were once the lands of Kilconnell Friary. Current owners the Gossips rescued it from a state of near complete dereliction and have cleverly restored it to its former glory. Paneled walls are painted in bold colors typical of the genre, rooms are tastefully furnished with pictures, antiques and collectibles. An impressive staircase sweeps up from the classic entrance hall to two floors of bedrooms above, the top floor rooms are tucked under the eaves. All have nicely appointed bathrooms en-suite and views over the surrounding countryside. Comfortable beds and crisp linens combine with the secluded surroundings to ensure a restful nights sleep. The comfortably furnished sitting room with black marble fireplace is a great place to curl up with a good book on those occasionally damp days. Breakfast (and dinner by appointment) is served in the blue paneled dining room on the long table in front of the fire and under the stare of one of Suzie's ancestors gazing down from his impressive gilt framed portrait on the wall. *Directions:* From Ballinasloe take the R438 towards Athenry. Pass through Kilconnell village then take the first left towards Capptaggle and immediately left again after 100 meters into an unsignposted lane. Continue past the houses and the lane leads to Ballinderry Park.

BALLINDERRY PARK   **New**
Owners: Susie & George Gossip
Kilconnell, Ballinasloe
Co Galway, Ireland
Tel & Fax: (090) 968 6796
4 Rooms, Double: €160–€200
Dinner: €50 (not Sun or Mon)
Open: Apr to Oct, Credit cards: MC, VS
Hidden Ireland
Country house
www.karenbrown.com/ballinderrypark.html

Behind a traditional downtown Kilkenny shopfront sits Zuni (the name of a native American tribe adopted on a whim by Paula), a swish complex of bar, restaurant, and accommodation where ornamentation is kept to a minimum. The narrow bar—the kind where you sip martinis rather than gargle pints of bitter—opens up to the restaurant, where vermilion-red walls contrast with black-and-cream decor and swathes of stainless steel can be seen in the adjacent kitchen. Of course, the food is modern and fun—more Mediterranean than Irish. You find the same modern, minimalist look in the bedrooms, all identically decorated in soft cream with a vermilion-red wall adding a splash of color behind the bed. Beds are heavenly, with crisp white cotton linens and plump duvets. Rooms are by and large snug in size so ask for 101 to 104 or 201 to 204, the larger rooms, or 300, the largest with a queen and two single beds and a big bathroom. Zuni's excellent central location allows you to walk to everything in town. *Directions:* Arriving in Kilkenny from Dublin on the N10, follow signs for City Centre, which bring you down John's Street. Cross the River Nore and you see the castle on your left. Go straight at the traffic lights into Patrick Street and Zuni is on your right after 200 meters. Park in front and collect a map that directs you to nearby parking.

ZUNI
Owners: Paula & Paul Byrne
26 Patrick Street
Kilkenny
Co Kilkenny, Ireland
Tel: (056) 7723999, Fax: (056) 7756400
13 Rooms, Double: €90–€170
Dinner: from €27.50
Closed: Christmas, Credit cards: all major
Restaurant with rooms
www.karenbrown.com/zuni.html

You would never dream that all the hurly-burly of Killarney town is just down the road when you look out of Coolclogher House to the rolling sheep pastures and distant hills of Killarney. Mary and Maurice Harnett hail from Ireland, and spent a good few years in London where Maurice restored homes in need of complete TLC, a skill he has honed to perfection with Coolclogher House—for the place was a complete disaster when they purchased it. Now it's in perfect condition with each spacious room stylishly decorated. I was especially enchanted by the dining room which opens up to a conservatory with a giant camellia that was a mass of pink blooms. While the Harnetts welcome individual guests on a bed and breakfast basis, do not be disappointed if you cannot secure a reservation for an individual room as they also rent the house on a self-catering basis (sleeps 10-12). When the house is rented the Harnett family decamps to a ground floor two-bedroom apartment. There's not a small room in the place which gives you lots of scope to make yourself comfortable. For dinner guests are directed to the great variety of restaurants in town. Whether viewed from a boat or a pony and trap, the lakes of Killarney are beautiful, but in summer the town can get very crowded. *Directions:* From Killarney take the Muckross road (N71) towards Kenmare. Take first left turn into Mill Road (after metal bridge). Gates on right after 1 km.

COOLCLOGHER HOUSE
Owners: Mary & Maurice Harnett
Mill Road
Killarney, Co Kerry, Ireland
Tel: (064) 35996, Fax: (064) 30933
5 Rooms, Double: €190–€240
1 House: €5,500 weekly
Hidden Ireland
Country house & self-catering
www.karenbrown.com/coolclogher.html

Killarney is a pleasant town, best to explore after the crowds of daytime visitors have departed. Staying at Earls Court gives you the opportunity to go sightseeing out of town during the day, return in the evening for a cup of tea, and then walk into town for dinner. Emer and Ray purpose built the property and while the exterior is modern, the inside is more traditional, for Emer is a great collector of English and Irish antiques. Guests sign in at reception adjacent to a writing desk once owned by President Cearbhaill O'Dalaigh. Several of the delightful bedrooms have balconies with views of the distant mountains across the trees. Larger rooms have the advantage of spacious sitting areas, king-sized beds and larger bathrooms with a tub and a walk in shower. There's a fully equipped handicap room on the third floor. All bedrooms have delightful antique furniture, (several are four-poster and one an exquisite brass bed), excellent bathrooms with power showers, satellite TV, and phones. Several also have an extra single bed and two bedrooms have an interconnecting door, making them ideal for families. Golfers are spoiled for choice, with Killarney, Waterville, Dooks, Tralee, and Ballybunion the most popular courses, and there's a golf room for clubs. *Directions:* Arriving from Cork on the N22, take a left-hand turn 1 km before the first roundabout in Killarney (or go to the roundabout and retrace your steps). Proceed for 2 km and Earls Court is on your right.

EARLS COURT
Owners: Emer & Ray Moynihan
Woodlawn Junction
Killarney
Co Kerry, Ireland
Tel: (064) 34009, Fax: (064) 34366
30 Rooms, Double: €120–€190
Open: Mar to mid-Nov, Credit cards: MC, VS
Guesthouse
www.karenbrown.com/earlscourt.html

Walk through the front door and you realize the pink façade of the 100 year old building is concealing something different. The lobby, white paneled ceiling, black marble floor, brushed stainless steel trim and luminescent green lighting speaks of a contemporary style more usually found in the chic townhouse hotels of Dublin or Belfast. Inside the trend continues, pink lighting illuminates the dark corridors leading to the guest rooms where muted earth tones are offset with brilliant splashes of color. Modern furnishings, plush bedding and immaculate marble and white bathrooms provide all the creature comforts demanded by today's traveler. All rooms have views across the town or the churchyard. The Lanes cafe bar with its large flat screen TV's is open to the public, a great place to rub shoulders with the locals. A sweeping polished wood and glass staircase leads down to the dining room, "Cellar One". Exposed limestone walls, innovative lighting, wine racks on the wall, and the signature brilliant pink and green upholstery. The shops and restaurants of Killarney are on your doorstep. It's a short walk to Ross Castle or you can take a jaunting car from in front of the hotel. *Directions:* Proceed to Killarney town centre. Park your car at the Killarney Park Hotel and walk across the street to the hotel (next to the church). A porter will collect your luggage.

🍽 ✧ 🖪 ⛶ @ P ⅋ 🏃 👥 🐎 🐎

THE ROSS HOTEL   New
Owners: Janet & Padraig Treacy
Manager: David Ruttle
Town Centre
Killarney, Co Kerry, Ireland
Tel: (064) 31855, Fax: (064) 27633
29 Rooms, Double: €190–€300
Dinner: from €30
Closed: Christmas, Credit cards: all major
City hotel
www.karenbrown.com/rosshotel.html

You can be sure of being well fed when you stay at Ballymakeigh House for Margaret is a well know chef—she has written cookbooks, and operated a very successful local restaurant. Whenever possible Margaret uses only the finest organic local meats, fish and vegetables. She does a set four course dinner having discussed your likes and dislikes beforehand—there's an extensive wine list. At breakfast you'll be spoilt for choice—organic porrige and strawberry muffins are specilties. Relax in the sunny conservatory or on the Victorian sofas in the cozy sitting room, all decked out in shades of cream and green. Bedrooms are named after local rivers and are all attractively decorated with well-chosen antique furniture, interesting paintings, wallpaper, and fabrics—four have six-foot beds. All have electric blankets. There are masses of things to do in the area: Youghal (pronounced "yawl") is famous for its old buildings and Midleton Jamestown Centre tells the history of Irish whiskey production. You can motor up the coast to Waterford, down the coast to Kinsale and inland to Cashel and its famous rock. *Directions:* Killeagh is on the N25 between Youghal and Cork. Turn at The Old Thatch Tavern, then after 1 km turn right: Ballymakeigh House is on your right after 1 km.

BALLYMAKEIGH HOUSE
Owners: Margaret & Michael Browne
Killeagh, Co Cork, Ireland
Tel: (024) 95184, Fax: (024) 95370
6 Rooms, Double: €130–€140
Dinner: €45
Open: Feb to Nov, Credit cards: MC, VS
Farmhouse B&B
www.karenbrown.com/ballymakeighhouse.html

Flemingstown House, an 18th-century farmhouse, is just an hour's drive south of Limerick and Shannon airport, a quiet countryside world away from the hustle and bustle. Walk round the farm and chat with Imelda as she works in her spacious kitchen; for the two things that Imelda loves are cooking and taking care of her guests. It would be a shame to stay and not eat, for Imelda prepares tempting meals in which, following the starter and soup, there is a choice of meat or fish as a main course and always three or four desserts and farm cheeses made by her sister and her husband. The intricate stained-glass windows of the conservatory-style dining room were made by the same artist as those in the local church. Upstairs the bedrooms are top of the line, beautifully appointed and provided with a variety of twin and king-size combinations that can accommodate families of all sizes. Each bedroom has a small shower room. Nearby Kilmallock has the ruins of two friaries and the remains of its fortified wall weaving through the town. Guests find this a good base for touring counties Limerick, Tipperary, Kerry, and Cork. *Directions:* From Limerick take the N20 (Cork road) for 30 km and turn left to Kilmallock (10 km). From Kilmallock take the Kilfinane road (R512) for 3 km and the house is on your left.

FLEMINGSTOWN HOUSE
Owner: Imelda Sheedy-King
Kilmallock, Co Limerick, Ireland
Tel: (063) 98093, Fax: (063) 98546
5 Rooms, Double: €100–€135
Dinner: €40
Open: Feb to Nov, Credit cards: MC, VS
Farmhouse B&B
www.karenbrown.com/flemingstownhouse.html

Maeve Coakley purpose-built this fantastic bed and breakfast set high up over the town. In a place where accommodations are traditional, Maeve's is modern, bright and airy, decorated in utterly peaceful colors. The bedrooms were particularly alluring with their soft-white walls, linen curtains and bedcovers turned down to show Killarney wool blankets, crisp cotton sheets and large square pillows. The largest room is king-bedded with the rest being either queen or twin-bedded. All have immaculate bathrooms with power showers above the tubs, modem sockets, satellite TV, phone, a tea and coffee tray and a trouser press. There's a cozy little sitting room where you can chat by the fire. Breakfast has lots of good things on the menu: fresh fruits and juices, farmhouse cheese and yogurts, organic muesli and hot dishes with smoked salmon and scrambled eggs and catch of the day, as well as the traditional full Irish breakfast. There's several ways to walk into town where you can enjoy views across the sheltered harbor all manner of restaurants and a great many interesting shops. *Directions:* Go straight up the main street in Kinsale (Pearse Street) to the end, turn left and keep going till you see Fishy Fishy restaurant of the right and church on left. Follow the church wall to the left, narrow bend, and Blindgate House is on the left in 400m. There's lots of parking—a real bonus for Kinsale.

BLINDGATE HOUSE
Owner: Maeve Coakley
Blindgate
Kinsale, Co Cork, Ireland
Tel: (021) 477 7858, Fax: (021) 477 7868
11 Rooms, Double: €135–€180
Open: mid-Mar to mid-Dec, Credit cards: all major
B&B
www.karenbrown.com/blindgate.html

Sitting near the harbor, the Old Bank House occupies a prime heart-of-the-action location in this busy town. At one time these two Georgian townhouses served as a bank and the post office for the community, but now they have achieved a new lease of life as premier accommodation overlooking the sailboat-filled harbor. Here you are at the heart of town, having finally managed to secure a spot for your car on the street. On the ground floor guests have a little sitting area perfect for browsing through the menus from nearby restaurants and toasting their toes on a chilly evening. In the morning enjoy a lavish breakfast before heading out for the day. Bedrooms at the front enjoy the best views and the higher you go, the better the view over the roofs of the town—fortunately there is an elevator. The largest room is the Postmaster's Suite, with a spacious sitting area and fireplace. Beds are twin or king-sized if you request that the twin beds be zipped together. All the rooms have phone, TV, bath with shower over the tub, and Egyptian-cotton towels and bathrobes. The location at the very heart of this most attractive harbor town is ideal: you can stroll round the shops perusing the restaurant menus as you go. *Directions:* Follow the main road into Kinsale (Pearse Street)—the Old Bank House is on the right as you come into town. Parking is on the well-lit street.

OLD BANK HOUSE
Owner: Ciaran Fitzgerald
Pearse Street
Kinsale, Co Cork, Ireland
Tel: (021) 4774075, Fax: (021) 4774296
17 Rooms, Double: €180–€250
Closed: Christmas, Credit cards: all major
B&B
www.karenbrown.com/oldbankhouse.html

Beyond the yacht-filled harbor, the narrow streets of Kinsale terrace upwards to high ground. Here you find The Old Presbytery, the home of Noreen and Philip McEvoy who offer a choice of bed and breakfast or self-catering accommodation. The three-bedroom, three-bathroom self-catering apartments offer a sitting room with cheery gas fire in an antique grate, an extra bed that can be pulled down from a wall cupboard, and a kitchenette equipped with light cooking facilities. The Penthouse has a narrow circular staircase going from the living room to the bedrooms where you have views across the rooftops to the harbor (an excellent choice for a party of four). Bed and breakfast guests can choose accommodation that ranges in size from cozy to spacious (a family room with a double and two single beds), with all rooms found up a narrow staircase—leave your large cases in the car. Philip, who used to be a seafood chef, now concentrates his culinary efforts on breakfast, offering everything from traditional Irish fare to crepes filled with fruit in the breakfast room, where an antique Irish pine credenza takes pride of place. *Directions:* Go straight up the main street in Kinsale (Pearse Street) to the end, turn left, first right, and first right, and The Old Presbytery is on the right. Park in the yard.

THE OLD PRESBYTERY
Owners: Noreen & Philip McEvoy
43 Cork Street
Kinsale, Co Cork, Ireland
Tel: (021) 4772027, Fax: (021) 4772166
6 Rooms, Double: €100–€170
3 Apartments: €500–€1,000 weekly
Closed: Dec 1 to Feb 14, Credit cards: MC, VS
B&B & self-catering
www.karenbrown.com/oldpresbytery.html

Laura and Andrew Corcoran have given a new lease of life to this grandiose Victorian edifice overlooking the harbor in Kinsale. Previous owners have all implemented their particular visions of grandeur and it is a tribute to the Corcorans' skills that they have consolidated all of the previous changes into a unified whole. A perky fire radiates a welcome in the vast reception hall (plenty of room for all guests to arrive at once) and the sitting and drawing rooms are large enough to provide a seating spot for every guest. Non-public rooms, however, are of more normal proportions. Bedrooms come in all shapes and sizes, from spacious junior suites to snug double rooms. All are attractively decorated in a traditional vein and priced according to their location—how wonderful if they all had harbor views! No matter—you step out the front door onto the harbor and into the heart of this lively town. Our favorite rooms are the four most luxurious tower suites—try to snag room 33 which has French doors opening to its own private courtyard. A buffet breakfast is included in the tariff and there is no shortage of restaurants nearby for dinner. *Directions:* Follow the main road into Kinsale (Long Quay)—Perryville House is on the right just as you come to the harbor. The hotel has several parking spaces opposite the hotel, next to the harbor.

🖵 🖬 ☎ P ⬆ 🏃 🚶 🐎 🏄

PERRYVILLE HOUSE
Owners: Laura & Andrew Corcoran
Long Quay
Kinsale, Co Cork, Ireland
Tel: (021) 4772731, Fax: (021) 4772298
22 Rooms, Double: €200–€380
Open: Apr to Oct, Credit cards: MC, VS
B&B
www.karenbrown.com/perryville.html

Visitors will truly appreciate the central location of The Pier House. This boutique B&B stands in its own secluded garden, a mere few steps from the harbor, restaurants, shops, and lively pubs of Kinsale. The house has a crisp air of contemporary upscale elegance. Its rooms are bright and airy, with dark wide plank floors offset by walls painted in fresh white and adorned with paintings by a local artist. The accent colors are taupe and burgundy. Goose-down comforters and immaculate white linens adorn the sleigh beds. The en-suite bathrooms have gray slate floors, black counters, gleaming white fixtures, spacious walk-in showers, and feature toiletries by Gilcrist and Soames. Three of the second-floor rooms have small balconies with harbor views. Those desiring some extra relaxation will find a hot tub and sauna on an outdoor private deck. A sumptuous breakfast is graciously served and many will appreciate the privacy of individual tables. Long-time residents Ann and Pat Hagerty are more than willing to offer advice on where to dine and how to spend your time in Kinsale and the surrounding area. The Pier House has two entrances: one on the harbor side and another from Main Street, a side avenue filled with colorful eateries and shops. *Directions:* Coming from Cork arrive at the Kinsale waterfront with SuperValu on your right, turn left, next left at the tourist office and Pier House is on your right, opposite the carpark.

PIER HOUSE   New
Owners: Ann & Pat Hegarty
Pier House, Pier Road
Kinsale
Co Cork, Ireland
Tel & Fax: (021) 477 4475
10 Rooms, Double: €120–€150
Closed: Christmas, Credit cards: MC, VS
B&B
www.karenbrown.com/pier.html

On the next bay down the coast from the Cliffs of Moher Moy House, a lovely hotel caressed by wispy breezes rising off the sea, has waves lapping at the bottom of the garden. Built as a stylish holiday home in the early 1800s, the property has undergone a complete transformation with all but three bedrooms having superb sea views—several have window seats in the bedroom and the bathroom. Relax with a drink from the honesty bar in the chic drawing room and contemplate the delectable offerings on the menu before going down the narrow spiral staircase to the conservatory dining room. Locally produced produce enhances the dining experience. Downstairs bedrooms Kilmaheen and Kilfarboy are particularly spacious and have large bathrooms, with separate bathtubs and showers. Upstairs, Moymore is a favorite with lots of room and a window seat in its bay window. For the most spectacular view, clamber up the narrow stairs that take you to the top of the tower. At low tide wander along the quiet beach and round the headland to the bustling little holiday town of Lahinch. While golfers head for the popular Lahinch golf course, sightseers drive along the coast. Visit the Cliffs of Moher and The Burren. *Directions:* From Ennis take the N85 through Ennistymon to Lahinch. Go up the main street and take the first left, then turn left again following signposts for Miltown Malbay. After 2 km the entrance to Moy House is on the right.

☎ ☕ 🍽 💳 ☎ @ P ⑂ ⛵ ⑄ 🚶 🐎 ⚓

MOY HOUSE
General Manager: Brid O'Meara
Lahinch, Co Clare, Ireland
Tel: (065) 7082800, Fax: (065) 7082500
9 Rooms, Double: €210–€325
Dinner: €55
Closed: Jan to mid-Feb, Credit cards: all major
Ireland's Blue Book
Country house hotel
www.karenbrown.com/moy.html

Delphi Lodge with its surrounding estate was for centuries the sporting estate of the Marquis of Sligo. This wild, unspoilt, and beautiful valley with its towering mountains, tumbling rivers, and crystal-clear loughs was acquired in 1986 by Jane and Peter Mantle. Fortunately for those who have a love of wild, beautiful places, they have restored the Marquis' fishing lodge and opened their home to guests who come to walk, fish for salmon, relax, and enjoy the camaraderie of the house-party atmosphere. In the evening Peter often presides at the head of the very long dinner table (guests who catch a salmon take the place of honor) where guests enjoy a leisurely meal and lively conversation. A snug library and an attractive drawing room are at hand and guests often spend late-night hours in the billiard room. Bedrooms are all furnished in antique and contemporary pine. On a recent visit we especially admired rooms 3 and 4, two larger rooms with spacious bathrooms and fabulous views of the lake. Such is the popularity of the place that it is advisable to make reservations well in advance to secure a summer booking. Five deluxe, self-catering cottages are also available on the estate. *Directions:* Leenane is between Westport and Clifden on the N59. From Leenane go east towards Westport for 3 km, turn left, and continue along the north shore of Killary harbor towards Louisburgh for 8 km. Delphi Lodge is in the woods, on the left after the adventure center.

DELPHI LODGE
Owners: Jane & Peter Mantle
Leenane, Delphi, Co Galway, Ireland
Tel: (095) 42222, Fax: (095) 42296
12 Rooms, Double: €200–€260
5 Cottages: €600– €1,250 weekly
Dinner: €50
Open: mid-Jan to mid-Dec, Credit cards: MC, VS
Hidden Ireland
Country house & self-catering
www.karenbrown.com/delphi.html

Rosleague Manor is a lovely Irish hotel—a comfortable country house hotel overlooking Ballinakill Bay and an ever-changing panorama of wild Connemara countryside. This is a quiet, sparsely populated land of steep hills, tranquil lakes, and grazing sheep, where narrow country lanes lead to little hamlets. Manager Mark Foyle is much in evidence, making certain that guests are well taken care of. The hotel is beautifully furnished with lovely old furniture, and the sitting rooms are cozy with their turf fires and comfortable chairs. The garden-style conservatory is a popular place for before- or after-dinner drinks. Bedrooms are most attractive, my preference being for those with views across the gardens to the sea and distant hills. Two particularly lovely ground floor rooms are perfect for those who have difficulty with stairs. The dining room is my favorite room in the house: tall windows frame the view and lovely old tables and chairs are arranged in groupings. There is an à-la-carte menu as well as the fixed-price menu that offers four or five choices for each course. Dishes vary with the seasons and include a wide selection of locally caught fish and Connemara lamb. This is a peaceful place to hide away and a well-located base for exploring the ruggedly beautiful countryside of Connemara. *Directions:* Take the N59 from Galway to Clifden then turn right at the church for the 10-km drive to Rosleague Manor.

ROSLEAGUE MANOR
Owner: Edmund Foyle
Manager: Mark Foyle
Letterfrack, Connemara, Co Galway, Ireland
Tel: (095) 41101, Fax: (095) 41168
20 Rooms, Double: €170–€210
Dinner: €48
Open: Easter to Nov, Credit cards: all major
Ireland's Blue Book
Country house hotel
www.karenbrown.com/rosleague.html

One of the joys of coming to stay with Beryl and James is that you get to see the completion of their various projects, first the house, then acres of gardens—the Japanese and French gardens, the conversion of the stables to a restaurant and the addition of seven spacious suites with a living room on the ground floor and bedroom above. The imposing house was built in the 1740s for the Cuffe family and was later the residence of the land agent who oversaw the Earl of Longford's estates. The upstairs drawing room boasts specially commissioned chandeliers and period furniture. Also on the first floor is a particular favorite, a very spacious suite which has a sitting room with open fire and a spacious bathroom. On the top floor Purple is the room to request not only for its vibrant color but also for its spaciousness. Breakfast is served at small tables in the ground-floor breakfast room with its beautiful fan-vaulted ceilings. Viewmount House is an ideal base for trips to Clonmacnoise, Birr Castle, and Newgrange. Garden enthusiasts head for Strokestown House with its 6 acres of gardens and Tullynally Castle with its Chinese and Tibetan Gardens. Longford's golf course is just across the back fence. *Directions:* Coming from the south, leave the N4 (Dublin to Sligo road) at the first roundabout in Longford towards Longford town. After the speed limit sign you see Viewmount House's sign. Turn very sharp left and the house is on your right in 500 meters.

VIEWMOUNT HOUSE
Owners: Beryl & James Kearney
Dublin Road
Longford
Co Longford, Ireland
Tel: (043) 41919, Fax: (043) 42906
13 Rooms, Double: €110–€160
Dinner: €55
Open: all year, Credit cards: all major
B&B
www.karenbrown.com/viewmount.html

Kilkenny is a most attractive, historic town, and there is no more perfect a base for exploring its many charms than Blanchville House, a 15-minute drive away. Acres of farmland give this handsome Georgian home seclusion. You'll know you've arrived when you see a tall, square, church tower-like folly. Inside Blanchville House, tall-ceilinged, generously proportioned rooms are the order of the day, and Monica has several pieces of furniture that were made for the house. One of these is the half-tester bed that graces the principal bedroom. Apparently Sir James Kearny, a great eccentric, was fond of waxing and singeing his mustache, an operation he performed in his bed. One day, while practicing this routine, he set fire to the bedding and narrowly escaped burning the house down. There's a portrait of Sir James in the drawing room, which has the wallpaper hung in 1823: guests enjoy a drink here before going in to dine together round the long polished table. Three lovely self-catering cottages (one handicap friendly) are found in the old stables and gardener's cottage (sleeps 3 to 6). *Directions:* Leave Kilkenny on the N10 (Carlow/Dublin road) in the direction of Dublin. Take the first right 1 km after The Pike pub, 6 km out. Continue over railway crossing following signs to Denbell. Turn left the first crossrods, Connolly's pub, and the first large stone house on your left after 2 km. There is no village of Maddoxtown and Dunbell is Connolly's pub.

BLANCHVILLE HOUSE
Owners: Monica & Tim Phelan
Dunbell, Maddoxtown, Co Kilkenny, Ireland
Tel: (056) 7727197, Fax: (056) 7727636
6 Rooms, Double: €110–€130
3 Cottages: €500–€700 weekly
Dinner: €45 (not Sun or Mon)
Open: Mar to Nov, Credit cards: all major
Hidden Ireland
Country house & self-catering
www.karenbrown.com/blanchville.html

Set back from the road in its own gardens and surrounded by green fields Newforge House is an oasis of calm scarcely thirty minutes drive from Belfast and both of its airports. Built in the late 1700's by a successful linen merchant, (remnants of his mill are still standing at the back of the property) the house has been in the family of its current owners for six generations. It was lovingly restored and renovated over a two year period by John and Louise Mathers and opened to receive guests in 2005. Food is a major focus, local produce is sourced and prepared personally by John. Comfortably proportioned sitting and dining rooms are beautifully furnished, collectibles and modern furniture blend with carefully restored architectural features; plaster cornices, wooden window shutters, marble and black iron fireplaces. Bedrooms, named after various ladies in the family history, are to be found on the second and third floors. I particularly liked the four poster and half tester beds in the superior rooms. Standard rooms on the third floor, while a trifle simpler and with slightly lower ceiling are also very lovely. All are provided with elegant en-suite bathrooms. Visiting the Giants Causeway makes a great day out while closer at hand are Belfast and an array of interesting houses and gardens. *Directions:* Leave the M1 West at exit 9 signpost Moira A3. After 5km, in Magheralin, turn left at Byrne's pub and the house is on your left after the speed limit sign.

NEWFORGE HOUSE   *New*
Owners: Lou & John Mathers
58 Newforge Road
Magheralin, BT67 0Q4, Northern Ireland
Tel: (028) 9261 1255, Fax: (028) 9261 2823
6 Rooms, Double: £110–£150
Dinner: £29.50 (not Sun or Mon)
Closed: Christmas & New Year, Credit cards: MC, VS
Ireland's Blue Book
Country house
www.karenbrown.com/newforgehouse.html

The sheer size of Longueville House takes your breath away. Set on a hill overlooking the River Blackwater, this wonderful country house offers you the very best of Irish hospitality. It was built by Richard Longfield, who was spurred on to grander things by a sum of money he received for supporting the British Act of Union. The house is now owned by the O'Callaghan family whose forebears had the estate confiscated from them by Cromwell in 1650. The O'Callaghans take great pains to make sure that you enjoy your stay: Aisling makes certain you are well cared for and made to feel completely at home while William ensures that you are well fed. Longueville is almost completely self-sufficient with vegetables, salmon, lamb, and herbs coming from the estate. The dining room in soft shades of pink is a picture and extends into the Victorian conservatory (1862), while the adjacent library provides a snug place to dine. Each and every bedroom is beautifully decorated and accompanied by a splendid modern bathroom. Reservations can be made for salmon and trout fishing on the nearby Blackwater. There are several 18-hole golf courses within easy reach of Longueville. *Directions:* The hotel is located on the N72, 5 km west of Mallow on the Killarney road.

LONGUEVILLE HOUSE
Owners: Aisling & William O'Callaghan
Mallow, Co Cork, Ireland
Tel: (022) 47156, Fax: (022) 47459
20 Rooms, Double: €235–€360
Dinner from €60
Closed: Jan 7 to Mar 15, Credit cards: all major
Ireland's Blue Book
Country house hotel
www.karenbrown.com/longuevillehouse.html

The 5-foot-thick wall in the dining room, the stone arch that leads to the kitchen, and the ancient defense wall in the garden are remnants of the 15th century keep that stood atop this rocky promontory. It's a "home" that has been added to over the years—a good bit of the house is over 300 years old with the most recent addition being shower rooms for each guest room. Beds are large and rooms are most attractively decked out. My favorite bedrooms were Lady Mary's room with its big bay window looking across the garden wall to miles of countryside and Deedee Walsh, a spacious room at the back. Joan and her daughter Catherine are the most welcoming and attentive of hostesses. They strongly believe in keeping you well fed: breakfasts have to be seen to be believed—a vast array of fruit dishes alongside fresh scones and a variety of hot dishes. Scones and a pot of tea (sometimes homemade pie) are served in the afternoon to keep you going between lunch and dinner. It's a delightful spot just a few minutes from the main roads that whisk you into Waterford and Cork. There are some lovely drives in this area (The Vee and Nire Valley to Clonmel) and several castles (Cahir and Lismore), and the sea with Dungarvan and Youghal is just over the hills. *Directions:* From Dungarven take the N72 towards Cork for 9.5 km (after Cappagh) and turn right on the R761 signposted Clonmel. After 5 km turn right in Millstreet, cross the bridge and the property is on your right.

CASTLE COUNTRY HOUSE
Owners: Joan & Emmett Nugent
Millstreet, Cappagh, Co Waterford, Ireland
Tel: (058) 68049, Fax: (058) 68099
5 Rooms, Double: €90–€100
Dinner: €30
Open: Mar to Nov, Credit cards: MC, VS
Farmhouse B&B
www.karenbrown.com/castlefarm.html

Amongst the scattered modern holiday cottages surrounding the village of Miltown Malbay, a popular Irish holiday destination; you find a traditional Irish farmhouse that is now a welcoming guesthouse, restaurant, and cookery school operated by Rita Meade. Rita offers cookery courses for adults, teenagers, and children. The heart of the house is the country kitchen with its large central island designed for cooking classes. There are comfortable chairs in the sitting room with its old country dresser. The adjacent dining room has been extended with a sunny conservatory. Dinner has four to five choices in each of the three courses. The country theme is continued in the bedrooms with their pine furniture and old beds topped with quilts. All bedrooms have televisions and compact shower rooms and three rooms have a double and a single bed. There is a small ground-floor double-bedded room for those who have difficulty with stairs. The nearby Cliffs of Moher are a great attraction but you can use Berry Lodge as a base for visiting Bunratty Folk Park, Craggaunowen Megalithic Centre, the Aran Islands, exploring The Burren, and sailing to Scattery Island. *Directions:* From Ennis (on the Limerick to Galway road) take the N85 to Inagh then the R460 to Miltown Malbay (32 km total). Take the N67 Spanish Point Road in the center of the village, pass the caravan park, cross the bridge, take the second left, and Berry Lodge is first on the right.

BERRY LODGE
Owner: Rita Meade
Miltown Malbay, Annagh, Co Clare, Ireland
Tel: (065) 7087022, Fax: (065) 7087011
5 Rooms, Double: €84–€90
Dinner: €40
Closed: mid-Jan to mid-Feb, Credit cards: MC, VS
B&B
www.karenbrown.com/berry.html

Lough Owel Lodge is a modern house set between Lough Owel and a quiet country road that runs into Mullingar. While the house has no architectural distinction, this is a tranquil country spot where you can cycle down quiet roads, stroll the shores of Lough Owel, and generally enjoy the peace and quiet of the center of Ireland. Aideen and Martin Ginnell find that the house works really well for raising a family of four children and providing bed and breakfast; for it is divided into two parts, the front being for guests and the back for their family. I particularly appreciated the large car port which sheltered me from the rain as I arrived. A large sitting room with comfortable sofas and floor-to-ceiling windows offering views of the garden and lake adjoins the dining room with its lovely old table and chairs. Upstairs, the two premier rooms are Lough Ennell with its king-sized, four-poster bed and Lough Owel with its family heirloom mahogany half-tester double bed. A family suite consists of a small double bedroom leading to a small twin-bedded room and a bathroom. Guests often wander down to the lough, enjoy a game of tennis, and make use of the children's game room. Tullynally Castle, Carrickglass Manor, Belvedere House, Fore Abbey, and Athlone Castle are within an hour's drive. *Directions:* Take the N4 from Dublin towards Sligo. After passing the third exit for Mullingar, Lough Owel Lodge is signed to your left after 1 km.

LOUGH OWEL LODGE
Owners: Aideen & Martin Ginnell
Mullingar, Cullion, Co Westmeath, Ireland
Tel: (044) 9348714
5 Rooms, Double: €75–€80
Open: Apr to Oct, Credit cards: MC, VS
B&B
www.karenbrown.com/loughowel.html

Readers' letters praise the warmth of welcome, the delectable food, the quality and utter charm of this country house—and the fact that Mornington is an hour and a half's drive from Dublin airport, making it an ideal first or last destination in Ireland. I totally concur; for a stay at Mornington House with Anne and Warwick, the fifth generation of his family to call this home, is also something I find completely delightful. The O'Haras have an easy way of making guests feel at home. They chat with them in the drawing room after dinner, and put a lot of trouble into helping them with their activities and sightseeing in this unspoiled region with its lakes, canals, and gently undulating countryside. Anne is a talented cook, producing delicious dinners and outstanding breakfasts. Families are welcome and children can be served an early tea. The two front bedrooms are enormous: one has a large brass bed sitting center stage while the other has a Victorian double bed and shares the view across the peaceful grounds. The third bedroom, a delightful twin-bedded room, looks out to the side garden and the woods. The oldest wing of the house contains two smaller bedrooms overlooking the kitchen garden. *Directions:* From Dublin take the Sligo Road to the Mullingar bypass. Exit for Castlepollard and go 10 km to Crookedwood, where you turn left by The Wood pub. After 2 km turn right and Mornington is on your right after 1 km.

MORNINGTON HOUSE
Owners: Anne & Warwick O'Hara
Mullingar, Mornington–Multyfarnham
Co Westmeath, Ireland
Tel: (044) 9372191, Fax: (044) 9372338
5 Rooms, Double: €150
Dinner: €45
Open: Apr to Oct, Credit cards: all major
Hidden Ireland
Country house
www.karenbrown.com/morningtonhouse.html

A mere stone's throw from Galway Bay, Mount Vernon was built in the late eighteenth century as a residence for Colonel William Persse of Roxborough. In spite of serving on the "wrong" side in the American War of Independence, he became a friend of George Washington with whom he shared an interest in plants and gardens. The walled garden contains stone terraces and Cypress trees thought to have been gifts from the American President. The house eventually fell into the hands of Lady Augusta Gregory, Persse's great-granddaughter and an avid supporter of the arts. During her tenure, she entertained such luminaries as W.B. Yeats, George Russel and George Bernard Shaw. The house contains several architectural features, fireplaces, an Arts and Craft staircase, Batiks and painted panels of that era. Current owners Mark Helmore and Aly Rafery have caringly renovated and extended the house to include five very smart bedrooms featuring antique furniture and stylish collectibles from their world travels. Go to Doolin to catch a boat to view the cliffs of Moher or head for Kilorglin to learn all about the Burren landscape. *Directions:* Leave the N18 at Kilcolgan and follow the N67 through Kinvarra and continue on the cost road for 6km. Turn right across the middle of a small lake signpost Linnane's Lobster Bar. Turn left at the lobster bar and right at the art gallery, proceed along the shore and Mount Vernon is the fourth house on your left.

MOUNT VERNON   New
Owners: Ally Raftery & Mark Helmore
The Flaggy Shore
New Quay, Co Clare, Ireland
Tel: (065) 7078126, Fax: (065) 7078118
5 Rooms, Double: €220
Dinner: €55 (not Mon or Tue)
Open: Apr to Dec, Credit cards: MC, VS
Hidden Ireland
Country house
www.karenbrown.com/vernon.html

The O'Donnell family's picturesque farmhouse has great appeal. It is over 200 years old and has received a sensitive restoration. There's a snug little lounge with a low thick stone arch that was one of the original doors in the house attesting to the fact that folks must have been much smaller in days gone by. A bay window nook overlooks the front garden and provides a perfect place for laying out your map and planning the days activities, returning home for one of Ber's excellent home-cooked dinners. Upstairs there are three guest bedrooms: 1: a tiny double with en suite shower (usually rented as a single), 2: a snug twin with bathroom, and 3: a larger room with zip-link beds with an en suite shower room. Take a stroll round the lovely garden and walk down to and along the riverbank. Trout fishing is a great draw. Walkers head for the hills—Kilmaneen is surrounded by the Comeraghs, Knockmealdowns, and Galtee Mountains. Kevin can either take you out for the day in a group walking or supply you with maps. Sightseers have lots to keep them busy with driving The Vee and visiting Lismore, Cahir, Cappoquin, and Swiss Cottage. If you have a family, enquire about renting the adjacent little two-bedroom cottage, either for bed and breakfast or on a self-catering basis. *Directions:* Go through Newcastle, towards Cloheen, at the Y-junction bear right down a narrow, winding lane, and Kilmaneen is on your right after 2 km.

KILMANEEN FARMHOUSE
Owners: Bernadette & Kevin O'Donnell
Newcastle, Clonmel, Co Tipperary, Ireland
Tel & Fax: (052) 36231
3 Rooms, Double: €85–€90
1 Cottage: €250-€550 weekly
Dinner: €30 (not Sun)
Open: Apr to Dec, Credit cards: MC, VS
Farmhouse B&B & self-catering
www.karenbrown.com/kilmaneen.html

When Lord Inchiquin sold Dromoland Castle in 1963, he moved five minutes up the hill to Thomond House, a large Georgian-style mansion. Now it is home to his nephew Conor O'Brien (the present Lord Inchiquin and head of the O'Brien chieftancy) and his family—and what a delightful home it is, with its high-ceilinged rooms looking out through tall windows to the surrounding countryside. An air of quiet formality is the order of the day. Guests enjoy a comfortable drawing room, take breakfast in the dining room, and watch television in the library. A sweeping staircase leads to the upper gallery and bedrooms, which are beautifully outfitted and offer views of the parkland or the adjacent castle. Two additional lovely bedrooms are found in a ground floor wing. You might want to walk down to Dromoland Castle for a superbly formal meal or drive a few kilometers further to less expensive restaurants. Guests often play golf on the neighboring course or roam over the estate, while farther afield lies the Burren, Lahinch, Doonbeg and Ballybunion golf courses. It's a perfect first or last destination in Ireland if you are flying in or out of Shannon airport. *Directions:* From Shannon Airport take the N18 towards Ennis. Exit signpost Quin and Ballygirran (not Newmarket on Fergus) and take the Dromoland exit from the roundabout. After 1km, at the end of the Dromoland Castle wall , turn left into Thomond House's driveway.

THOMOND HOUSE
Owners: Helen & Conor Inchiquin
Newmarket-on-Fergus, Co Clare, Ireland
Tel: (061) 368304, Fax: (061) 368285
5 Rooms, Double: €240–€380
Closed: Christmas, Credit cards: all major
Country house
www.karenbrown.com/thomondhouse.html

Built on a sheltered site with distant views across Strangford Lough to the Mourne Mountains, Edenvale House is the lovely home of a most gregarious couple, Diane and Gordon Whyte. Relax with tea and cakes in the beautiful drawing room, plan your sightseeing forays, and enjoy the complete tranquility of this lovely spot. Try to snag one of the spacious front bedrooms with their spectacular views, dressing rooms large enough to accommodate a bed for a child, and spacious bathrooms with both bath and shower. (One's a queen-size four-poster, the other a king or twin.) The two other very lovely bedrooms have garden views and spacious shower rooms. There's a beautiful garden to wander in and horses and ponies to enjoy. Just down the road, Mount Stewart House has a splendid interior and a painting by Stubbs, but the acres of magnificent gardens are the main attraction. Nearby, the village of Greyabbey has lots of antique shops and the ruins of a Cistercian abbey. Dozens of old buildings have been brought from the countryside to the Ulster Folk Park where demonstrations of traditional crafts and farming are given. *Directions:* From Belfast take the A20 through Newtownards in the direction of Portaferry. After 3.2 km the entrance to Edenvale House is on the left.

EDENVALE HOUSE
Owners: Diane & Gordon Whyte
130 Portaferry Road
Newtownards,
Co Down, BT22 2AH, Northern Ireland
Tel: (028) 9181 4881
4 Rooms, Double: £80
Closed: Christmas, Credit cards: MC, VS
Country house
www.karenbrown.com/edenvale.html

Eoin's great-great-grandfather came to the Nire Valley to build the church. He married a local girl Hanora and together they lived in a little cottage adjacent to the church nestled beside the tumbling River Nire in this delightfully wild and isolated spot on the edge of the Comeragh Mountains. They would not recognize their little home for it has been extended to include a parade of sitting rooms, spacious restaurant, hot tub for eight in the conservatory, and array of large bedrooms. All bedrooms have Jacuzzi bathtubs—just for fun, reserve one of the six rooms whose bathrooms come equipped with Jacuzzi tubs for two. Whenever you come to stay, you can be sure of being well fed—Mary, Eoin's mum, lays out a feast of a breakfast for which there is always a variety of freshly baked breads. In the evening Eoin (pronounced Owen) and his wife Judith offer a set, four-course, dinner with lots of choices for starters and main courses. Packed lunches, maps, and directions are available for walks that range from leisurely rambles to challenging hill hikes. Non-walkers can drive to Lismore, Cashel, or over The Vee, returning in time for a visit to one of the nearby pubs for a drink and perhaps (more often in the summer months) a late-night Irish music session. *Directions:* From Clonmel or Dungarvan, follow the R672 as far as Ballymacarbry, where you turn left at Melody's Lounge Bar. Travel 5.6 km and Hanora's is beside the church just before the stone bridge.

HANORA'S COTTAGE GUESTHOUSE
Owners: Mary, Judith & Eoin Wall
Nire Valley, Clonmel
Co Waterford, Ireland
Tel: (052) 36134, Fax: (052) 36540
10 Rooms, Double: €170–€250
Dinner: €50
Closed: Christmas, Credit cards: MC, VS
Guesthouse
www.karenbrown.com/hanoras.html

Guests at Currarevagh House (pronounced "Curra-reeva") find themselves entering a world reminiscent of the turn of the last century. Tranquility reigns supreme and things are done the good old-fashioned way at Currarevagh House. However, do not be afraid that you will be deprived of central heating and private bathrooms, for this is not the case. If you book well in advance, you may be able to secure one of our four favorite rooms (1, 2, or 3 in the main house, or room 16 in the "new" wing with its lake views). There are several smaller rooms in the new wing. Try to arrive by 4:30 pm when tea and cakes are served—you will then have enough time for a brisk woodland or lakeshore walk to make room for a delicious dinner at 8. A gong announces dinner and while there are no choices, the helpings are of generous proportions. A tempting breakfast buffet of cold meats, cheeses, and traditional cooked breakfast dishes is spread on the sideboard and the hotel is happy to pack you a picnic lunch for your day's excursion. It's all very old-fashioned and un-decorator-perfect, but you will thoroughly enjoy it. Harry can arrange for fishing on the adjacent Lough Corrib. The gardens fringed by rhododendrons and hydrangeas have a croquet lawn and lovely views across Lough Corrib the second largest lake in Ireland. *Directions:* From Galway take the N59 to Oughterard, turn right in the center of the village, and follow the lake shore for the 6-km drive to the house.

CURRAREVAGH HOUSE
Owners: Harry, June & Henry Hodgson
Oughterard, Connemara, Co Galway, Ireland
Tel: (091) 552312, Fax: (091) 552731
15 Rooms, Double: €170–€208
Dinner: €45
Open: Apr to mid-Oct, Credit cards: MC, VS
Ireland's Blue Book
Country house hotel
www.karenbrown.com/currarevaghhouse.html

Carmel is the sixth generation of her family to live in the Oughterard area and the first to be more interested in interior design than the Connemara ponies that her family has always raised. Named Railway Lodge because it stands adjacent to a former railway line—now a walking path—the house has a modern exterior and country style interior. There's a snug parlor with a fire and a sunny conservatory overlooking the rolling gorse and distant mountains. Stylish bedrooms have queen-sized beds with crisp white sheets and duvets, and antique pine furniture—each with a top-of-the-line shower room. For dinner we walked the ten minutes into Oughterard and Carmel lent us a flashlight to guide us home. Breakfast proved to be a sumptuous affair. The offer of fresh-baked scones and bread and poached fruit led us to decline the offer of a cooked breakfast. If you would like to stay for a week Carmel has a lovely one bedroom cottage in the garden. If you have an interest in walking, local history or Connemara ponies, Carmel refers you to her father who lives nearby. Lough Corrib is a popular fishing venue. Non-fisher types enjoy spectacular drives through rugged countryside and trips to islands on the lough. *Directions:* Arriving in Oughterard from Galway you see the Corrib Hotel on the left, turn left beside it and then immediate right (do not go straight). Continue to fork in road and take a right and Railway Lodge is the 2nd entrance on the left.

RAILWAY LODGE
Owners: Carmel Geoghegan & Joe Howlett
Canrower
Oughterard, Co Galway, Ireland
Tel: (091) 552945
4 Rooms, Double: €100–€110
1 Cottage: €540–€590 weekly
Open: all year, Credit cards: MC, VS
B&B
www.karenbrown.com/railway.html

Portlaoise has been bypassed with a new road and you can once again enjoy the quiet in this heart-of-Ireland town. Situated close to downtown on a side street, Ivyleigh House is set back from the road, its immaculate Georgian façade heralds a first-class interior furnished and decorated in a delightful traditional style. A lovely sitting room is available for guests' use and for breakfast there's a handsome dining room, its large communal table decked out with china and crystal. Dinah does an excellent breakfast with the freshest of local ingredients including free-range eggs, local bacon, and natural yogurt with geranium jelly. Then there's perfect porridge with cream, homemade brown bread, tea made with leaf tea, and freshly brewed coffee. The spacious bedrooms are particularly comfortable with top-of-the-line beds, linen sheets and pillowcases, and large shower rooms with power showers. One is located downstairs on the garden level. There is no shortage of restaurants for dinner. Portlaoise is well placed for visiting Tullamore, Kildare, Kilkenny, and Carlow, the Slieve Bloom Mountains, Emo Court, and the Rock of Dunamase, an ancient fort. A 2 bedroom cottage at Killenard is available for weekly rental. *Directions:* Approaching from Cork, turn off the N8 for Portlaoise. In Portlaoise drive straight through two roundabouts onto the N80 for 30 meters, turn right at the railway bridge, and Ivyleigh House is the second house on the left.

IVYLEIGH HOUSE
Owners: Dinah & Jerry Campion
Bank Place, Church Street
Portlaoise
Co Laois, Ireland
Tel: (057) 8622081, Fax: (057) 8663343
6 Rooms, Double: €125–€150
1 Cottage: €800–€900 weekly
Closed: Dec 23 to Jan 2, Credit cards: MC, VS
Guesthouse
www.karenbrown.com/ivyleigh.html

Ardeen country house is situated in the heritage town of Ramelton overlooking the River Lennon. This Victorian house gives you a homey relaxed feeling the moment you walk through the front door. Ardeen is the onetime home of Nurse Black who was the private nurse to King George V. The book King's Nurse, Beggar's Nurse tells her story. Anne and Bert Campbell have been welcoming guests into their lovely home for many years. Anne enjoys baking and will spoil you with afternoon tea and home made scones as soon as you arrive. Breakfast is served around the beautiful antique dining table and includes fresh fruits, home made brown bread and scones as well as the traditional Irish breakfast. The bedrooms are all very nicely furnished and individually decorated and in keeping with the house. Four are en suite and a twin room enjoys a large private bathroom. The adjacent stable has been converted to a snug holiday cottage with an exposed stone living room, attractive kitchen and three bedrooms, one of which is en suite. Ardeen is an ideal base for exploring the Donegal coastline and visiting Glenveagh National Park and the Glebe Art Gallery with its fine collection of Irish paintings. *Directions:* If you are arriving from Donegal, take the N56 to Letterkenny and on the outskirts of the town look for the T72, signposted for Rathmullen. It's an 11-km drive to Ramelton. When you reach the river turn right, following the bank, and Ardeen is on your right.

ARDEEN
Owners: Anne & Bert Campbell
Ramelton, Co Donegal, Ireland
Tel & Fax: (074) 91 51243
5 Rooms, Double: €70–€80
1 Cottage: €350–€500 weekly
Open: Easter to Oct, Credit cards: MC, VS
B&B & self-catering
www.karenbrown.com/ardeen.html

Frewin was a rectory for over 150 years and its earlier fortified annex dates back to the 1600s. Thomas, a restorer of old homes, antique collector, and raiser of rare-breed animals, found a family link while he was refurbishing the house: his great-aunt Susan had written her name on the back of one of the cupboards in the maid's room in 1912. If you do not mind having your own private shower room down the hall, you can stay in Aunt Susan's room. The other three bedrooms are small suites with sitting room areas—one has a claw-foot tub in the bathroom and the other two have showers. Our favorite, the green room, has a king-sized bedroom and, through the shower room, a private library which can double as a sitting room. There's lots of interesting furniture (a praying wall and sideboard from Glenveagh Castle) and pictures (the library is covered with old Vanity Fair prints). Regina and Thomas are hospitable and easygoing. Several of Thomas's finds are for sale in a little courtyard store. If you want to stay for a week, there are two little cottages tucked into quiet corners of the 2-acre garden. Ramelton is a 17th-century town with handsome houses and old riverside warehouses. A scenic route winds up Fanad Peninsula to Rathmullan and Portsalon. *Directions:* From Letterkenny take R245 towards Ramelton. Travel 11 km, pass the Shell station (on right), continue 800 meters and turn right at speed limit sign—Frewin is 400 meters along on the right.

FREWIN
Owners: Regina & Thomas Coyle
Ramelton, Co Donegal, Ireland
Tel & Fax: (074) 9151246
4 Rooms, Double: €120–€180
1 Cottage: €500–€550 weekly
Dinner: €45
Closed: Christmas, Credit cards: MC, VS
Hidden Ireland
Country house & self-catering
www.karenbrown.com/frewin.html

Rathmullan House has the most tranquil setting amidst mature trees and rose gardens that slope down to a sandy beach, with views of the mountains across Lough Swilly. The second generation of the Wheeler family run the hotel creating a relaxing and friendly atmophere. It's a delightfully rambling house with large sitting rooms (one in an Indian Raj style) leading to Batt's bar presided over by the portrait of Mrs. Batt who had Rathmullan house built as her summer home in the 1800s. Here you can enjoy drinks and lighter fare. Three-or four-course dinners are served in the dining room where meters of fabric are gathered into peaks dotted with fairy lights to create softest of lighting and the most romantic of dining atmospheres. Bedrooms are either "view" (garden and lough) or "not" and fall into three categories: Regency; (delectable, subtly themed, oh-so-spacious rooms with terrace or balcony and grand bathrooms of which the two penthouses offer the ultimate in luxury); Balcony (spacious rooms with top of the line bathrooms, terrace or balcony); or Main House (mainly high-ceilinged rooms divided between no view and lough view rooms—try to snag one with a spacious bay-window). Enjoy a walk on the beach, a swim in the pool, a game of tennis or a relaxing massage in the Solace room. *Directions:* From Letterkenny take the R245 through Ramelton and Rathmullan. The hotel is on the right as you pass the Catholic church upon leaving the village.

RATHMULLAN HOUSE
Owners: Mark, Mary, William & Yvonne Wheeler
Rathmullan, Letterkenny
Co Donegal, Ireland
Tel: (074) 9158188, Fax: (074) 9158200
32 Rooms, Double: €160–€320*
*Service: 10%, Dinner: from €42.50
Open: all year, Credit cards: all major
Ireland's Blue Book
Country house hotel
www.karenbrown.com/rathmullan.html

Hunter's Hotel has adopted Samuel Johnson's words as a creed and they certainly describe it: "There is nothing which has yet been contrived by man by which so much happiness is produced as by a good inn." Dating back to the 1720s, the hotel retains its old-world charm with creaking wooden floorboards, polished tile floors, old prints, beams, ancient sofas covered in old-fashioned chintz, and antique furniture. The Gelletlie family has owned the inn since 1820, and now Tom and Richard Gelletlie (the fifth generation) ably assist their mother, Maureen. There is a delightful feeling of another age, which endures in the tradition of vast, Sunday roast lunches (1 pm prompt: book ahead) and afternoon teas of oven-fresh scones and strawberry jam—a particularly delightful feast when enjoyed in the garden on a warm summer's afternoon. You can sleep in bedrooms that kings have slept in—the king of Sweden has paid several visits. I loved my room 17 a spacious ground floor twin. Be sure to request a room with a view of the flower-filled gardens stretching beside the hotel down to the River Vartry. Some interesting gardens and houses are a short drive away: Powerscourt with its grand gardens, Mount Usher with its informal gardens, and Avondale House with its wooded parklands. *Directions:* Take the N11 from Dublin to Rathnew and turn left in the village for the 1-km drive to Hunters Hotel.

HUNTER'S HOTEL
Owner: The Gelletlie family
Rathnew, Co Wicklow, Ireland
Tel: (040) 440106, Fax: (040) 440338
16 Rooms, Double: €190–€210
Dinner: €45
Closed: Christmas, Credit cards: all major
Ireland's Blue Book
Inn
www.karenbrown.com/hunters.html

Tinakilly House maintains the purpose for which it was designed—gracious living. The house was built in the 1870s by Captain Robert Halpin, the commander of the ship Great Eastern, which laid the first telegraph cable connecting Europe to America. Tinakilly House's ornate staircase is reputed to be a copy of the one on this ship. Whether or not this is true is a matter of conjecture, but the Captain certainly spared no expense when he built this classical house with its fine, pitch-pine doors and shutters and ornate plasterwork ceilings. The Powers bought the house as a family home before deciding to open it as a luxurious country house hotel. They have done a splendid job, extending the home and adding rooms that fit in perfectly, furnishing the house with appropriate Victorian furniture, and adding a welcoming charm to the place. Some of the bedrooms have four-poster beds, while all twenty junior suites and two captain suites have sea views. Dining is a delight. Tinakilly is an ideal countryside base for exploring Dublin, Glendalough, and the Wicklow Mountains. *Directions:* From Dublin take the N11 (Wexford road) to Rathnew village. Turn left, towards Wicklow, and the entrance to the hotel is on your left as you leave the village.

TINAKILLY HOUSE
Owners: Josephine & Raymond Power
Rathnew, Co Wicklow, Ireland
Tel: (040) 469274, Fax: (040) 467806
51 Rooms, Double: €300–€725
Dinner: €65
Closed: Christmas, Credit cards: all major
Ireland's Blue Book
Country house hotel
www.karenbrown.com/tinakillyhouse.html

Simon O'Hara is the seventh generation of his family to call Coopershill home since it was built in 1774. It is one of those wonderful places that offer the best of both worlds— the luxury of a country house hotel and the warmth of a home. You can even rent the entire place on a weekly basis for a house party. Simon welcome guests to his family home through the massive front door into the stove-warmed hall whose flagged floor is topped by an Oriental rug, and where rain gear hangs at the ready. Beyond lies a parade of lovely rooms tastefully decorated and beautifully furnished with grand, antique furniture, much of which is as old as the house itself. All but three of the bedrooms have the original four-poster or half-tester beds, but, of course, with modern mattresses. All the bedrooms are large and have private bathrooms. The only one with its bathroom down the hall requires an instruction manual to operate its magnificent shower! Ancestors' portraits gaze down upon you in the dining room, set with tables to accommodate individual parties. After an excellent dinner, guests chat round the fire over coffee. Secluded by 500 acres of farm and woodland, there are many delightful walks. Boating and fishing are available. There is enough sightseeing to justify spending a week here. *Directions:* From Dublin take the N4 to Drumfin (18 km south of Sligo). Turn right towards Riverstown and Coopershill is on your left 1 km before the village.

COOPERSHILL
Owner: Simon O'Hara
Riverstown, Co Sligo, Ireland
Tel & Fax: (071) 91 65108
8 Rooms, Double: €238–€271
1 House: €6,000 weekly
Dinner: €57
Open: Apr to Oct, Credit cards: all major
Ireland's Blue Book
Country house
www.karenbrown.com/coopershill.html

In summer, the driveway of Rosturk Woods is lined with wild red fuchsias that lead you to the low white house hugging a vast expanse of firm, sandy beach on the shores of Clew Bay. Home to Louisa and Alan Stoney and their young family (Alan grew up in the imposing castle next door, while Louisa's mother lives close by), the house has the feel of an old cottage, though it is only a few years old. Bedrooms have stripped-pine doors and several have pine-paneled, sloping ceilings. There's a lot of old pine furniture, antique pieces, and attractive prints and fabrics. The house cleverly divides so that a wing of two or three large bedrooms, a living room, and a kitchen can be closed off and used as self-catering accommodation. A delightful self-catering cottage has four beds and is equipped for handicapped guests. Louisa can sometimes direct you to nearby places where traditional Irish music is played. You can play tennis on the Stoneys' court, or hire their boat for a full- or half-day trip on Clew Bay. In contrast to the lush green fields and long sandy beaches that hug Clew Bay, a short drive brings you to the wilder, more rugged scenery of Achill Island. To the south lie Newport and Westport. *Directions:* From Westport take the N59 through Newport towards Achill Island. Before you arrive in Mulrany, cross the Owengarve river and after 500 meters turn left into the woodland to Rosturk Woods.

ROSTURK WOODS
Owners: Louisa & Alan Stoney
Rosturk, Mulrany, Co Mayo, Ireland
Tel & Fax: (098) 36264
3 Rooms, Double: €100–€150
1 Cottage: €750–€1,500 weekly
Dinner: €40
Open: Feb to Nov, Credit cards: none
B&B & self-catering
www.karenbrown.com/rosturk.html

Built as a hotel in the 1880s, by a sea captain who also served as the local rector, Grove House has over the ensuing years attracted famous literati to the extent that Katarina Runske has named her rooms after them. Somerville and Ross (who wrote "The Irish R. M.") are two queen bedded rooms that look out across the garden to the water. Yeats (the famous painter and brother of the poet), Carberry, and Shaw are the most spacious; Shaw having the original loo in its bathroom. With only one bathroom in the house in times past it is fairly certain that all these men of letters used it. Dinner is a real treat cooked by Katarina, her mum and son Nico. Max, Katarina's other son, makes sure guests are well taken care of. Toast your toes by the fire in the sitting room and decide where you would like to go the next day. You'll be spoilt for choice: a ferry to the beautiful Cape Clear or Sherkin Island, a summer evening boat trip to Fasnet Island Lighthouse (Ireland's tallest most southerly lighthouse—the last piece of Ireland emigrants saw as they sailed for America), golf, walking, diving, or visiting scenic Mizen Head. *Directions:* The Mizen Peninsula is off N71 (Cork to Killarney road). Arriving is Schull turn left opposite the AIB into Colla Road and the house is about 500m on the right hand side.

GROVE HOUSE   New
Owners: Katarina Runske & family
Colla Road
Schull, Co Cork, Ireland
Tel: (028) 28067, Fax: (028) 28069
5 Rooms, Double: €100
Dinner: €40
Open: all year, Credit cards: all major
Country house
www.karenbrown.com/grove.html

Ballymaloe House is a rambling, 17th-century manor house built onto an old Norman keep surrounded by lawns, a small golf course, and 400 acres of farmland. Run by members of the extended Allen family, Ballymaloe has established a reputation for outstanding hospitality and superb food, yet everything is decidedly informal. Families are made especially welcome (play equipment, outdoor heated pool in summer, childrens' meals) and several of the rooms can be `linked` together to accommodate them. Guests gather before dinner in the lounge to make their selections from the set menu, which offers four or five choices for each course. The bedrooms in the main house come in all shapes and sizes, from large and airy to cozy. For peace and quiet opt for one of the lovely garden rooms several of which have little patios and direct access to the garden. Surrounding a courtyard, the smaller stable bedrooms offer country-cottage charm—and beamed ceilings for those on the upper floor. Blarney and Kinsale are within easy striking distance but allow time to play a game of croquet, go for a walk or a bike ride; and explore the coast with its small rocky inlets, fishing harbors, and lonely headlands. Need a gift there`s no need to go further than the car park where the Ballymaloe shop offers the best of all-things Irish. *Directions:* Ballymaloe is signposted from the N25 (Cork to Waterford road)—3 km beyond Cloyne on the Ballycotton Road.

BALLYMALOE HOUSE
Owner: The Allen family
Manager: Hazel Allen
Shanagarry, Midleton, Co Cork, Ireland
Tel: (021) 4652531, Fax: (021) 4652021
32 Rooms, Double: €275–€330
Dinner: €70
Closed: Dec 24 to 27, Credit cards: all major
Ireland's Blue Book
Country house hotel
www.karenbrown.com/ballymaloehouse.html

The K Club began life as The Kildare Hotel & Country Club but as everyone shortened the name, they changed it. Stay here and you get preference for tee times on the championship golf courses designed by Arnold Palmer. If you do intend to play, enquire about the golf packages that include accommodation and green fees. Even if you are not a golfer, this is the most sumptuous of places to stay—the grandest of houses with a parade of luxurious, beautiful rooms. The artwork is exquisite, with a room devoted to Jack Yeats's paintings. Taking pride of place in the magnificent dining room is The Byerly Turk, a massive 17th-century portrait of one of the three stallions that sired every thoroughbred in the world. Fine cooking is an essential ingredient here and the menu includes Irish classics such as roast Wicklow lamb as well as more nirvana-like fare. Pamper yourself in the health spa, splash in the pool, or just stroll through the acres of gardens and revel in the sheer luxury of the place. Exquisite self-catering apartments are available. It is easy to understand why The K Club represents an ideal of luxury for so many people. *Directions:* Take the N7 (Kildare road) out of Dublin to Kill where you turn right for the 5-km drive to The K Club, on your left just before Straffan.

THE K CLUB
Manager: Michael Davern
Straffan, Co Kildare, Ireland
Tel: (01) 6017200, Fax: (01) 6017299
69 Rooms, Double: €280–€900
24 Apartments: €675 daily
Dinner: €65–€75
Open: all year, Credit cards: all major
Ireland's Blue Book
Luxury resort & self-catering
www.karenbrown.com/kclub.html

I arrived on a windswept stormy day to be revived by hot tea and a slice of cake. The journey was quickly forgotten as I became engrossed in Patricia's tale of training the new rooster to begin his song at 8 am, instead of dawn, to give guests a good lie in. Patricia and her husband Austin (passionate about all-things golf) are welcoming hosts, generous with their time and experts at planning trips—one along the coast and across the little ferry to Waterford is a favorite with guests. Their farmhouse dates back to 1703 and over the years various owners have made additions and changes with, most recently, Austin and Patricia's transformation. Incredibly, the soaring garden room, where you toast your toes before the fire and gather for sherry before dinner, was recently a crumbling piggery. Bedrooms come in all shapes and sizes are priced accordingly. Patricia's dinner celebrates good country food with local, organic produce. Austin offers a short, value-for-money, wine list. If you are traveling to Ireland via the Rosslare Ferry, a stay at here is an excellent introduction to Ireland or a great place to spend your last nights in the Emerald Isle. *Directions:* Tagoat is on the N25, 6 km north of Rosslare harbor. Turn between the church and pub onto R736. Churchtown House is on your left after 1 km.

CHURCHTOWN HOUSE
Owners: Patricia & Austin Cody
Tagoat, Rosslare, Co Wexford, Ireland
Tel: (053) 9132555, Fax: (053) 9132577
12 Rooms, Double: €120–€150
Dinner: €40 (not Sun or Mon)
Open: Mar 1 to Nov 1, Credit cards: all major
Country house
www.karenbrown.com/churchtown.html

Tir Na Fiúise offers you a perfect base for exploring the mid-west and Shannon region. Inez and Niall Heenan have converted the barns just down the lane from their farmhouse to self-catering accommodation rented by the week. The delightful cottages are decorated with a simple, fresh, country look. The kitchen/living areas feature solid-fuel stoves and modern appliances such as dishwashers and microwaves. The Hawthorns is a one- or two-bedroom cottage with king-sized beds. The Granary is a one-bedroom cottage just perfect for a couple getting away from it all to a cozy little nook, while The Stables has two bedrooms, making it more suitable for a family or larger group. The Lime Kiln also has two bedrooms and is larger than the Stables. The area has some excellent restaurants and local pubs, which also serve great food. Inez and Niall encourage guests to explore their organic farm and adjacent bog land. You can cycle along the quiet lanes, try your hand at fishing in the nearby lough, and join in village activities. On Thursday nights, May to September, there is Irish music and dance in the village hall. If you must rush off to tourist spots, Bunratty Folk Park is a 90-minute drive away (as is Shannon airport). Closer at hand are Clonmacnois and Birr Castle. *Directions:* Leave the N7 in Nenagh and travel through Borrisokane and Ballinderry to Terryglass. The lane leading to Tir Na Fiúise (1 km on your left) is opposite the bridge in the village.

TIR NA FIÚISE
Owners: Inez & Niall Heenan
Terryglass, Nenagh, Co Tipperary, Ireland
Tel & Fax: (067) 22041
4 Cottages: Granary €260–€380 weekly
Stables €310–€510 weekly
Lime Kiln €320–€550 weekly
The Hawthorns rate depends on number of bedrooms
Open: all year, Credit cards: MC, VS
Self-catering
www.karenbrown.com/tirnafiuise.html

Only in Ireland can you have a village that does not exist! Inch House is the only building in Inch while the nearest village, Bouladuff, is known and signposted only as "The Ragg" in spite of being marked as Bouladuff on maps—hence we list Inch House under Thurles! Follow the directions and you'll reach this stately Georgian home surrounded by miles of farmland. The house was built in 1720 by the Ryan family. Nora and John Egan originally came here to farm with their eight children who are now grown. Daughter Maureen works closely with her parents and chances are you'll meet one or two of the other children around the place. It's a real treat to stay here for it is quintessentially Irish and incredibly homey in spite of having ballroom-sized drawing and dining rooms resplendent with 15-foot-high ceilings. Michael Galvin is in charge of the kitchen and his set dinner menu (plenty of choices for each course) focuses on local produce. A grand sweep of polished oak stairs lead up to the bedrooms where room 26 is large enough to hold a party, room 24 has a stupendous half-tester bed, and room 27 offers a four-poster. Cashel with its famous rock is a half-hour drive away. *Directions:* From the N8 (Dublin to Cork road) take the turnoff to Thurles. Go to the town square and take the Nenagh road for 6 km past "The Ragg" and the driveway to the house is on your left.

INCH HOUSE
Owners: Nora & John Egan
Thurles, Co Tipperary, Ireland
Tel: (050) 451348, Fax: (050) 451754
5 Rooms, Double: €140
Dinner: €55 (not Sun or Mon)
Closed: Christmas, Credit cards: MC, VS
Country house
www.karenbrown.com/inch.html

Fortview house is a traditional stone built, slate roofed, Irish farmhouse that has been thoughtfully expanded. Full of antiques, collectibles, quiet nooks, pine floors and exposed beams, it hunkers down next to the country road, sheltering from the prevailing wind off the not-too-distant Atlantic Ocean. Richard works the farm and guests are welcome to visit and learn the intricacies of dairy herd management first hand. Violet pours heart and soul into operating the bed and breakfast. Five country-comfortable rooms with brass beds and small, but well equipped en-suite bathrooms, are all named after local flowers. An airy conservatory provides guests with a sunny spot to relax with a cup of tea or coffee. Breakfast is served in the dining room with its rough-wood mantled brick fireplace and its black iron stove. A large pine country dresser, matching chairs and tables covered in blue and white checkered table cloths complete the scene. In addition to your cooked breakfast there will be local cheese, home made jams, fresh baked bread, scones and hot croissants to accompany, fresh squeezed juice, compote and potato cakes with crème fraiche and fresh salmon. Drive West Cork's peninsulas: Mizzen Head, Sheeps Head and the Beara Peninsula; visit Bantry House and Glengarrif Island; and take the ferry to Cape Clear. *Directions:* Located 2km from Toormore on the road to Durrus. (R591). Fortview House is 12km from Durrus and 9km from Goleen.

FORTVIEW HOUSE   **New**
Owners: Violet & Richard Connell
Gurtyowen
Toormore, Goleen
Co Cork, Ireland
Tel & Fax: (028) 35324
5 Rooms, Double: €100
Open: all year, Credit cards: none
Farmhouse B&B
www.karenbrown.com/fortview.html

Ardtara, a grand home with well-proportioned rooms and lovely stained-glass windows, was built in 1856 by the Clark family, owners of the village linen mill. A downturn in the Clark family fortunes shut the gates for many years, and the house lay sleeping until it received a new lease on life as a country house hotel. Central heating and modern bathrooms were added, but care was taken in keeping architectural details. Many of the 16 original fireplaces have been converted to open gas fires, which give the house a cheerful warmth. All but one of the bedrooms has a cozy fireplace. It's a comfortable place where the staff, many are locals, offers a warmth welcome. The restaurant has gained an excellent reputation for his food and takes great pride in his locally sourced produce. The impressive dining room has a hunting frieze and a ceiling dominated by an enormous glass skylight, a perfect place to enjoy Olivier's food. Just a 5 minutes drive from major roads, Ardtara is a perfect location for a day trip along the Antrim coast to visit the famous Giant's Causeway. Derry town is an hour's drive away and guests often take a guided walk around the city walls. *Directions:* From Belfast take the M2 motorway to A6 (Londonderry road). After Castledawson, take A29 towards Coleraine. Just beyond Maghera, turn right at the Upperlands and Kilrea signpost. Go through the village of Upperlands. The hotel is on your left.

ARDTARA COUNTRY HOUSE
Manager: Valerie Ferson
8 Gorteade Road
Upperlands,
Co Londonderry, BT46 5SA, Northern Ireland
Tel: (028) 796 44490, Fax: (028) 796 45080
9 Rooms, Double: £150–£180
Dinner: £30
Open: all year, Credit cards: all major
Country house hotel
www.karenbrown.com/ardtara.html

Foxmount is the sort of house that feels like home from the moment you walk in the front door. David and Margaret have been taking guests on their family farm for over forty years, and they very much enjoy welcoming guests from all parts of the world to enjoy the homely comforts and experiences of a family run country house on a working farm. Margaret is a natural at hospitality while David loves to talk about the farm and give advice on what to do and see in the area—the Waterford crystal factory is a big draw. Margaret feeds her guests lavish breakfasts. Tasty porridge cooked on the Aga with lots of cream. Scones that melt in your mouth with lashings of raspberry jam. Walk up the garden and see the fruits that she uses: strawberries, raspberries, gooseberries, apples, and rhubarb fresh from the garden. There's no shortage of places to go for dinner and you are welcome to relax and make yourself at home in the drawing room. Upstairs, the extremely comfortable bedrooms have very nice bathrooms—two with showers over the tub and two with their shower cubicles tucked into separate little closets. One has an extra bed, making it ideal for families. Just down the road is the Passage East Ferry which takes you across the river to the pretty Hook peninsula. *Directions:* Take the road from Waterford toward Dunmore East. Three km after passing the hospital, take the left fork toward Passage East. Foxmount Farms is signposted on the right after 500 meters.

■ ✤ @ P ⚲ ⚴ ⚹ 🐎 ⚽

FOXMOUNT FARMS COUNTRY HOUSE
Owners: Margaret & David Kent
Passage East Road
Waterford
Co Waterford, Ireland
Tel: (051) 874308, Fax: (051) 854906
5 Rooms, Double: €110–€130
Open: Mar to Oct, Credit cards: none
Country house
www.karenbrown.com/foxmountfarm.html

Youghal (pronounced "you all" with an American southern drawl), a workaday fishing port, is beginning to flaunt its historic past: drab, gray buildings are being restored, empty shopfronts are coming to life. Standing amongst them, Aherne's old-world pub exterior is decked out in shiny new paint. Owned by the Fitzgibbon family since 1923, Aherne's includes a seafood restaurant and bedrooms. There's an old-world, traditional atmosphere in the bars where you can enjoy a pint with the locals and an array of tempting bar food. The restaurant specializes in locally caught seafood and the menu changes daily, depending on what is fresh and available. In the guests' sitting room, a cozy fire is flanked by comfortable sofas and a coffee table stacked with books on all-things Irish. Three ground-floor bedrooms offer easy access, with one specially equipped for wheelchairs. I particularly enjoyed the upstairs rooms, which have little balconies facing the courtyard. All guestrooms have attractive decor, antique furniture, and large firm beds, each accompanied by an immaculate bathroom. For a stay of longer than a couple of nights the Fitzgibbons have two studio apartments adjacent to the hotel and a luxurious, two-bedroom penthouse apartment with breathtaking views of the harbor. *Directions:* Youghal is between Waterford and Cork on the N25. Aherne's is on the main street in town.

AHERNE'S
Owners: Gaye, Kate, John & David Fitzgibbon
163 North Main Street
Youghal, Co Cork, Ireland
Tel: (024) 92424, Fax: (024) 93633
13 Rooms, Double: €160–€240
3 Apartments: €400–€1,800 weekly, Dinner: €48
Closed: Christmas, Credit cards: all major
Ireland's Blue Book,
Restaurant with rooms & self-catering
www.karenbrown.com/ahernes.html

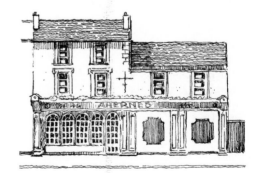

Index

C

Index

Index

Karen Brown's
2007 Readers' Choice Awards

Most Romantic
Quay House
Clifden

Warmest Welcome
Ballyvolane House
Castelyons

Greatest Value
Ballaghtobin
Callan

Splendid Splurge
The Merrion
Dublin

Be sure to vote for next year's winners by visiting
www.karenbrown.com

KAREN BROWN wrote her first travel guide in 1976. Her personalized travel series has grown to 17 titles, which Karen and her small staff work diligently to keep updated. Karen, her husband, Rick, and their children, Alexandra and Richard, live in a small town on the coast south of San Francisco.

JUNE EVELEIGH BROWN'S love of travel was inspired by the *National Geographic* magazines that she read as a girl in her dentist's office—so far she has visited over 40 countries. June hails from Sheffield, England and lived in Zambia and Canada before moving to northern California where she lives in San Mateo with her husband, Tony, their two German Shepherds, and a Siamese cat.

BARBARA MACLURCAN TAPP, the talented artist who produces all of the hotel sketches and delightful illustrations in this guide, was raised in Sydney, Australia where she studied interior design. Although Barbara continues with architectural rendering and watercolor painting, she devotes much of her time to illustrating the Karen Brown guides. Barbara lives in Kensington, California, with her husband, Richard, and is Mum to Jono, Alex and Georgia. For more information about her work visit *www.barbaratapp.com*.

JANN POLLARD, The artist of the cover painting has studied art since childhood, and is well known for her outstanding impressionistic-style watercolors. Jann's original paintings are represented through The Gallery in Burlingame, CA and New Masters Gallery in Carmel, CA. *www.jannpollard.com*. Fine art giclée prints of her paintings are available at *www.karenbrown.com*.